THE
DEADLOCK
OF DEMOCRACY

THE
DEADLOCK
OF DEMOCRACY

James MacGregor Burns

Four-Party Politics in America

Englewood Cliffs, N. J.
PRENTICE-HALL, INC.

The Deadlock of Democracy
by James MacGregor Burns

© 1963 by James MacGregor Burns

Library of Congress Catalog Card Number: 63-8455

Printed in the United States of America

19694-T

PRENTICE-HALL INTERNATIONAL, INC.
(*London, Tokyo, Sydney, Paris*)

PRENTICE-HALL OF CANADA, LTD.

PRENTICE-HALL DE MEXICO, S.A.

BOOKS BY JAMES MACGREGOR BURNS

*The Deadlock of Democracy: Four-Party
    Politics in America*

John Kennedy: A Political Profile

Roosevelt: The Lion and the Fox

Government By the People (with Jack W. Peltason)

Congress on Trial

Okinawa: The Last Battle (co-author)

Guam: Operations of the 77th Division

For Margaret and Eunice

Each in her own way. . . .

Contents

Prologue: The Politics of the Cave   1

PART I
THE MADISONIAN MODEL

1   *Madison and the Strategy of Checks*   8

     THE ROAD TO PHILADELPHIA   10
     THE "PROFOUND POLITICIAN" AND "SCHOLAR"   14
     THE THEORY OF MINORITY CHECKS   17

2   *Jefferson and the Strategy of Parties*   24

     THE FIRST CONGRESSIONAL REPUBLICANS   26
     JEFFERSON BUILDS A PARTY   32
     THE THEORY OF MAJORITY RULE   38
     THE CHECKING AND BALANCING
         OF JAMES MADISON   42

3   *The Splintering of the Parties*   47

     THE FLOWERING OF THE PARTIES   51
     WHIGS: THE EROSION OF THE CENTER   58
     DEMOCRATS: THE STRATEGY OF DISRUPTION   61
     WHY DID THE PARTIES FAIL?   65

4   *The Pulverization of Party*   70

     THE SEESAW OF THE PARTIES   75
     THE PARTIES UNDER ATTACK   80
     AMERICAN HYBRID: A LOOK BACK AND AHEAD   87

ix

PART II
THE JEFFERSONIAN IMPULSE

5 *Roosevelt and Taft: Which Republican Party?*   93

    THE COLONEL AND THE BOSS 95
    A "REGULAR WITH A CONSCIENCE" 99
    TAFT AND THE CONGRESSIONAL REPUBLICAN 106
    CONSCIENCE WITHOUT REGULARS 112

6 *Woodrow Wilson and the New Democracy*   119

    THE SCHOLAR AND THE BOSS 123
    MASTER OF HIS PARTY? 130
    WILSON V. LODGE: NO ADVICE, NO CONSENT 136
    WILSON AS A JEFFERSONIAN LEADER 142

7 *Roosevelt: The Art of the Possible*   148

    THE EDUCATION OF FRANKLIN ROOSEVELT 151
    ROOSEVELT AND THE GRAND COALITION 156
    THE CRUMBLING OF THE COALITION 161
    ROOSEVELT AS A POLITICAL STRATEGIST 167
    THE TWO ROOSEVELTS: AN EPITAPH 173

8 *Eisenhower and Taft: Which Republican Party?*   177

    THE EDUCATION OF ROBERT TAFT 179
    THE ROUT OF THE REGULARS 182
    THE GENERAL AND THE SENATOR 188
    SUMMARY: THE FOUR-PARTY SYSTEM
      IN HISTORY   195

PART III
THE MADISONIAN SYSTEM TODAY

9 *The Balance Wheels of Politics*   204

    REGULARS AND IRREGULARS 206
    THE WEB OF LEADERSHIP 212
    THE ANATOMY OF BALANCE 218

9   *The Balance Wheels of Politics* (Cont.)
   THE OUTSIDERS   222
   THE OUTSIDER INSIDE   229

10   *The Structure of Coalition Politics*   234
   STATE PARTIES: THE SHRIVELED ROOTS   236
   THE CONGRESSIONAL PARTY SYSTEM   241
   THE PRESIDENTIAL PARTY SYSTEM   249
   FOUR-PARTY POLITICS   257

11   *The Whirlpools of Change*   265
   THE CITIES AND THE SUBURBS   267
   SOUTHERN POLITICS: RIM AND HEARTLAND   271
   IS PARTY REALIGNMENT INEVITABLE?   275

12   *Which Republican Party?*   280
   THE CONGRESSIONAL PARTY: REARGUARD
      STRATEGY   283
   THE PRESIDENTIAL PARTY: STRATEGY OF THE
      CENTER   288
   COALITION AND COMBAT   295

13   *The Dilemma of the Democrats*   301
   KENNEDY AND THE PRESIDENTIAL DEMOCRATIC
      PARTY   306
   CONGRESSIONAL DEMOCRATIC STRATEGY   311
   WHAT STRATEGY FOR THE NEW FRONTIER?   317

14   *Strategy for Americans*   323
   THE POWER IN THE PEOPLE   332
   LEADERSHIP: THE ART OF THE IMPOSSIBLE?   336

Acknowledgments   341

Sources   343

Index   377

THE
DEADLOCK
OF DEMOCRACY

Prologue

THE POLITICS of the CAVE

B ehind the fascination with political personalities and election gladiators there is in this country, I think, a vast boredom with politics. Because it has failed to engage itself with the problems that dog us during our working days and haunt our dreams at night, politics has not engaged the best of us, or at least the best in us. If people seem complacent or inert, the cause may lie less in them than in a political system that evades and confuses the real issues rather than sharpening and resolving them. Anyone active in everyday politics knows of concerned, civic-minded people who give hundreds of hours and dollars to fund drives, the Red Cross, and other worthy local causes but will have nothing to do with politics. It frustrates them, alienates them, bores them to tears. They are failing their political obligations —but perhaps politics is failing them.

1

But never has politics needed them more. We are at the critical stage of a somber and inexorable cycle that seems to have gripped the public affairs of the nation. We are mired in governmental dead-lock, as Congress blocks or kills not only most of Mr. Kennedy's bold proposals of 1960, but many planks of the Republican platform as well. Soon we will be caught in the politics of drift, as the nation's politicians put off major decisions until after the presidential campaign of 1964. Then we can expect a period of decision, as the voters choose a President, followed by a brief phase of the "politics of the deed," as the President capitalizes on the psychological thrust of his election mandate to put through some bits and pieces of his program. But after the short honeymoon between Congress and President the old cycle of deadlock and drift will reassert itself.

This cycle is one reason for the disenchantment with politics of those most concerned with political issues. It has led to a government by fits and starts, to a statecraft that has not been able to supply the steady leadership and power necessary for the conduct of our affairs. Historically there has been a serious lag—once a near fatal lag—in the speed and effectiveness with which the national government has coped with emerging crises.

The record is a disturbing one. The steady, moderate action on slavery that was so desperately needed in the 1840's and 1850's finally came, immoderately and at frightful cost, in the 1860's and 1870's. American participation in the first real efforts at collective security came after World War II instead of World War I. The anti-depression measures so critically necessary in the 1930's, if not long before, became governmental and political commitments only in the 1940's and 1950's. The most elementary types of federal control over economic power were delayed for years. The social security and other welfare measures needed to protect men against the insecurities of the modern economy should have been adopted at least by the turn of the century; they had to wait for the New Deal of the 1930's. The economic internationalism that characterized the Marshall Plan and its successor programs in the last fifteen years was missing in the 1920's, when our nationalistic economic policies helped bring on the world depression. Our admirable concern today with the developing countries would have paid off many times over if we had come to it sooner; as it is, we are trying to influence revolutions that in many cases have moved out of the narrow orbit of American influence. The cost of delay has also been high in countless other areas of hardly less importance: urban decline, conservation, tax reform, medical care, governmental organization. We have reacted to change rather than dominated it.

We have often been too late, and we have been too late with too little. Whether we can master depression in peacetime is still in doubt, for we pulled ourselves out of the Great Depression only by the bootstrap of war. Currently baffled by a sluggish economy, we seem unable to promote long, sustained economic growth. Negroes still do not share the basic rights of citizenship promised in the 14th and 15th Amendments. We have done almost nothing about the old dream of a coordinated and vitalized transportation policy. Our social welfare measures are inadequate, especially in medical care. We cannot play our full economic role abroad because of inhibiting forces in Congress. Our structure of transportation is inequitable and archaic. We have hardly begun to adapt our federal and state policy-making machinery to the heavy demands on it.

One can view this drift and delay with a certain philosophical calm. In the end American government, like the belated hero in the horse opera, seems to come to the rescue. Delays may be hard, of course, on certain persons. A man whose working life stretched from 1900 to the mid-thirties might be a bit concerned in retrospect over the delay in federal social welfare programs. A twelve-year-old boy working in a textile mill during the 1920's, or even in the 1930's, might wonder, if he had a chance to wonder about such things, how a great nation like the United States had been unable to outlaw child labor despite general condemnation of it, while most of the civilized world had accomplished this primitive reform years earlier. A Negro in the 1960's might not be so detached toward states' rights and congressional obstruction as some of his fellow Americans. Still, most of us could reflect that progress has almost always come in the long run, even if the run has been longer for some than for others. And the slowness of change has meant, perhaps, less tension and disruption of the social fabric.

Today, however, the notion of the beneficent inevitability of gradual progress is open to challenge. For one thing, the furious pace of social and economic change at home and abroad makes delay in government action far riskier than before. We do not enjoy a cushion of time in adjusting to such change, just as we no longer enjoy a cushion of time in coping with enemy attack. We may not possess, for example, an extra decade or two to respond to the demands of a revolution in Africa or Asia or Cuba. Then too, crisis does not seem so productive of federal action as in former days. Judging by the Democratic and Republican platforms of 1960, the campaign speeches of the presidential candidates, and the bulk of opinion in the press, at the pulpit, and in academia, most American opinion leaders agree that the international situation calls for mobilization of educational, scientific, industrial, manpower, health, and physical resources, as well as military strength. But despite this weight of opinion, key domestic proposals of both the Eisenhower and Kennedy administrations in such areas have been stalled in Congress. It is notable that Kennedy's major foreign-policy proposal of 1961—long-term financing of foreign aid—failed at the very time that the nation was aroused over crises in Berlin and Southeast Asia. Perhaps the American people have become so benumbed by constant emergency that a crisis no longer serves the old function of providing broad support for government action.

Another reason that the habit of delay and devitalization may have to be abandoned, however, lies in the nature of the competition that the nation faces. Never before have we confronted an enemy that, over so long a period, challenges so formidably as does Soviet Russia, our ideology, our economic system, our democratic ways, and our international role. It is clear in the 1960's that the nation faces a period of years and perhaps decades during which it must strain every nerve and marshal every resource to maintain its own strength and to nourish that of the free world. Soviet Russia has shaped a governmental and political system that, whatever its failings and terrors and deprivations, has shown itself capable of mobilizing Russians for a sustained effort. The Chinese colossus, imposing perhaps even greater sacrifices, is building up its own hard strength. The question is whether Americans, without harming the substance and the processes of democracy, can empower and invigorate their own society for the long pull.

Yet, serious as these failings are, I have still not expressed the main reason that so many concerned people are aliens to the political process. The main reason, I think, is that politics to them seems dominated by old and sterile issues and appears unable to grapple with the two cardinal problems of late 20th Century civilization. These problems are the style of life of urban man, and the need for fresh and creative ventures in foreign policy.

By 1980, it is expected, over four-fifths of all Americans will be living in metropolitan areas. By the year 2000 a nation of 300,000,000 will embrace vast patches of almost solid urban settlement: the Eastern seaboard; the West Coast; and an urban Midwest fusing the urban and suburban areas of a dozen cities from St. Louis to Buffalo. We have become, as Walter Lippmann has said, in large part a mass society living in congested urban agglomerations. This inexorable trend poses the question of whether men will become further dehumanized and corrupted in megalopolis, or whether a national government sensitive to urban needs can take the leadership, through policy on education, cultural subsidies, television and other mass media, city planning and redevelopment, recreation, transportation, expansion of civil rights, in making megalopolis not only habitable but hospitable to man.

The other problem is how to break out of immobilism in foreign and military policy. However much we may be balked by Russian intransigence in such areas as disarmament and East-West trade, there are other creative possibilities that we have hardly begun to exploit. Vastly stepped up educational and cultural exchange, broadening of the powers of the United Nations, more sophisticated and longer range programs of economic aid to the new nations, the establishment of international universities and cultural centers, increased international collaboration in social and natural science and in space technology, follow-up action to the President's "declaration of interdependence" of the Western nations—the possibilities are almost limitless.

It is in these two areas, with their exciting potential for creative statesmanship, that our politics has, I think, seemed most crabbed and irrelevant. One wonders, indeed, whether we have advanced much beyond the cave man in the stakes and style of our politics. He fashioned shelter, gathered food, and doled out sustenance to the weaker members of the clan; he and his fellows huddled together in defense against the outside foe. And in Plato's famous

allegory of another cave, he often took shadow for substance in trying
to grasp the great world beyond his narrow vista. So too we produce
and distribute goods and grant welfare to the poor; we huddle with
our allies behind our nuclear weapons; and we act politically in a
shadowland of old governmental fetters and outworn stereotypes.
Politics is still mainly a matter of brute economics and sheer survival.

While the main reason for our political futility and frustration is
the political system described in this book, the ultimate source is
intellectual. The root trouble, I think, is on our own minds. Like
the people in the cave, we have been hypnotized by the shadows of
our own political images and by the echoes of our old incantations.

We have been too much entranced by the Madisonian model of
government that I will describe in the first chapter. This model was
the product of the gifted men who gathered in Philadelphia over
175 years ago, and it deserves much of the admiration and venera-
tion we have accorded it. But this is also the system of checks and
balances and interlocked gears of government that requires the consensus of many groups and leaders before the nation can act; and
it is the system that exacts the heavy price of delay and devitalization
that I have noted.

In glorifying the Madisonian model we have undervalued—have
even been frightened by—the great competing system of Jefferson
that I shall describe in the second chapter. We have underestimated
the powerful balances and safeguards that are built into a system of
majority rule and responsible parties. We have thwarted and fragmentized leadership instead of allowing it free play within the
boundaries of the democratic process.

Partly because of these miscalculations, we still underestimate the
extent to which our system was designed for deadlock and inaction.
We look on the current impasse in Washington as something extraordinary rather than as the inevitable consequence of a system
we accept. We look on the failure of the national government to
act as the result of poor leadership or bad luck or evil men, and we
search for scapegoats. Some conceive that Mr. Kennedy today can
break the impasse by some magic feat of manipulation or some deft
bit of persuasion or by some grand appeal to the people, but they
are ignoring the weight of American experience. Typically the Madisonian system has made us go slow; only under extraordinary combi-

nations of circumstances have we moved vigorously ahead on many fronts. As some of these chapters will show, even the strongest and ablest Presidents have been, in the end, more the victims of the Madisonian system than the masters of it.

And so today we face the Madisonian idea built into a system of entrenched power. We face a four-party system that compels government by consensus and coalition rather than a two-party system that allows the winning party to govern and the losers to oppose. While the demands on our government pile up at a feverish pace, the system shows no sign of relaxing its grip on the levers of action. This system is rooted in our constitutional arrangements, electoral behavior, party institutions, and machinery of government.

Above all, it is rooted in our minds. "We are at one of those uncommon junctures of human affairs when we can be saved by the solution of intellectual problems and in no other way," John Maynard Keynes said in the 1930's. So we are today. Our need is not to win an election or a leader; we must win a government. To do this we must disenthrall ourselves of the shadows and echoes that draw us away from reality. We cannot unfreeze our politics until we unfreeze our minds.

I

The
Madisonian
Model

1

MADISON and the STRATEGY of CHECKS

O n the morning of May 2, 1787, a short man of
36 years strode down a Manhattan pier and
stepped onto an open boat that would take him
across the Hudson River to Paulus' Hook, now Jersey City. Few
loungers on the pier that morning would have taken special notice
of the traveler, for he was rather ordinary looking, with his hair
combed to conceal a low forehead, and doubtless dressed in a sedate
black. But this was James Madison, member from Virginia of the
impotent national Congress then meeting in New York City, and
he was embarking on one of the most fateful enterprises in American history. For he was headed toward Philadelphia to take the
leading part in the framing of a new Constitution for the American
states.

All winter and early spring Madison had fretted in New York—

fretted over the "thinness" of Congressional business, over snags to the approaching convention in Philadelphia, over reports of turbulence in various states. But he had turned his time to good account. Each day after Congress recessed he changed from politician to scholar and worked far into the night on a long study he titled "Vices of the Political System of the United States."

In his small, even handwriting Madison listed eleven failings of the system. The states were failing to comply with constitutional requirements. They were encroaching on the federal authority of the Articles of Confederation and were disrupting foreign relations. They were trespassing on one another's rights and were unable to work together where their common interest required it. They were not guaranteed by the Articles against internal violence. Even worse, the government of the Confederacy could not back up the laws passed by its own Congress. Indeed, some states had not actually ratified the Articles. Finally, the states passed too many laws, changed them whimsically, and many of these laws were unjust.

What should be done? Temporizing would simply "foment the internal malignity of the disease," he had written George Washington two weeks before leaving. Radical changes were necessary. Between state independence and "consolidation of the whole into one simple republic," he went on, he was seeking middle ground—proper supremacy for a national government but maintaining "local authorities wherever they can be subordinately useful." To Thomas Jefferson, another eminent fellow-Virginian and his closest ally, Madison also poured out his grievances over the inadequacies of the existing Congress.

And now, as his boat ploughed slowly across the Hudson this May morning, Madison could see a striking example of the problems of the Confederation. This was the port of New York. Into the broad mouth of the Hudson sailed packets and schooners with madeira, rum, farm machinery, ironware, watches—and the state of New York had established its own customshouse to collect duties on such imports from abroad. Who should get the money? Congress and the New York legislature had squabbled long and hard over the matter, and Congress had lost. But to Madison this was only one item in a darkening scene. Why should New York levy customs at all? Why should the states have their own foreign relations? Why should Congress, now almost bankrupt, be forced to beseech states for funds, like a beggar with a cup?

"The nearer the crisis approaches, the more I tremble for the issue," he had written shortly before leaving for the convention.

The Road to Philadelphia

At Paulus' Hook Madison boarded a towering, deep-bellied stage-coach, drawn by four horses. This was the "American Flyer," a diligence widely advertised as outspeeding all competitors. Inside were hard benches facing forward; if the day was wet or cold, leather curtains could be pulled down over the open windows. Under the benches the passengers could stow their belongings. It is quite possible that somewhere on the dusty floor of the American Flyer, between cobbled shoes and small valises, sat for some time the basic plan for the new Constitution—or at least that part that was not in Madison's head.

For the Virginia congressman had already mapped out the essentials of the new system. The proposed national government must be armed with "positive and compleat authority in all cases which require uniformity," such as trade and taxes, he wrote Washington and Jefferson. The legislative department should be divided into two branches, one chosen at brief intervals directly by the people or their state legislatures, the other to be smaller with long, overlapping terms. There must be a national judiciary, with some power over the states. And there must be a national executive—but here Madison admitted that he had not thought through the question of executive power.

It was Madison's part in the framing and enacting of this plan that would give him his rightful accolade of "Father of the Constitution." Yet it is doubtful that Madison was thinking so much of political mechanics as of political philosophy that May day as the Flyer rumbled over a trembling causeway of logs through the New Jersey swamplands. For he was a political theorist as well as a practitioner—a man with a genius for seeing the necessary relation between the nature of man and his political institutions.

The nature of man—this was the crux of the problem. Some of his friends—Alexander Hamilton, for example—looked on the mass of people as grasping, ignorant, slavish, in short, as incapable of self-government. Others—including Jefferson at times—seemed to have unlimited faith in man's goodness and reason. As usual Madison took middle ground. To him man combined wisdom and folly, avarice and altruism, good and evil. "As there is a degree of depravity in mankind which requires a certain degree of circumspection and distrust," he said in his prim way, "so there are other qualities in human nature which justify a certain portion of esteem and confidence." Which qualities win out? This depended largely on man's political arrangements. Republican government more than any other form might bring out the best in man—but it also demanded a high degree of virtue and talent.

Later in the day the Flyer lumbered into Princeton and pulled up at Nassau Tavern. Madison, who had graduated from Princeton (then the College of New Jersey) in the class of '70, must have remembered earlier days when the students eagerly crowded around the stages to hear the latest news from New York and Philadelphia. At Princeton he had continued his studies in the old and newer classics, begun as a youngster in Virginia. After college he had continued to read Aristotle, Polybius, Locke, Montesquieu, and he had read men scorned at Princeton, such as Hume. And hunting down books for him in Paris was about as fine a book collector as a Virginia Republican could want, Thomas Jefferson himself.

Out of the writings of such men Madison had forged his own theories of government. On the one hand, as a republican, he believed that the people, not kings or aristocrats, should rule. On the other hand, if people ruled themselves, how would they control their natural tendencies to invade the personal and property rights of others? Would the people's elected representatives control such tendencies? No, because politicians sought office more for ambition and selfish interest than to serve the people. How easily were base and selfish measures masked by pretexts of public good! How often would honest but innocent legislators become the dupes of popular heroes and demagogues!

Since Princeton was an overnight stop for the Flyer, Madison probably spent the night near his Alma Mater in the cramped garret room that the Philadelphia line provided. He was off again early the next morning. A good conversationalist, Madison must

have talked readily with any fellow travelers; only a year later a
Frenchman taking the same trip noted that a member of Congress
sat next to a laborer who voted for him, and chatted with perfect
familiarity. But conversation was difficult in the noisy, jolting carriage, and we can presume that Madison spent most of the long
hours looking out at the passing New Jersey countryside, at the log
cabins and cleared fields, and snatching a few minutes to stretch
his legs on the scow that carried the stage over the Delaware at
Trenton. Here in the New Jersey hinterland he could reflect on the
perverseness of mankind. At heart, like his friend Jefferson, he was
an agrarian, convinced that the independent farmer was the foundation of public liberty and the bulwark of public safety. But how
far could one trust any section of society? These New Jersey farmers,
burdened by debts and falling prices, had forced the little state's
legislature to issue paper money. New York and Philadelphia treated
the paper with contempt, and it depreciated further. The rage for
paper money had flared up in Rhode Island too. When a farm-
dominated legislature issued cheap money and forced creditors to
accept it, Providence merchants closed their doors, riots broke out,
and all over the state harried creditors fled from their debtors, some
barely escaping over the state line.

But the worst news had come from Massachusetts. Under Daniel
Shays, war veterans and farmers had actually taken to arms against
mortgage foreclosures, steep interest rates, and imprisonment for
debt. Blocking the entrance to the Northampton courthouse, they
had stopped the judges from issuing foreclosures. They had been
put down—but only after sending a spasm of fear down the spines
of substantial citizens. Would people suffer such "disaffected and
desperate characters to involve this rising empire in wretchedness
and contempt"? Washington wrote Madison. But for Madison the
aftermath had been even more galling. The same farmers that
backed Shays had helped elect a new Massachusetts governor who,
in Madison's eye, was "not a little tainted by a dishonorable ob-
sequiousness to popular follies." Then Rhode Island had given asy-
lum to Shays' refugees and capped it all by refusing to send delegates to the coming Philadelphia convention. "Nothing," Madison
lamented on hearing this, "can exceed the wickedness and folly
which continue to reign there."

Madison was not only a philosopher. His knowledge of government was distilled not merely from books or from reports of "turbulent scenes in Massachusetts and infamous ones in Rhode Island," as he called them. Even at 36 he was a seasoned legislator. He had served three years in the Virginia Assembly and four in Congress. He possessed clear insight into the ways of politicians. He had borne his share of political knocks at the hands of frivolous voters; once he had failed of re-election because he refused to hand out free whiskey. He knew the pushing and hauling of groups; he had worked for Virginia's commercial interests against New York's; he had fought religious factions in politics; he had helped kick his political foe, Patrick Henry, out of the legislature upstairs into the weakest governorship in America. He knew all the Byzantine maneuvers of local politicians.

The latent causes of faction, he had decided, were sown in the nature of man. "All civilized societies," he had written in New York that spring, "are divided into different interests and factions, as they happen to be creditors or debtors—rich or poor—husbandmen, merchants, or manufacturers—members of different religious sects—followers of different political leaders—inhabitants of different districts —owners of different kinds of property, etc., etc." Where there was no real basis for conflict the most frivolous and fanciful differences could excite passionate hatreds.

How control these factions? In particular under a republican government, where the majority rules, how prevent that majority, when united by some interest or passion, from trampling on the minority or on individuals? Enlightened self-interest? Statesmen with vision would not always be at the helm. Public opinion? The average man—even the average legislator—thought in terms of local interest. Did a Rhode Island Assemblyman, Madison demanded, care what France or even Massachusetts thought of his paper money? Religion? This did not restrain men individually; it had even less effect on the masses. Indeed, religion could lead to oppression as well as to justice.

How, then, to curb the "notorious factions and oppressions" of corporate towns and little republics? Madison's answer brought him back to the grand strategy of the Philadelphia convention. The solution was not to try to remove the causes of faction, for a free society would always produce differences among men. The solution was to control the effects of faction by enlarging the sphere of government and hence breaking society into a greater variety of interests and passions, which would check one another, while "those who may feel a common sentiment may have less opportunity of communication and concert." And this was the main purpose of the convention —to set up a strong national government and hence check the power of local majorities to invade the rights of others.

This was the great solution to the "vices" of the Confederation that Madison had worked out and written up shortly before leaving New York. The actual national machinery for breaking up the thrust of the majority—the system of checks and balances—he would shortly present to the convention. As the Flyer sped through the flat country north of Philadelphia Madison doubtless knew that much depended on his ability, as a practical politican, to convert these ideas into the reality of a new national Constitution.

The "Profound Politician" and "Scholar"

The Flyer rattled over the pebble stones of Chestnut Street and pulled up at Philadelphia's famous Indian Queen Tavern on Fourth Street. Nearby, in Mrs. House's neat little rooms, Madison was to take his lodgings, as he had often done before; there he waited for Washington and other members of the Virginia delegation. The eager Madison was the first delegate to show up; no other arrived for ten days. He had time to talk tobacco prices with the local merchant who handled the crop from Madison's fields at Montpelier, and to pay a call on the venerable Benjamin Franklin under a big mulberry tree off Market Street. On May 13 there was a great clatter outside Mrs. House's. It was Washington, escorted by the City Light Dragoons and hailed by the booming of artillery and the huzzas of a great throng. He was promptly taken off by financier Robert Morris to his fine brick mansion. During the next few days Governor Edmund Randolph and the other Virginians arrived and took lodgings near Madison.

The Indian Queen Tavern now became the scene of probably the most significant state caucus in American history. Every day the shrewd group of Virginians met for two or three hours "to form a proper correspondence of sentiments," as one of them said. Out of this caucus came the Virginia plan, essentially a recasting of the proposals that Madison had sent from New York to Jefferson, Washington, and Randolph during the spring. The plan called for a national government with three branches. The legislature would be divided into two houses, one directly elected, the other indirectly. The executive was to be chosen by the national legislature, but he could have only one term. A national judiciary would have jurisdiction over questions involving the "national peace and harmony."

Madison could not be sure of Randolph, who had been too busy with his gubernatorial duties in the spring to give the new Constitution much thought, and who often leaned toward a states' rights position unless Madison pushed him the other way. So Madison, to get Randolph on record, agreed that the governor should present the Virginia plan to the convention and that he should do so in the guise of a correction and enlargement of the Articles of Confederation, which had been the official reason for calling the convention. Their plans set, the Virginians waited for more delegates to arrive. By May 25 most of them had finished their long trips by stages and ships: governors, legislators, judges, financiers, lawyers, politicians—almost all of them men of action, men of thought.

Everything went off smoothly for the Virginians when the convention got under way in the Philadelphia State House. George Washington was unanimously elected president; Madison took up a seat in front so that he could keep a full record of the proceedings; and after the convention had been organized, Randolph took the initiative and presented the Virginia plan. In the discussions at the State House, and afterwards at the Indian Queen, Madison quickly impressed the delegates with his lucid, low-voiced exposition of political and constitutional problems. He took the lead in managing every great question, a Georgia delegate noted; he "blends together the profound politician with the scholar."

We do not need here to review in detail the work of the Framers during that hot summer of 1787: how the Virginia plan served as the basis of discussion for two weeks; how a fight broke out between the big states and the small over representation in Congress, and how the New Jersey plan, reflecting small-state attitudes, countered the Virginia plan with a proposal for a single chamber with equal representation for all states; how the delegates boiled up over this question and the convention seemed on the verge of dissolution; how the delegates from Connecticut, a middle-sized state then as now, offered the famous compromise that would give states equal representation in the upper chamber and proportional in the lower; how the practical-minded delegates accepted myriad other compromises on other ticklish questions, such as three-fifths representation for slaves and indirect election of senators, "sawing boards to make them fit," as Franklin said; how in mid-September 1787 Washington and 39 other delegates representing twelve states signed the document; and how the weary delegates adjourned to the City Tavern for a feast and leave-taking. All this is well known.

But of all the convention's actions we should especially note two that would shape the strategy of American politics for decades to come. One of these was as carefully and brilliantly calculated as the other was faltering and negative.

The first was simply the establishment of a national government, ruling the people directly instead of through the states, but a national government checked and balanced by different branches representing different groups of people. The capacity of the Framers to rise above state jealousies and to achieve unity by agreement was their noblest achievement—one that has served as inspiration ever since to those seeking peaceful federation in other lands. But we must remember that federation was won only at a price—the establishment within the national government of a "balance of checks" that prevented the government (and hence any popular majority working through the government) from wielding too much power. Only when delegates from the smaller states knew that their states would have equality in the Senate were they willing to sacrifice states' rights to the new nation. The cost of greater national power was the lodging of ample state power within the new Congress.

All this showed the genius of the Framers, and we can call the new national government, with its balance of checks, the Madisonian system not because he thought it up all by himself, not because he inflicted it on his colleagues, but because he articulated a series of proposals in his earlier planning, led the Virginia caucus to adopt them, and in his dexterous operations on the floor of the convention captured the consensus of the Framers. But Madison also shared in the floundering that marked the second vital action of the convention.

This second action was the establishment of the Presidency. Everyone knew on coming to Philadelphia that there would be a new national Congress, and probably a judiciary—but what about the executive branch? As we look back today from the vantage point of the powerful presidency that has developed in the past century, the Framers' backing and filling on the executive seems almost ludicrous. When on June 1 James Wilson of Pennsylvania boldly suggested a single executive, there was a long pause in the chamber, and a delegate remarked on the "shyness of gentlemen" on this subject. Questions quickly arose. A single or plural executive? How chosen? How much power? On these questions Madison did not demonstrate his usual intellectual grasp. This was the one great question, let us recall, that he had left open in his letters to Washington and Jefferson during the spring. Like most of the delegates he was caught between popular fears of a new monarch and the obvious need of an efficient executive to administer the laws passed by Congress. Both the Virginia and New Jersey plans had provided for selection by the legislature.

Reading the debates today one watches suspensefully as the Framers again and again come to the brink of letting Congress choose the President and then teeter off in the reverse direction. For we know now that legislative selection of the executive would have radically changed the new Constitution and its balance of checks— would have given us a parliamentary system, and probably one much more like the 3rd or 4th Republics of France, I think, than Great Britain's system of strong executive leadership. None of the Framers save Hamilton glimpsed the potential uses of executive power—and Hamilton, with his demand for a strong President in a strong national government, was about the least influential delegate in Philadelphia. The question was finally handed over to a committee on postponed matters.

In the end, the Framers acted mainly by not acting. They in effect left open the specific reach of the President's power and his eligibility for re-election. They set forth his method of election in a clumsy and faulty provision for an electoral college, but all in the expectation that the college would often fail to choose the President, so the decision would revert back to Congress—where many delegates still felt it belonged. The Framers saw the President as a wise magistrate who would carry out the laws of Congress, who would have a vague inherent power of his own, and who, with his modified veto, could defend his office against the power of the legislature and check any dangerous passions in the more popular branch. It is the great paradox of the Constitution—otherwise the world's foremost example of audacious and effective political planning—that what would turn out to be its most creative element, the Presidency, was one on which the Framers' grip was most unsure.

While the other delegates left Philadelphia for home, Madison conscientiously filled out his notes on the debates, like the good scholar he was, and then hastened to New York where he helped persuade the old Congress, neglected during the fateful days in Philadelphia, to agree to transmit the new Constitution to the state legislatures for submission to state conventions. No state was more crucial than his own, and back in Virginia his friends were urging him to return to lead the fight for ratification. But Madison tarried in New York, for Hamilton had approached him with an exciting proposal. Would Madison join him and John Jay in a series of articles for the local *Independent Journal* defending the Constitution against its busy detractors? Madison saw his chance for a national rostrum. By fall he was hard at work with Hamilton and John Jay on what were to become the classic Federalist papers.

The Theory of Minority Checks

Sometimes the printer had to wait while Hamilton dashed off the last sentences. Madison doubtless had less trouble with his deadlines, for many of his pieces were the fruit of ideas that had been blossoming during the spring and summer. In his first paper, Number 10, he came to grips with the crucial problem of breaking and controlling the violence of faction, which he defined as a "number of citizens, whether amounting to a majority or minority of the whole, who are united and actuated by some common impulse of passion, or of interest, adverse to the rights of other citizens, or to the permanent and aggregate interests of the community." The origins of such factions were in the nature of man, in his passions and interests, economic, religious, and otherwise. The cause of faction, Madison wrote, could not and should not be removed, for that cause was liberty, which must never be suppressed. But the effects of faction could be controlled by enlarging the society to be governed, since the larger the society, the greater the "variety of parties and interests" and the less likely that any one faction will have a majority. The greater variety could be found in a broader Republic, with its national Congress representing many sections and groups and hence able to break and control the violence of faction, whether of a popular majority or minority.

Like a careful cook, Madison wanted to dissolve indigestible lumps and fiery spices in the blander waters of a large pot. His crucial assumption here was that the broader republic would overcome faction. Why? If, say, inflationists in one state could get control of the state legislature, why could not inflationists in all states join hands and gain control of the new Congress? Here Madison marshaled his arguments convincingly. For one thing, he said, in a large republic the people would have to delegate decisions to representatives of bigger constituencies, and hence factional feelings would be refined and tempered by carefully chosen leaders whose views were more refined and broad minded than factional leaders. To be sure, factional and even sinister representatives might get elected and betray the people, but this would be less likely where representatives had to appeal to a "greater number of citizens in the large than in the small republic." The new Constitution, providing for two layers of government, would be a fine balance, a "happy combination" of local and general representation. But even more important, under a greater variety of parties and interests, "you make it less probable that a majority of the whole will have a common motive to invade the rights of the citizens; or if such a common motive exists, it will be more difficult for all who feel it to discover their own strength, and to act in unison with one another." Thus inflationists in different states could not easily join together because in the broader sphere other differences would keep them apart—for example, Madison had noted prophetically, the basic conflict between North and South.

But Madison still was not satisfied. There was still the possibility

that even in the new Union a majority of the people might gang
up on the minority. To be sure, Montesquieu's old safeguard might
work: divide up national power among different officials, legislative,
executive, and judicial, "for the accumulation of powers . . . in the
same hands . . . may justly be pronounced the very definition of
tyranny." But even this might not be enough, for what if the different officials—Congressmen, President, and federal judges—got
together and pooled their power for the interests of some oppressive
majority?

The answer to this question became the archpin of the whole
constitutional framework. That answer was the system of checks and
balances. "The great security against a gradual concentration of the
several powers in the same department, consists in giving to those
who administer each department the necessary constitutional means
and personal motives to resist encroachments of the others," Madison
wrote in the fifty-first paper, which rivals the tenth in intellectual
sweep and power. ". . . . Ambition must be made to counteract
ambition. The interest of the man must be connected with the
constitutional rights of the place." Was it a reflection on human
nature that such devices should be necessary to control the abuses
of government? Yes, Madison admitted, and reverting to his first
premise as to the nature of man, he asked: "But what is government
itself, but the greatest of all reflections on human nature? If men
were angels, no government would be necessary."

"Ambition must be made to counteract ambition"—in these seven
words Madison drove straight to the heart of the whole problem;
here he showed his genius as a political scientist. For he was not
content with a flimsy separation of power that lunging politicians
could smash through like paper. He was calling for barricade after
barricade against the thrust of a popular majority—and the ultimate
and impassable barricade was a system of checks and balances that
would use man's essential human nature—his interests, his passions,
his ambitions—to control itself. For Madison's ultimate checks and
balances were political; they built into the engine of government
automatic stabilizing devices that were sure to counterbalance one
another because they were powered by separate sources of political
energy. The ambitions of Presidents and Senators and Representatives and judges were bound to collide because each was responsible

to separate constituencies in the "greater variety of parties and interests of the new federal republic." And each official, of course, had some kind of constitutional weapon—the President's veto, for example, or the Senators' power over treaties—that could be used against other officials and the sectional or economic or ideological interests they represented.

It was a stunning solution to the Framers' problem of checking the tyranny of the majority. Yet the solution contained a major flaw, or at least inconsistency, in the thinking behind it—a flaw so relevant to our later analysis that we must note it even in the same breath that we pay tribute to this profound scholar and politician.

The trouble was this: if, as Madison said, the first great protection against naked majority rule was the broader diversity of interests in a larger republic and hence the greater difficulty of concerting their "plans of oppression," why was not this enough in itself? Why would not any popular majority representing such a variety of interests perforce become so broad and moderate in its goals as never to threaten any major or even minor or individual interest? Why was it necessary to have what Madison called "auxiliary precautions" of checks and balances built right into the frame of government? Because, he said, experience had taught men the necessity of them. What experience? Madison must have meant the experience of societies so deeply divided between rich and poor, between master and slave, between sections, between religions, that victory for one side meant coercion or annihilation of the other. But the America he knew was not such a society. No ideological conflict racked the nation; as Louis Hartz has shown, Americans were united—to the extent they thought about such things—over the liberal creed of John Locke. No sharp class or religious conflict had torn the country into two warring halves. The same diversity that Madison used as an argument for broader union would have required any majority to appeal to so many interests, to straddle so many issues, that it must act in a moderate, broadly representative fashion.

The key to Madison's thinking is his central aim to stop people from turning easily to government for help. Today, when many people want protection by or through government, and not just protection from government, the power of a minority to stop the majority from acting through government may be as arbitrary as

majority rule seemed to Madison. The fact is that Madison believed
in a government of sharply limited powers. His efforts at Philadelphia
to shift powers from the states to the new national government were
intended more to thwart popular majorities in the states from passing
laws for their own ends than to empower national majorities to pass
laws for *their* ends. For the new national government was supposed
to tame and temper popular majorities—which some states had been
unable to do. This meant weaker government—but it was Madison,
after all, who said that the necessity of any government was a mis-
fortune and a reflection on human nature. Government, in short,
was a necessary evil that must be curbed, not an instrument for
the realization of men's higher ideals or a nation's broader interests.
Hence he could sponsor what Richard Hofstadter has called a har-
monious system of mutual frustration.

Still, if Madison was very much a child of his age, his analysis
has long outlived him. Because of his brilliant linking of man's basic
drives and man's formal institutions, of political forces and governmental mechanisms, Federalist No. 51 is still the best short analysis
of the foundations of the American system. How far Madison extended his insights into political dynamics is not wholly clear. His
concern—almost obsession—with factions suggests that he well understood the instincts of politicians to collect groups of followers and
to build positions of power, for "the interest of the man must be
connected with the constitutional rights of the place."

Certainly the implications of Madison's insight are clear today.
Around every position established under the new Constitution—
around "the interest of the man," whether President, legislator, or
even judge or bureaucrat—a circle of sub-leaders and followers would
also grow, the size of the circle depending on the importance of the
office and the appeal and skills of the leader. Other factions would
grow around politicians outside government, trying to get in. And
of course the Constitution left intact a proliferation of offices in the
states, counties, and localities, which in turn were the centers of
thousands of other little circles of political action and influence.

These officeholders, their rivals, and the circles of sub-leaders
and personal followers around them comprise a web of influence
stretching across the formal governmental system. This is not to
deny the importance of political parties and interest groups, of opin-

ion-shaping agencies such as the press, of the thick crust of traditional habits and attitudes, of ideological and social forces, and of other factors. It is to say that, given the stability and durability of our constitutional system, these offices establish the main structure of political combat and governmental power.

Because Madison took the lead in thinking out and articulating this balance of checks, because he helped in masterly fashion to establish it, he stands today as one of the supreme strategists of American politics.

2

JEFFERSON and the STRATEGY of PARTIES

Jt is ironic that within fifteen years of the adoption of the Constitution, the Madisonian model was suddenly overturned. The man who stood Madison on his head was seemingly the least likely author of such a revolution, Thomas Jefferson. "There are very good articles in it; & very bad," he had said when a copy of the Constitution first reached him in Paris. "I do not know which preponderate." He approved the three coordinate departments, the system of checks and balances, and the indirect election of the Senate. He regretted the absence of a Bill of Rights and the eligibility of the President for re-election. Slowly he warmed up to the charter. "It is a good canvass," he finally granted, "on which some strokes only want retouching."

The Jefferson that feared national power and presidential tenure in the new Constitution is the Jefferson that has emerged most vividly in our national heritage. This was Jefferson the ideologist, who believed that states' rights should be predominant; that the small rural property holder was the foundation of the good society; that large cities were the source of corruption, and city mobs "the panders of vice and the instruments by which the liberties of a country are generally overturned"; that the hope of America lay in an easy, self-regulating system of agriculture that would cultivate the virtues of honest and virtuous yeomen; that the threat to America was urbanization, industrialization, centralized finance, a landless proletariat, and a consolidated national government that would vigorously direct economic development; that that government was best which governed least; and hence that the division of powers between nation and states, and the separation of powers between President and Congress and judiciary, were the great safeguards of the peoples' liberties. Closely akin to this Jefferson was the dreamer and revolutionary who made radical statements about the need of occasional revolutions, for "the tree of liberty must be refreshed from time to time with the blood of patriots & tyrants. It is its natural manure."

There is another, quite different Jefferson that needs to be brought much more sharply into our national vision. This is Jefferson the politician, who grew up in the Virginia tradition of public service; won a seat in the House of Burgesses at twenty-six; led the Virginia reformers in abolishing primogeniture and entail, in disestablishing the Anglican church, and in defending freedom of thought and religion; served unhappily as war governor of Virginia; represented the new nation in France; and became in turn Secretary of State, Vice-President, and President. Closely akin to this Jefferson was the tinkerer and practitioner who devised a leather buggy top, a swivel chair, and a dumb waiter; invented a hemp-beater and the formula for a mold board plow of least resistance; conceived the American decimal system of coinage; and was curious about everything around him. He wrote his daughter: "Not a sprig of grass shoots uninteresting to me."

This second Jefferson, the politician and pragmatist, is, I think, as "real" a Jefferson as the first, and far more relevant to the America of the 1960's.

The First Congressional Republicans

In May 1791, four years after Madison's journey to Philadelphia, Secretary of State Thomas Jefferson took the same road but in the opposite direction. Vexed by the political distempers in the nation's capital, he had persuaded Madison to join him on a long trip through the Northern states. The object was to study the botany of the region, with perhaps a little politicking on the side. For Jefferson was still the naturalist and philosopher as well as statesman and politician. His carriage, equipped with an odometer to measure the distance traveled, had no sooner left behind the noise and bustle of Philadelphia when he was happily breathing the country air and listening for the whippoorwill's cry. His odometer had clicked off over 100 miles when he reached the Hudson ferry and made his way to Madison's house.

New York was no place to escape politics. Local Federalists watched the Republican leaders narrowly. What were they up to? Alexander Hamilton, leader of the New York Federalists, got word that there was "every appearance of a passionate courtship" between the visitors from the Old Dominion and local Republicans Aaron Burr and Robert Livingston. The British consul reported to London that "the Secretary of State's Party and Politicks gain ground here." When Jefferson and Madison, after tarrying in New York only two days, left for Albany by carriage and boat, suspicions did not die. The botanical expedition was just a pretext, it was said; the Republican leaders were travelling to Albany and New England to "sow a few tares" and spread their dangerous doctrines. The fauna and flora that interested them were really political, not natural.

Like most politicians the Federalists were, in a way, too suspicious. Although the travelers probably visited Governor Clinton in Albany and one or two other Republican leaders along the way, what actually excited them most were the flowers and fish, the trees, game, insects, soil, streams, lakes, scenery, and battlefields. They were congenial travelling companions, though the two men contrasted sharply. Jefferson was tall, loose, rangy; he usually had a relaxed, lounging air about him, compared to the younger man's bounciness and vigor. But philosophically they were twins. And as they made the long journey up Lake George to Champlain, down through Vermont to Bennington (where they were stranded for a whole Sunday by a law against Sabbath travel), then overland to the Connecticut Valley and down to Hartford, and finally across the Sound to Long Island, the two men had a chance to compare notes on Republican politics in the Northern states and across the nation. And word seeped out to the surrounding countryside that the famous Virginians had come through.

So in a most fundamental sense the Federalists had every right to worry about the Virginia tourists and their travels. Powerful political currents were loose in America, and the two men were in the middle of the turbulence.

How does a great party get started? Some historians have pictured the founding of the first Republican party as a stroke of genius on Jefferson's part. Like a commander surveying the battlefield, it is said, he rallied people and politicians behind him, built a mighty national machine, and swept on to win the presidential battle of 1800. What really happened was more complicated but no less instructive for understanding American politics, nor less testimonial to Jefferson's key role. Actually, the first Republican party grew out of a series of gropings and blunderings, small ambitions and great issues, petty politics and superb national leadership. And it originally grew up in Congress, not around the Presidency.

Most Americans in the early 1790's did not want parties. Not only the exalted George Washington, who was trying to be President of all the people, but Jefferson, Hamilton, and Madison railed against the spirit of party. "If I could not go to heaven but with a party," Jefferson exclaimed, "I would not go there at all." An anonymous Philadelphian spoke for many Americans when he wrote in a local paper: "We want no *Ticket Mongers*: let every citizen exercise his own judgment, and we shall have a good representation—intrigue, favoritism, cabal and party will be at rest." Party stood for selfish faction and petty maneuver. But the impulse toward political organization was inexorable. As Madison said, men tend to be selfish and aggressive; they attach themselves to one another and to ambitious leaders; and they find plenty of things to quarrel about, sensible and silly. Factions spring up behind leaders contending for place and power. Much of the fighting occurs on a darkling plain of ignorance, but not all is confusion. What gives order to the combat is the structure of political and governmental offices. Around every desired position, administrative, legislative, judicial, develop little clusters of aspirants and their circles of supporters.

Since the Constitution of 1787 set up a new system of national offices—President, Senator, and so on—it might be expected that the first tendencies toward national parties would focus on contests for national offices, especially for Congress and the Presidency. Such was the case. But since Washington was "above politics," the first national party contests revolved around battles for seats in the House and Senate. During most of Washington's first term, congressional politics was personal, fluid, placid on the surface, and sometimes vicious underneath. Politicians ran for Congress and voted in Congress on their own. Such a wholly individualistic politics could not last; inevitably politicians would join forces with like-minded men in order to concert and broaden their power. The only question was when and how.

The man who unwittingly threw down the gage of party battle was Washington's Secretary of the Treasury, Alexander Hamilton. While his chief denounced politics, Hamilton went about the tricky business of organizing congressional support for the Administration's measures—for the national bank, assumption of state debts by the national government, federal subsidies, and the other parts of Hamilton's famous "system." For the New Yorker saw that his program could not be enacted without pressure and persuasion and hard bargaining from the top. If Washington would not provide political leadership, Hamilton would. He forced through his program, but only at the price of uniting the opposition.

The heart of that opposition was the Virginia delegation in Congress, and the head of it was James Madison. As Washington's first term came to an end, the alert Virginian was busy converting the anti-Federalist irregulars in Congress into an organized phalanx. People even spoke of the "Madison party." The anti-Federalists were not content simply to oppose Hamilton's measures. They organized forays against his position in the Administration. They set up a Ways and Means committee in the House to clip his financial powers. They backed Jefferson's successful effort to have the Mint shifted from Hamilton's department to his own. They swore they would topple Hamilton from his "fiscal throne."

Foreign affairs widened the breach. During the mid-1790's Americans were taking sides over the French Revolution. The fall of the Bastille set off a wave of sympathy in revolution-minded America, checked later by news of the execution of Louis XVI and of other excesses. As hostilities flared up between Paris and London, Republicans tended to attach themselves to the French cause, Federalists to the English. And both domestic and foreign conflicts were interlaced with disputes over the very style of government. Republicans charged their foes with secretly wanting monarchy under Washington and Adams; Federalists denounced the Republicans for seeking to subordinate the executive to a radical legislature.

Soon the political winds were full of epithets. The Republicans charged that the Federalists were not really Federalists but Monarchists (or Monocrats), Tories, Royalists, aristocrats, the British party. Federalists countered that Republicans were not really Republicans but Democrats, Jacobins, and Frenchified. By early 1797, when Washington gave his farewell speech against parties, the language of party dialogue was complete.

It was a time of numerous newspapers—Philadelphia alone had twelve—and many of these threw themselves into the party battle. Some were the kept organs of a party leader. Hamilton gave printing patronage to the Federalist *Gazette of the United States* and loaned money to its editor, John Fenno. Disgusted by the "hymns & lauds chanted" by this "paper of pure Toryism," Jefferson, with Madison's help, asked a New York journalist, Philip Freneau, to set up a Republican newspaper in Philadelphia. Jefferson sweetened his bid with the offer of a clerkship for Freneau, official advertising for the paper, and inside information from the State Department. Soon the *National Gazette* was fulminating against Hamilton, who complained indignantly to Washington about Jefferson's hireling.

Alarmed at Hamilton's influence, tired by political abuse and squabbles, Jefferson quit Washington's cabinet at the end of 1793 and returned to the tranquillity of Monticello. He left Madison in full command of the Republican party in Congress. During the mid-nineties, with the expected departure of the nonpartisan Washington from the presidency and the likelihood of a party fight over the succession, the Republicans in Congress were becoming more organized. Although party unity was still rough, party lines were tightening in Senate and House. "No disciplined Prussians or enthusiastic French, adhere more firmly to their ranks than the differing members of Congress to their respective standards," a South Carolinian complained, with some exaggeration. Madison was a brilliant congressional tactician, keeping in touch with Jefferson and other Republican leaders outside Congress, planning parliamentary strategy, holding his ranks firm through persuasion and bargaining, occasionally calling his men into caucus.

But the Republican party was not just a group in Congress; gradually during the 1790's it built electoral strength in the states and districts. Earlier members of Congress had won office through small, informal groups of friends and neighbors, with no extensive organization in the modern sense. As the party cleavage widened, members of Congress sent out increasingly partisan circulars to their constituents. In 1796 congressmen in several states campaigned on party tickets. Sometimes the tickets bore partisan labels, sometimes not, but the party groupings behind the ticket were made clear to all. Madison gave some direction to the effort; one of his best grassroots organizers and reporters was House Clerk John Beckley (who was promptly sacked when the Federalists regained control of the House). Even more, the Republican party in Congress dominated the party's presidential effort in 1796. Meeting in informal caucus, its leaders easily agreed on Jefferson as their presidential nominee. The sage of Monticello was not consulted.

By the end of Washington's second term, in short, America had its first national party in the Republicans. Significantly, it was a congressional party, organized in Congress, around members of Congress and candidates for Congress, with rough party discipline, and reaching out to embrace networks of followers in the constituencies. The Federalists had identity and some organization too, but it was limited; the Federalists were more likely to assume their right to office and less inclined to hustle at the polls. (After the fatal Federalist setback of 1800 Hamilton proposed that the party organize local clubs, debate issues, and set up real party machinery, all under national party control, but by then it was too late for both Hamilton and the Federalists). It was the Republican party in Congress under Madison that pioneered in America's early experiments in nation-wide organization.

At this point Jefferson's role was uncertain. As Secretary of State he had quietly led the Republican cause: not only had he got the *National Gazette* started under Freneau, but he had encouraged Republican politicians to seek office; he had stimulated Republican pamphleteering against Hamilton; and on his own he had disseminated Republican philosophy and policies. But when he quit Washington's cabinet in 1793 he also quit his role as party chieftain and left everything to Madison. He wanted Madison to run for President in 1796; Republicans feared, however, that their congressional leader could not carry the crucial mid-Atlantic states. So they ran a reluctant Jefferson who, after sitting the campaign out at Monticello, came in second to John Adams and hence became the new Vice-President. The congressional Republicans were not yet strong enough to elect a President.

Like vice-presidents ever since, Jefferson found his position an awkward one for directing a national party. But now he was back in the swirl of politics, and he could not escape the rising political temper. "Men who have been intimate all their lives," he noticed, "cross the streets to avoid meeting, and turn their heads another way, lest they should be obliged to touch their hats." Madison had retired from Congress, so political intelligence between the two men ran in the opposite direction. In Philadelphia Jefferson led the Republican congressional opposition to Adams and tried to get a new paper started; in Monticello he talked with state politicos that passed by, and corresponded with others.

That Jefferson still had no clear idea where he and his party were headed, however, was shown by a sharp change in his political strategy in 1798. This was his leadership in drafting the Virginia and Kentucky resolutions. A protest against Adams' alien and sedition laws, these resolutions by state legislatures declared the Federalist measures unconstitutional and—far more important—affirmed the right of states to judge for themselves the constitutionality of acts of Congress. There was even the hint of a right of secession. The resolutions failed; to most informed Americans they were a long step backward toward the weak Articles of Confederation that the

Virginians had taken the lead in abandoning. They were the Madisonian formula but carried to such an extreme as to be a caricature. They were the reverse of the strategy of party opposition, which assumed that the way to overcome a bad national administration is not to play the politics of Chinese warlords and pull out but to win enough votes at the next election to drive the administration out of power.

The Jeffersonians were still floundering. It was not conscious political planning but the election of 1800 that impelled them to create a great national party.

Jefferson Builds a Party

When Jefferson returned to Philadelphia shortly before New Year's, 1800, he was already planning to run for President. Gone were the doubts and vacillations of earlier days. Bombarded by the Republicans and undermined by Hamilton and his anti-Adams guerrillas, the Adams administration was an easy target. But to Jefferson the Federalists still seemed formidable. To be sure, he considered them inferior in numbers, comprising mainly, he said, "old refugees & tories," British and American merchants, speculators in public funds, federal jobholders, a "numerous and noisy tribe" of office hunters, and "nervous persons, whose languid fibres have more analage with a passive than active state of things." But the Federalists, he noted, were concentrated in the cities and hence could influence government in a way that the Republicans, dispersed in the back country, could not easily overcome.

Jefferson did not campaign across the country, as presidential candidates do today. Stumping was against his nature, and against the custom of the day. Indeed, the masses of voters often did not need to be approached directly, for in some states the presidential electors were not chosen directly by the voters, as they are today, but by state legislatures. Jefferson's presidential campaign was in large part an effort to elect state legislators who would choose the right electors to pick the right man for President.

During 1800 Jefferson decisively asserted control over the Republican party. He had already drawn up a set of party policies—frugal government, reduced national debt, smaller national defense, "free commerce with all nations" but "political connections with none," freedom of religion, press, and speech—and during the year his followers used these policies as a rough party platform in their own campaigns. Jefferson did not answer Federalist charges, however, "for while I would be engaged with one," he said, "they would publish twenty new ones." His tactic was to out-organize the Federalists, not merely out-debate them.

Jefferson's main strategy, however, was simply being Jefferson—Jefferson the revolutionary, the framer of the Declaration of Independence, the author of the Virginia statute for religious freedom, the intellectual leader and symbol of the Virginia Republicans, the great successor to Franklin in Paris, the Secretary of State, the philosopher and politician. Actually Jefferson was a complicated man, so mixed and shifting in his point of view as to appear irresolute to his friends, arrantly hypocritical to his foes, and a puzzle to later historians. But at the time the Jefferson image was glowingly clear, especially to the back-country people living in a long crooked swath from the interior of Maine through the Green Mountains and the Berkshires down the long uplands to his own Virginia country and then on to the inland South and the Southwest.

But Jefferson realized—and this was his supreme achievement as a party leader—that it was not enough to solicit the old centers of Republican support. He must broaden his appeal in order to reach into the cities. He played down his earlier warnings about the city mobs, while his Republican supporters in the cities played up his opposition to speculation, high taxes, usury, British seizure of American ships, and similar matters that vexed mechanics, sailors, and other city dwellers.

Indeed, the first great election test, according to Jefferson's calculations, would come in the nation's largest city, New York. At the end of April 1800, New York state would elect its legislature, which in turn would choose a slate of electors that might hold the balance of power between Jefferson and Adams in the electoral college. Sizing up the political terrain, Jefferson sounded much like any political analyst a century and a half later: "If the city election of New York is in favor of the Republican ticket," he wrote Madison, "the issue will be Republican; if the federal ticket for the city of New York prevails, the probabilities will be in favor of a federal

issue because it would then require a Republican vote both from
New Jersey and Pennsylvania to preponderate against New York, on
which we could not count with any confidence." In charge of the
Republican group in Manhattan was Aaron Burr. Jefferson had
always been a bit dubious about the slick New Yorker, but this was
no time for squeamishness. During the winter Burr made a quick
trip to Philadelphia and the two men discussed strategy.

In the next three months Burr staged a masterly political campaign. He faced severe odds, for the Federalists were ably led by
his old adversary, Alexander Hamilton, who had won the previous
election decisively, and the Republicans were divided. Burr quietly
persuaded the older party leaders to unite on one ticket of eminent
local Republicans; shrewdly waited to announce his ticket until
after Hamilton had pieced together an inferior one (Hamilton had
shortsightedly chosen his own satellites instead of eminent Adams
supporters); organized his lieutenants solidly on a ward-by-ward
basis; card-indexed the voters, their political history, attitudes, and
how to get them to the polls; set up committees to canvass for funds
from house to house; put the heat on wealthy Republicans for bigger
donations; organized rallies; enlisted in his cause the members of
the Tammany Society, then a struggling fraternal group; debated
publicly with Hamilton; and spent ten hours straight at the polls
on the last day of the three-day election.

A superb local tactician behind a great strategic leader—Burr
could hardly fail. The entire Republican ticket for the assembly carried by an average of almost 500 votes, and there was a good deal
of straight-ticket voting. Word was dispatched to Jefferson in Philadelphia: "We have completely and triumphantly succeeded." Such
a hubbub rose in the Senate that it had to adjourn. Federalists were
downcast; Republicans exclaimed that the New York returns presaged
Jefferson's success nationally.

They were right. During the summer Republican candidates for
state legislature and the electoral college toured their districts and
talked to crowds wherever they could find them—even "at a horse
race—a cock fight—or a Methodist quarterly meeting." The Federalists, solidly based in New England, fought hard to retain the balance-
of-power states, but in vain. Although nowhere else did the Republicans have an organization rivalling New York's, the backwoods

seemed alive with Jeffersonian politicians who were acting with unprecedented unity and who seemed to have a bottomless supply of pamphlets and printed lists of nominees.

It was well for the Republicans that they fought as hard as they did, for in the end they gained only a narrow victory over the divided Federalists: Jefferson and Burr both won 73 electoral votes, Adams 65, General Charles Pinckney 64, and Jay one. The Jeffersonians' elation was dimmed by the tie vote between their leader and Burr. They had produced party regularity in the elections without really understanding it; now party regularity was playing a mean trick on them. The election was thrown into the strongly Federalist lame-duck Congress. For thirty-five ballots the House was stalemated. Only because the Congressional Republicans stuck together while the Federalists were divided, and because Burr dared not connive with the Federalists, while Jefferson (evidently) indicated through intermediaries that he would carry on certain Federalist policies, was the Virginian able to win out on February 17, 1801.

So Jefferson was President. But would he really be *President?* He had made the Republican party into a tool for winning a presidential election. Could he continue to run the party, or would the party run him? Everything seemed to point to a period of executive weakness. No one had preached with more unction than Jefferson about the sanctity of the separation of powers and checks and balances. He had seemingly looked on his party as something to win through, rather than as something to rule through. And now he faced the Republican majority in Congress, enlarged by the election, prepared to carry out their doctrines of congressional supremacy in a weak national government. Independent, divided, jealous of their legislative powers, the congressional Republicans, after years of carping at Washington, Hamilton, and Adams, had now come into their own.

So they thought. But they underrated the steel in Jefferson's gangling frame and his knack for overlooking general principles when faced with practical politics. "What is practicable must often control what is pure theory," he said blithely, "and the habits of the governed determine in a great degree what is practicable." Not only did Jefferson accept much of the Federalist policy, such as the Bank. He went far beyond Federalists in broadening executive power.

And in the Louisiana Purchase he took a step that he considered unconstitutional, telling Congress that it must ratify the agreement with Napoleon, "casting behind them Metaphysical subtleties," and throw themselves on the country for approval of the step at the next election.

What astonishing doctrine! Here was the first Republican President saying in effect that his party should support his unconstitutional act because the voters would sustain the party at the next election. It was a daring move, and wholly successful. Not only was the Louisiana Purchase magnificently vindicated in history, but Jefferson was vindicated in the presidential election of 1804, winning by 162 electoral votes to 14, while the congressional Republicans enlarged their already big majority.

Above all, it was in his leadership of Congress that Jefferson upset old Republican notions of the executive-legislative balance. Considering himself the national head of the party, he gave close and constant leadership to his forces in Congress; he personally drafted bills and had them introduced into Congress; saw to it that the men he wanted took the leadership posts in Congress; induced men he favored to run for Congress by holding out promises of advancement; made the Speaker and the floor leader of the House his personal lieutenants; changed the leadership as he saw fit; used Ways and Means and other committees as instruments of presidential control; dominated the Republican caucus in the House. In short, he took the machinery that the congressional Republicans had built up against Federalist Presidents and turned it to his own uses.

Some Republicans complained bitterly, but they were helpless. Jefferson followed every measure with a hawk's eye, applied pressure where necessary, wined and dined the legislators, and used his Cabinet members and other subordinates as his agents on the Hill. He did not crack the whip publicly, nor did he need to. He simply threw into the balance every ounce of his political, administrative, and moral power—power all the greater because Jefferson had created the electoral foundations of the party.

And he knew how to deal with his enemies, by attacking them from the rear, on their own ground. One of his foes—or so Jefferson thought—was his Vice-President, Aaron Burr. Jefferson not only denied patronage to Burr and his friends; he set out deliberately to destroy the dapper little New Yorker's power in his home state by giving patronage to Burr's adversaries there. Then Jefferson denied him re-nomination for the Vice-Presidency, completing Burr's isolation and helping, in the end, to make an adventurer out of him. John Randolph was another Republican run over by Jefferson's party machine. At first a rising star, a parliamentary leader and chairman of the potent Ways and Means Committee, the stormy young Virginian turned against the President. At the right moment Jefferson simply eased him out of the chairmanship, and then out of the leadership. A few years later Jefferson's lieutenant and son-in-law, John W. Eppes, took up residence in Randolph's district and defeated him for Congress; whether Jefferson's fine hand was behind this *coup de grâce* is for once hard to say.

There were, of course, limits to Jefferson's power. Before leaving office John Adams had carefully packed the judicial branch with staunch Federalists. The enemy had taken refuge in the courts, Republicans noted, but how much power would they have? The right of judicial review had not yet been established in the national government; if the courts tried to invalidate good Jeffersonian measures, Republicans calculated, the President would simply defy the Federalist judges. But the Republicans underestimated the new Federalist Chief Justice, John Marshall—surprisingly, since he was a Virginian. In the famous case *Marbury* v. *Madison,* he invalidated not a great Republican measure but a minor part of a bill that had given certain technical powers to the Supreme Court. It was a brilliant stroke, for Marshall set forth the vital precedent of judicial review, but in such a way that Jefferson could not retaliate, for there was not even a specific court order that he could refuse to obey. The President had no better luck in his impeachment of Supreme Court Justice Samuel Chase, an intemperate Federalist propagandist. Conviction of Chase would have prepared the way for an attack upon Marshall, but the Senate Republicans could not muster the necessary two-thirds vote to convict Chase.

Marshall himself had astutely predicted at the outset that Jefferson would repudiate old Republican principles of congressional supremacy. "Mr. Jefferson appears to me to be a man," Marshall wrote Hamilton, "who will embody himself with the House of Representatives . . . and become the leader of that party which is about to constitute itself the majority of the legislature." What Marshall did not see was that in doing so Jefferson would augment rather than weaken the Presidency. Because Jefferson repudiated the anti-national ideas of the old guard of the Republican party, because he adopted the strong legislative methods of the "presidential" Federalists, because he built a new Republican party to win a presidential election and then governed through it—because of all this Jefferson was the father of the first truly national Republican party, as Madison had been of the Constitution, and again like Madison, one of the grand strategists of American politics.

The Theory of Majority Rule

Timid ladies in Boston, so it is said, had hid their Bibles under their beds on the eve of Jefferson's Inauguration. They had been frightened by Federalist alarms that March 4, 1801, would usher in a hideous new revolution with "the loathsome steam of human victims" offered in sacrifice to a new Goddess of Reason. As steady a man as the new Chief Justice, John Marshall, had written on Inauguration morning that the democrats were divided into "speculative theorists & absolute terrorists," and he was not sure in which class to put the new President. But Marshall, unlike the ladies in Boston, would attend the Inaugural, since he had to administer the oath. By the afternoon of March 4 he was feeling much relieved, for the Inaugural speech had struck him as judicious and conciliatory.

Despite the fierceness of the election contest, Jefferson had told the crowd, all would now abide the result. "All, too, will bear in mind this sacred principle, that though the will of the majority is in all cases to prevail, that will to be rightful must be reasonable; that the minority possess their equal rights, which equal law must protect, and to violate would be oppression. . . ." Events abroad had divided Americans, he granted. "But every difference of opinion is not a difference of principle. We have called by different names brethren of the same principle. We are all Republicans, we are all Federalists. If there be any among us who would wish to dissolve this Union or to change its republican form, let them stand undisturbed as monuments of the safety with which error of opinion may be tolerated when reason is left free to combat it."

"We are all Republicans, we are all Federalists"—these words must have fallen like soothing music on Marshall's ear. And ever since, the famous phrase has been quoted as a lofty and patriotic expression of nonpartisanship. Actually, Jefferson was making a partisan gambit. Recognizing that his election majority had been perilously thin, he saw that he must detach moderate Federalists from the extremists, keep the support of his own party, and thus consolidate his position. He was not pretending that he would follow Federalist principles or even neutral ones; most of his speech called for good Republican measures. He was arguing that no deep division of principle separated him from moderate Federalists.

The Inaugural speech was, indeed, an almost perfect expression of the practical operation of majority rule. The will of the majority must always prevail, Jefferson said, but it must be and would be reasonable. The Republicans would not press extreme party doctrines. Opponents—even those preaching disunion—would be left free. Jefferson was implying that in order to hold and expand his majority, he must embrace policies so broad and so moderate that no minority party or group would be imperiled. We do not need to infer Jefferson's strategy only from his public speeches. In letter after letter he made his plan crystal clear—to bring over moderate Federalists into the Republican camp and thus to create an invincible majority behind the new Administration. Jefferson had an ingenious nomenclature for this strategy. Moderate Federalists he termed "Republican Federalists," and the radicals in his own party he called "Sweeping Republicans." Jefferson served as umpire, connector, and ultimately as unifier of the two groups, as the 1804 triumph proved.

It was Jefferson's actions, however, more than his words, that revealed the anatomy of majority rule. On the one hand he carried on many of the more moderate Federalist policies; and despite Republican grumbling he left in office Federalists who were not extremely partisan or "monarchical." On the other hand, he put good Republican measures through Congress and saw to it that his own loyal followers were rewarded as much as possible. But the high point of Jefferson's majoritarianism, as we have seen, came in the Louisiana Purchase. When the chips were down, when a great decision had to be made and pressed quickly, Jefferson violated congressional rights, by-passed accepted constitutional processes, refused to go through the long process of a constitutional amendment, and threw himself and his party on the mercy of the new popular majority that he was building up.

From both Jeffersonian words and practice, then, we can draw some basic elements of the strategy of majority rule:

1. Majority rule in a big, diverse nation must be moderate. No majority party can cater to the demands of any extremist group because to do so would antagonize the great "middle groups" that hold the political balance of power and hence could rob the governing party of its majority at the next election. A democratic people embodies its own safeguards in the form of social checks and balances —the great variety of sections and groups and classes and opinions stitched into the fabric of society and thus into the majority's coalition.

Since "tyranny of the majority" has long been a term to scare little children with, we must note again that the Jeffersonian system had internal checks and balances, just as Madison's formula had. But the two types differ radically. Madison's formula turned on the "Swiss watch" concept, as Saul K. Padover has aptly termed it, of checking government through major "opposite and rival" interests, any one of which, through its branch of government, could stop extremist action by the majority. Jefferson's system assumed that in a nation like the United States, where sectional, economic, and other group lines cut across parties in a maze of overlapping memberships, and hence where neither major party could abuse any major interest without alienating people in its own ranks—that a governing majority in such a nation could not afford politically to be immoderate, because it could not afford to alienate moderate voters holding the balance of power.

2. The Jeffersonian formula of majority rule allows more government action than the Madisonian model of checks and balances. Once a majority party had been pieced together—no easy job—and its leaders had taken over the three branches of the national government, the majority could govern rather freely and vigorously within its broad mandate, as Jefferson did. But the Madisonians would require that even after a majority had thus won power, strong mi-

nority interests—farmers, say, or Southerners or creditors—would still have a veto power over government action. In a sense the difference between the two systems was quantitative—the Jeffersonian formula required leaders to gain and keep the support of a simple majority of the people—say 55 per cent—behind federal action, while the Madisonians demanded clearance with a far larger proportion of the people (since any major group held a veto power). But this was one of those differences in degree that became a major difference in kind when it came to the capacity of government to act.

3. Jeffersonian majority rule had a more popular, egalitarian impetus than the Madisonian. To win majorities a party leader must reach out to embrace new voters, while holding on to his present supporters; otherwise the opposition party might get the jump. It did not matter if the new voters were poor or ignorant, if they were aliens or even women—every effort must be made to enfranchise more voters and to get the warm bodies to the polls. Madisonian politics lacked this impulse. Whether or not the "veto groups" had wide popular backing was not crucial; such groups could often get their grip on some lever of government whether or not they had broad support among the voters.

To operate properly majority rule required a reliable mechanism: a vigorous, competitive party, under strong leadership. To be sure, majority rule in one sense is not the same as a strong two-party system; the liquid, ever-changing majorities, embracing different coalitions, that form and re-form in a New England town meeting, a city council, or the French Assembly, can do so apart from durable party lines. But effective majority rule on a national scale in a continental nation demands a durable popular majority organized by a leader who can depend on his following in moments of need, as in Jefferson's case. This makes the national majority something more than a mere expedient, a mere holding company for a collection of minorities. Moreover, the majority party—and the opposition that hopes to supplant it—must be competitive; if either one forsakes victory in order to stick to principle, as the Federalists did after the turn of the century, it threatens the whole mechanism of majority rule. Majoritarian strategy assumes that in the end politicians will rise above principle in order to win an election.

Madison's system demanded a reliable mechanism too: interlocking gears of government, each one responding to different thrusts originating in different groups of the electorate. To get the gears to mesh demanded endless bargaining and adjusting among the groups who had their hands on the gears—and hence demanded high-level negotiators who could deal with group leaders. It also meant that government action could be feeble and halting, as agreements among hostile groups might be overly compromised and meaningless. Madison's formula, like Jefferson's, could be abused—especially if one group became so adamant and rigid that it refused to bargain.

So much—for the moment—for the competing formulas. The important point is that by the end of Jefferson's second term the nation was trying to operate both systems. Would such a hybrid work?

The Checking and Balancing of James Madison

James Madison succeeded Jefferson as President in March 1809 and promptly ran into trouble. The big Republican majority in Congress, which Jefferson had barely been able to hold together at the end, now began to get out of hand. The machinery that Jefferson had used to control Congress—the Speakership, floor leadership, caucus, committees—was now used by the congressional party to thwart and sometimes to control the President.

Madison was not allowed even to construct a Cabinet of his own choosing. He wanted to appoint the talented Albert Gallatin, Jefferson's Secretary of the Treasury, as Secretary of State, but congressional Republicans compelled him to keep Gallatin where he was and to select as ranking Secretary the incompetent brother of an influential Senator. Four years later the same faction forced Gallatin out of the Treasury against Madison's will. The power of the Senate to ratify executive appointments—a power that the Father of the Constitution had once seen as a check against presidential oppression—was now being used against Madison himself.

Soon Jefferson's whole system of legislative leadership was crumbling under his successor. During Madison's first two years no Republican group in Congress was able to dominate legislation; rather the old Jeffersonian majority fell into factions strong enough only to defeat Administration measures. Madison's Vice-President, George Clinton, was unfriendly to him; James Monroe had wanted the Presidency and was still sulking; John Randolph returned to the House to head a faction of Old Guard Republicans, the Quids. Gleefully—and correctly—a Federalist predicted that "though there may not be a Federal majority in the House against (Madison), there will be one composed of Federalists, Monroeites and Clintonians. And the D—l would be in it, if we could not handle Mr. Madison then." Within a few months Madison was complaining to Jefferson that Congress was in an "unhinged state."

Madison's great failing was that he refused to be the hinge. When the recharter of the National Bank came up, he let Gallatin support it but refused himself to put pressure on Congress or even take a public stand. The Senate split evenly on the bill, and Vice-President Clinton cast the deciding ballot against the Administration. Heartsick, Gallatin submitted his resignation to the President in a letter that deserves extensive quotation, for it described many Administrations yet to come:

". . . In a government organized like that of the United States, a government not too strong for affecting its principal object,—the protection of national rights against foreign aggressions . . . ,—it appears to me that not only capacity and talents in the Administration, but also a perfect heartfelt cordiality among its members, are essentially necessary to command the public confidence and to produce the requisite union of views and action between the several branches of government. In at least one of these points your present Administration is defective, and the effects, already sensibly felt, become every day more extensive and fatal. New subdivisions and personal factions, equally hostile to yourself and to the general welfare, daily acquire additional strength. Measures of vital importance have been and are defeated; every operation . . . is prevented or impeded; the embarrassments of government, great as from foreign causes they already are, are unnecessarily increased; public confidence in the public councils and in the Executive is impaired, and every day seems to increase every one of these evils." Madison was able to keep Gallatin in the Treasury for another two years, but the latter's fears for the "administration party," as the Madison faction of Republicans was called, were soon vindicated.

The midterm congressional elections in 1810 produced a tidal wave of new Congressmen, many of them Westerners bent on a tougher policy toward England. Their leader was Henry Clay of Kentucky, whom they promptly chose as Speaker of the House. Clay was a new breed in the Speaker's chair: young, independent, militant, and commanding. At the rostrum he was not merely an umpire; he was a political leader who took clear positions on questions before the House, voted even when there was not a tie and manipulated the rules to suit his needs; managed the debate; incessantly pressured the members on and off the floor; and organized committees as he wished, not as the President wished. This dazzling new chief of the congressional Republicans simply supplied from the rostrum the leadership that Madison would not provide from the White House. Soon he had wrested the initiative from the President.

The judgment of history is harsh. Madison "could write a constitution of divided powers," Herbert Agar has summed it up, "but he could not administer one."

Why could not Madison duplicate Jefferson's success? Was it because he was weak, soft, just a "withered little apple-john," as his enemies said? But this was the same Madison who had tenaciously steered his measures through earlier legislatures, who had impressed the "demi-Gods" of Philadelphia (as Jefferson called them) with the strength of his ideas, who had a rare understanding of politicians' ambitions and passions. Was it lack of political skill? Evidently not; Madison was a resourceful legislative politician who knew all the tactics of parliamentary chieftains. The reasons lie deeper and bring us back to the competing strategies of politics.

For one thing, Madison wanted less from the national government than Jefferson finally did. Logically, one can believe in a relatively strong President while opposing a strong national government. Practically, the two go together; an active Presidency has always meant an expansion of national power. Jefferson, above all a pragmatist, was willing to forsake his old preference for checks and balances in order to do what must be done. Madison, a supreme theorist, was not willing to forsake his basic principles in order to do what he was not sure had to be done.

Secondly, the different careers of the two men influenced their presidential effectiveness. While Madison may not have been politically inept, his earlier political influence had been largely legislative. Jefferson's had been mainly executive; as governor of Virginia he had had a particularly harrowing time with the state legislature. He had learned what an executive must do to protect himself. Without drawing the line too sharp, we can say that Jefferson's instinct as President was to master the legislators, using both the carrot and the stick. Madison was a negotiator and bargainer, a behind-the-scenes manipulator—qualities necessary but not adequate for the Presidency. He demonstrated early that congressional experience does not guarantee that a President will know how to master Congress.

Finally, Madison's political situation was different from Jefferson's. He inherited his predecessor's mantle but not the power relationships that Jefferson had developed. Jefferson had built a "presidential" party rooted in the electorate; he could deal with Congressmen on superior terms because he had a political base in their own states that rivaled theirs. Hence he was able to curb men like Burr and Randolph, for he had the kind of power that politicians most respect—power in the electorate. Madison had been a good congressional leader but his strength rested on his ability to negotiate with independent men. And of course he lacked the older man's vast moral authority and nationwide appeal.

The whole story offers many ironies: the Republicans denouncing the Federalist methods of executive influence and then taking them over; Jefferson, whose theories of limited government are still quoted in behalf of every cause, repudiating them in the face of necessity; the Federalists, in opposition, turning to states' rights, congressional supremacy, and other governmental checks that once they had spurned; Madison finally checkmated by his own formulas. But the supreme irony, for our purposes, was that the Madisonian system, which above all aimed at balance, moderation, adjustment, and a harmony of interests, was soon to be perverted by extremists into a caricature of itself, and to help produce a tragic disruption of government and breaking of the nation.

But we must not dismiss Madison too cavalierly. He was no less a great theoretician for having been a second-rate President. To be sure, Jefferson turned his system upside down, but not for many years, if ever, would any other President prove as effective as the great Virginian in organizing his party and Congress in defiance of the Madisonian formula. And even Jefferson, after all, had failed to take control of the judiciary—the final barricade erected by the Madisonian system against majority rule. In the years ahead the country would try to manage a strange hybrid of both majority rule and checks and balances, but Madisonian theory much more than Jeffersonian practice would dominate the strategy of American politics.

3

THE SPLINTERING
of the PARTIES

During the two terms of Madison's successor, James Monroe (1817-1825), the nation's politics completed a cycle that nations recently engaged in political development have made familiar to us today. Americans under Washington had started with a one-party system that had given way under Adams and Jefferson to two national, competitive parties. The Republicans achieved such wide electoral support under Madison and Monroe that the nation seemed to be slipping back into one-party politics. "Now is the time to exterminate the monster called party spirit," Andrew Jackson—of all people—wrote President-elect Monroe in 1816. Paradoxically, this one-partyism tended toward a multi-party system, for in the absence of a strong opposition a regime tends to dissolve into numberless factions.

So the nation under Monroe faced the classic political problem:

could American politics regain a middle way between a one-party system, with its anti-democratic cast, and multi-party chaos, with every politician running for office on his own and then setting up little centers of political free enterprise in the government? Much depended on the health of the opposition party.

But the Federalist party was dying. For two decades its leaders had elevated principle over party; in the end they kept the former and lost the latter. Actually, the Federalists never established a party in the modern sense, for they failed to plant political organization throughout the country; they were simply a small congressional grouping. In 1816 the Federalists nominated for President one of their own, the able, austere Rufus King, leader of the nine Federalists in the Senate, who gained 34 electoral votes, all from Massachusetts, Connecticut, and Delaware, against 183 for Monroe. In 1820 the Federalists nominated—no one.

In their last years the Federalists seemed to do everything wrong politically. They opposed the War of 1812 and hence took on the color of disloyalty. They failed to maintain strength outside New England. They in effect sponsored the Hartford Convention, which like the anti-Federalists of an earlier day toyed with secession and drafted constitutional amendments designed to hobble those in the seats of power in the nation's capitol. Above all, the Federalists simply lost touch with the great currents of American life, with the whole Jeffersonian movement, with frontier expansion, nationalism, agrarianism, rustic politicking. They failed to develop national leaders who would make deals, adjust platforms, compromise policies, and hence they were unable to build a national coalition.

In thus rigidly sticking to their old principles the Federalists left the Republicans in control of a one-party government. Monroe presided over a period known later as the "era of good feelings." Actually there were plenty of bad feelings in the politics of this period, but they were not channeled into conflict between two national parties and hence were easier for chroniclers to ignore.

But one party cannot maintain a monopoly very long in a free and robust society. The men in power cannot satisfy all the varied interests, and certain politicians will calculate that by splitting off from the "ins" they can win concessions or perhaps even overthrow the government. This is what happened, despite Monroe's efforts to keep the squabbling factions together. The big question was whether the one party would give way to two, or to a multitude. This question turned in part on whether the new cleavage would take a sectional or ideological or class or economic form. To some extent it took all these forms, but the immediate fight was among politicians using whatever political weapons came to hand. And the immediate question was who would succeed Monroe when his second term expired in 1825.

If things went according to custom, the issue was already settled. For years Secretaries of State had gone on to the Presidency through the mechanism of the congressional caucus, a meeting of the dominant party's representatives in Congress. And eagerly waiting in the wings was Monroe's Secretary of State, John Quincy Adams. But the mechanism went awry in 1824. Because the Republican party was everything it was nothing. Monroe gave it no leadership on the crucial question of the succession. One faction lined up behind William H. Crawford, the Secretary of the Treasury, but only 66 members of Congress showed up in support of him, while the rest of the pack ignored the action. King Caucus was de-throned. The pack was a large one—Adams, John C. Calhoun, Henry Clay, Andrew Jackson, besides Crawford. All these men were Cabinet members or leaders of Congress. All but one were members of the Republican Establishment. The exception was Jackson, a Senator, but a man who, as a national hero, a general, and an outlander, had kept his distance from the insiders who ran the nation's affairs.

The presidential campaign that followed was one of the murkiest in American history. The attitude of the people could hardly be discerned, as Dangerfield writes, from an election that "had been cooked in the legislatures (as in New York), hampered by district systems, tax qualifications, and the slow death of old political machines, and finally vitiated by an evident feeling among the voters that, even if they could make a choice among this constellation of candidates without platforms, the old-line politicians in the end would be too many for them. As, in the end, they were." All that we can report with some certainty is that Jackson, as the only candidate with extensive strength across the nation, won the most popular and electoral votes, but not a majority. Adams, Crawford, and Clay came in second, third, and fourth, in that order, so the issue had to be turned over to the House of Representatives, with each state delegation, large or small, casting a single vote. Hence Clay was left out of the race, but with a little bag of votes that could decide the outcome.

It was the perfect opportunity for political insiders, and they made the most of it. Only the choice of French premiers in the 1930's or 1950's can compare with the bargaining, maneuvering, and finagling that took place in Washington in the winter of 1824-5. The fact that the attitude of each candidate toward every other ranged from dark suspicion to intense dislike did not inhibit the making of deals and coalitions. Adams swore to himself and to his friends that he would not stoop to ordinary politicking, but he did. His consummate deal was with Clay over the Secretaryship of State, a job that the Kentuckian saw as putting him in a commanding position to win the Presidency four years later. There was no outright bargain between the two, as their enemies later charged; the deal was made in the politician's soft currency of unwritten understandings backed up by mutual advantage.

On an afternoon in February 1825 the results of this and other deals became evident in the voting in the House of Representatives. Clay delivered his own votes to Adams; he and other allies of the New Englander even secured the votes of Representatives from states that had backed Jackson in the electoral college. Adams won on the first ballot. The President-elect promptly went through with his end of the bargain by appointing Clay Secretary of State.

"The Judas of the West has closed the contract and will receive the thirty pieces of silver," Jackson cried. The country was angry; the hero of New Orleans had lost out to a gang of politicians, and a corrupt bargain had turned the trick. King Caucus, seemingly toppled the year before, had suddenly been re-enthroned. The West had been ignored by the Adams-Clay Republicans, just as it had by Federalists in the days of an earlier Adams. The hinterland—the upland farmers, the small planters of the South, the mechanics, the back-country people and the Jacksonian politicians who aroused them—had been left out. But what to do?

The Flowering of the Parties

Martin Van Buren knew what to do. The New Yorker was one of those strategists to whom a situation of indescribable disorder was a grand opportunity. Still in his early forties, the "little magician" had learned the trade of politics as an apprentice and leader of the Albany regency, which ran the politics of New York through a tight caucus. Van Buren had the perfect candidate in Jackson; through the hero of New Orleans he could exploit the rising feeling against the dour Adams in the White House; he could prey on the ambitions of the innumerable politicians who felt that Adams' close-to-the-belly deals like the "corrupt bargain" with Clay had left them out in the cold. No campaign has proved better than that of 1828 Brooks Adams' quip that the art of politics is the art of the systematic organization of hatreds.

Van Buren knew that first he must knit Northern and Southern Democrats, who had split off from the parent Republican party, behind Jackson. Just as two Southerners, Jefferson and Madison, once had taken their symbolic trip up the Hudson, Van Buren made a political pilgrimage through the Southeast. He steered a tight course between the Calhoun and Crawford factions, who had little more liking for each other than they did for the Adams and Clay forces. Van Buren promised Calhoun the Vice-Presidency under Jackson. Back in New York, where Adams had a good deal of strength, Van Buren dexterously kept the state out of the Administration's hands.

The New York politician was not merely trying to elect Jackson; he confided to intimates that he sought the "substantial reorganization of the old Republican Party" after its demoralization under Monroe. He proposed, in his words, to combine "Genl. Jackson's personal popularity with the portion of old party feeling yet remaining," by re-establishing the old coalition "between the planters of the South and the plain Republicans of the North," with party lines once again drawn between Jeffersonians and Hamiltonians. Only a party cutting across North and South rather than between them, he argued, could hold the two sections together.

Van Buren was called the "little magician" by his friends and the "fox of the Vanderkill" by his enemies, but he was more than this; he was an able strategist who understood that he must move party politics outside the confines of Congress and small congressional constituencies and build a wide electoral following. His was not, of course, a solo operation, for he was allied with a host of other astute Jacksonians, but Van Buren had the best understanding of the situation. In all this Jackson played the proper role. He kept quiet on burning issues in Congress, he did not campaign, and he quit the Senate as if to dramatize his remoteness from the congressional and Administration juntas in Washington. The results were dramatic. Just as the Jeffersonians had immensely broadened political participation in 1800, so the Jacksonians drew thousands of new voters to the polls in establishing a new national coalition. Voting for President, as best we can measure it, more than doubled between 1824 and 1828. The election results of 1828 also showed how the Jacksonians had nationalized their campaign in beating Adams, for they carried the Northwest, the South, all of Pennsylvania, and a majority of New York's electoral votes. Four years later Jackson showed the breadth of his national support by winning 219 electoral votes to Henry Clay's 49.

With Jackson in the White House for two terms, and with Van Buren as his Secretary of State during the first term and Vice-President during the second, the nation once again saw in the White House the magic combination of two men, one a great presidential leader and the other a shrewd political strategist, as in the days of Jefferson. The story of Jackson's great feats as "tribune of the people"—of his fight with Nicholas Biddle and with the congressional leaders over the Bank, his use of the veto power, his defiance of the nullifiers in South Carolina, his compelling the Senate to expunge its motion of censure—does not need to be retold here. But it is well to remember that Jackson could act with boldness because he knew that he was not dependent on congressional support and that his strength lay ultimately with the party-in-the-electorate, as Ralph Goldman has called it.

The real test of Van Buren's strategy, however, was not the success of a national hero, but whether the new Democratic party, which embodied the democratic elements of the old Republican party, could be institutionalized as a durable national organization. Could the party be fashioned to elect *non*-heroes? Here the Jacksonians turned to the notion of a national party convention to choose its top leadership.

The convention was not a new idea. For years the parties in the states had been holding such musters, complete with speeches, parades, and revelry. The Federalists had convened "the original national nominating convention," as it has been called, in 1808, but it fell short of nationwide representation and did not stay the party's demise. In 1831 the National Republicans nominated Clay against Jackson in a national convention, but Clay's defeat was the end of that party. In 1832 the Democrats held a national convention to re-nominate Jackson and to nominate Van Buren for the Vice-Presidency over Vice-President Calhoun, who had turned against the President. Van Buren won easily, but this was a test of Jackson's personal prestige rather than of national party organization.

The test facing Van Buren was whether he could convert Jackson's personal popularity into party strength. Aware that opposition to him was growing among some factions in the party, Van Buren had the convention convened early, for May 1835. The conclave, packed with Administration men, many holding patronage jobs, duly chose Van Buren. The permanent chairman of the party gave the reason for the convention when he said that the Democrats had "been forced to look to a national convention, as the best means of concentrating the popular will and giving it effect in the approaching election. It is in fact, the only defense against a minority President."

It was precisely on this score—concentrating the popular (that is, majority) will behind one national candidate—that the opposition forces had trouble in this same year. The opposition was now dominated by a new party, the Whigs. By the mid-thirties they had inherited much of the old National Republican strength. Born in opposition to Jackson, pledged to states' rights, defense of property, and the "American system" of economic development, the Whigs were a logical opposition party to the Democrats. But they were centered largely in Congress and in the South, and they were sorely divided. The result was a curious arrangement, achieved through chance as well as calculation, to run three sectional candidates, with the hope that Van Buren would be deprived of an electoral majority and the election thrown into the House, where a good Whig could be chosen. For the Whigs it was a logical tactic, for it was a reversion to the minority politics of King Caucus. But it failed; Van Buren won a decisive majority of electoral votes.

Nothing educates like failure; four years later the Whigs used the national convention to broaden their appeal and to win the Presidency. Once again Clay wanted the nomination, and if matters had been left to the old congressional caucus, the Whigs doubtless would have chosen their Senate leader. But, refusing to burn their fingers again, the Whig leaders convened their first national nominating convention, to meet in December 1839 at Harrisburg. Clay had a plurality of votes on first ballot, but his enemies combined against him and chose an aging war hero, William Henry Harrison.

The campaign that followed has been pictured in most histories as a carnival of hokum and bunkum, as the Whigs merchandised Old Tippecanoe, the log cabin, and hard cider on a platform of "Harrison, two dollars a day, and roast beef." Doubtless much of it was absurd. But the outcome—Harrison over Van Buren by a narrow popular but huge electoral vote—had a logic of its own. Van Buren, an able second man but not a strong leader, had presided over a lackluster administration; and he had been damaged politically by the panic of 1837. The Whigs, like the Jeffersonians and Jacksonians before, had broken out of their congressional and sectional confines to bring thousands of new voters to the polls, and on their side. The jump of about 60 per cent in voting between the presidential elections of 1836 and 1840 has never since been equalled.

The increase in voting was also a response to a vigorous party politics. By the 1840's the American party system was reaching its full bloom. It had three characteristics of a stable, mature and democratic politics:

First, the parties were well organized, for the most part. They were rooted in a multitude of local committees that elected members of county committees that elected members of state committees. To nominate candidates for most offices the parties held conventions at which politicians fought in open combat on the floor and in closed combat in smoke-filled rooms as they do at national conventions today. Party committees undertook the fun and drudgery of politics, running barbecues and torchlight parades, managing campaigns, pamphleteering the neighborhood, collecting funds, working up lists of voters, and printing party ballots. It was a crude, noisy politics, usually vulgar and often corrupt, but vigorous and broadly based.

At the top of the party pyramids stood the party conventions, clothed with a new prestige and legitimacy, especially after 1844, when the Democratic convention proved its ability to by-pass the front-runners and to choose the first "dark horse," James K. Polk, for its presidential nominee. During the 1840's the parties regularized convention procedures, the manner in which delegates were chosen, and the apportionment of delegates to the states. During this period also the parties organized permanent national committees run by chairmen and secretaries. The parties began adopting national plat-forms. Backing the new organizations of the national parties was the President's prestige and his control of thousands of jobs. And both parties had the strident support of partisan newspapers.

Secondly, the party politics of the 1840's was a more democratic politics than before. By this decade Americans had almost completed their long struggle to extend the vote to all adult white males, re-gardless of wealth. Party politicians played a central part both in breaking down the legal barriers in the states and in enticing and dragging voters to the polls. The more ardent the party struggle, the more zealous party leaders were to extend the franchise to new groups—immigrants, the unpropertied, the illiterate, and others—in order to outvote the opposition. The voters, moreover, had gained more direct control of their political institutions. Almost all members of the presidential electoral college were now chosen directly by the voters rather than by state legislatures; and it had long been un-written law that the electors select for President not their personal choice but their party choice. And the rise of the national convention had made that party choice a direct expression of popular feelings. It had overcome the two great defects of King Caucus: its inability to give representation to areas where the party had no Senators or Representatives in Congress, and its control by men elected years before the presidential contest and for reasons that had little to do with current national issues. All this helped make the Presidency a more direct expression of the majority will.

Third, and above all, American politics had become competitive politics. Sharp rivalry marked the national presidential battle. In the four elections after 1836 control of the White House shifted between Whigs and Democrats four times. Congressional leadership, especially in the House, broadly reflected the ebb and flow of party fortunes and popular sentiment. Intense party competition appeared in most of the states too. There was, for the most part, a fairly easy articulation between the national parties and the state parties; a Whig politician could stand for roughly the same things in Boston as a fellow Whig in Philadelphia or New York. Neither party, of course, was wholly united or homogenized—it could not be in a diverse society—but each stood for a general philosophy and a set of policies and promises and each had the machinery to carry them out.

This party balance showed that the Jeffersonian formula could work, and was working. The party balance had been able to reassert itself after the long era of Republican monopoly. The balance, moreover, was not of section against section, but within sections; it was significant that in 1836 Van Buren broke into hitherto solid New England to pick up electoral votes. Studying the electoral maps of the 1836-1852 period, one is struck by their checkered appearance. Aside from the solid Democracy of the sparsely settled states of the Midwest, neither party had a monopoly of any section. In particular the big populous states like New York, Pennsylvania, and Ohio, shifted from party to party. Significantly, there was no "Solid South."

It was a polity of balance but not of stagnation. The system permitted presidential leadership, as Jackson and Polk demonstrated, but it also required compromise. The system refused major-party nominations to extremists like Calhoun, and to sectional spokesmen like Calhoun and Webster, and hence it kept them out of the White House. A moderate like Clay, on the other hand, won major-party nominations twice. If he had been something more than a strictly congressional leader, if he had been a little more adept at building nationwide coalitions outside Congress, and if he had had a bit more luck, Clay probably would have won the Presidency. It was Clay who made the immortal statement "I would rather be right than President"; it was also Clay who said wryly toward the end that his sentiment had been "applauded beyond its merit."

Two defects marred this happy picture. One was the two-thirds rule in the Democratic national convention. Adopted for obscure reasons at the first Democratic national convention in 1832, the rule required that a vote of two-thirds of the convention (of those voting, but sometimes interpreted as two-thirds of the entire authorized voting strength) was necessary to nominate the standard bearer. "The record from 1832 to 1860, taken as a whole," according to David, Goldman, and Bain, the leading authorities on the convention, "suggests that the two-thirds rule was a major factor in producing the weak executive leadership of the period, since its normal effect was to eliminate anyone with sufficient character and record to have aroused serious opposition." The two-thirds rule became part of the arsenal of the congressional Democrats in choosing and dominating weak Presidents in the 1850's. And it seriously handicapped the Democrats in recruiting strong national leadership.

The second weakness was related to the first, but intellectual rather than institutional. This was the emergence of a complete philosophical defense of human inequality, white supremacy, states' rights, anti-majoritarianism, minority power. The chief of this school was John Calhoun, and his main contribution the doctrine of concurrent majority rule—rule by a consensus of all the major sections and interests rather than by a simple majority of the people cutting across regions, groups and classes. Calhoun's doctrine was a reversion to the Articles of Confederation; it was a perversion, though perhaps a logical one, of the Madisonian model. His brilliant argumentation, his orderly marshaling of his dogmas, and the wide scope of his work produced a bible from which Southerners could cite chapter and verse to defend their caste and sectional ambitions.

Still, the two-party politics of the 1830's and 1840's was an impressive achievement for so young a nation. With his marvelous insight Tocqueville had seen in 1831 the absence of "great political parties"; instead, he said, the United States "swarmed with lesser controversies; and public opinion is divided into a thousand minute shades of difference upon questions of detail." But the deeper he

penetrated behind the strange and even puerile disputes into the
inmost thought of these parties, "the more do we perceive that the
object of the one is to limit, and that of the other to extend, the
authority of the people." It was the genius of the American parties
that during the sunburst of political energy that characterized the
Age of Jackson, they contributed so mightily to the spread of democratic politics and to the softening of sectional cleavage.

Whigs: The Erosion of the Center

The Democratic and Whig parties attained maturity during a decade of rising tension between South and North. Could the leaders
of these two great national organizations cope with sectional
cleavage? Congressional adoption of the Compromise of 1850
seemed to show that they could. Shaped by Whigs Clay and
Webster and by Democrat Stephen A. Douglas of Illinois, the bill
distributed its favors nicely; the North got the admission of California as a free state and the abolition of the slave trade in the District of Columbia; the South got a fugitive slave law with teeth and
the organization of Utah and New Mexico as territories free to
enter the Union with or without slavery. For men of principle north
and south the settlement was not ennobling—few compromises are
—but it was one that people could live with. High feeling in both
sections subsided.

At the start of the 1850's the competitive party balance seemed
to be working. At the end of the decade one party had disappeared
and the other was shattered into pieces, and the nation was on the
verge of civil war. How can the dizzying collapse be explained?

The prime causes of the disruption of American democracy have
been analyzed by historians with loving care (and with some
polemics): the cultural nationalism of the South; the rise in the
North of abolitionist feeling stemming from the spread of humani-
tarian and democratic ideas; the social and economic cleavages between the two sections; divisive issues such as Free Soil and the
tariff; the rise of a moral issue so profound that it could not be resolved without conflict. The question then is: granted these ultimate
causes, what were the immediate reasons for political and governmental failure to deal with the widening fissure?

To this narrower question too, historians have given their answers: the failure lay in the witless politics of a "blundering generation." Or in the absence of statesmanship. Or in the weak leadership of the feeble Presidents. All this can be granted too, but we must relentlessly press the question. Why did this generation of politicians blunder? Why was there an absence of leadership? Why were the Presidents weak? Was this simply chance—a willful halt in the run of good luck that Americans seemed to enjoy? Or, granted the power of the external pressures on President, Congress, and party, were there internal forces that disrupted the Jeffersonian balance of parties and the moderating force of national competition?

It is possible, of course, that the impact of all the exploding forces was so titanic that no political system could have contained them. But we must not underestimate the tensile strength of the webs spun by ambitious politicians as they seek to weave their fortunes together. No party could gain the Presidency or control of Congress without building alliances that stretched across the nation, and without making the compromises necessary for such alliances. Because practical politicians realized this, both parties by 1850 were national in scope. And as long as they were national, their leaders would have the political foundations for gradual adjustment. As it happened, though, the foundations crumbled during the 1850's and the decade was filled with embittering crises instead of attempts at adjustment. Why?

A foreshadowing of political disruption was the plight of the Whig party in the early 1850's. After winning the Speakership in 1846 and the Presidency in 1848, the party of Clay and Webster saw its ranks in Congress steadily erode away. In 1852 the Whigs' presidential candidate, General Winfield Scott of Mexican War fame, lost to Democrat Franklin Pierce by a small popular but heavy electoral vote. In winning only four states the Whigs proved the boast of their Democratic rivals that the Democracy had nationwide appeal. The Whig party now split in two, its southern wing inundated in a rising tide of Democrats, its northern section amalgamating with Republicans and Know Nothings. In 1856 it failed to offer a presidential ticket; like the Federalists it was dead.

An autopsy of the Whig party cannot be definitive. It did not perform the simple feat of the Federalists and perish from lack of contact with popular trends; in 1852 Scott managed to win 46 per cent of the major-party vote. It did encounter bad luck; Clay, its "great pacificator," and Webster, its supreme orator, both died in 1852, but major parties usually survive the demise of their leaders. The Whigs were badly rent by hostility between the "Cotton Whigs" of the South and the "Conscience Whigs" of the North, but the Democrats also had a Southern and Northern conscience, and that party held together until the nation was on the edge of the abyss. And the Whigs more than the Democrats had the chance to capture the image of national unity, for their congressional leadership, especially Clay, had shaped and symbolized union for a generation.

But under the impressive front the heart of the Whig party often seemed to beat feebly. Born in opposition to Jackson, it always was most vigorous in attacking executive leadership and federal authority rather than uniting behind a positive program. It had won both its presidential victories on the cheap, by nominating military heroes, who proceeded to die in office. The Whigs tried the same trick again with Scott, and unsuccessfully; this time, as Herbert Agar said, the general survived but the Whig party did not. Unlike the Democrats, the Whig party had never built itself solidly as a national party; indeed, it seemed to fear the spirit of party. More than the Democrats it had failed to develop intense party fervor and loyalty. It had failed to develop a stable constituency in key states like Pennsylvania. It had neglected to perfect machinery in Washington that could serve the needs of the party as a national organization. The military men had not been political organizers; the resources of patronage had slipped into the hands of congressional leaders, so that a national party had never been firmly built around the President, as suggested by the fact that neither Tyler in 1844 nor Fillmore in 1852 was able to gain nomination for another term. The Whig party was hard on its own Presidents as well as the opposition's.

What the Whigs needed after 1852 was a political strategist who could rally the party behind a moderate, constructive program and out-general the divided Democrats. What happened was that power trickled into the hands of the small congressional blocs that remained after 1852. Whig congressional strength had dwindled in the South, and worse than this, it had been shattered in the great swing states of New York and Pennsylvania. The party of Clay and Webster

simply lacked the materials out of which to rebuild a national political organization. Once again the trend toward one-partyism led
also to its paradoxical counterpart, multi-partyism. Whig decline
left a political void quickly filled by Know Nothings, Free Soilers,
and other third-party groups. The Whigs' final disgrace was the
nomination in 1856 of their last President, Fillmore, by the Southern
Know Nothings. The Whigs had died without a whimper.

The disruption of a major party always brings turmoil to American politics. During the mid-fifties the political panorama looked
like a Tolstoyan battlefield, filled with vast marchings and counter-
marchings as units were cut off from the main forces and wandered
in confusion. But all was not chaos; dominating the battlefield was
the Democratic party with its secure grip on the Presidency and its
huge majorities in House and Senate. With the Whigs disintegrating, with new political movements quickly taking on a sectional cast,
everything now seemed to depend on the capacity of this old party
to keep intact its own ranks and thereby save the union.

Democrats: The Strategy of Disruption

When the Democrats won all but four states with Pierce in 1852,
they boasted that they had re-established themselves as *the* national
party. Pierce had endorsed the Compromise of 1850, and under his
leadership the "grand old party" of the time seemed the likely bond
to hold the country together. But halfway through Pierce's term the
post-Compromise mellowness and the Democratic party were both
shattered by a single blow.

The shattering agent was the Nebraska bill reported into the
Senate by Stephen A. Douglas early in January 1854. The immediate object of the measure was to organize the Great Plains as the
territory of Nebraska in order to expedite Douglas' pet project of a
transcontinental railroad. But the bill had a wider sweep; it would
extend the principle of states' rights by letting the people in the
new territory decide for themselves whether or not they wished to
have slavery. A calculated sop to the South, "squatter sovereignty"
had frightening implications in the North, for it would repeal Henry
Clay's mighty settlement, the Missouri Compromise of 1820, which
forbade slavery north of 36° 30'. Leading congressional Democrats

from the South eagerly took up the bill. With the help of Jefferson Davis and others in Pierce's cabinet, they persuaded the complaisant President to make it a party measure.

The impact on the nation was stunning. "Douglas had asserted that he wished to mollify the sectional conflict and give direction and unity to the party," Nevins has said. "Instead, he had torn open all the wounds of 1848-50; . . . he had split the Democratic Party asunder; he had completed the destruction of the Whig Party, so recently, under Clay, Crittenden, and Webster, a potent force for union; and he had set the scene for the entrance of a powerful new sectional party." Free Soilers in Congress issued a rousing appeal to the nation, people in the North and West crowded into churches and halls to organize "against Nebraska," and Douglas himself said that he could find his way from New York to Chicago by the light of his own effigies.

Why did Douglas take this fateful step? Historians have long discussed the conundrum. A total miscalculation as to the reaction in the North? Douglas was too shrewd a politician to make such a blunder; and we know that he anticipated the Free Soilers' outbursts. An effort to propitiate the South in order to promote his railway interests? Douglas was not the type to risk his national standing for the sake of a dubious local advantage. To divert criticism from a water-logged Administration? The Illinois Senator had no reason to rescue Pierce. To forward his presidential ambitions by earning Southern backing? This is what Douglas' enemies charged and he indignantly denied. He actually discouraged talk of the presidency, but a man who tried for the White House three times straight, beginning in 1852 at the age of 40, can hardly be suspected of a sudden lapse of this fiercest of politician's ambitions.

The question is not whether Douglas wanted to be President—he did of course—but how he planned his route to the White House. That route was commanded by Southern Democrats. They controlled in varying degrees the House, the Senate, the Supreme Court, the Cabinet, the President, and the national convention. Douglas did not mean to open a Pandora's box. He calculated that squatter sovereignty was a sufficient basis of compromise because it left the question to the states and thus removed it from the strained councils of the nation. When he first brought up his Nebraska bill, he evidently hoped to leave uncertain its relation to the Missouri Compromise and hence to leave the nation's calm undisturbed. But as he dealt with Southern leaders he was forced step by step to a new version of the bill that explicitly repudiated the 36° 30′ restriction on slavery. Why he let himself be forced into an extreme position we can answer only by putting ourselves in the Illinoisan's position.

He was a practical man who dealt with many public issues besides slavery: Western homestead bills, railroads, land grants, tariffs, river-and-harbor bills. He wanted to advance the interests of the Northwest, and he could not succeed without the help of the veto-wielding Southerners. Not to solve the smoldering question of slavery—impossible to do for some time anyway, he believed—but to settle the concrete problems facing an expanding nation was his immediate concern. By getting action on a host of practical measures he could establish a national reputation as a doer at a time when the national government seemed muscle-bound. Too, he doubtless believed, or rationalized, that once he gained the Presidency he could deal with the Free Soil issue from a position of power.

Like many practical politicians before and since, Douglas simply undervalued the moral and emotional reaction to Nebraska in the North. The protest was not the usual quick tempest that politicians can depend on to blow out before the next election; it led directly to anti-Nebraska fusion movements by Free Soil Democrats, Whigs, and other elements, to the formation of the Republican party and its triumph in the next congressional elections (in 1854), and eventually to the re-casting of the whole pattern of American party politics. And, ironically, the passion over the Nebraska bill and the civil war in Kansas helped to deprive Douglas of the Democratic presidential nomination in 1856. The South preferred a man not so exposed to the counterblast of events, and they found the perfect neutralist in James Buchanan of Pennsylvania, who had been Pierce's minister to London and thus insulated from direct involvement in the sectional dispute. Buchanan carried the electoral college, but with only 45 per cent of the popular vote against 21 per cent for Fillmore and 34 per cent for the Republican nominee, John C. Fremont.

So once again the nation was headed by a Northern man with Southern principles, by a *roi fainéant* who seemed immobilized by crisis. And the 1850's boiled up into one crisis after another: "Bleeding Kansas," Northern outrage over the return of fugitive slaves, the Dred Scott decision, Preston Brooks' assault on Charles Sumner in the Senate chamber, John Brown's murderous raid on Harper's Ferry. A brilliant leader might have turned these crises to advantage by rallying the great moderate elements of North and South behind a program of compromise and adjustment. But Presidents Pierce and Buchanan were tools of Southern congressional forces, when they were not inert. They tried to substitute maneuver for creative leadership. In his inaugural address, for example, Buchanan asked the nation to accept cheerfully the Supreme Court's imminent decision in the Dred Scott case, however it might turn out; not only did he know ahead of time that the Southern-dominated court would invalidate the Missouri Compromise but he had actually influenced the court toward its fateful decision.

Toward the end of 1857 Douglas broke with Buchanan over the President's pro-slavery policy in Kansas. The Illinois Senator, who was up for re-election the next year, knew that anti-Administration feeling was rising in his home state, as Buchanan followed a pro-Southern policy. Douglas knew too that the Democratic party was headed toward defeat in 1860 unless it could re-orient its policy and recapture the support of moderates in the North. It was a tribute to Douglas' skill that he could muster enough strength in Illinois to win re-election on the platform of squatter sovereignty over the prairie lawyer and rising Republican politician, Abraham Lincoln. Then the Little Giant began campaigning for the Democratic nomination for President. By the time the Democratic convention opened in Charleston in April 1860, he had won a string of delegations in the North and Northwest.

But Douglas had committed the unpardonable sin of turning against the Southern leaders of the party. They had disciplined him in Congress by deposing him as chairman of the Senate Territories Committee; now they set out to block his nomination or, failing that, to make his nomination worthless. Desperately the Douglas forces yielded to the Southern irreconcilables on the slavery plank in the party platform. No use—the cotton delegations walked out of the convention when their even more extreme demands were refused. What was left of the convention adjourned to Baltimore and duly nominated Douglas. The bolters held a rump meeting and chose Vice-President John C. Breckinridge of Kentucky on a platform of slavery extension. Remnants of the old Whig party nominated Senator John Bell on a "Constitutional Union" ticket, and the Republicans, meeting in the Chicago Wigwam, chose Lincoln.

The splitting of the Democratic party led inexorably to the fateful events of the next twelve months: the election of Lincoln, the shifting of power in the South to the firebrands; the secession of South Carolina; frantic efforts at last-minute compromise; Fort Sumter; general secession; and civil war. The election map tells the tragic story of the political disruption that preceded war. Breckinridge swept the South and Lincoln the North. Bell carried three states on the border. Douglas, the candidate of the "center," drew almost as many popular votes as Bell and Breckinridge combined, but his vote was spread so evenly across the nation that he won only a dozen electoral votes. The moderate candidates had been ground to death between two sectional ones; the compromisers had given way to the extremists. The center had been devitalized.

Why Did the Parties Fail?

The decline of the Whigs and the disruption of the Democrats were the prologues in each case to the two crucial political steps toward civil war: the passage of the Nebraska bill and the election of a sectional candidate as President. The Jeffersonian balance of parties had failed. Granted again that social, economic, and ideological forces were the basic causes of the civil war, we may still ask: what caused the party balance to topple, the moderates to yield to the extremists, the two national, unifying parties to give way to the two sectional, disrupting ones?

To answer this question we might consider for a moment how a healthy and competitive party system deals with controversial issues. First of all, strong parties do not fear such issues; they live off them. As policy questions move from the possession of a few zealots and attract national concern, one or both parties moves in on them, perhaps filching them from a third party, exploits them, offers "solutions" to them, and ultimately achieves a new political equilibrium. Such one-time pressing problems as the currency, graduated

income taxation, anti-trust, business regulation, and social security
have moved across the whole political front from the Socialist party
or some other third party, into the hands of the liberal wing of one
or both of the major parties, finally to be grudgingly accepted by
the Old Guard. This is how parties, often in a clumsy and half-
hearted way, have handled scores of economic and social issues for
over a century and a half. The system demands that the parties deal
with problems in the early stages, before they have become burning
issues, and in a spirit of moderation and conciliation. Hence sharp
issues have their teeth drawn before they cut the nation into warring
and irreconcilable camps.

Such an ideal system requires imperatively that moderates control
at least one of the parties, in the short run, and both parties in the
long run. A party will of course embrace extremists who refuse to
compromise on issues, and sluggards who refuse to act until the
problem is almost insuperable, but it must have a "vital center" that
deals quickly and sensitively with problems still in their adolescence.
Neither party dares become too radical or too inert for fear of alienating the moderate elements who hold the balance of power in the
next election. This means that each major party comprises conservatives who grumble that it is going too fast, activists who complain
about its inertia, and moderate party leaders who seek to hold the
two groups together and put the party in the right tactical position
for engaging the enemy. The price of letting any element get out
of hand is a harsh one for politicians: defeat.

This argument turns on a key assumption: that the nation is
operating under two coherent, stable, highly competitive parties—
the Jeffersonian system. With each party embracing both extremist
and centrist elements, power will focus more in the latter than the
former. Voters in the center, independent of either party, always
have an easy alternative: they can shift over to the opposition party
if extremists get control of their own. Extremist voters, on the other
hand, find the opposition party even more obnoxious than the dominant elements in their own, so for them to desert their party or to
sit on their hands would be suicidal; they must go along with their
own party as the lesser of two evils. To such extreme rightists or
leftists, politics must always be the strategy of the second best.

I hope that my use of the terms moderate and extremist, or centrist and radical, do not carry any disparaging implications. Quite the contrary. It would be a dead society that had no radicals or extremists of the right or left. I assume that a free society generates a competition of ideas and interests among leaders and among sub-leaders, that on major issues divisions will appear within the leadership clusters and within their followings, that a rough spectrum of attitudes will result, and that in a mixed and reasonably affluent society enough leaders and their followings will be found between the polar positions to provide support for various middle ways. The problem is not one of radicals versus centrists—we need both—but of how a political system can harmonize these differences by finding a middle way that has a vitality of its own.

If all this is how a rational and moderate political system deals with hot issues and deep cleavages, the parties before the Civil War followed precisely the opposite course.

Perhaps the decisive event was the election of an overwhelmingly Democratic Congress in 1852, largely as a result of Whig weaknesses noted above. The Democrats outnumbered the Whigs 37 to 21 in the Senate and 159 to 71 in the House. The Whig decline in the South produced an unusually large number of Democrats from that area. Within the Democratic caucus the Southerners had the votes to select their own men for the leadership of Congress. The congressional leaders—the Speaker of the House and the President of the Senate—had sweeping powers over the choice of committee chairmen, the composition of committees, the clearance of bills, and parliamentary procedure. This was the background to the Nebraska bill; only because the pro-slavery forces had such tight control of Congress could they pass such an extreme measure.

Power in the Democratic party in Congress, in short, lay with the Southern radicals rather than the moderates. If the competitive, two-party formula had worked, the Democrats should have paid the price in 1856—defeat at the hands of a moderate party which would have gone to the people for a mandate against Southern extremism. Unhappily, 1856 was a time of collapse for the Whigs, beset by their own sectional problem, and of the concurrent rise of splinter parties. The Democrats won an undeserved victory over the divided opposition. In 1860 Douglas tried to steer his party back to a "national" and conciliatory course, but it was too late; he could carry only the moderate elements of the party with him.

Why were the moderates never able to take control of the national Democratic party during this crucial decade? Because they were dealing not merely with pro-slavery majorities among congressional Democrats, but with a system of power rooted in Capitol Hill and ramifying through the whole government. Not only did the congressional leaders rule the Senate and House, but with their pro-slavery allies in the Cabinet they had direct lines into the Pierce and Buchanan administrations. The two-thirds rule in the Democratic national convention gave them a veto power in the one agency that, because of its representation of non-congressional forces, might have served as a moderating influence in the party.

The power of the congressional leadership was pervasive. It was not by chance that neither Democratic President in the 1850's could gain re-nomination. The men who did win Democratic presidential nominations did not go directly to the voters; much of their campaigns were taken over by congressional Democrats, who thus managed to insert themselves between the President and the people. Even if Presidents had wanted to defy Congress on the slavery issue, they could do so only at the risk of losing out on other issues on which they wanted legislation. Even the presidential veto was negated when the congressional leaders, invoking party discipline (their own), could override the White House. Influential Senators and Representatives also laid claim to much of the President's patronage. Hence there was never a powerful Administration party that could build a solid link with moderate elements in the North and in the border states. The congressional leaders also cracked the party whip; when Douglas balked at some provisions of the Nebraska bill he was threatened with loss of his chairmanship of the Territories Committee, a post he considered vital to his legislative and political hopes, and a post he finally lost, as we have seen, when he turned against the Southern extremists.

Pierce and Buchanan have been called weak Presidents, and so they were. They had been chosen to be weak. But one wonders how they could have been "strong." How does one deal with an interlocked system of power? The Southern Democrats were not just a thin line on the Hill; essentially they were a political party in their own right, with Jefferson (as they interpreted him) as their party hero, Calhoun as their party philosopher, states' rights as their party platform, and the Senate as their party forum. Many of their leaders ate together and lived together in Washington; they enjoyed a common heritage; they shared a mutual goal, the protection of slavery.

Parties failed in the 1850's because power drained into the hands of immoderates. Presidents failed because they could not build a vital center as a basis for their influence. The crucial step, politically, toward the Civil War was not simply the splitting of parties; it was the centering of power in wings of the parties that saw the crisis of the 1850's as pretexts for more extremism rather than as warnings of the holocaust to come.

4

THE
PULVERIZATION
of PARTY

*T*he thunderous political skies of 1860 had suddenly exploded and revealed not two parties but four: the Southern Democrats, led nationally by the congressional extremists; the Constitutional Unionists, a moderate party inheriting much of the old Whig leadership and sentiment; the Douglas Democrats, also seeking compromise; and the Republicans, dominated by congressional radicals who were politically astute enough to settle on a moderate, Lincoln, for President. But the stupendous pressures of the year had simply brought into sharp relief a four-party system that was always latent in the Madisonian tendency for parties to organize around presidential and congressional leaders. The events leading up to 1860 had also shown that in certain circumstances one of the parties, even a congressional party, could virtually control the whole national government.

70

But if the congressional Democrats gave a classic demonstration in the exercise of national power during the 1850's, the congressional Republicans more than matched their feat during and after the Civil War—and again with fateful results. The Radical Republicans in Congress, like the pro-slavery Democrats, had their party heroes (William Lloyd Garrison and even John Brown), party philosophers (mainly Abolitionists), and party platform (freedom for the Negro). Shrewd and determined men, they had gambled and won on an antislavery strategy and now took the seats of authority in Congress; Thaddeus Stevens, chairman of the House Ways and Means Committee; William Pitt Fessenden of Maine, chairman of the Senate Finance Committee; Ben Wade, eventually President of the Senate; and a score of others. Their power had been immensely bolstered, of course, by the wiping out of the old Southern representation on the Hill.

The Radicals had planned in 1861 to parlay control of their congressional faction into control of the whole national government. But first they had to deal with Lincoln. To the seasoned men on the Hill the new President had looked quite manageable when he took his oath of office on March 4, 1861. He had a reputation as a rustic politician, a calculating, fence-sitting moderate, a compromiser and finagler. Most of his life a Whig, he had often attacked Presidents' use of executive power, and he himself had never held an administrative position of any importance. The prairie lawyer had shown his compromising tendencies even before taking office. In the teeth of the gale from the South he built a "Union" Cabinet out of fragments of the old parties. Radicals could find comfort in the presence of several old Free Soilers who could serve as a channel of congressional influence on the Administration.

Like many others, including perhaps Lincoln himself, the Radicals underrated their man. As civil war broke out during the spring of 1861, the new President solved the old problem of executive-congressional deadlock very simply: he governed without Congress. To be sure, he called the lawmakers back to Washington for a special session—but he set the date for many weeks after the opening of hostilities, and in the meantime he governed by orders and proclamations. He expanded the army and navy, called for volunteers, raised and spent money, all on his own authority. Congress duly legitimized these actions when it finally convened.

But during the next two years, as Northern armies met staggering reverses in the field, the Radical Republicans sensed that the political situation was changing in their favor. Capitalizing on popular impatience with the lagging war effort, the Radicals set up a Joint Committee on the Conduct of the War dominated by themselves. The President, said Sumner, was only the instrument of Congress under the Constitution, and Congress had its own objectives. Above all the Radicals wanted to free the slaves through act of Congress. Concerned about the divided feelings toward slavery in the border states, Lincoln had proceeded slowly on emancipation. As pressure mounted in 1862, he struck a series of shrewd blows: he sent to Congress a detailed plan for compensated emancipation, threatened to veto a congressional alternative he disliked, forced Congress to pass the bill he preferred—and then, after Congress adjourned and dispersed, he issued the Emancipation Proclamation.

Still, affairs were going badly for Lincoln in late 1862. Democratic gains in the fall elections hurt the Administration's prestige and strengthened the Radicals, for many Republican moderates lost their seats in the swing. On December 13 came the disaster of Fredericksburg. Three days later Republican Senators met in secret caucus on Capitol Hill. Their immediate target was the Secretary of State, William H. Seward, a moderate whom they considered the prime minister and evil genius of the Administration, but ultimately they had a far more sweeping goal—to force Lincoln to replace his coalition cabinet with a group of ultras who would then, as a kind of modern French-style Cabinet, govern the country through Congress, with Lincoln as a feeble premier. "Quarrels between Congress and President have been common enough," an authority on Lincoln's Cabinet has said, "but a fairly ferocious attempt of the legislature to seize the executive power, to dictate cabinet removals and appointments, was something new. . . . It was an attempt to transfer the seat of executive power from the White House to the Capitol."

How a desperate Lincoln parried this thrust is a fascinating case study in presidential politics. Seward had tendered his resignation on hearing of the caucus opposition to him, but Lincoln wished to keep the New Yorker in his Cabinet, in part because he did not want to bow to the Radicals. Knowing that his Secretary of the Treasury, Salmon P. Chase, was conniving with the ultras, the President arranged a showdown meeting between his Cabinet and the congressional leaders. Caught in the open between both sides, Chase put on so poor a show that he wrote out his resignation too. This he offered reluctantly to Lincoln, who almost tore it out of his hand. "This cuts the Gordian knot," the President exclaimed with a triumphal laugh. He would not accept either resignation; he had shown up Chase; he had put his two leading cabinet members on an equal plane; he had demonstrated his own supremacy. "Now I can ride," he said, "I have got a pumpkin in each end of my bag."

Lincoln could ride the storm because his tactics of balance were an expression of a strategy of moderation. Harriet Beecher Stowe noted perceptively that Lincoln's power was of a peculiar kind. "It is like the strength not so much of a stone buttress as of a wire cable . . . swaying to every influence, yielding on this side and on that to popular needs, yet tenaciously and inflexibly bound to carry its great end. . . ." As a moderate trying to keep the support of people in the border states and of War Democrats generally, Lincoln submerged the Republican party in a broader Union party embracing all the pro-war elements. He gave hundreds of jobs, including officers' commissions, to Democrats; he proposed post-war policies of conciliation toward the South; he chose a War Democrat, Andrew Johnson, for his running-mate on a Union ticket in 1864, and he governed as much as feasible without Congress. At his last Cabinet meeting, on April 14, 1865, he said "he thought it providential that this great rebellion was crushed just as Congress had adjourned, and there were none of the disturbing elements of that body to hinder and embarrass us."

That evening Booth's bullet snuffed out not only Lincoln's life but any hope that his strategy could be pursued after the war. Johnson lacked Lincoln's political dexterity and national standing. Their numbers augmented in the previous year's elections, the Radicals now proceeded to capture and consolidate political power.

Historians have exposed and belabored the Radical "Directory" so vigorously that strictures here would be superfluous. Instead we might simply note the way in which the Radicals extended their

influence into every nook and cranny of the elected branches. It was
a virtuoso performance. The Radicals seized the whole legislative
power by systematically overriding Johnson's vetoes. They disciplined pro-Johnson legislators. They arranged that Congress could
be in almost ceaseless session so that Johnson would never have
Lincoln's freedom to act and could not even use pocket vetoes.
They set up the Congressional Campaign Committee to help elect
Republicans to Congress; soon this committee, according to Ostrogorski, was penetrating deeply and continuously into local political life. And they moved to take over the Executive's central
power, control of personnel, by passing, over Johnson's veto, the
Tenure of Office Act, which denied the President the right to remove civil officers, even Cabinet members, without the Senate's
consent. The President was instructed to issue all military orders
through a general whom he could not remove. And when Johnson
finally tried to sack his Secretary of War in a challenge to the Tenure
of Office Act, the House of Representatives impeached the President. If Johnson had lost out, Ben Wade, by now the radical president of the Senate, would have become the new chief executive.
Although the Senate failed by one vote to muster the necessary
two-thirds for conviction, Johnson was now broken politically. The
Directory was virtually the Cabinet, Thaddeus Stevens almost a
premier.

The Radicals had a grand strategy. They wanted to keep Southerners out of Congress while they fashioned Reconstruction to their
own liking. Ultimately they hoped to enfranchise the freedmen so
that they could create a coalition of Northern Republicans and
Southern Negroes. Once they had hamstrung Johnson they proceeded to operate on this master plan. They overturned earlier Reconstruction policy, set up in the South five military districts ruled
by generals, appointed carpetbaggers and Negroes to key posts, and
took control of Southern elections. But the Radicals overreached
themselves. The excesses of the new rulers have been exaggerated,
but the significance of the Southern reaction cannot be. The Radicals both drove moderate Southerners to join their extremist fellows
in the Democratic party and removed the possibility for decades to
come of temperate, competitive, two-party systems in the South.

And they did not even succeed in their original and laudable aim of permanently enfranchising the freedmen.

Still, the Radical Republicans on Capitol Hill had shown that they could govern. They may not have governed wisely or well, but they did show their power to seize and administer political authority on behalf of their policy and ideological goals. They had turned the Constitution upside down—all in the name of fidelity to the Constitution—and they had upset the balance of national party politics. How long would the imbalance last?

The Seesaw of the Parties

That the national party system righted itself so quickly after the Civil War was testament to the tenacity of the Democrats and the persistence of the thrust toward party competition. In 1861 the Democratic party was split into War Democrats and Peace Democrats in the North and was shorn of its old heartland in the South. It was labelled the party of treason. Douglas, its only talented national leader, was dead. The party seemed totally unable to hold its own against Unionists and Republicans.

The post-war rise in the pulse of the national Democracy was dramatic. By 1871 the Democrats had carried the House of Representatives. Five years after that, in 1876, they outpolled the Republicans in the popular vote for President (but Hayes defeated Tilden in the famous electoral college deadlock and manipulation) and two years later the Democrats won a majority in the Senate. Later Grover Cleveland gained popular-vote pluralities three times in a row, although the second time, in 1888, Benjamin Harrison won the Electoral College.

Historians often describe the post-war period as an "era of Republican supremacy"; actually the national parties were amazingly well balanced once the southern states were re-admitted. The 1880's were much like the 1840's. The Senate was divided in 1881, 37 to 37; two years later by 38 to 36, with the Republicans holding the edge. The Presidency seesawed between the two parties. House elections followed their old pattern of giving the newly elected President a majority of his own party, and then slashing his strength

in the non-presidential or "off" years. During the decade the Democrats carved heavily into the Republican vote of the "Solid North,"
and at the end of it, in 1890, Democratic candidates for Congress
swept scores of northern districts that had been considered Republican to the death. State elections outside the South were becoming
more competitive too, and even in the South Republicans were
gaining strength. Moreover, as national and state elections were
increasingly held on the same day, there was a greater tendency
toward voting a straight ticket for both national and state candidates and hence toward articulation of national and state politics.

Thus the two main parties, like great awkward giants, were
grappling on more and more even terms. And party leaders once
again had to learn the harsh lessons of competitive politics. The
Radical Republicans could afford to nominate a stalwart, General
Ulysses S. Grant in 1868 and 1872, for he was a war hero, the South
was still partly disenfranchised, and the Republicans could pose as
the patriotic party. But in 1872 reform and independent Republicans split away from the stalwarts to nominate Horace Greeley,
and the Democrats rejected their own stalwarts to support that
reform ticket. Even though Greeley was not very popular with
many reformers, he polled a big popular vote. Only by nominating
a reform Republican, Rutherford Hayes, were the Republicans able
to defeat Tilden in the Electoral College in 1876, and eight years
later, when the hard-core Republicans ventured "one of their own,"
the old congressional hand James G. Blaine of Maine, they lost
to Grover Cleveland. Clearly, the Democratic tacticians understood
the game of competitive politics. Knowing that they must win the
swing states, they by-passed their congressional leaders and nominated a series of candidates—Seymour, Greeley, Tilden, Cleveland—
who came from New York, with its big clump of Democratic voters.
Ultimately this tactic won them the Presidency.

As the balance between parties became closer, so did that between presidential and congressional power. Hayes, Garfield, Arthur,
and Cleveland fought to restore the President's authority over the
executive branch, and Congress put its own house in order. The
lower chamber had been disorganized almost to the point of anarchy
during the early 1880's. A young graduate student at Johns Hopkins
named Woodrow Wilson had noted that power "is nowhere con-

centrated; it is rather deliberately and of set policy scattered amongst many small chiefs." At the end of the decade, by a masterful demonstration of personal authority, Speaker Thomas B. Reed, a conservative Maine Republican, re-asserted the leader's authority over the House. And veteran Senators of the Republican party, which held a majority in the Senate almost unbroken for three decades, controlled the upper chamber through their tight grip on caucus and committees.

It was not, to be sure, a time of elevated politics. The issues over which the parties clashed so furiously—the tariff, civil service, corruption, and so on—were often trivial compared with the mighty decisions made by the captains of finance and industry; the latter, as Matthew Josephson has said, spoke little and did much, while the politicos did as little as possible and spoke all too much. Rarely has the nation seen such naked representation of economic interest. As William Allen White observed, by this time Senators were more than spokesmen for a state or region; they "represented principalities and powers in business." It is true too that a handful of congressional leaders dominated affairs in both houses and in both parties. But the system was basically healthy because it was competitive. If new problems arose, if popular attitudes changed, at least one of the parties would have to respond to new conditions. If congressional oligarchs froze their party into immobility, the price would be paid at the polls. And so it seemed to work. The Republican congressional leadership chose for President in 1888 a stodgy conservative, Benjamin Harrison, who proceeded to lose heavily to the Democrats at mid-term and to Cleveland two years after that.

Then, in the 1890's, the competitive situation collapsed and the collapse precipitated a whole new alignment in American politics.

The cause of the overturn was the fateful combination of sectional cleavage and a catastrophic failure of political machinery, as in the 1850's, but now intensified by class tension. Cleveland's second term was a time of social convulsion—financial panic, industrial failures, desperate strikes, jobless men roaming the nation. Above all, this period culminated years of rising protest in the rural West and South against Eastern finance and politics. A bold and active President might have coped with some of these problems, but Cleveland, like the Federalists of old, refused to desert his rigid, conservative principles. The man who had once balked at using federal funds to send seed corn to Texas after a drought now refused to use federal power to cope with economic crises, except on behalf of capital. By 1896 fanatical silverites had captured the southern and western wings of the Democratic party and were set to repudiate Cleveland and his eastern goldbugs.

The vibrant Cross of Gold speech by William Jennings Bryan before the Democratic convention in Chicago in 1896, and his dramatic nomination, appear in popular histories as the Democratic party's logical shift to the left into the willing embrace of silverites and Populists. The truth was less simple but more ominous for the future of the party. Bryan was no barefoot boy from the buttes. Elected to Congress in 1890, he had won appointment to the Ways and Means Committee as a freshman and had worked closely with the southern and western leadership of Congress. That leadership, by 1896, had become bitterly anti-Cleveland and planned to take control of the party from the eastern wing. In this plan they were brilliantly successful. A "Senatorial clique," as Nevins has called it, dominated the 1896 convention, its rules, credentials, and procedure. While the congressional leaders had their own candidate in "Silver Dick" Bland, Bryan's nomination fit their purposes better, for it gave them a popular champion who in his own orating and politicking across the land had captured considerable support from southern and western Populists. And shortly the Populist party, at the urging of silverites in Congress, also nominated Bryan and engulfed itself in the Democratic party.

Brilliant tactics for the congressional Democrats—but a fatal strategy for the Democratic party. For Bryan's victory in Chicago was a sectional victory and a rural victory, and this was not enough for a party seeking to retain its national power. In the face of solid Republican strength in the East and Midwest, the Democrats' only hope was a union of farmers in the South and West with workers in the East. In 1892 the Populists had called for such a union. "The interests of rural and civic labor are the same; their enemies are identical," proclaimed the national platform, which went on to urge government control of railroads, telegraph, and telephone, a graduated income tax, and postal savings banks, as well as free silver and rural reforms. Four years later the Democratic platform, aside from fulminating against "importation of foreign pauper labor," was simply a farm and silver platform. The congressional leaders from South and West who controlled the resolutions committee left the platform naked of urban appeal.

The Great Commoner himself was essentially an agrarian and a Westerner. The key passage in his brilliant convention speech was not the "Cross of Gold" climax quoted by a million schoolboys since, but a downgrading of the cities. "Burn down your cities and leave our farms, and your cities will spring up again as if by magic," he orated, "but destroy our farms and the grass will grow in the streets of every city in the country." Years later Mencken said that the only truly "sincere" thing in the man was his love of the country and his suspicion of city folks. Even Bryan's life in Washington had been among rural legislators from West and South. To be sure, he tried in his city campaigning to appeal to urban labor. But his heart never seemed to be in it. Once he referred to the East, and to New York in particular, as "the enemy's country."

The savage reaction of the East to Bryan's candidacy must have deepened the Nebraskan's suspicions of the city. Republican newspapers called him an anarchist, an assassin, a revolutionary "slobbering demagogue"; Bryan "would steal from the creditors of the nation half of what they saved," thundered Theodore Roosevelt. Breaking ranks, Gold Democrats in the East set up the National Democratic party to take votes away from the Bryanites. Publicly Cleveland assumed a guarded position because he feared to antagonize congressional Democrats during his remaining eight months in office, but privately he said that the Bryanites had committed a crime against the Democratic party worthy of the penitentiary. Said another New Yorker in an immortal phrase: "I am a Democrat still— very still."

The election returns made mercilessly clear how badly Bryan had failed in the East. For Republican enthusiasts it seemed like 1860 all over again. The Republicans won every county in New England and every Northern state east of the Mississippi. But it was the margin of the Republican victories that staggered the politicians. States that had been closely competitive in 1892 and before, such as New York, Illinois, Wisconsin, New Jersey, went for McKinley by top-heavy majorities. New York, which had voted Democratic in 1892 by 46,000 votes, now went Republican by 268,000. It was clear from the Republican sweep of the ten biggest cities in the nation that labor had rallied to the Grand Old Party. McKinley's promises of prosperity, his advocacy of the tariff as a means of protecting labor, his generally sympathetic attitude toward unionism won him the votes of workers who simply were not reached by the man from Nebraska. McKinley, not Bryan, had turned out to be the coalition-builder.

Doubtless the Democrats would have lost in any event in 1896, for Cleveland's failures were too much for any party to bear. But the future was to see the party veer away even further from competitive politics. Left as a national party largely in the possession of rural congressmen who survived the holocaust of '96, the Democrats renominated the Commoner in 1900 and lost by an even heavier margin than before. Not only did the Democrats offer less to labor than the Republicans; but their whole program and style—their isolationism in foreign policy, their crabbed view of federal power, their unconcern about any except currency reforms—alienated the burgeoning middle classes which, with their liberal elements, often held the balance of power in the more urban states.

At the dawn of the Twentieth Century, as the nation moved deeper into the age of industrialism and urbanism, the Democratic party was galloping back into the Nineteenth.

The Parties under Attack

In historical perspective the election of 1896 was not just another tilt in the party seesaw. It was a "critical election," a major recasting of electoral forces. It was a substitution of party competition *between* sections for competition within sections. Democratic party politicians of the day did not possess the hindsight of history, and they waited for the seesaw of party politics to swing back again. After their second failure with Bryan in 1900, Democratic leaders sought a new formula for victory. Reversing field, in 1904 they chose instead of the spirited Westerner just the opposite: Alton B. Parker, an Easterner, a judge, a conservative, a Cleveland Democrat. The result was the worst popular defeat in history for the Democrats. Swamped outside the South, Parker won only 38 per cent of the popular vote.

The Democrats had tried the old post-war tactic of nominating an Easterner with assured southern support. Why had the tactic failed so badly this time? The answer lay largely in the person of another Easterner, the bespectacled, square-faced Theodore Roosevelt. In his three years in the Presidency he had re-oriented the Republican party toward a Square Deal, as we will note in the next chapter. As the hero of San Juan, a reform Republican (but not too reformist to alienate the regulars), a lover of the West, a "friend of labor," a lusty Chief Executive with a genius for public relations, he had won vast support throughout the North and West. Sadly the Democrats noted that the mountain states, which had given the GOP only 18 per cent of their vote in 1896, now had flipflopped back to the Republicans with a heavy vote for the Rough Rider.

In 1908 the desperate Democrats reversed field again and once more chose Bryan. And once again the Peerless Leader led the party to defeat. This loss was the most ominous of all, for it came at the hands not of a great politician-President but of a Cabinet member who lacked Roosevelt's flair and finesse. Yet William Howard Taft swept the North and West, though with a smaller popular vote than his predecessor. Ominous too for the Democrats was their plight in Congress. The Republicans outnumbered them in the Senate two to one, and held a decisive margin in the House, during the whole decade.

The great Republican tide in national politics swept through state and local elections too. In 1905 the Republicans held all three major statewide offices—the governorship and the two United States senatorships—in over half the states. In northern New England Democrats were almost totally excluded from power. In Michigan no Democrat won the governorship after 1890 until 1912 when the GOP split there as it did in the nation. In about twenty northern, mid-western and western states the Republican party held almost as strong a position as the Democrats enjoyed in the Solid South.

This near-monopoly of the Republicans outside the South now precipitated a profound transformation of the American party system —one that still decisively influences the shape of American politics.

In the early years of this century the state and local parties were still choosing their candidates in conventions. As long as parties were fairly evenly matched in national, state, and local elections, the convention system worked well. It worked well because the mechanism of the conventions gave considerable power to party leaders, and the leaders knew that the price of selecting an undistinguished party regular was to play into the hands of the opposite party, which could choose a man of more appeal to moderate and balance-of-power voters. There may not have been much democracy within the parties, for affairs were often run by an inner core of bosses. But there was a good deal of democracy "between" the parties in that each had to be on its best behavior to please a majority of the voters.

But all this presupposed substantial competition between the two parties. After 1896 this could not be assumed. When the pendulum swung heavily to the Republicans and seemed to stick there for a dozen years, the great safeguard against convention excesses disappeared. For now regular Republican chieftains could count on such heavy party support in most Northern states that they could choose the safest, most regular, most stand-pat candidate and get away with it. There were, of course, limits to this freedom, and there were many exceptions to the rule. But in general the convention came to be an instrument of the conservative elements of the Republican party and hence an instrument of the industrial and financial interests of the nation.

Southerners had faced the same problem when the Democracy monopolized state and local offices in the Solid South. Here and there insurgent Democrats in the South tried to solve the problem of Old Guard control by instituting the direct primary, which enabled members of a party to choose party nominees directly in elections rather than by sending delegates to conventions. But the shift toward primaries in the South did not go very far; its main importance was to help Populist forces overcome entrenched conservative leadership.

In the North, however, the "one-party era" after the turn of the century coincided with the upthrust of a potent new force in American life. This was the progressive, muckraking revolt against the oligarchs that had ruled American business and politics since the Civil War. In part a movement of professional, salaried, and small-business elements in the growing "new middle class," this revolt focused not only on patent-medicine frauds, adulterated foods, life-insurance malpractices, prostitution, and graft in general; but it also aimed at the trusts and rings in both business and politics. In short, as Hofstadter and others have shown, the progressives were revolting against "machines" that supposedly controlled the conventions, the Senate, and the cities, just as they controlled food packing, oil, and the utilities. What gave the progressives immense momentum was the fact that they were attacking both the machines and the conservative, often corrupt purposes to which they were put to use.

In the world of politics this attack focused on the conventions, where the party bosses in back rooms made their corrupt deals with one another and with their fellow-oligarchs in the citadels of big business. This was the progressive image of the machine, and not always a false one. What to do about the convention? The remedy was drastic but simple: Abolition. The dismantling of the conventions went with amazing speed. Wisconsin passed the first state-wide primary law with teeth in 1903; within a dozen years virtually all but a handful of the states had established primaries, most of them mandatory. The battle cry of political progressivism was "direct democracy" and its motto, "The only cure for democracy is more democracy." And democracy meant direct participation by the people in managing political affairs, with as little control by leaders as possible.

The direct primary was backed up with other techniques to bring the government "back to the people." The Initiative enabled the voters directly to propose a new law, by-passing their elected representatives, who were usually under party influence. The Referendum allowed the people to vote directly on bills already passed by the legislature. The Recall permitted voters directly to remove erring officials. Straight-ticket voting was discouraged by eliminating party-column listing on the ballot. Efforts multiplied to pass Civil Service laws, or to strengthen existing ones, against the attacks of the patronage-mongers. All these devices, in varying degrees, weakened party organization and leadership.

But it was in the cities that the most devastating assault on parties took place, for there the reformers proposed to abolish party itself. And with some reason, because the national political alignment had raised hob with the normal balance of party competition in many

localities. What had questions of schools and sewers and local corruption to do, demanded reformers, with national divisions over
tariffs and money and foreign policy? The answer was the nonpartisan election, which sought to shift city politics out of the hands
of local leaders adhering to the two great national parties and into
the hands of local groups and their leaders.

The sweep of the assault on parties varied from state to state.
New York adopted the primary and other anti-party reforms, but so
powerful and competitive were the two parties in that state that
their leaders were able to overcome the divisive impact of the changes,
and the convention is still a powerful party instrument in the
Empire State. California followed the opposite course. After Hiram
Johnson and his fellow progressives took control of the Republican
party, they proceeded systematically to dismantle the state party
system. Between 1911 and 1913 California authorized presidential
primaries and the direct election of United States Senators, discouraged straight-ticket voting by removing from the ballot the circle
in which a straight party vote can be cast by marking but one X,
introduced cross-filing (allowing candidates to run for more than
one party's nomination), and made all city and county elective
posts nonpartisan. As a result the legal party organization was so
fragmentized, according to a student of Golden State politics, that
a political vacuum was created for decades. Most states fall between
the New York and California extremes, but closer to the latter.

The most spectacular attack on the "party machine" came on the
national stage. There, in the House of Representatives, Speaker Joseph G. Cannon was carrying on the absolutist rule established by
Reed 20 years before. He operated through the Congressional Campaign Committee, which granted or denied funds to Republican
aspirants to the House; through the Rules Committee, which he
chaired and which regulated the order of business; from the rostrum,
where he could see or ignore members clamoring for recognition;
and above all through his own power to grant or withhold prized
committee chairmanships and memberships. By the time Roosevelt
left office in March 1909, the progressives were leveling their guns
on the "autocrat" of the House. A few days after Taft's inauguration, 31 progressive Republicans voted against Cannon on the question of adopting the old rules of the House; only by winning over

some Southern and Tammany Democrats was Cannon able to stave off the attack.

But Uncle Joe's days were numbered. Patiently waiting to dethrone him was a progressive Republican-Democratic coalition headed by George W. Norris, a young Nebraskan who was the political antithesis of the Speaker. Cannon came from an ultra-safe Illinois district; he was now in his 36th year in the House; he was an incorrigible conservative who once remarked that most proposals for change were conceived in corruption and the rest in ignorance. Norris was hardly out of his freshman year as a congressman. He represented an insurgent district in a plains state, which he had held in 1908 by a majority of only 22 votes; originally a bitterly partisan Republican, he had steadily swung over to the progressive cause. Cannon had denied him the committee memberships and other recognition that he wanted. On St. Patrick's Day in 1910 Norris found his chance. Making use of a parliamentary technicality, he submitted a resolution he had been carrying around in his pocket so long that the paper barely held together. It provided for election of the Rules Committee by geographical groups—with the Speaker ineligible to serve on it. A tempestuous floor fight followed. In the end Cannon was routed, as 44 Republican insurgents deserted the regulars to support Norris' dethronement of the Speaker. The next year, in an equally important but far less publicized action, the Speakership was further emasculated when it was deprived of the power to appoint standing committees.

The Senate too felt the wrath of the insurgents. The equivalent of Cannonism in the upper chamber was "Aldrichism," and although Senator Nelson W. Aldrich retired in 1909, for years afterwards his rule remained the symbol of Old Guard control of the Senate. Chairman of the mighty Senate Finance Committee, Aldrich had ruled the disintegrate upper chamber less through formal authority than through his astute handling of men, his knowledge of Senate machinery, and his personification of Old Guard interests and attitudes. When the Republican regulars tried in April 1911 to pass Aldrich's mantle on to an equally conservative gentleman from New Hampshire, they ran straight into the solid, bristling figure of Robert La Follette. The Wisconsin Senator and his progressive cohorts delayed and harassed the Old Guard in its efforts to organize the Senate, and although the insurgents failed to gain the committee assignments they sought, they had aroused the public once more against the evil party machine. Public indignation over the Senate oligarchy bore fruit in 1913 with the passage of the 17th Amendment requiring the election of Senators directly by the people rather than by the state legislatures.

Probably the high-water mark of anti-organization idealism came around 1910 when the reformers were struck by an intoxicating thought: if governors and Senators could be nominated in state primaries, why not Presidents in national primaries? Why not strike at King Convention in its strongest form? The idea seemed all the more attractive in 1912 when Taft—so the reformers felt—"stole" the presidential nomination from TR in a "rigged convention." The idea won influential backing but ran into insuperable odds; a constitutional amendment would be necessary, and many states opposed the idea of being swallowed up in one big mass primary. But in many states the reformers did help institute presidential primaries for selecting delegates to national conventions, and this reform further eroded the power of the party leaders.

Not all progressives favored "direct democracy." Herbert Croly, the brilliant advocate of powerful national government and strong political leadership, warned that direct democracy would endanger majority rule and hence democratic government. "Direct primaries will necessarily undermine partisan discipline and loyalty," he wrote in 1914. Devices like the initiative and referendum, he contended, actually produced minority rule. To Croly the real test of party or of any other political organization was whether it strengthened or weakened executive leadership. But Croly's own vision dimmed when he came to party politics; he did not see the potential link between strong parties and strong leadership. It remained for a practitioner in the White House once again to demonstrate the vital possibilities of that relationship. Other progressives, less probing than Croly but more cynical, felt that primaries and other popular reforms would not stop the really evil party bosses, who would find some way to turn the new machinery to their own uses.

But the heyday of progressivism was no time for skepticism about popular rule. Liberals, radicals, moderates, and mugwumps were almost unanimous: the cure for democracy was more democracy.

American Hybrid: A Look Back and Ahead

By the middle of the second decade of the 20th Century, the essential structure of the American party system, as we now know it, had been formed. Before discussing the ways in which Presidents during the new century dealt with this system, we might do well to summarize developments to that point. What had happened in over a century to the Madisonian and Jeffersonian strategies of politics?

The Madisonian model, it will be recalled, was designed to prevent popular forces working through government from being too strong or tyrannical. The formula was a system of checks and balances among the different branches of government, such as executive and legislative, and between the different levels of government, especially the states and the nation. Madison's system was more than a mechanical or legal arrangement of checks; it assumed that around each of the elective offices established or retained under the 1787 Constitution factions of leaders and followers would organize. Hence it assumed, for example, not merely that the Senate would check the President, or that a governor would veto an act of a legislature, but that the political forces embodied in, or organized around, the Senate or a legislature would balance and check those speaking through a President or a Governor. Institutional checks, in short, were embedded in and bolstered by political checks which in turn reflected the social and economic diversity of the nation. Men's conflicting ambitions powered both the active and the restrictive levers in the governmental engines of the new republic.

In an extreme form the Madisonian system assumed a highly individualistic politics, with scores of separate officeholders, each backed up by some kind of constituency, engaged in an endless series of negotiations. Out of the bartering and bargaining would come progress, for the system postulated an open society with a good deal of rationality, and access to decision makers by a great variety of groups and persons. But the system was not anarchical, for it required that men negotiate their differences in order to make the system work, and that they operate through a constitutional system with a prescribed set of procedures.

The system assumed that the American people would not become sharply divided on a class (horizontal) basis. For if they did—if, for example, a swelling, unified proletariat should develop *à la* Marx, or if, to take Madison's own example, a debtor class should gain majority support in every state and elective district—then the debtors would capture control of every decision point in the government and could tyrannize the minority. But the Madisonian system assumed —quite rightly, as it turned out—that American society as a whole was so diverse, and would remain so diverse, that no such unified class would grow up or be able to take power. But the system also assumed something less likely—that American society would not become sharply divided on a sectional (vertical) basis. For if it did —if, for example, sharp economic or cultural or ideological forces should split the nation into two warring sections—either side could build up so much power in some part of the government as to disdain the bargaining necessary for conciliation. This is what happened in the 1850's.

The Jeffersonian strategy, fashioned from experience rather than theory, stressed majority rule as against the Madisonian system of minority checks. It depended on strong, national parties under aggressive leadership to shape and reflect powerful attitudes on domestic and foreign policy and on the style of government. Given such leadership and such attitudes, most politicians hungering for office would find it expedient to concert their policies and their political tactics with those of the national party leadership. This concert of politicians behind national leaders—especially behind the President or candidate for President—would be able to govern because the leadership would act through the directly elected branches of government and, if its strength held out, eventually would control the judicial and administrative organs.

In a mixed society such as the American, the Jeffersonian system would make for moderate policy—slightly left or slightly right of center—because an immoderate policy would play into the hands of the opposition party. Neither the ruling party nor the chief opposition party would become the party only of debtors, for example, because such a single interest would not, under normal conditions, become solid or intense enough to take control; too many other interests would be represented in the majority. Under the Jeffersonian strategy, a leader and his party must broaden and moderate their appeal in order to secure office. The system assumed that minority forces would counter-organize against an extremist or overbearing majority, and that the balance in the system would be provided by hot competition between the two sides.

It is clear from our review of the first century of American political parties that neither the Madisonian nor the Jeffersonian model has been followed with any exactness or consistency. Most of the time American politics has shown rather mixed tendencies. During Jefferson's two terms the nation had seen the closest approximation to party government and majority rule. During the Jackson-Van Buren period and the close party balance that followed in the 1840's, and again in the 1880's, there were periods of close national party competition. What was missing, except during part of Jackson's and perhaps Polk's administrations, was the presidential leadership that could shape and exploit a majority coalition for positive purposes of government. Generally speaking, there were neither strong parties nor strong leadership in American government during the first century.

A seeming exception to this absence of party strength consisted of the party machines in some cities and a few states. Here the party chiefs were true bosses, working closely with private interests, handing out jobs, favors and money; running charitable and recreational activities such as Christmas baskets for the poor, relief for the widows and orphans, and excursions up the river; controlling conventions; delivering the vote on election day; and enforcing their control by judicious combinations of force, fraud, and favors. In such circumstances politicians sought and administered government office in a concerted effort under central party control. But despite all the publicity given the bosses by reformers and muckrakers (and received with gratitude, perhaps, by party chiefs who wanted to maintain their image), the machines were not typical of American politics, and often they were far less disciplined and unified than their critics thought. And they usually flourished in areas of one-party domination rather than in situations of party competition.

Most of the time, we can conclude, the American system has operated much closer to the Madisonian model than to the Jeffersonian. Most politicians dealt with one another from a relatively autonomous basis of power. Partly because the Constitution decreed separate and independent constituencies, partly because the thousands of districts were differently affected by the variety of interests and attitudes in a pluralistic society, and partly because of an individualistic ethic that operated in politics as well as business, politicians tended to build and nourish their own power centers. There was, to be sure, a great deal of concerting of efforts among politicians who saw profit in running together on party tickets, or in informal alliances based on mutual coattail-grabbing. But typically it was every man for himself.

As the national parties came into equilibrium after the Civil War and post-bellum disruptions, there were hints of tendencies toward more national party centralization and solidarity. But the 1880's were not an auspicious period for the kind of presidential leadership that might have given the parties verve and focus, and in any case the post-1896 imbalance precipitated a reversal of whatever trend there was. The imbalance combined with the progressive impulse produced a drive toward "direct democracy" that undermined and pulverized the party system. The strongest anti-party instrument was the direct primary, which separated candidates from party organization and leadership, forced them to develop their own sources of support in personal organizations, local boosters, and interest groups, and hence compelled politicians, even more than they had before, to run (and to govern) on their own.

It was in the Deep South that the breakdown of parties went the farthest. Before the Civil War the Whigs and the Democrats had carried on a vigorous party battle in many areas of the South. After the war the Radical Republicans naturally forced most Southerners into the Democratic party. Republicanism came to symbolize Negro and carpetbagger rule. Southerners breaking away from dominant Democratic rule met, as Key has said, social ostracism, economic coercion, and election chicanery. Since political battles were waged mainly within the Democratic party, the party became simply an arena in which office seekers backed by personal organizations fought out their individual battles. Adoption of primaries further disrupted the state Democratic parties in the South. A minor but hopeful Republican revival and the possibility of more party competition was cut short by the Populist fervor that swept the South in the

1890's. Dominant white forces, fearing that party competition might lead politicians to cater to the Negro vote, beat back the Populist attack, destroyed the possibility of durable Democratic-Populist competition, and forced the party struggle back inside the shell of the Democratic party. The four decades after 1860 left most of the South with a one-party monopoly, a restricted franchise, a highly personal and fluid politics, an array of techniques to bar Negroes from the polls, a highly developed system of party primaries, and almost complete party disorganization. But the South was only an extreme example of tendencies found in most of the rest of the nation, especially after the turn of the century.

Party organization had declined in Congress too. The power of party leaders in House and Senate, which reached its apogee shortly after the turn of the century, was subverted in the revolts against Cannonism and Aldrichism, in the adoption of direct election of Senators, and in the growth of mandatory direct primaries. Other institutions were altered. Power became broadly dispersed in both chambers. The cluster of state and local conventions that had vivified (and sometimes degraded) American politics since Jacksonian days gave way to primary elections, and in most states conventions disappeared or became ritualistic gatherings of the party devout where a party platform was adopted which most of the party's candidates would ignore once they won office. Even the national convention came under sharp attack, but it survived. The decline in party vigor was accompanied by a decline in voting and in party spirit. "The most striking feature of the over-all picture is the persistent decline in the proportion of eligible voters making use of the franchise from 1896 to 1924," Lane says. Party spirit is harder to measure, but the stories of the old political battles—the huge crowds, the parades, the unabashedly partisan oratory, the occasional partisan fisticuffs—suggest also, perhaps, a decline in the intensity of party competition.

It was significant and ironic that America entered the 20th Century with an increasingly pulverized party system. For that century would see the intensified concentration of capital and industry, vast military establishments in two world wars, stronger nation-wide farm, labor, and professional associations, huge newspaper and magazine chains with national circulations, mass entertainment industries, enlarged federal, state and big-city government bureaucracies, and other agencies of mass unification and control. Could the national political parties remain as loose coalitions of amorphous committees in the face of growing institutionalization and bureaucratization of American society? Would either the Madisonian or Jeffersonian strategies prove relevant to the political demands of the new century?

II

The Jeffersonian Impulse

5

ROOSEVELT and TAFT: WHICH REPUBLICAN PARTY?

A political aspirant in the United States," Tocqueville observed, "begins by discovering his own interest, and discovering those other interests which may be collected around and amalgamated with it. He then continues to find out some doctrine or principle which may suit the purposes of this new association, and which he adopts in order to bring forward his party and secure its popularity." Tocqueville was describing one of the oldest and simplest acts of politics—the effort of the Greek magistrate or the Roman senator, of the Russian revolutionary or the British squire, to piece together a following big enough to win power in a legislative assembly or a political party or a popular election.

Equally old is the dread of such a man—especially of the man who sought to organize the *demos*, the rabble, the masses against the rich, the comfortable and the well born. Democratic politics, said a cynic, was the art of obtaining money from the rich and votes from the poor, on the pretext of protecting the one against the other. The men who wrote the American Constitution feared the demagogue who might organize a majority of the poor and propertyless into a faction that would take undue advantage of the republican principle of majority rule; hence they set up barricades against a simple majority.

The idea that the poor could be easily banded together against the rich stemmed from the 19th Century concept of economic man —from the notion that people would act in politics, as they did in the market place, in terms of a calculus of economic self-interest. This notion underplayed the fact that the 20th Century has unhappily made only too clear—that men are moved also by noneconomic motives, by base instincts and lofty ideals, by strange mixtures of selfishness and generosity, rationality and stupidity. Such non-economic motives made things much harder for most politicians, for moralistic attitudes were too wayward and intangible to be converted easily into the balance accounts of the political market place.

Compelling moral issues have raised hob with American politics and parties. During the decade before civil war the old party methods of bargain and adjustment suddenly seemed no longer to work. The kind of small concession that usually quieted the struggle over economic spoils was as likely as not to arouse rather than propitiate Northern abolitionists or Southern states' righters. It had been possible to cut the economic loaf many ways, and into the thinnest slices; slavery was a moral question and hence a more flammable type of political commodity. So politicians like Douglas, adept at calculating every ounce of pressure and every dollar of advantage, found themselves on strange political ground. They made terrible miscalculations, and they ended that decade with their old party system in a shambles.

The first decade of the 20th Century posed a new set of moral issues. Politics had never had such a nakedly economic basis and thrust as during the years from Grant to McKinley; now many people, especially affluent, middle-class people, seemed more concerned with matters that had high moral overtones: honest government, child labor, women's rights, regulation of big business, conservation, bossism, more democracy in politics and government, white slavery, pure food and patent medicine scandals. These much publicized problems sharpened the old tension between "Cotton Republicans," many of whom were party regulars interested in the party as a vehicle for economic rewards, and the "Conscience Republicans," who were often more independent of party. Presiding over the party, and over the America of this reformist decade, was a Republican regular who was also one of the most vocal moralists of American politics. By the end of the decade the Republican party was splitting, as the Democrats had a half century before.

The Colonel and the Boss

The long and stormy engagement between Theodore Roosevelt and the regular Republican party began one day in the fall of 1880 when the young Harvard graduate marched into a saloon at 59th Street and Fifth Avenue, climbed a dingy flight of stairs, and presented himself to the occupants of the Twenty-first District Republican Club. Doubtless it was a painful occasion. Roosevelt, with his spectacles, shrill voice, and fancy side whiskers, must have seemed the very personification of the "Diamond Back Republicans," the local nabobs from whom the organization was delighted to accept campaign contributions but otherwise kept its distance. And to Roosevelt this room, with its canonical furniture, spittoons, and dusty portrait of Grant, and its seedy, expectorating, cigar-chewing denizens, must have symbolized the party machine against which he had been warned.

The warnings had been plentiful, and edged with derision. When Roosevelt had inquired as to the whereabouts of the local Republican headquarters, he said later, his prominent friends in business and law had laughed at him, telling him that politics was "low," that the organizations were controlled not by gentlemen but by saloon-keepers, horse-car conductors, and other rough and brutal types. "I answered," Roosevelt remembered, "that if this were so it merely meant that the people I knew did not belong to the governing class and that the other people did—and that I intended to be one of the governing class." The young Harvard man had already developed an instinct for power. Within a year he gained the confidence of a rebellious group in the club, won the Republican nomination for state assemblyman, and easily carried the election in his heavily Republican district.

Regular Republicans were one thing, regular Democrats something else. Early in January, 1881, on taking his seat in the legislature in Albany, Roosevelt saw for the first time Democratic leaders as a body. "Vicious, stupid looking scoundrels with apparently not a redeeming trait," he scrawled in his diary. ". . . The average Catholic Irishman of the first generation as represented in this Assembly, is a low, venal, corrupt and unintelligent brute. The average Democrat here seems much below the average Republican. Among the professions represented in the two parties the contrast is striking. There are six liquor sellers, two bricklayers, a butcher, a tobacconist, a pawn broker and a type setter in the house—all Democratic; but of the farmers and lawyers the majority are Republicans. . . ."

Still, all these men, Democrat and Republican alike, held the levers of power, and it was Roosevelt's great task to get along with them so that he could become one of the real "governing class." During the next two decades, as he served three terms in the Assembly, took a bad beating in a three-way contest for mayor of New York, became a member of the Civil Service Commission in Washington under Harrison and Cleveland, and returned to New York for a hitch as head of the city's Board of Police Commissioners, Roosevelt had to hold the confidence of the "regulars" in his party without alienating the independent Republicans, the independent Democrats, and the independent Independents who often held the balance of power in New York elections. Two things made Roosevelt's task difficult. He was possessed of a supercharged sense of moral indignation about corrupt bosses in both parties, "socialistic" labor unions, selfish and shortsighted businessmen, and, above all, the reformers, whom he denounced as impracticable and worse. The reformers, for their part, were suspicious, inflammatory types who looked on Roosevelt as a man likely in a showdown to side with the Republican regulars.

They were right. The first clear test of Roosevelt's regularity came in 1884, when the Republicans nominated Blaine for President. Before the convention Roosevelt strongly opposed the Plumed Knight and his "decidedly mottled record." Right after the convention he was furious with the delegates' choice, and his indignation boiled over when he talked with a reporter. It seemed that he might bolt. But after brooding for a few weeks he decided against joining the Mugwumps, who had renounced the Republican party for Cleveland. At first he stood on the ground of expedience. "It is impossible," he said, "to combine the functions of a guerrilla chief with those of a colonel in the regular army." By fall he was taking higher moral ground. The Mugwumps, he said, were suffering from a "species of moral myopia, complicated with intellectual strabismus."

Clearly Roosevelt was "safe." During the '80's and '90's he roundly berated the Republican regulars when occasion arose, but he stayed prudently within the party. Stung by the reformers' criticisms, he showered more epithets on them than on any other group in New York. Mentally dishonest, vain, hypocritical, mendacious, lunatic, mentally diseased, slanderous, criminal were items from a large vocabulary Roosevelt used privately against the "professional reformers" like Oswald Garrison Villard, editor of the *New York Evening Post,* and Charles Henry Parkhurst, a noted foe of municipal sin. Where he wanted to stand, he said, was in the "just middle," along with practical reformers and independent Republicans.

Roosevelt's tactic, in short, was to keep barely inside the big GOP tent and then to claim that he was taking high moral ground. The middle way was advantageous politically too. In 1898, Senator Tom Platt, the boss of the New York State Republican organization, was looking around for a candidate to succeed the incumbent governor, Frank S. Black, who was politically vulnerable because of lax handling of the Erie Canal Scandals. Although Platt had picked Black two years before, he now was ready to dump him for the sake of the party. Presently his eye fell on Roosevelt just back from Cuba and covered with glory as the hero of San Juan Hill. To Platt Roosevelt was a "perfect bull in a china shop," but he might be just regular enough to work with the Senator and just independent enough to appeal to the independents and hence hold the governorship for the GOP.

Platt broached the idea to Chauncey Depew, head of the New York Central. Depew concurred. He liked to be practical about

these things, Depew said. If Black were the candidate again and if
he were speaking for him, Depew said, some heckler would stand
up and say, "Chauncey, we agree with what you say about the
Grand Old Party and all that, but how about the Canal Steal?"
But if Roosevelt was nominated, Depew went on, he could answer
the heckler: "I am mighty glad you asked that question. We have
nominated for governor a man who has demonstrated in public
office and on the battlefield that he is a fighter for the right and
always victorious. . . ." Then, said Depew, he would "follow the
colonel leading his Rough Riders up San Juan Hill and ask the
band to play the Star-Spangled Banner."

Platt said impulsively, Depew recalled later, "Roosevelt will be
nominated."

A most elaborate courtship followed between the Boss and the
Colonel. In the end, through an intermediary, Roosevelt agreed to
respect Platt's position as head of the Republican organization, to
avoid factional activity in the party, to consult with the Senator
freely and fully before making decisions on all important measures.
Platt agreed to treat Roosevelt as the Governor and not as a mere
figurehead, to expect cooperation but not slavish obedience, and to
let Roosevelt act on his best judgment provided he kept the party
united and the organization intact. Platt also let Roosevelt pretend
that this was no deal or bargain but only what the Colonel wanted
anyway, so that Roosevelt could get the job and keep his conscience
clear too.

At the same time he was flirting with Platt, Roosevelt was con-
ducting an equally elaborate back-door negotiation with the reformers. The independents hoped to nominate a complete ticket
of their own, headed by Roosevelt, whom the Republicans would
have to nominate too. Then the reformers would follow Roosevelt
on their local tickets with young good-government candidates who
would beat Platt's regulars. Both Platt and the reformers, in short,
hoped to use the Colonel for their own purposes. Which way would
Roosevelt jump? He wanted both the Republican nomination and
independent endorsement, but this was impossible because it left
unsettled the question of the rest of the ticket. Finally, after a summit conference with Platt and his men that ratified the previous
negotiations, Roosevelt decided to stay regular. He told the inde-

pendents that he must announce himself as exclusively the Republican candidate.

The reformers were indignant. Although they themselves had been divided over tactics, and though Roosevelt had made no hard-currency promises, they now denounced Roosevelt's lack of "honor." By accepting Platt, said one, the Colonel had become the "standard bearer of corruption and demoralization. Where is the courage of San Juan?"

Platt saw his tactics magnificently vindicated when Roosevelt squeaked through by 17,794 votes. But as the months passed he found the new Governor even more unmanageable than he had feared. Roosevelt treated him as head of the organization, consulted him, negotiated with him, defended him, flattered him—but in the end acted as he saw fit. Eventually he was boasting to reformers that during his administration he had "had the kernel and Mr. Platt the husk." In one condescending note to Platt he said that he would not go back on a promise he had made on an appointment, nor should Platt expect him to; the letter ended, "it is not your style, Senator."

Clearly Platt had a bear by the tail. He could deny the Governor re-nomination, but this might touch off an uproar in the party and a big switch by independents to the Democrats. The easiest way to get the Governor out of state politics was to kick him upstairs into the vice-presidency in 1900, when that office became available because of the death of the incumbent. The main obstacle was Roosevelt himself. The Governor had favored the idea at one point, but he turned away from it, especially as he saw Platt's motives. He wanted to run for Governor again, as a stepping stone to a Cabinet post or some other high national office. He feared the vice-presidency because it was a dead end politically and it offered so little action. "I would a great deal rather be anything, say professor of history, than Vice-President," he wrote Platt gloomily.

Once again the long-suffering Platt had to take Roosevelt's future in hand without rasping the Governor's high-blown sensibilities. One difficulty was the national Republican chairman, Mark Hanna, who had no wish that Platt's problem should become his own. "Don't any of you realize that there's only one life between this madman and the White House?" he was said to have demanded. On the other hand, Roosevelt had strong backing among western delegates who wanted the Rough Rider to brighten up the ticket headed by the respectable McKinley. Roosevelt himself, while outwardly protesting, had come to the convention in a wide-brimmed, black hat suggestive of his Cuban exploits—"an Acceptance Hat," an old Republican politico noted. In the end, after a complex series of maneuvers, Roosevelt was drafted kicking and screaming as McKinley's running mate, but in such a way that he could boast that the "New York machine" had actually been against him.

In the fall Roosevelt took to the hustings against "all the lunatics, all the idiots, all the knaves, all the cowards and all the honest people who are slow-witted," all of whom, it seemed, had gathered to Bryan's side. While McKinley received delegations at home, the Governor made a campaign of phenomenal intensity, by the standards of the day; it was estimated that he traveled 21,209 miles and appeared before three million people. McKinley's respectability and Roosevelt's ardor paid off. On November 6, 1900, the Republican ticket overcame Bryan for the second time with the largest plurality since Grant's re-election campaign.

A "Regular with a Conscience"

Lincoln Steffens told of the time that Jacob Riis, the crusading journalist, burst in on his friend Roosevelt shortly after the latter's appointment as police commissioner, and asked bluntly whether he was running for the presidency. "T.R. leaped to his feet, ran around his desk, and fists clenched, teeth bared, he seemed about to strike or throttle Riis, who cowered away, amazed. 'Don't you dare ask me that,' T.R. yelled at Riis. 'Don't you put such ideas into my head. Don't you ever mention that to me again.'" If he got to thinking of the presidency, he went on, he would become careful, calculating, cautious—and he would beat himself.

The story rings true, for Roosevelt was forever tantalizing himself with notions of future glory, while openly denying his ambitions and privately despairing of his chances of achieving them. He took to power as some men do to drink, and like the addict who keeps his bottle out of sight, as if to ease his conscience, Roosevelt was forever assuring people that he had no political future. While Governor he complained that he could not get re-nominated; as Vice-President he said that he was at the end of the road. But all the time he was constantly weighing his position and calculating his chances. While Vice-President he wrote to a number of eminent lawyers asking their advice as to how he might resume the study of law and gain admission to the bar. A few weeks later he was writing William Allen White as to how he might gain the presidency after McKinley. Even while McKinley lay wounded by an assassin's shot in September 1901 (and was expected to recover), Roosevelt was planning a discreet political tour of the Midwest.

Early in the morning of September 14, 1901, while the Vice-President was racing out of the Adirondacks on a buckboard to the nearest railroad station, McKinley died. It has been said that both Roosevelt and the Republican party were lucky that this "regular with a conscience," as John Blum has called him, came into power just as the Grand Old Party had to tack to port in order to catch the rising wind of reform. Was it just luck? Roosevelt had been nominated mainly in response to pressure from rank-and-file delegates who wanted to balance the ticket, and with the acquiescence of McKinley and other party leaders, had gained power through the ancient and orthodox ways of American politics. How would he use power as President?

In the few days that Roosevelt had presided over the Senate he had been "immensely amused and interested from the standpoint of an historical observer" by what he saw going on before him in the upper chamber and in Washington. As President he could not be quite so detached. At this time the Republican Old Guard in the Senate was in the zenith of its power. The Old Guard was buttressed by pervasive financial and political power. Platt was boss of New York Republicanism and tied to financial interests; Matthew Quay was Republican boss of Pennsylvania and a spokesman for its steel and coal magnates; Mark Hanna was national Republican chairman as well as head of the party in Ohio; Nelson Aldrich—"Morgan's floor broker in the Senate," some called him—was chairman of the Senate Finance Committee as well as party kingpin in Rhode Island. Such men, elected and re-elected by the state legislatures,

had the security that goes with long tenure; William Allison of Iowa
had been Senator for 36 years, chairman of the Appropriations Committee for 27, head of the party caucus for 11.

Roosevelt approached this citadel warily. "During the coming
three years I hope to keep in closest touch with you and to profit by
your advice . . ." he wrote a conservative Senator. "Whenever
possible I shall pay the utmost heed to your advice," he wrote another. He treated Speaker Cannon with marked deference; he carefully allotted New York jobs to Platt, and to his own people; he
handed out patronage positions chiefly through the Senators. Roosevelt was not squeamish about acting like a politician. No more
malodorous boss took the Senate floor than Matt Quay; Roosevelt
made one of Quay's friends postmaster in Philadelphia and another,
collector of internal revenue.

The President was not out to reform the Senate or to reorganize
his party; he was out to get through some legislations on which he
had set his heart. Sometimes, despite his honeyed words, he outmaneuvered rival politicians as he once had Platt. But his basic
method was to live and let live. Through an unceasing stream of
letters, chats, and indirect messages, he flattered, cajoled, negotiated,
bargained, pressured. He recognized that men like Aldrich and Cannon had their independent power bases that he must respect. But
he demanded that they work with him to reorient the Republican
party toward moderate reforms after its long period of standpattism.
Essentially he was working within the Madisonian system.

With all his zest and bombast, Roosevelt rarely forgot the limits
of his strength; he had an instinct for nice calculations of his own
and his opponents' power. During the critical coal strike of 1902,
when the miners were stubborn and the mine owners truculent,
the President wrote a revealing letter to Lodge. How could he get
concessions from the owners? "Unfortunately, the strength of my
public position before the country is also its weakness. I am genuinely
independent of the big monied men in all matters where I think the
interests of the public are concerned. . . . But when I do not grant
any favors to these big monied men . . . it is out of the question
for me to expect them to grant favors to me in return. I treat them
precisely as I treat other citizens; . . . In return, they will support
me, in so far as they are actuated purely by public spirit, simply ac-

cordingly as that I am or am not doing well; and so far as they are actuated by their private interests they will support me only on points where they think it is to their interest to do so. The sum of this is that I can make no private or special appeal to them, and I am at my wit's end how to proceed. . . ." In the end Roosevelt obtained a coal settlement more by maneuver and stratagem than by an exercise of power—in sharp contrast to John Kennedy's curbing of Big Steel sixty years later.

With Congressmen, too, Roosevelt employed the arts of bargain and barter. Like a good cavalryman he knew that he could not always—or even usually—attack all across the line. His main legislative goal in 1904 was to vest the weak Interstate Commerce Commission with real power over railroad accounts, private railway equipment, and, to a limited extent, railroad rates. A second objective was revision and reduction of the tariff. It was soon clear that he could not have both. Railroad legislation was closer to the President's heart, for he had firm ideas about the abuses of organized corporate power. Tariff reform he considered less central to the task of regulating the national economy; and while rate regulation would antagonize the railroad magnates, reduced tariffs would arouse thousands of little manufacturers and businessmen across the country. "There is no question that there is dynamite in it," he wrote an anti-tariff leader, Nicholas Murray Butler. He would not break his party over it.

Roosevelt's way out of this dilemma was ingenious: he used the threat of tariff revision to compel Congress to back railroad legislation. To Speaker Joe Cannon, who could not stomach tariff reform, he sent a draft of a special message proposing some changes and more executive control of tariff schedules. A few days later, while Cannon was mulling over this disturbing document, Roosevelt asked Congress for railroad legislation. Subsequently, the President made a deal with Cannon by which the tariff question was dropped in favor of massing the Rooseveltian forces in the House behind the railroad bill. Massed they were, and the bill passed by an overwhelming majority. The Senate, more conservative than the House, was harder to overcome. By careful indiscretions the President kept the threat of tariff reform alive, even threatening to call a special session. Aldrich, the Old Guard leader, tried to upset Roosevelt's plans by turning over floor control of the bill to a Democratic demagogue Roosevelt despised, "Pitchfork Ben" Tillman, of South Carolina, and to a Republican progressive he distrusted, Robert La Follette. The President quickly called Aldrich's hand by entering into negotiations for a stronger bill with Tillman through a third party. Tillman could not deliver enough Democratic support, however, so Roosevelt turned back to the Old Guard, who were now willing to settle for his original bill. The result was passage of the famous Hepburn Act of 1906.

At the same time that the President was willing to barter with Congress in its sphere of legislation, he tried to keep his own executive power inviolate. This was especially true in foreign policy, where the Constitution and the coercion of events give the President wide latitude. Most of his party, and much of the opposition party, was incorrigibly isolationist. He used his treaty and recognition powers vigorously in getting the Panama Canal underway, letting "Congress debate, and while the debate goes on," as he said later, "the canal does also." He helped end hostilities between Russia and Japan. He expanded the Monroe Doctrine to police the Caribbean and check intervention from the Great Powers of Europe. He fought the efforts of Bryanites to withdraw from our imperial commitments in Cuba and the Philippines. And he exuberantly dispatched the fleet around the world; as Agar has said, Congress had to pay the bills or allow the ships to rot away in some foreign port.

In his role as party leader, too, Roosevelt used the traditional powers of the Presidency. He insisted on complete control of the national party organization, of course, but mainly because he knew this was indispensable for his nomination in 1904. First he had to deal with the national chairman, Hanna, the rugged, outspoken Ohioan who had run the party under McKinley. "I trust you will command me if I can be of any service," Hanna had said just after Roosevelt took the oath of office on McKinley's death; but he didn't really mean this, and Roosevelt knew that he didn't. As 1904 approached, Hanna declined to line up behind the President. Possibly he wanted to be President himself; more likely, as an old "pro," he wanted the regular Republican party to become something else than the tail to Roosevelt's kite. Matters came to a head when Roosevelt's friends put up a resolution in the Ohio Republican convention endorsing the President for 1904. Just as the Roosevelt forces hoped, the resolution compelled Hanna to take a stand. Which way would he jump? Seeking a neutral corner, he wired the President that the endorsement had come in such a way that he must oppose the resolution. "When you know all the facts I am sure you will approve my cause." Roosevelt would not let him escape. ". . . Those who favor my administration and my nomination will favor endorsing both and those who do not will oppose," he told Hanna coldly. The national chairman meekly backed down. When Hanna still refused to support Roosevelt's nomination Roosevelt gave patronage to the other Senator in Ohio and even attacked Hanna indirectly on the stump. Hanna's death early in 1904 destroyed any potential opposition to Roosevelt's nomination.

Despite all the histrionics Roosevelt was careful during his first term not to move much outside the traditional orbit of the President's party leadership. Accused once of trying to form a "Roosevelt Party in Congress," he said that no one in the White House had dreamed of it. When he tried to depart from custom he ran into trouble. For example, he so admired Joseph W. Folk, a Democrat running for Governor of Missouri, that he urged Missouri Republicans to nominate him too; but the Missouri regulars went ahead and chose their own man. Glumly, Roosevelt endorsed him, amid charges that he still preferred Folk. He did prefer Folk (who won), but he was not willing to antagonize Republican regulars and jeopardize his own chances of carrying Missouri.

What Roosevelt tried to do as party leader, in short, was to establish his own independent power base from which he could deal with other sovereign politicians. He in effect formed his own party, a presidential party, that could insure him the nomination. He bargained with Senators and Congressmen, mediated their disputes, gave them patronage and favors in return for support, but he did not challenge their autonomy. He built a presidential coalition of Republicans, dissident Democrats, independents, friendly labor leaders, and Southern Negroes, but this was his personal political following, and he did not try to re-align the basis of the regular Republican party. In 1904 he ran largely on his own; when state politicians battled over fierce local issues, Roosevelt pleaded with them to emphasize state matters less and the Square Deal more. But on his own part he played down certain issues that might alienate support, and in foreign affairs he tried to appear as less of a saber rattler. Mr. Dooley, the philosophical bartender, remarked to Hennessey that he had been authorized "to deny th' infamous rayport that th' Prizident was iver at San Joon Hill. At th' time of this gloryous an' lamintable performance, th' good mon was down with the measles conthracted at th' Internaytional Peace Convintion."

Since Roosevelt respected the independent power of the congressional Republicans, the measures that the President signed almost always were sharp compromises with his original hopes. But throughout his Presidency Roosevelt was still so adept at making compromises seem exciting and beneficent rather than drab and timorous that he gave the appearance of vigorous forward movement even while dragging anchor. He was still so effective in portraying the extremists as the criminal rich and the criminal poor, as lunatics, fools and idiots that the President's way ended up not simply the middle way but the right way—and the only right way.

Roosevelt brought such zest and gusto and craft to American politics that his style was often taken for substance. And his task was easier as a result of the work of La Follette and the other reformers whom he assigned to the lunatic fringe. Only because Roosevelt and his main body of troops were well back of the skirmish line of reform, only because he was able to pull back when the battle became too hot, was he able to survive and flourish politically. "I wanted to go a little ahead of my party in the right direction," he said once, "but not so far ahead that they won't follow me." Because he both cherished power and accepted the responsibility that went with it, because he made his followers face up to the foreign and domestic problems of the new century, because he wielded his own executive power with such verve and effect, he still stands as both hero and modernizer of the presidential Republicans.

Taft and the Congressional Republicans

Of all Roosevelt's major public acts the most uncharacteristic was his voluntary surrender of the Presidency on March 4, 1909. Why he gave up the position and the power he loved so much is still not clear. He had, of course, made his famous statement on election night in 1904 that he would respect the two-term tradition and that "under no circumstances will I be a candidate for or accept another nomination." But this reckless pledge—so typical of Roosevelt's ambivalence toward power at the very moment he drank so heavy a draft of it—could have been annulled by any of the myriad devices used by politicians. A more important reason for his retirement from the White House was probably the momentum of national affairs during the last two years of Roosevelt's regime.

This was the heyday of the crusading journalist, the exposing magazine article, the social gospel, civic reforms, the conservation movement, moral uplift. City bosses, traction magnates, Wall Street financiers, avaricious exploiters of natural resources, patent medicine manufacturers, life insurance companies, the United States Senate— all these and more were "exposed" month after month in the popular journals of the day. "Time was," Mr. Dooley said to Mr. Hennessey, "when these magazines was very ca'ming to the mind. . . . But now when I pick me fav-rite magazine off th' flure, what do I find? Iverything has gone wrong. . . ." Prodded by the reformers, respectable middle-class America was taking a fresh and critical look at American life.

Roosevelt leveled the choicest of his old epithets against the reform movement and invented a new one: muckraker. But also in his own way, at his own pace, with his own style, he responded to it; and more important, he contributed to it. During his last two years in the White House he veered sharply left. His rhetoric took on a new militance. "I have been appalled recently by the many revelations of crookedness in high places," he wrote Lodge in 1908. "Ten years ago I did not believe there was anything like the amount of corruption high up in business and political circles that there actually is." By now he was describing himself almost casually as a "radical" and he was attempting to make Republicanism the party of "progressive conservatism" or "conservative radicalism"—he was not sure which. By now Roosevelt's rhetoric was no longer outrunning his recommendations for legislation. By the end of his term he had proposed adoption of an inheritance and income tax, regulation of railroad securities, limitations of labor injunctions, extension of the eight-hour day, national incorporation and regulation of interstate business, and other reforms that deeply pained the Old Guard.

Roosevelt's shift to the left sharpened and deepened the split within the Republican party. Not only did he carry a large number of urban, middle-class Republicans with him, he also mobilized a good deal of new support, especially in the ranks of labor. And in some cases he institutionalized this support. For example, in the field of conservation alone the President in 1908 created the National Conservation Congress, the National Country Life Commission, and the Inland Waterways Commission to frame and support national action. Other groups, such as reform and labor organizations, were already in being but gained impetus as a result of presidential recognition. These and other less formalized groups were not only policy instruments. They were also political instruments, for the group interests mobilized through them became part of a broad Roosevelt coalition operating across the jurisdiction of the regular Republicans.

The upshot was that by March 1909, Roosevelt was leading a large body of troops toward new goals, at the same time that the conservative wing of the party was standing almost absolutely pat. Aldrich still reigned in the Senate, Cannon in the House. Unrest was growing among sections of the congressional rank and file, especially in the House, but the old chieftains governed unperturbed in caucus and committee rooms. Roosevelt had indiscriminately supported Republican congressional candidates of all hues in 1906; now, with his personal power drawing to an end, he had no way of effecting a union with the reform elements, some of whom lacked faith in the durability of Roosevelt's progressivism. And he had won the lasting enmity of the Old Guard. "The ruling clique in the Senate, the House, and the National Committee, seem to regard every concession to decency as merely a matter of bargain and sale with me, which I must pay for in some way or fashion," he wrote a friend in May 1908. ". . . I think I can get to the end of my term without a break." He barely did so, but by the time he left the White House, Congress, as he recognized, was in an ugly mood.

Such was the state of affairs when the jovial William Howard Taft became President in March 1909, and Roosevelt left for hunting in Africa and a triumphal tour of Europe. At first Taft evidently had no clear idea of how he would conduct his relations with Congress and the party regulars. Certainly he did not plan to submit to the Old Guard; his career had been executive and judicial rather than legislative, and he had won attention as a leader of the Rooseveltian forces. Indeed, at one point Taft must have been highly critical of the congressional Republicans, for in 1903 Roosevelt had taken him mildly to task for being "unjust" to Aldrich and the rest. The new President, moreover, personally disliked Cannon "and his nest of standpatters in his House," although he also had friends in the party's right wing.

For a time Taft, like many Presidents before him, followed a fluctuating mid-course between the conservative and progressive forces in his party. On the one hand, he made plans to help insurgent Republicans to de-throne Cannon as Speaker, or at least to reform the rules of the House; he moved to ask Congress for tariff revision downward; and he proceeded to administer existing reform legislation, such as anti-trust, with even more vigor than had Roosevelt. On the other hand, he generally kept his distance from the progressive wing of the party; he took a cramped view of the President's role as chief legislator because of deeply held constitutional views of presidential power; and he chose a cabinet dominated by corporation lawyers who, while not conservatives of the Aldrich stamp, could be expected to administer their departments without the histrionics of some of Roosevelt's men. Taft's cabinet appointments, in fact, were a direct truce offer to Aldrich & Company. He hoped, the new President said, that his proposals to Congress would be received "with respect and a desire to support them by those men—leaders in Congress—who would certainly oppose recommendations made by a cabinet consisting of the more radical members of the party."

How long could Taft's middle way work? It was doomed from the start. To hold an independent course between the party wings, to play one group against another, to avoid inexorably alienating either side, called for rocklike self-confidence, enormous energy, a sense of basic direction, and a willingness to exploit and even expand presidential power. These qualities were not Taft's. He did not possess the steady will power and direction that enables the strong man, with all his twists and turns, to move toward his target; rather, as Pringle has said, Taft had only the stubbornness of the uncertain man. He was indolent, too; his personal political voltage was not high and steady enough to energize the circuits of power leading out of the White House. He was too high-minded to use some of

Roosevelt's blustering, bullying methods, and he lacked what Mowry has called Roosevelt's catlike political touch.

Taft's attack on Cannonism was a case study in presidential ineptitude. Encouraged by the President's rumblings against the Speaker, 30 Republican Congressmen boycotted the party caucus and thereby announced a revolt against Cannonism in March 1909. Soon Taft had a visitation from Cannon, Aldrich and the chairman of the House Ways and Means Committee, who warned him that a defeat for the Speaker on rules would jeopardize the President's plan for tariff revision. The congressional leaders offered, in effect, a deal: if Taft would call off his efforts against Cannon, the three leaders would go along on tariff revision. Taft consented, to the consternation of the insurgents. But once Cannon was re-elected Speaker, under the old rules, and with Taft's help, he cooly ignored his pledge to support tariff revision, at least as the President understood it. The President stood by helpless while Cannon stripped the rebel Congressmen of choice committee assignments and while the Republican Congressional Campaign Committee, under the Speaker's influence, moved to oppose insurgent candidates in the forthcoming primary elections during 1910.

If Taft lacked the power and craft to make his middle way work, which direction would he take when he had to choose? His ultimate decision was largely controlled by compelling circumstances in the Republican party.

In inheriting the Presidency, Taft also might have inherited the "Square Deal" presidential party that Roosevelt had built out of moderate and reform Republicans, independent Democrats, and other elements. It did not work out that way; Taft quite naturally wanted to be President in his own right and not a slavish projection of Roosevelt, even if that had been possible. But in constructing his own Cabinet, in dropping some of Roosevelt's friends from the Administration, in edging into the Republican "center" and out of TR's "center left," Taft began to snap the ties that might have held a large body of Rooseveltians in his train. Holding their allegiance would have been a hard job at best, since nobody could take Roosevelt's place in the hearts of the Square Dealers, who cast hopeful glances at their departed hero with the tantalizing thought, "Back from Elba." But Taft made things worse with his clumsiness.

Once the President began swinging right there was no place he could stop short of the Old Guard wing in Congress. For institutionally, politically, organizationally, there was no support for a middle way between the left and right wings except for a politician who might have slowly built up some kind of following over the years. This Taft had not done. For him, the choice was Roosevelt's presidential party or Aldrich and Cannon's congressional party. Because of pressures both in him and outside of him, he made the latter choice.

His situation can be put much more simply. He needed friends—friends who could be depended on, who had power of their own, who were organized and available and exploitable. It was partly a psychological need. "When you and Senator Aldrich are both absent from the Senate," Taft wrote to the highly conservative Senator Hale of Maine in June 1910, "I feel much anxiety as to whether the measures in which I am so much interested will receive proper consideration. In other words, I yearn for the presence of an old parliamentary hand." To Aldrich he wrote early the next year: "I long for your presence. I feel about you as Scott said of Rhoderick Dhu. A blast upon your bugle horn were worth a thousand men."

The more Taft succumbed to the Old Guard embrace, the more he was caught in the network of obligations and pressures surrounding the congressional party. The mishaps that studded Taft's administration—his calling the Payne-Aldrich Tariff Act "the best tariff act" ever passed, his public praise for Aldrich and other standpatters, his cold-shouldering of Republican progressives, his failure to exert influence in Congress—were not haphazard blunders. They were implicit in Taft's allegiance to the congressional Republicans. Thus his most dramatic mistake, the dismissal of Gifford Pinchot as head of the Forestry Bureau, was not only a matter of conflicting personalities, policies, and ideologies. Taft simply had to back up his Interior Secretary, Richard Ballinger, because he had to respond to a power system that not only embraced Western Senators hostile to conservation and the interests they represented, and included the supporters of Ballinger in Congress (whose investigating committee later exonerated him), but also upheld the idea, as Taft said, that progress in conservation, as in other fields, should be made "through statutes" and not by a free-wheeling President.

But if Taft needed the regulars, they needed him too. They wanted a President who would not brandish his veto power or try to dominate Congress, for any self-limitation of presidential power automatically strengthened congressional power. The President also possessed weapons of discipline, such as patronage, that could be used to help the congressional leaders maintain their own strength on Capitol Hill. The sanctions that Taft had failed to bring to bear on Cannon he was ready, by 1910, to use against the liberals in Congress. Sluggishly Taft threw his weight into the Republican primaries. He planned with Aldrich to use party funds to help "orthodox Republicans"; he induced regulars in several states to stop squabbling among themselves, so that they might mass their strength against insurgents; he sent his aged Vice-President, James Sherman, to Wisconsin to show the administration's support for the regulars against La Follette. He encouraged the formation of Taft Republican clubs, who were shortly doing battle with "Progressive Republican" clubs.

In June 1910, in the middle of this Republican ruckus, Theodore Roosevelt came home.

Conscience Without Regulars

Even today, 50 years later, the events of 1911-12 have a perverse and enigmatic quality. Why did Roosevelt, who had sided with Blaine in '84 and, when the chips were down, with the regulars ever since, proceed in his mid-fifties to shatter his old bonds with his party? How could he tie his fortunes to a movement led by the very types of "fools" and "lunatics" he had denounced so long? How could the man who loved power so and used it so deftly, lead—deliberately and knowingly—both his old party and the new movement to defeat at the hands of the Democratic party he had fought for thirty years? It was not strange that he broke with his successor; Roosevelt being Roosevelt, this was doubtless inevitable. What was strange was that he could go on to break the party and the system in which he had so prospered.

He had, of course, plenty of provocation. Even while in Africa, runners brought him news of Taft's dalliance with the Old Guard. Pinchot intercepted him in Europe with a long bill of complaints from outraged progressives. He arrived home in June 1910 to find Taft using the machinery of the congressional party to purge some of his old friends from office. Root had extracted a promise from the Colonel that he would forbear from politics for two months after his return; the cooling-off time became a warming-up period as Roosevelt's old friends streamed to Oyster Bay carrying tales against the administration. The time was hardly up when the Colonel plunged back into New York state politics by challenging the regulars under William Barnes, Jr., a far less reputable boss than Platt had been. Taft clumsily gave the impression of supporting Barnes. In November came the Administration's staggering losses to Democrats and insurgents in the congressional elections. The President was now exhibiting weakness as well as conservatism—a dangerous combination in front of a roaming Bull Moose.

Still, Roosevelt was desperately uncertain of his role in this strange new situation. The problems he had pushed away by fleeing to Africa now rebounded in harsher form. For a time he tried again to be a regular with a conscience; while reserving the right to speak out he maintained pleasant relations with most of the regulars, including Taft, whom he now flatly placed in that category. He made some effort in the fall elections to support Republican candidates, both regular and insurgent, he still bellowed at the "wild irresponsible folly of the ultra-Insurgents" (while also denouncing the "sordid baseness of most of the so-called Regulars"), and he even put in a word for the Payne-Aldrich tariff. But his heart was not in it. "I have never had a more unpleasant summer," he complained to Root.

Roosevelt could no more keep to his wavering middle course than Taft had been able to do a year earlier. Political circumstances were simply too much for him. Roosevelt's absence and Taft's shift toward the Old Guard had left unled a great body of troops who were now turning to Roosevelt for leadership. La Follette had tried to take command, but he lacked the former President's wide political appeal and prestige. During 1911 the pressure on Roosevelt to run built up relentlessly.

This pressure came largely from Roosevelt's old presidential party, minus the regulars who were staying with Taft for reasons of patronage and ideology. By 1912 this party was both steering and riding the tide of reform that had been building up for a decade. Its leaders, as Hofstadter had said, were the spiritual sons of the old Mugwumps who had fought Grantism and Blaine, but they had dropped some of the old ideological baggage. "Where the Mugwumps had been committed to aristocracy, in spirit if not in their formal theories of government," Hofstadter says, "the Progressives spoke of returning government to the people; and where the Mugwumps had clung desperately to liberal economics and the clichés of laissez faire, the Progressives were prepared to make use of state intervention wherever it suited their purposes." This activist concept of national government set the Progressives sharply apart from the great body of Taft's regulars.

This new breed of Mugwumps came largely out of the nation's waxing, upper middle-class in the cities. They were mostly businessmen, editors, lawyers, with a scattering of professional workers, college professors, writers, doctors, and clergymen. Most of them born and bred Republicans, they had kept their distance from other reform movements, from the country populists, the silverites, the trust busters, the city labor groups. Many of them ran their own businesses or were self-employed as lawyers and editors; hence they were an independent lot. They had had little experience with institutional discipline, political or otherwise.

Roosevelt was one of them. Thoroughly an upper-class Eastern city man, despite his cowboy trappings, and a writer and thinker of extraordinary range and brilliance, he was also a hero to them. During Taft's administration Roosevelt carried the Progressives with him toward a broader and more sophisticated brand of urban progressivism. While abroad he had read Herbert Croly's *The Promise of American Life;* soon after returning he had had the author out to lunch at Oyster Bay; and Croly's ideas had confirmed Roosevelt's own beliefs, stemming from his second presidential term, in the need for a stronger national government and wider executive power to achieve the general welfare. In his famous speech at Osawatomie Roosevelt called for a vigorous national effort to master the social consequences of the industrial revolution: he wanted nationally graduated income and inheritance taxes, broadened efforts to conserve the nation's resources, comprehensive labor legislation, publicity for political spending. He demanded, above all, national power to grapple with the evils of (but not to break apart) large-scale financial and industrial combination. And he urged a governmental system that could master corporate economic power and thus put the national need before sectional or personal gain.

The New Nationalism, he said, was "impatient of the utter confusion that results from local legislatures attempting to treat national issues as local issues. It's still more impatient of the impotence which springs from overdivision of governmental powers. . . . This New Nationalism regards the executive power as the steward of the public welfare. It demands of the judiciary that it shall be interested primarily in human welfare rather than in property, just as it demands that the representative body shall represent all the people rather than any one section or class of the people."

Thus by the dawn of 1912 a Roosevelt party still existed, strongly rooted in the social and political fabric, and fully equipped with its own ideology and platform, zealous troops, and an unemployed hero. There was needed only the spark to bring it to life.

That spark was struck from Roosevelt's smoldering ambition. Throughout 1911, of course, he insisted that he was not a candidate for President, and would not be. After all, he had been President, and why stake his place in history on a long and probably fruitless quest for the nomination and election? But into his letters late in 1911 crept a note that might have stirred the memory—and the suspicions—of any who knew well the earlier Roosevelt. "I very emphatically feel that to me personally to be nominated in 1912 would be a calamity," he wrote a friend in December 1911. There followed 500 words of tortured reasoning against his running. But then the fateful sentence: "Moreover I am absolutely certain that it would be criminal folly under any circumstances to nominate me unless it could be made clear as day that the nomination came not through intrigue or political work, not in the least to gratify any kind of wish or ambition on my part, but simply and solely because the bulk of the people wanted a given job done, and for their own sakes, and not for mine, wanted me to do that job. . . ." Ten years earlier Roosevelt had written to a friend: "If my nomination is to come at all, it has to come at the initiative of the people."

Roosevelt took only a few more weeks to discover that the movement for him did come from the "people at large." It is easy to dis-

miss all this as the old Rooseveltian trick of demanding and arranging one's own draft. It would be easier—and quite correct—to say
that once again Roosevelt had shown his neurotic need to legitimize
the power he wanted so badly. Root astutely compared him to a
"thirsty sinner." But it would be just as true, and more relevant to
our inquiries here, to note that more than most politicians taking
this demagogic line, Roosevelt was responding to a clear party call.
The hundreds of progressive leaders who visited him or wrote to
him bespoke the genuine need of a political movement that had to
have Roosevelt as presidential candidate.

Quickly the progressive leaders picked up their cue. Early in
February 1912 seven progressive governors in a letter that reads
suspiciously as though the Colonel drafted it himself, urged him to
run and asked whether he would accept the nomination if it came
"unsolicited and unsought." He would, Roosevelt replied. So coherent and unified was the old presidential party that the structure
of the Roosevelt organization was virtually complete by the end of
February.

The frenetic events of the next few months—Roosevelt's radical
speeches, Taft's replies, Roosevelt's charge of deliberate stealing of
delegate votes by his enemies, the furious primary fights in which
the two old friends called each other "demagogue" and "fathead,"
the roaring convention with Roosevelt beaten by the "Taft steamroller" (which was in fact the Congressional party steamroller), the
bolt of the progressives—such events can be understood as a battle
between two parties, not simply as a fight within a party. Rarely have
Democrats and Republicans hated one another as bitterly as did Republican regulars and Republican progressives in 1912. Nor was
there ever a more fervent party rally than the Bull Moose convention
in early August, nor a more rapturous reception for a hero than
Roosevelt received when he came to the platform to offer his "Con-
fession of Faith." As he stood on the platform in his old familiar
style, his body rocked back and forth to the rhythm of the cheers.

"Fifteen thousand people roared their welcome," Mowry reports.
"For fifty-two minutes, wildly waving red bandanas, they cheered
him as they had never cheered anyone else. Here were no claques,
no artificial demonstration sustained by artificial devices. None were
needed. Men and women simply stood on their feet for an hour

because they liked him and believed in him. When Roosevelt himself finally sought to stop the demonstration, the crowd once more broke into song."

> Thou wilt not cower in the dust,
>   Roosevelt, O Roosevelt!
> Thy gleaming sword shall never rust,
>   Roosevelt, O Roosevelt!

Out of this convention came the authentic voice of the old Republican party conscience—the conscience of the Abolitionists, of the crusaders against spoils, of the middle-class respectables who hated the vulgar new rich who bought and sold politicians, of the new urban reformers who glimpsed the great collective needs of 20th Century urban America. Morality was not all on one side. Taft, too, had his ethic—one that turned more to older, small-town notions of decency and enterprise and self-reliance and freedom from corporate or governmental bigness—just as men who stuck with him, like Root and Stimson, had theirs. But by the force of circumstances, Taft had been left presiding over a party of regulars, many of whom looked on the Republican party as an enterprise in which they conducted their private business. He had been left with the cotton whigs of 1912. The party conscience had bolted with Roosevelt.

But the Progressives were a party without regulars, a conscience without power. The old Colonel who had united the two so effectively in the Square Deal now found himself commanding cavalry without foot soldiers. No wonder that a reporter watching him at the convention noticed that he seemed bewildered at the wild welcome of the crowd: "They were crusaders; he was not." And victory demanded more than a crusade. Not only were the bulk of the troops still with Taft. These troops manned the state and county and city parties where election battles are won and lost. And because the Progressives were unable to build state and local organizations to fight for their own candidates throughout the maze of the American electoral system, many politicians, including some Progressives, who might otherwise have followed Roosevelt stuck with the regular party.

Unlike some of his disciples, Roosevelt knew very early that his cause was doomed. He said that he did not care, that the fight had to be fought because it was a fight for morality. But he did care, because he had always loved power, and known its strange and intoxicating ways. At the end of the campaign he had lost to the Democrats, and his party was broken after 16 years in power; now an enormous effort at healing was in order. He spent the last six years of his life trying to re-unite conscience and power. He was still trying to mass his party against his real enemy, the Democrats, when, on January 4, 1919, he suddenly died.

6

WOODROW WILSON
and the
NEW DEMOCRACY

$\mathcal{E}$arly in 1879 an editor of the *International Review* read with approval a remarkable essay submitted by a college student. The editor was Henry Cabot Lodge, 29 years old, a proper young Bostonian, a Republican, and a tutor at Harvard; the contributor was Thomas W. Wilson, 22, a Southerner, a Democrat, and a senior at Princeton. Lodge published the article in the August issue of the *Review*. Entitled "Cabinet Government in the United States," the essay opened with a gloomy view of American government. "A marked and alarming decline in statesmanship, a rule of levity and folly instead of wisdom and sober forethought in legislation threatened to shake our trust" both in the nation's leaders and in its basic principles of government.

What, demanded Wilson, was the real cause of anxiety? It was the "absorption of all power by a legislature which is practically irresponsible for its acts." In the long paragraphs that followed the young Princetonian laid a heavy indictment against Congress. It did not deliberate. It did not debate. It was not responsible. It acted through little committees in which cunning and trickery thrived. As he wrote, Wilson's criticism sharpened. ". . . We are ruled by scheming, incompetent, political tradesmen, whose aims and ambitions are merely personal, instead of by broad-minded, masterful statesmen, whose sympathies and purposes are patriotic and national." The solution? Reverse the decision of the Framers to isolate the President from Congress. Let the Chief Executive choose his Cabinet from members of Congress. Let this Cabinet link President and Congress in support of a system of party government.

"Eight words contain the sum of the present degradation of our political parties: *No leaders, no principles; no principles, no parties.*" Responsible cabinet government would mean talented national leadership.

And so, a hundred years after James Madison left Princeton for the career in which he helped set up the system of checks and balances in which he was finally enmeshed, another Virginian entered Princeton and concluded from his studies that the Framers had been wrong, that executive and legislature must be joined so that the nation could be led and governed. That, perhaps, was wholly coincidental, but it was not coincidental that the Republican congressional party that had governed the South so harshly should have provoked this attack from a Southerner who had been born in Staunton, Virginia, five years before Fort Sumter and who had grown up in Georgia and South Carolina during and after the Civil War. In 1885 Wilson published a longer and even more devastating attack on legislative supremacy and irresponsibility in his first book, *Congressional Government.* Greeted warmly by reviewers, the book quickly became a classic and established Wilson's name in academic political science.

Recent critics have been less friendly toward Wilson's early analysis and prescription for our governmental ills. He grossly underestimated the potential of the President; he slighted the role of economic factors in politics; he borrowed heavily from the recent writings of other men, not always with full acknowledgment; he was

neither very profound nor very original. He had never even seen
Congress or its committees at work. Wilson later had to correct his
underestimation of the President and his absurd idea that United
States Senators were removed from class or vested interests. It seems
clear, too, that Wilson's idea of cabinet government would not have
worked in America. Certainly Wilson was heavily influenced by
Walter Bagehot's admiration for the British cabinet system. When
the Princeton senior wrote that "a complete separation of the executive and the legislative is not in accord with the true spirit of those
essentially English institutions of which our Government is a characteristic offshoot," he was coming perilously close to saying that
the Madisonian system of checks and balances was un-American because it was un-English.

Still, in the midst of Wilson's floundering and miscalculations,
one central idea gleams powerfully. This was his belief in leadership. It was the decline in great political leadership that had produced the mediocrity of American political life, and only the revival
of leadership would make possible a brilliant American statecraft.
This idea, in various forms, marks virtually all Wilson's early writings and speeches; it is, indeed, the dominant theme in his whole
intellectual life. And political life too—for not only did Wilson want
to think and write about political leadership, above all he wanted to
practice it. This, as Walter Lippmann has said, was his true vocation.
Hence he quite deliberately made his life into a unity of thought
and action—and incidentally made it a test of an intellectual's capacity to put his ideas into action.

Wilson's background and early life were ideal for this kind of
test. Growing up in a South that had been wrenched out of the
nation, inspired by the moral imperatives of his Calvinist faith,
nourished on English political ideas, especially Manchester liberalism, he was, like a number of other world leaders, something of an
outsider to his own culture. He could view his nation's institutions
with a critical detachment even while he committed himself pas-
sionately to what he conceived to be his nation's loftiest ideals. Not
until his late 40's did he plunge into the midstream of public affairs.
He had practiced law briefly in Atlanta but the higgling and haggling
over tiny, specific problems—mainly money—repelled him. "Who can

lead an intellectual life in ignorant Georgia?" he demanded of a
friend. So he returned to academic life where he could study and
dream of leadership and statecraft.

But what purposes would great leadership serve? During his early
years Wilson seemed much less interested in specific public policies
than in the thrust and parry of great party orators. What policies he
espoused stemmed from his background. Basically he was an old-
fashioned Manchester liberal. His battle cry was individual liberty.
He frowned on labor unions, Populists, and excessive regulation by
government. He saw evils in big business, too, but these were largely
the failures of individuals, not of the business system. He opposed
the Bryanites and doubtless voted for the Gold Democrats in 1896.
He admired Cleveland, including the reactionary Cleveland of the
second term. Wilson was—in 20th Century terms—an economic conservative. But as Hofstadter has said, his conservatism made room
for organic change and gradual reform.

An economic conservative, a constitutional reformer—this was
Wilson's political posture when he became president of Princeton
in 1902. During the next ten years he virtually reversed this combination. Absorbed in university problems, he seemed during his
first years cut off from the Square Deal and muckraking fervor of
the day. Then came two dramatic Princeton campaigns that ended
in failure: his proposal that the exclusive Princeton eating clubs give
way to a more democratic arrangement, and a tough battle to control the location and direction of a proposed graduate college. The
first failure demonstrated the heavy imprint on education of ma-
terialism and snobbishness and other false values, Wilson felt; the
second failure, which was caused largely by the sudden receipt of
millions to be used for a graduate college plan favored by Wilson's
university foes, demonstrated the direct influence of wealth. Wilson
started neither fight for democratic goals; but he came out of them,
as Arthur S. Link has said, with the conclusion that the forces of
wealth were hostile to social and educational democracy. Once in
speaking to the Pittsburgh alumni, he converted the graduate college fight—essentially an issue of educational policy and control—
into a great democratic struggle. "I have dedicated every power that
there is in me," he cried, "to bring absolutely democratic regeneration
in spirit."

By the time he quit the Princeton presidency in 1910 Wilson had turned vaguely and idealistically to the left. He had also worked out far more perceptive and less reformist views of American government. He was still highly critical of the pulverization of policy in the committees of Congress. But by now, thanks to Cleveland, McKinley, and Roosevelt, he had glimpsed the leadership that the Presidents could supply. He had a better understanding of American parties, with all their problems and promise. And he saw that under American conditions, the President as party leader, rather than cabinet government, could be the great unifying and energizing force in national government.

So by 1910, Wilson had had his schooling and apprenticeship in political leadership; he was ready for public affairs. And public affairs were ready for him. In 1910 Democratic politicians were looking for a man who could restore the New Jersey governorship to the Democracy after years of Republican control. Wilson, a battler against snobbishness and privilege, seemed just the man behind whom the regulars could win office in what was clearly a progressive year. In September the Democrats drafted him as their candidate for governor.

The Scholar and the Boss

"God! Look at the man's jaw!" a ward boss was heard to say as Woodrow Wilson pushed through cheering Democrats in the Trenton Opera House, to accept the nomination for governor. It was a prophetic remark. As he faced the throng, he must have realized that the cheers came much more from the organization regulars in front of him than from the independent reform Democrats. For at this point Wilson was the machine candidate. He had won the nomination largely because ex-Senator James Smith, Jr., of Newark, the biggest boss in New Jersey's seedy Democratic organization, saw Wilson as a popular and respectable figure behind whom Democrats could unite and win. Smith also expected that his man might pull enough Democrats into the legislature to fulfill Smith's fondest dream—re-election after years of exile to the United States Senate.

The reform Democrats watched Wilson skeptically as he started his acceptance speech. They suspected darkly that Smith would never have taken this man unless certain understandings had been reached. They were right. Through an intermediary Smith had let Wilson know in June that he would make no demands as to "principles, measures, or men," but he did want assurances that as governor Wilson "would not set about fighting and breaking down the existing Democratic organization and replacing it with one of your own." Word for word Wilson had made that pledge. He would not build up a personal machine, he promised the intermediary, adding only that the arrangement would last as long as he was left absolutely free in the matters of measures and men. Smith was satisfied. In his political world party control was crucial; whoever mastered the party ultimately controlled measures and men.

But now there was that jaw jutting out into the opera house, and there were those progressive Democrats wondering if he was anything but Smith's catspaw. Wilson opened his speech with the customary thanks for the nomination. Then his manner suddenly changed. "As you know," he said, his long earnest face alive with missionary zeal, "I did not seek this nomination. It has come to me absolutely unsolicited, with the consequence that I shall enter upon the duties of the office of Governor, if elected, with absolutely no pledge of any kind to prevent me from serving the people of the State with singleness of purpose. . . ."

"The future is not for parties 'playing politics,'" Wilson went on, "but for measures conceived in the largest spirit, pushed by parties whose leaders are statesmen not demagogues, who love, not their offices but their duty and their opportunity for service. We are witnessing a renaissance of public spirit, a reawakening of sober public opinion, a revival of the power of the people. . . . We shall serve justice and candour and all things that make for right. Is not our own ancient party the party disciplined and made ready for this great task?" By now the progressives were cheering. "Thank God, at last, a leader has come!" one cried out to another. The candidate ended his prepared speech but the delegates shouted "Go on, go on!" and Wilson turned back to them to say that great tasks lay before the party, that Americans had to reconstruct their economic order and hence would reconstruct their political organization.

Smith could hardly have been disturbed by Wilson's disclaimers of political debt; they were the traditional rhetoric of an acceptance speech. The Democratic leader busied himself with initiating Wilson into practical politics—no easy task since the candidate said he was unable to conduct a handshaking, baby-kissing campaign, and even had the notion that he could run his campaign for a few hundred dollars out of his own pocket. But as Wilson swung into the momentum of the campaign Smith began to have misgivings. For this was 1910, the climax of a reformist decade, and New Jerseyites were more aroused than ever about party machines and financial trusts and the links between the two. When Wilson in his early speeches was fuzzy about specific reforms he got a bad reception from insurgent Democrats and Republicans and from the independent press. The more he campaigned, the more specific, searching and meaningful his utterances became. Challenged by progressive Republicans to state his independence from Smith, Wilson asserted that he would be absolutely free of the boss system. Then in his climactic campaign speech in Newark, the heart of Smith's Essex County bailiwick, Wilson pushed his position even further.

"When I was approached with regard to the nomination for the Governorship, I understood it to be distinctly represented to me that the purpose of those who asked my leave to use my name for that purpose was that I should be invited to take the leadership of the Democratic party. . . . I was asked to take it with the understanding that I was absolutely free from pledges and obligations of any kind. . . . I regard myself as pledged to the regeneration of the Democratic party."

It is said that Smith, sitting in the audience, wept as Wilson closed his speech; it may have been Wilson's eloquence that moved him, but more likely mortification over this incredible turn of events. Anyway, there was nothing he could do now but accept the gage of battle. When Wilson handsomely carried the election in November 1910, winning 56 per cent of the two-party vote, and when Smith soon afterwards indicated that he would ask the newly elected Democratic legislature to make him United States Senator, the stage was set for a direct contest between the scholar and the boss. Progressive Democrats were backing a lack-lustre Bryan Democrat, James Martine, mainly because Martine, a perennial candidate for office, had won a preference primary for Senator. The primary was nonbinding, but by 1910 any kind of primary had become a sacred cow for independents.

Then came the extraordinary spectacle of the scholar from Princeton systematically destroying the political career of the old party pro from Newark. Taking the offensive from the start, the Governor-elect carried the battle into Smith's home territory by conferring directly with party leaders and legislators. He undermined Smith's support even in the old Senator's own county. Smith fought back only to find himself the object of a crusade. Wilson pictured him not as he really was—a run-of-the-mill party boss—but as evil personified, a party despot, a symbol of corruption and predatory control by the rich. Frantically Smith charged Wilson with dishonesty and trickery; but few would take the word of a boss over the word of a high-minded professor. Actually Wilson's motives were probably more political than moralistic. The progressives had put great pressure on him to back Martine; he needed their support in the legislative session ahead. And the mood of 1910 welcomed a battle against political sin. Not that Wilson disbelieved his own oratory; but he also saw that a moral crusade aroused more support than a fight over power and pelf. Smith was badly beaten in the legislative balloting in January 1911.

"You poor scholar and amateur in politics!" a friend wrote the elated Wilson. "I feel so sorry for you. Why don't you get an expert like Smith to advise you?"

By trouncing Smith, Wilson had made himself leader of the New Jersey Democracy. What, asked the progressives, would he do with his new authority? They had their answer during the early months of 1911. Wilson focused his efforts on four campaign pledges: direct primaries and election reform; outlawry of corrupt practices; workmen's compensation, and public utilities regulation. Moving quickly and surely, he prepared the legislative program, marshaled public support behind it, conferred with Republican legislators, took his case personally to the Democratic caucus, dramatized his battle against the bosses by ordering out of his office State Democratic Chairman James R. Nugent, a crony of Smith; maintained steady pressure on the legislators—and got all four bills enacted almost exactly as he wanted them. By April, when the legislature adjourned, the whole nation seemed to be watching this display of political leadership. New Jersey progressives were jubilant. "In less than four months," wrote one editor, "he has turned New Jersey from one of the most conservative and machine-dominated states into a leader in the forefront of progressive commonwealths."

During the next few months Wilson acted swiftly to consolidate control of his party. Nugent conveniently blundered by publicly and drunkenly offering a toast to the Governor, "an ingrate and a liar," and was soon ousted from the state chairmanship in favor of a Wilson man. With the Governor's support progressive Democrats organized a Woodrow Wilson League in the heart of Smith-Nugent country. Independents formed Wilson-for-President clubs, and some old Bryan clubs turned now to the Governor. A number of organization leaders lined up behind Wilson. In the fall Wilson led this loose alliance in a strenuous attempt to carry the Democratic primaries for Wilson men. Aside from Smith's bailiwick, the Governor's forces won Democratic nominations throughout the state. Wilson then, in the fall of 1911, launched an assault against the Republican bosses and called for a Democratic legislature (then elected annually). But unlike those in 1910, when Wilson himself had been a candidate and had a definite reform program, the results were disappointing. The Republicans won control of both houses.

So after one glorious year in office the prime minister from Princeton had lost his first general election. The result in New Jersey was a dreary anti-climax. "In spite of his assurance of willingness to cooperate in close association with the legislators during the session of 1912," Link says, "the fact is that Wilson simply refused to provide leadership for the Republican majority; and, more important, at no time did he give any indication that he considered himself the leader even of the Democratic minority. It is startling, this contrast between Wilson in 1911, a vigorous, driving party leader, and Wilson in 1912, content for the most part to carry on the routine business of state. Not once did he meet in caucus session with the Democrats; not once did he attempt to determine party policy or coerce the legislature into enacting reform legislation by going to the people to rouse public opinion in support of some specific measures. The Grand Old Party was back in legislative power; the political honeymoon was over.

What had gone wrong? Part of the trouble was that Wilson's great advantages of the first year—the freshness of his appeal, his specific program that had been shaped by a generation of progressives, the fact that he was running for office and could carry Democrats in with him—were absent the second year. Perhaps more important, and certainly more significant for Wilson's future, he had disrupted the existing state party with his crusade against bossism and with his party primary and other reforms, without establishing in its place a tight, solidly rooted organization of his own. Smith and Nugent had still been strong enough to cut the Democratic ticket seriously in their county, and Wilson had not compensated for this by making inroads into Republican territory.

Anyway, by early 1912, Wilson was running for President and this effort was absorbing most of his energy. In one of the most intense pre-convention campaigns up to that time he crossed and crisscrossed the nation, delivering high-minded speeches, arousing a flurry of interest wherever he went, appealing to the middle-class liberals with a creed of vague, utopian liberalism and somewhat more specific political reform. He won the ardent support of churchmen, educators, and college students. Noted magazines like *Outlook* and the *Nation,* influential newspapers like the *New York Evening Post,* the *Baltimore Sun,* and the *Kansas City Star* backed him. Wilson clubs dotted the country.

During the spring of 1912, Wilson's campaign for the Democratic presidential nomination stalled and almost collapsed. For the more Wilson made his elegant appeals to independents and progressives, the more the state and city bosses eyed him with cold suspicion. Wilson's overthrow of Smith and his threat of doing the one thing party regulars fear most—replacing the party organization with a personal organization—had put bosses like Charles F. Murphy of New York and Roger Sullivan of Chicago on their guard. Their suspicions deepened when Wilson spurned the public support of George Harvey, the New York publisher who had been his early and ardent booster. Obviously, Democratic regulars decided, the man could not be trusted to come through. And the regulars, along with William Randolph Hearst, who lambasted the "Professor" furiously on his front pages, had an easy alternative in Speaker Champ Clark.

The Missourian was an old Capitol Hill pro, a Bryanite, and a man that the regulars could deal with.

State after state went to Clark. Enough went to Wilson to keep him in the race, but even states with presidential primaries—supposedly the great mechanism for overcoming the regulars—went to the Speaker in some instances. Clark beat Wilson in the Illinois primaries by almost three to one. Wilson Democrats in New York, including a young state senator named Franklin D. Roosevelt, failed to pry delegates from the tight grip of Murphy. Even in New Jersey, Wilsonites had to fight to keep Smith from winning an anti-Wilson slate; the Newark boss did elect four of his own men. Wilson had virtually lost hope by June. "Just between you and me," he wrote a friend, "I have not the least idea of being nominated, because the make of the convention is such, the balance and confusion of forces, that the outcome is in the hands of the professional, case-hardened politicians who serve only their own interests and who know that I will not serve them except as I might serve the party in general." It looked as though Smith, who would control the federal patronage in New Jersey if Clark should be elected, might yet have the last laugh on the Princeton scholar-in-politics.

The Democratic convention opened in Baltimore late in June 1912. Its dramatic moments have long been celebrated: Bryan's declaration against Morgan, Ryan, Belmont "or any other member of the privilege-hunting and favor-seeking class"; the rowdy demonstrations for Clark and Wilson; Tammany's attempt to stampede the convention to Clark by delivering him New York's 90 votes on the tenth ballot; Bryan's warning to the convention, amid a storm of cheers and boos, that he would withhold his vote from Clark as long as New York voted for him; the stalemate that settled on the conclave for ballot after ballot; the slow rise in Wilson's strength; the sudden delivery of Boss Sullivan's Illinois votes; Underwood's withdrawal; and the stampede on the 46th ballot. Perhaps more significant were the private episodes: Wilson's manager, William F. McCombs busily dealing with bosses while the candidate announced in Sea Girt "I will not bargain for this office"; Wilson's negotiations with Bryan, who nourished a tiny hope that the convention might turn back to him; Wilson's failure of nerve after the Tammany switch, only to be saved by McCombs, who later lost *his* nerve; all amid blunders, misunderstandings, and miscalculations in the smoky confusion of the contest.

Watching from Sagamore Hill, Theodore Roosevelt saw that Wilson's nomination made Democratic victory almost inevitable, for now the Colonel could not monopolize the progressive vote. At Baltimore Wilson had been the middle-of-the-road candidate between the Bryanites and the South; now he took the middle ground between Roosevelt and Taft, though much closer to the former. Wilson made a fumbling start in his presidential campaign, just as he had two years earlier in New Jersey; but once again, as the tempo of his campaign heightened, he established closer contact with the crowds, found a surer political touch, and even picked up some of the arts of the demagogue, as when he addressed some workers sitting on box cars as "gentlemen in the boxes." With the help of Louis Brandeis and others, he took more explicit stands on trusts, labor, and other dimensions of the New Freedom. His party, bosses and Bryanites alike, rallied to him, while Taft and Roosevelt drove a wedge deeper and deeper into the Grand Old Party. On November 5, 1912, Wilson won 6,293,019 popular votes and 435 electoral votes, to 4,119,507 and 88 for Roosevelt, and 3,484,956 and 8 for Taft. Election of a Democratic House and Senate gave Wilson's party control of the national government for the first time since Cleveland's second term.

In the midst of these great events James Smith of Newark decided that he would try again for his old love, the Senate. Wilson was on him like a tiger. The implacable scholar took time from his campaign to help mass the progressive forces against the old boss, and he journeyed to Hoboken and Jersey City to urge his repudiation by the party. Smith was beaten so badly in the primary that he quit politics for good.

Master of His Party?

"There has been a change in government," Wilson opened bluntly in his inaugural address on March 4, 1913. ". . . No one can mistake the purpose for which the Nation now seeks to use the Democratic party." In lofty terms he spelled out his vision of a more pure and just America. "This is not a day of triumph; it is a day of dedication. Here muster, not the forces of party, but the forces of humanity. Men's hearts wait upon us; men's lives hang in the balance; men's hopes call upon us to say what we will do. . . ."

Could the Democratic party serve as the nation's instrument in pursuing this great vision? Wilson himself had his doubts. To be sure, the party now controlled both houses of Congress, and the President was the undisputed national leader. But as a national organization the Democracy was a patchwork of old Cleveland Democrats, urban bosses, Bryan Populists, conservative Southerners, urban middle-class progressives, strung together in a jumble of city machines, state committees, independent Democratic groups, and personal factions. The party was torn by ancient divisions: farm prices, labor's rights, political reform. And the party had a heavy rural bias in Congress, where Southerners and others from one-party states and districts had been accumulating committee seniority and power. The Democratic party, one critic scoffed, was the organized incapacity of the country.

So dubious was Wilson about the possibilities of this ancient and creaking structure that for some weeks before his inauguration he toyed with the idea of reconstructing the Democratic party and aligning it with liberal-minded independents and Republicans. The time seemed ripe; he needed progressive allies, and many progressives who had gone down with Roosevelt were now looking to him with hope. He would, he promised a New Jersey audience, avoid narrow partisanship by choosing for his administration "progressives, and only progressives." Shortly after his inauguration he told Albert S. Burleson, his Postmaster General and chief patronage dispenser, "that on appointments I am not going to advise with reactionary or standpat Senators or Representatives."

Burleson reacted like the seasoned old party politician that he was. "Mr. President," he exclaimed, "if you pursue this policy, it means that your administration is going to be a failure. It means the defeat of the measures of reform that you have next to your heart. The little offices don't amount to anything. They are inconsequential. It doesn't amount to a damn who is postmaster at Paducah, Kentucky. But these little offices mean a great deal to the Senators and Representatives in Congress. If it goes out that the President has turned down Representative So and So and Senator So and So, it means that that member has got bitter trouble at home. . . . I know these Congressmen and Senators. If they are turned down, they will hate you and will not vote for anything you want. It is human nature. . . ."

In the end Wilson gave way. If he had any doubts about Burleson's argument they were resolved in the actual business of trying to enact his program. Of many episodes the case of James A. O'Gorman, Democratic Senator from New York, was typical. Colonel Edward M. House, Treasury Secretary William G. McAdoo, and other advisers hoped to re-vamp the New York state Democratic party which was racked by the ancient struggle between Tammany and the reform independents. The Wilsonites planned to use New York patronage to recognize independent, anti-Tammany Democrats and ultimately to reconstruct the New York Democracy. At once O'Gorman was on guard. Though no tool of Tammany, he feared that McAdoo might try to supplant the regulars with a presidential or personal machine. So O'Gorman warned the President that he would invoke his personal privilege as a senator (i.e., his right to brand a proposed appointee as "personally obnoxious" and hence to gain votes for rejection from his fellow Democrats, under the old practice of "senatorial courtesy") against Wilson's key appointment. Backing off, the President offered a compromise that O'Gorman found acceptable. In other states, too, the Wilsonites discovered Senators to be tied so closely to the regular organization that the price of state and local reform was obstruction on Capitol Hill. So Wilson decided to use the party pretty much as he found it.

It was a fateful move, this decision to operate through the existing party mechanism, and in the short run, at least, Wilson was magnificently vindicated. His management of Congress during 1913 and 1914 still stands as the copy book model of how a strong President drives his program through Congress. Building on his experience in New Jersey, Wilson appeared in person before Congress to present his proposals; he conferred frequently with party and committee leaders in the White House or on the Hill; he exploited the caucus to unify the congressional party behind his program; he threatened to employ his veto against obnoxious proposals; he denounced the lobbyists infesting Washington; he mobilized the influence of Bryan, now his Secretary of State, and other party leaders, against wavering Democrats. Largely because the President acted as "the responsible leader of the party in power," to use his own term, he was able to unite the Democrats behind a substantial tariff reduction and behind a federal reserve measure that had threatened time and again to cleave the party into its ancient divisions. Legislation establishing a federal trade commission to police unfair trade practices followed in 1914.

If there is anything more difficult for a party leader than the blocking of his program in Congress, it is the full enactment of it. By the fall of 1914 Wilson had carried out his major campaign promises. He had redeemed some of the long-standing pledges of his party to agrarians, small businessmen and anti-Wall Street Populists. Where would the Democrats go from there? The problem was especially critical for Wilson because of strategic political developments. As TR's Progressive party declined, millions of independents were turning back toward the two old parties. Which party would exploit the progressives' concern over labor, women's rights, tenant farmers, child labor, Jim Crow? Which would form a new coalition that might attract the poorer farmers, union labor, Negroes, and the liberal-minded members of the middle-class? As urbanization and industrialization proceeded apace, which party could better address itself to the 20th Century big-city problems? Which could better exploit the federal government in coping with economic concentration and industrial malaise?

In the face of this question of grand political strategy, Wilson seemed to flounder. He opposed a rural credits measure that would have enabled the federal government to support low-interest loans to farmers. He refused to support a federal child labor law on the grounds that it was unconstitutional. He evaded taking a stand on woman suffrage. He signed La Follette's bill to protect seamen, but with reluctance because of international complications. He fought the exemption of labor and farm organizations from the penalties of the Sherman antitrust act. He came around to a "strong" federal trade commission only at the eleventh hour. He supported some regulatory legislation but made some very conservative appointments. He acquiesced in race segregation and made little effort to rid even his own executive agencies of Jim Crow.

Wilson's situation was immensely complicated by the power in the interlocked machinery of Congress of the Southern conservatives and of a few boss-controlled Democrats from the North. It was also complicated by the outbreak in August 1914 of World War I, which threatened to disrupt old party alignments and the balance of conservative and liberal forces. But his main trouble was that, with all his long years of writing about political parties and leadership, he seemed to lack comprehension of the relation of his party to shifting economic problems and the new demands of a changing society.

In the end it was—ironically for a scholar in politics—practical election needs rather than broader intellectual comprehension that compelled Wilson to move toward the old progressives and the liberal Democrats. The congressional elections of 1914, which left the Democrats with shrunken majorities in both houses, suggested that the old Republican popular majority might be welling up again. By 1916 it was clear that the Progressive party was crumbling and that the Democrats nationally needed a large infusion of new blood to win in the fall presidential campaign. During that year, Link has said, Wilson became "almost a new political creature, and under his leadership, a Democratic Congress enacted the most sweeping and significant progressive legislation in the history of the country up to that time." Reversing himself on the rural credits bill, he urged that the government should establish and initially finance farm loan banks. He pressured a workmen's compensation law and a child labor bill through Congress. In a departure from traditional Democratic policy, he supported a cooperative effort by government and the export trade to give some protection to American business overseas. To prevent a railroad strike the President persuaded Congress to pass a bill imposing the eight-hour day for railroad workers.

Progressives—especially intellectual progressives—were elated. He would vote, said Walter Lippmann, "for the Wilson who is temporarily at least creating, out of the reactionary, parochial fragments of the Democracy, the only party which at this moment is national in scope, liberal in purpose, and effective in action." The party, Lippmann went on, "had earlier seemed to lack all power of cohesion, it showed no ability to plan comprehensively, and in the test of action it seemed to have an irresistible tendency to fly apart into sulky groups." But Wilson had become the master of his party, had fashioned an old party into something like a national liberal organization.

Had he? When other progressive independents and journals—Jane Addams, Herbert Croly, Edward P. Costigan, and the *New Republic*, the *Nation*, the *New York Evening Post*—came out for Wilson, it seemed that Lippmann was right. And when Wilson eked out his victory over Charles Evans Hughes in the November election, it seemed that the Democratic party might become, as Croly said, a purposive national organization, embodying a genuinely national democracy. But on second look the election results were ominous. The President had not carried the great urban states of the Northeast. Labor had divided its vote between Wilson and Hughes. Where Wilson was successful he probably won more on the peace issue of having "kept us out of war" than on the record of his recent progressivism. And the Democrats had lost control of the House.

Whether Wilson would have realized the hopes of his progressive supporters during his second term we will never know, for war came within six months, and with it a new alignment of political support for the Administration. As Chief of State and Commander-in-Chief he might have drawn internationalist, moderately liberal Republicans into political alliance. The war itself intensified issues —foreign commitments, a league to enforce peace, woman suffrage, transportation, resources, wages, prices, and the reach of federal power in these and other areas—that might have provided a program behind which progressives in both parties could have rallied. But Wilson was preoccupied by foreign and military policy. Politics, he said, was adjourned. He allowed the Democratic national organization—such as it was—to atrophy without trying to organize a political home, or even a foundation, for a new coalition.

It was inevitable, no doubt, that a war leader would have little time for domestic political operations. What was surprising was that as the war neared its end Wilson should decide to offer a blanket endorsement to all Democratic Congressmen, including some who had opposed him on war measures, and that he should ask a repudiation (in effect) of all Republican Congressmen, including some who had backed him. To be sure, Wilson had plenty of provocation. Roosevelt, Taft, and Lodge had been calling for a Republican victory to guard against a cowardly peace. Wilson wanted a show of support at home for his peacemaking abroad. On October 25, 1918, ten days before the election, twelve before the Armistice, he convened politics again.

". . . The difficulties and delicacies of our present task," the President said in a statement to the American people, "are of a sort that makes it imperatively necessary that the Nation should give its undivided support to the Government under a unified leadership, and . . . a Republican Congress would divide the leadership."

"The leaders of the minority in the present Congress have unquestionably been pro-war, but they have been anti-administration. . . ."

"In ordinary times, I would not feel at liberty to make such an appeal to you. . . . But these are not ordinary times. . . ."

Once again, as in New Jersey seven years before, the prime minister had asked for a mandate in what he conceived to be a general election, and once again he was rebuffed. In November 1918 the Republicans regained control of Congress. The new majority leader in the Senate, and chairman of the Foreign Relations Committee, would be Henry Cabot Lodge.

Wilson v. Lodge: No Advice, No Consent

Like the disruption of the union sixty years before, the failure of the United States to join the League of Nations still stands as one of the historic misadventures of American politics. The story of 1919 and 1920 is still a paradox. Probably a large majority of the American people favored joining the League, without reservation, or with mild ones. Most newspapers endorsed adherence without reservations; only one out of six or seven flatly opposed membership. Prominent Republicans such as Taft wanted to join on a meaningful basis. And Democrats, spurred and inspired by their leader in the White House, were almost wholly united in support of some kind of adherence. Yet the United States never joined the League, and its defeat had such an effect that twenty years later a bold campaigner for the Presidency, Franklin D. Roosevelt, shied away from a pro-League stand when he was accused of softness on the matter.

How could such a cause be lost, and lost so irretrievably? Many reasons have been advanced: Wilson's and Lodge's hate for each other; the stubbornness of both the President and the Republican leadership in the Senate; the two-thirds requirement for Senate ratifications; the post-war slump in missionary idealism and the upsurge of nationalism; Republican control of both Senate and House; failure of party leaders to follow a bipartisan policy in foreign policy. Doubtless all these factors played a part. Yet all of them could have been overcome, as similar difficulties had in earlier times. Democrats and Republicans, for example, had often disagreed about treaties and still managed to compromise. What was so insuperable about the cleavage in 1920?

The answer is the same for 1919-20 as it was for 1850-60. The struggle was not simply between parties or between leaders or between different branches of government; it was rooted in the electoral system, in group and party interests, in governmental machinery, in such a way that majority opinion could never be brought to bear on the issue. This is not to say that the system was at fault and not the leaders; the leaders are part of the system. It is to say that the protagonists had little leeway for conciliation because the political context in which they operated fortified their intransigeance and hence inexorably forced them toward a fatal deadlock. It was not simply a series of blunders and misunderstandings that kept the United States out of the League; the outcome was inherent in the situation; and only rare statesmanship and good luck could have brought adherence. This time Americans had neither. How the system operated can be seen by considering the designs of the main adversaries.

To Wilson the League had become a highly personal and desperately important matter. During his triumphal tour of Europe crowds in the streets had hailed him as a savior. He made major concessions on the treaty both to Lloyd George and Clemenceau, and to isolationist opinion at home. He had, for example, specifically protected the Monroe Doctrine in the League Covenant, as well as our right to withdraw from the League altogether. He believed that he could make no further concessions on the League and the treaty without blighting his whole idea of America's positive role in helping enforce peace. He believed too—probably wrongly—that further tampering would require re-negotiation with our allies and hence would heat up the European pot all over again. Knowing he could count on almost all the Senate Democrats, he presented the treaty to the proud upper chamber on essentially a take-it-or-leave-it basis.

Whether deep down in his heart Lodge really wanted a League is still an open question; probably he preferred a Rooseveltian policy of the big stick, international conferences, and the balance of power. In any event, the League was of secondary importance to the gentleman from Massachusetts; what he most certainly wanted was to block Wilson from getting his League and then using it as a vote-getting issue in the 1920 campaigns. His main interest, in short, was the Republican party—or at least his wing of it—not the League. Lodge's situation in the Senate was a ticklish one. Of the 49 Republicans, about a dozen were "mild reservationists" who would accept the treaty without major changes. These Republicans were close to the more moderate, international wing of the party headed by men like Taft, Hughes, and Root. On Lodge's right flank were about fourteen "irreconcilables" who stood bitterly and vocally opposed to the treaty in any form. Lodge's own troops consisted of about twenty "strong reservationists" who reflected Lodge's willingness to take a league but only on his own terms.

Washington politicians watched, fascinated, as these two veteran politicians, the crusading President and the shrewd old Senator, worked out their battle plans. Wilson calculated that if the Senate turned down his League, he could establish a dramatic issue on which the Democratic party could win the election in 1920. The President was probably ready to run for a third term if necessary to turn the 1920 election into a "solemn referendum." And he had made the League and the treaty essentially a party issue by appointing to the peace conference a delegation that included only one Republican, a diplomat who had little standing with the congressional wing of the party. And he scorned the mild reservationists who could have supplied enough votes to win majorities for Wilson on reservations and amendments (only final ratification of the treaty required a two-thirds vote). To keep the issue unentangled, focused, headlined, the President planned also to make a "swing around the circle."

Lodge's tactic was just the opposite—to delay, obfuscate, and finally to suffocate Wilson's League. This tactic called for room to maneuver, since it meant veering back and forth, working first with one Republican faction and then another, conciliating his followers, stiffening them, yielding to them, as the situation demanded. And here Lodge took a step that raises doubt as to whether he really wanted any kind of meaningful league. As majority leader and as chairman of the Foreign Relations Committee the Senator could select new Republican appointees to this high-prestige committee. He chose two strong reservationists (one of them Warren G. Harding of Ohio) and two irreconcilables (one of them Hiram Johnson of California). He offered a post to a mild reservationist, Frank B. Kellogg of Minnesota (later Secretary of State under Coolidge) but only on the understanding that he support Lodge on the League. Kellogg demurred; Lodge renewed his conditional offer, using the amiable Harding as an intermediary. Kellogg declined. Lodge wanted only those moderates who would go along with him, but at the same time he accepted—evidently without conditions—two bitter-enders who later helped put pressure on him to stand firm against the League.

Still, the gentleman from Massachusetts was operating within bounds set by the Republican party in the Senate, and he had to adjust to the compulsions of the system. So did Wilson. For after all, he too had "stacked his committee"—the delegation to Paris— and he was just as willing as Lodge to deadlock the treaty in the Senate if this would give him a clear case on which to appeal to the people. Each man in his own medium operated like a virtuoso. Lodge dulled and confused public discussion of the issue by endless delays. He read aloud to his bored committee the entire text of the 268-page treaty; held six weeks of public hearings; helped trigger outcries from minority groups, especially the Anglophobe Irish; and demanded from the President executive documents he knew Wilson would never surrender. As Lodge proved master of the Senate, Wilson prepared to go to *his* constituency, the American people.

Wilson's appeal to the people in September 1919 has become one of the nation's imperishable memories: the hopeful departure of the presidential train packed with reporters, clerks, secret service men, and the President's wife and his personal retinue; the mixed receptions to his speeches in the isolationist Midwest; the huge crowds, sometimes fervent, sometimes just friendly, but always reverent; the train puffing through the Rockies with a stop at Coeur d'Alene, in Borahland; the never-ending bustle and strain within the hot, crowded trains; the milling crowds in the far West, aroused to fever pitch by Wilson's eloquence; the pounding headaches that racked the President as he hunched over his portable typewriter; the climactic address in Pueblo where an exhausted President almost broke into tears as he described the burial places of American soldiers in France and asserted that this tragedy should not be enacted again; more racking headaches that night, now amid nausea; the anguished decision to cancel the rest of the tour; the return of the presidential special to Washington, with curtains drawn; then the thrombosis, the collapse, the semi-paralysis, and the long imprisonment in the White House.

Yet the fact seems to be that Wilson's appeal to the people, though made with brilliance and boldness and capped by tragedy, did not change a single Senator's vote. The President might almost as well have been campaigning in another country. The wise old Senators knew their political world just as the President knew his. They knew that the people were fickle, that their passions would ebb as the issue of the League was obscured and devitalized during the year that would elapse before the election. Indeed, only one third of the Senators would have to face the voters in 1920. But beyond all this, most of Wilson's foes in the upper chamber were confident of their strength back home. The crowds in Idaho and California might cheer the Commander-in-Chief, but Borah and Johnson and the others had their own support, built up by years of mulish independence nationally, combined with steady obeisance to local interests and attitudes.

So the Senate was unmoved, and the treaty and the League headed inexorably to defeat. Wilson still would not compromise or confer with Lodge; he still preferred to keep his treaty intact and turn 1920 into a great and solemn referendum. Lodge was stuck fast too; when he seemed at one point on the verge of making concessions to the moderates, the bitter-enders called a council of war, summoned Lodge, and threatened to oust him as majority leader. (Borah said later that he had never seen a man look so scared.) On March 19, 1920, the Senate took the final vote on the resolution of ratification, which incorporated the Lodge reservations. The vote was 49 to 35 in favor—a majority, but fifteen votes short of the necessary two-thirds. About half the Democrats went over to Lodge in order to support some kind of League, but the other half—all Southerners—stuck with the President. Combined with the irreconcilables, they killed the League. Once again, as in 1860, the moderate elements in the middle had shrunk; the extremists had carried the day. And the League, like the Union, was dead.

But dead for how long? Now Wilson, still ailing, looked toward the fall elections for a popular mandate for his party and his cause. It was not to be. Although the President seemed to make himself available for renomination on the eve of the convention, this was out of the question; and the Democrats chose an Ohio governor identified neither with the Administration nor with the cause. While James M. Cox and his young running mate, Franklin Roosevelt, endorsed the League in general, they ran on a Democratic platform that itself fuzzed over the crucial questions of reservations.

Perhaps Wilson's plan for a referendum would have worked if the Republicans had nominated the leader and symbol of the Senate opposition, Senator Lodge. But Lodge, whatever his failings, knew himself; he knew that he was a senatorial, not a presidential, type. Nor did he want such a clear-cut posing of the issue as his candidacy would afford. He and his colleagues simply made sure that they would dominate Republican strategy. The convention was "government of the Senate, by the Senate, and for the Senate," said *The New York Times*. Lodge was both keynoter and permanent chairman of the Republican convention, appropriately held in isolationist Chicago. His men dominated the platform committee, and it was essentially Lodge's clique in the Senate, after the leading candidates for the nomination had deadlocked, that gathered in Room 404 of the Blackstone Hotel to choose a fellow Senator whose slovenly intellect and wabbling ways could be depended on to drown the League issue in a flood of double-talk and verbiage.

Where were the moderate Republicans in all this—where were Hughes and Taft and Herbert Hoover? During the Senate proceedings they had tried to moderate Lodge's position, but their pressure on the Massachusetts Senator had not overcome the opposing pressure from the irreconcilables. During the convention the moderates had lacked a clear-cut contender of their own; Root and Stimson were not popular enough; Hughes, grieving other the loss of his eldest daughter, would not run; Herbert Hoover was tainted by his service under Wilson. So the moderates had to go along with Harding. During the campaign they tried to win middle-of-the-road support and to push the wavering Harding toward a more pro-League stand by issuing a public appeal stating that the issue was between an extreme Wilson League and a modified Harding League. This was the intellect and conscience of the Republican party speaking out, and it served only to muddy the waters further.

Harding and the Republican party duly swept to victory in November 1920; they carried the electoral college, 404 to 127, won 64 per cent of the two-party popular vote, and gained topheavy majorities in Congress. But no one to this day has determined whether the campaign turned more on the League or a host of other issues and personalities and popular moods. Wilson's scheme had failed; the great and solemn referendum of 1920, as Bailey says, had turned into a great and solemn muddlement.

Wilson as a Jeffersonian Leader

The President, Wilson wrote in 1908, "cannot escape being the leader of his party except by incapacity and lack of personal force, because he is at once the choice of the party and of the nation. He is the party nominee, and the only party nominee for whom the whole nation votes. . . . No one else represents the people as a whole, exercising a national choice; and inasmuch as his strictly executive duties are in fact subordinated, so far at any rate as all detail is concerned, the President represents not so much the party's governing efficiency as its controlling ideals and principles. He is not so much part of its organization as its vital link of connection with the thinking nation. He can dominate his party by being spokesman for the real sentiment and purpose of the country. . . ."

Wilson was sharply aware of the two great conflicting roles of the President, national leader and party (or majority) leader:

"For he is also the political leader of the nation, or has it in his choice to be. The nation as a whole has chosen him, and is conscious that it has no other political spokesman. His is the only national voice in affairs. Let him once win the admiration and confidence of the country, and no other single force can withstand him, no combination of forces will easily overpower him. His position takes the imagination of the country. He is the representative of no constituency, but of the whole people. When he speaks in his true character, he speaks for no special interest. If he rightly interprets the national thought and boldly insists upon it, he is irresistible; and the country never feels the zest of action so much as when its President is of such insight and calibre. Its instinct is for unified action, and it craves a single leader. It is for this reason that it will often prefer to choose a man rather than a party. . . ."

It is given to few men to portray political roles as evocatively and to perform those roles as brilliantly as it was to Woodrow Wilson. As leader of his party he unified it behind its historic planks against high tariffs, the trusts, and the money power. Working closely with his fellow Democrats and their leaders in Congress, he made the party deliver on its major promises to the people. He brought the party victories in two presidential elections; he was the first incumbent Democratic President to be re-elected since Jackson. And far more than most Presidents, he gave his party credit—perhaps too much credit—for the achievements for which the President could have claimed most of the responsibility.

As national leader, too, he lived up to his intellectual projections of 1908. Not only did he speak magnificently for the people as a whole, as he interpreted their wishes, during the war and post-war periods. He did something much more difficult—acting as a national leader, he made his party turn from some of its old shibboleths, tied it closer to the new needs of an urban and industrialized nation. The old Democracy of 1913-14, once it had acted for farmers and little businessmen and Southerners and Westerners, then began to deal with industrial problems by legislation and to shape the governmental tools (such as regulatory commissions) necessary to cope with such problems. Then, during his second term, Wilson converted his party into a source of support during the war and during his long campaign for the Versailles Treaty and the League.

Yet Wilson is remembered as much for his magnificent failures as for these political feats. The main failure was, of course, the League, but there were others. As party leader, Wilson was never able to re-fashion the state and local Democratic parties in the national Wilsonian image; they remained—perhaps inevitably—the disorganized, often corrupt organizations, he found them to be in 1912. He left behind him a weak national party that in 1920 suffered one of its worst defeats in history. He made serious miscalculations on the capabilities of the Democracy in non-presidential elections. And it seems likely that Wilson's turn to urban progressivism, had it not been blurred by the war, would have involved him in serious difficulties with his party in Congress during his second term.

Against the background of Wilson's dazzling triumphs, how can we account for his failures? A main reason was Wilson's faulty grasp of the workings and limitations of the Democratic party, his failure to build strong party organization at party headquarters in Washington or in the field. This was paradoxical, for both as political scientist and as politician he had always emphasized the role of party. Perhaps too much so, for Wilson was prone to put a much greater burden on his party than it could bear.

In New Jersey, in 1911, he seemed to assume that his nationally celebrated achievements during his first year would be reflected in Democratic victories in the legislative elections; they were not. After his victories during his first two years as President, he probably expected another vote of confidence in the congressional elections of 1914; the Democrats lost heavily (but not their majority) and Wilson was heartsick. In 1918 he appealed for a Democratic Congress and this time lost his "mandate." Every time Wilson ran for office he won; every time his party ran without him on the ticket, his side lost.

Clearly something was wrong with the workings of the party at the congressional and local level. Wilson seemed to sense this on taking office in 1913, when he told Burleson that he would not give patronage to some of the old standpatters on Capitol Hill. Burleson was quite right in arguing that Wilson should use his minor appointments to win congressional support for the New Freedom. But Burleson and Wilson missed the longer term implication—that to give jobs and recognition to the congressional Democrats was to strengthen them both in Congress and in their constituencies, to add to their political resources, and hence to make them more formidable in the long run.

The most celebrated of Wilson's errors on this score was his call for a Democratic Congress in 1918, after all but ignoring the

Democratic party during his months of wartime, nonpartisan leadership. But perhaps the most significant miscalculation was a curious scheme of Wilson's during the struggle over the League. The scheme was to settle the issue by direct reference to the voters; since there would be no regular election for a year, he proposed that Senators who opposed him—he drew up a list of them—resign their seats and run for re-election on the basic issues. Wilson would promise the nation that if a majority or more of these Senators won re-election, he would appoint one of the Republican leaders (Lodge?) as Secretary of State; then the President and the Vice-President would resign, and the Republican Secretary of State would automatically become President.

It was an incredible idea. Since most state constitutions did not provide for special elections but left appointment to the Governors, the scheme was technically impossible. Politically it was suicidal; presumably only those Senators like Borah and Lodge, who felt completely safe in their districts, would resign their seats, and Wilson would be stuck with the results. It is unfair to hold Wilson wholly accountable for the scheme, of course, because he concocted it while in bed half-paralyzed. But it is too akin to Wilson's appeal of 1918 and his old liking of open parliamentary combat, and even his Princeton article of 1879, to be considered wholly aberrant. In any event, his associates talked him out of it.

Even Wilson's ablest move as party leader—his re-orienting of the Democratic party toward urban progressivism in 1916—betrayed his infirm grasp of party organization. In that year Wilson was able to pick up considerable support from the Progressives of 1912, and he brought over internationalist Republicans during the war. But he never made room for them in the Democratic party; by leaving the state and congressional and local parties unreformed and undisturbed, he made it impossible for most liberal and internationalist Republicans to take part in the Democracy at the lower levels. He created no new base for a realigned Democratic party. And when he reverted to his role as partisan leader in 1918 and called for a Democratic Congress, he lost the support of Republicans who were for him but not for his party. Wilson made a similar mistake after the war. He could have won the aid of internationalist Republicans if he had put a Taft or a Hughes on the peace commission, if he had worked with the mild reservationists in the Senate and accepted their essentially innocuous changes.

So entranced was Wilson with his dream of politics as a grand encounter between the forces of light and darkness that he never seemed to comprehend the world of lesser politics, where almost everything is grey. While aware of the importance of the state parties, he seemed not to grasp the routine of the regulars: the low-voltage politics of little deals, favors, bargains, local problems, and practically no national issues. As Austin Ranney has pointed out, for one who expected so much unity, discipline, and organizational strength from parties, Wilson had no clear idea of how to strengthen the party at the base. He had a stunted view of the local party foundations on which he hoped to erect such an elaborate super-structure of national policy and program. He never saw clearly the role of the party regulars as compared with the party independents and reformers and potential Republican supporters; he was never able to organize them into a national party backing a national program.

Intellectually he never was rid of his youthful idea that the American political struggle could be made essentially a politics of clear party encounters and splendid parliamentary debates. At crucial moments he acted like a British prime minister leading a unified cabinet, in a setting of strong national parties, rather than in the Madisonian setting of disorganized parties, local politics, and federalized and divided government. This view in turn stemmed largely from Wilson's moralism. "His basic, lifelong faith," says Blum, "was in the individual as a distinct moral agent, inspired by and accountable to God; in the individual as the special object of a Christian education; in this individual, so accountable and so educated, as the judicious artificer of his own political and economic life. This was the essential belief of the America of Wilson's time, a belief derived from Calvin and Adam Smith and Emerson at least. It presumed, as Wilson did, that normative man was a kind of William Gladstone, that a normative nation consisted of a mass of separated human particles, each like him. But within the United States in the 20th century, giving these particles a chance to compete was not enough; they needed also help and cohesion." National politics needed leadership at the top, such as Wilson gave it, but it needed reorganization and realignment at the base.

So in the end the President who called for a Democratic Congress in 1918 and a senatorial mandate a year later was not so far removed from the Princeton senior who complained of the decline of statesmanship in the essay he sent Henry Cabot Lodge. Wilson was to break his own body, and to break the heart of the world, in his effort to make America face its world responsibilities. His defeat was so magnificent, so tragic, so clear-cut that he set the stage for his victory at San Francisco twenty-five years later. But all this was too late for Wilson, and perhaps too late for the world.

For his statecraft ended on March 4, 1921. On the morning of that day, Senator Harding's Inaugural, it was touching that the man who had had so much to say in scholarly journals, to his students, to his fellow Democrats, to his nation and to the world—should have delivered to a hated leader of Congress, as Hofstadter has said, a last symbolic message which closed his public life: "Senator Lodge, I have no further communication to make."

7

ROOSEVELT:
The ART
of the POSSIBLE

*W*hen conservative Republicans contend today that their party can win the Presidency only with a "real" (i.e., conservative) Republican rather than a "me-too" candidate, they can point to three inescapable facts. Warren G. Harding and Calvin Coolidge trounced their Democratic opponents almost two-to-one in the major-party split of the popular vote in 1920 and 1924, and Herbert Hoover cut deep into the hitherto Solid South in 1928. Of all these victories Harding's was the most spectacular. Running against the incumbent party, he gave the Democrats the worst defeat they had ever suffered in a two-party fight. Thus did the voters render their verdict on the man nominated by a senatorial cabal in a convention described by William Allen White as more dominated by predatory forces than any he had ever seen.

148

"We have torn up Wilsonism by the roots," Lodge could soon boast. The New Freedom disbanded. Cox returned to Ohio to begin his long and graceful career as an elder party statesman. McAdoo became counsel for the oil tycoon Edwin Doheny, at an annual retainer of $50,000. Wilson moved to a house on S Street in Washington, where he lingered a few years, a broken man. And Cox's vigorous young running-mate, Franklin Roosevelt, returned to New York to recoup his political fortune, only to be struck down by polio and removed permanently, it was believed, from the political scene.

In Washington the men who sat around the new President's Cabinet table personified the yawning gap of attitude and style between the two Republican parties. On Harding's right was Charles Evans Hughes, the new Secretary of State, battler against insurance company wrong-doing in the age of the muckrakers, already a symbol of rectitude, and later the Chief Justice of the United States. On his right sat former Senator John Weeks, Secretary of War, the most regular of Massachusetts party regulars. On his right sat Will Hays, Postmaster General, later the czar and morals-keeper of the movies. On his right sat former Senator Albert Fall, Secretary of the Interior, who would soon lease government oil reserves to Doheny and Harry Sinclair in return for $400,000 and become the first cabinet officer in history to go to jail. And on his right sat Herbert Hoover, Secretary of Commerce, internationalist, World War I relief administrator, who with Hughes would stay clear of the corruption issue of the Harding administration. Neither man, an English observer later commented in wonder, "seems ever to have concerned himself with the issue; nor did the public treat it as one in which their honor was in any way involved." A like situation in a British Cabinet was inconceivable. The Englishman might have understood this phenomenon if he had seen that Hughes and Fall were members, in all but name, of two different parties.

Once again an alliance of the Cotton Whigs and the Conscience Whigs ruled the nation, with the former as senior partner. "Never before, here or anywhere else," exulted the *Wall Street Journal*, "has a government been so completely fused with business." The regime was an experiment in single-interest government under the auspices of the Republican regulars. The central question of the politics of the 1920's, William Leuchtenburg has said, was "whether the business interest, given full support by a cooperative government, could maintain prosperity and develop social policies which would redound to the benefit not merely of itself but of the whole American people." The answer would come at the end of the decade.

Conservatism gripped the nation's politics, as progressivism had ten years before, and as liberalism would ten years later. Harding was perfectly equipped to preside over a regime barren of fresh ideas, one that would gloss over the deep-lying economic and social malaise of the nation. His speeches, said McAdoo, "leave the impression of an army of pompous phrases moving over the landscape in search of an idea; sometimes these meandering words would actually capture a straggling thought and bear it triumphantly, a prisoner in their midst, until it died of servitude and overwork." Alice Roosevelt Longworth found in the White House a general atmosphere of "waistcoat unbuttoned, feet on desk, and spittoons alongside."

While the Republicans plastered over their cleavage, the Democrats opened theirs for all the world to see at their convention in Madison Square Garden in 1924. The convention came at a moment when the rising urban forces of the Northeast seemed in exact balance with the old regulars of the rural South and West, who had power in Congress; a motion not to mention the Ku Klux Klan by name in the platform passed by 543 3/20 to 542 3/20. For 17 days and 102 ballots the delegates deadlocked between Al Smith and McAdoo, in the wilting heat; the century-old two-thirds rule was still plaguing them. Then came the ludicrous anticlimax, nomination of a colorless Wall Street lawyer, John W. Davis, for President, with Bryan's younger brother as his running-mate—an all too obvious sop to the populist and fundamentalist wing of the party.

It was a time of fusty politics. Harding's death brought to the White House a flinty Vermonter whose most famous aphorism summed up his party's philosophy: "The business of America is business." Labor and farm elements of Theodore Roosevelt's progressive following broke away from the regular Republicans again in 1924 to nominate their old hero, Robert La Follette. To the Progressive convention came Fiorello La Guardia to "let you know there are other streets and other attitudes in New York besides Wall Street. I speak for Avenue A and 116th Street, instead of Broad and Wall."

The Progressives promptly ran into the same situation that had thwarted them in 1912: they lacked state, county, or local parties to support the national candidates with local tickets. While La Follette carried only Wisconsin and helped give Calvin Coolidge his landslide, his feat in winning twice as many votes as the Democrats in 17 states west of the Mississippi carried a warning to both the major parties.

Four years later the mounting urban and ethnic forces in the Democratic party finally overcame rural power and nominated Al Smith for President. But the country was not ready for a Catholic, a New Yorker, and a wet. Smith's appeal, wrote the Tennessee editor and historian George Fort Milton, was "to the alien, who feel that the older America, the America of the Anglo-Saxon stock, is a hateful thing which must be overturned and humiliated; to the northern Negroes, who lust for social equality and racial dominance; to the Catholics who have been made to believe that they are entitled to the White House, and to the Jews who likewise are to be instilled with the feeling that this is the time for God's chosen people to chastise America yesteryear. . . ." The Republicans carried Virginia, Tennessee, Texas, North Carolina, Florida, and Kentucky. But the cities were more prophetic of the next political generation. Harding in 1920 had carried every borough in New York City. Coolidge had won the twelve largest cities in the country by a margin of over a million. Four years later Smith carried the same cities, though barely, and strongly challenged the Republicans' long dominance in the Northeast.

And the Democrats scored another important recovery that year, though few might have guessed its dimensions at the time. Franklin D. Roosevelt, still on crutches but back in politics for good, was the new Governor of New York.

The Education of Franklin Roosevelt

In 1910, just 30 years after Theodore Roosevelt burst in on the regular Republican Club of the 21st district, his 28-year-old cousin Franklin had suddenly begun to show up at Democratic party affairs in Dutchess County. Local Democrats must have felt pretty much as the regulars had about Theodore—the young man was an outsider, definitely not one of the boys. They knew of Franklin vaguely as a rich man's son from a big house on the bluff over the Hudson in Hyde Park. He had been away at school and college for years; since his graduation from Harvard in 1904 he had worked in Manhattan, and Hyde Park saw him mainly during summers and weekends. And not much of Hyde Park saw him—he was active in the Hudson River Ice Yacht Club and the Episcopal Church, but these circles were hardly populated by rank-and-file Democrats.

Now they watched this young man from Hyde Park, with his spare figure, gold-bowed spectacles, and his disconcerting habit of staring fixedly down his long nose at a point about two inches over the head of the person he was talking to. What was he doing there anyway? some of the regulars must have wondered. His father, they knew, had been a Cleveland Democrat much concerned about the rise of Bryanism. But Roosevelt was a Republican name, and they might have suspected (correctly) that Franklin had voted for his cousin Theodore in 1904. Certainly he had not bothered with the Dutchess County Democracy.

But Roosevelt knew exactly why he was there. He was bored with the law, eager to dive into politics, and suddenly aware of an opportunity. The Democratic nomination for state senator was open. No other Democrat seemed interested, since no Democrat had won this seat in a straight party contest in 64 years. But 1910 looked like a Democratic year, even in Dutchess County, and in any event the experience of running might do him good. First it was necessary to cultivate the regular party leaders. This he did, so convincingly that they agreed to steer his nomination through the senatorial district convention. In his acceptance speech Roosevelt sounded much like his cousin Ted—and like another newcomer to politics, Woodrow Wilson, over in Jersey.

"As you know," Roosevelt said, "I accept this nomination with absolute independence. I am pledged to no man; I am influenced by no special interests, and so I shall remain." Then he struck a Teddy Roosevelt note. "We are going to have a very strenuous month!"

The strenuous month lengthened into a strenuous decade. He beat his Republican opponent for the Senate, an Old Guard state senator, on the issue of bossism. In the legislature he made a name

for himself by leading a dramatic effort to stop Tammany from sending a shopworn politico, William F. Sheehan, to the United States
Senate. He was a leading Wilsonian in New York State in 1912
and hence in line for recognition in Washington. As Assistant Secretary of the Navy for eight years, he dealt with a multitude of political
problems in Washington and on the waterfront. He ran for United
States Senator in the Democratic primary in New York in 1914,
and was badly beaten. He capped the decade in 1920 by winning
the nomination, at the age of 38, as James Cox's running-mate, only
to go down to a shattering defeat.

Perhaps more important to Roosevelt's later career than the political ups and downs of the decade were some of the lessons he
learned.

He learned, first of all, that it was much simpler to denounce
"bossism" on the hustings than it was to deal with it in practice. In
the fight against Sheehan, it was exciting to negotiate with Boss
Murphy on equal terms, to hand out statements to the press, to look
like a Sir Galahad to the voters back home. But Tammany, he discovered, was not quite so monolithic, nor Murphy so diabolical, as
he had imagined. The regular organization was not really a machine
but a collection of men with crisscrossing loyalties and motives. And
some of these men commanded Roosevelt's respect: for example,
the young legislators from New York, Al Smith and Bob Wagner.
The regulars, moreover, were often far more dependable than the
independents; they were hard to deal with but once a deal was
made, they lived up to it.

Roosevelt also learned something of the intricate relationships of
party and faction to different types of elections. He ran in 1910 as
an independent Democrat and he denounced Democratic and Republican bosses with fine impartiality. He virtually ignored the state
Democratic party and ticket. He allied himself with "good" Republicans, such as Uncle Ted and Governor Hughes. But two years
later, during the presidential contest of 1912, it was more advantageous to tie himself to the Democratic national party. Roosevelt
and his friends established the "Empire State Democracy" made up
of pro-Wilson independents and progressive Democrats. The plan
was to threaten to set up a state ticket to run against Murphy's reg-

ular Democratic ticket, and hence force Murphy to jettison his Tammany slate in favor of a "good" Democrat. Murphy's astuteness and divisions among the independents ruined the plan.

Another vivid political lesson came in 1914, when Roosevelt decided to try for the Democratic nomination for either governor or United States Senator. He hoped that President Wilson would back him over any candidate that Murphy might put up. Wilson was sympathetic; but his hands were tied. When he tried to help the anti-Tammanyites through patronage and other forms of recognition, he set off an uproar in the Tammany camp. Worse than this, Murphy's men in Congress, including the chairman of the House Appropriations Committee, warned the President, in effect, to keep hands off. More concerned about his legislative program than party reform, Wilson sheered off from the affair. Roosevelt plunged into the senatorial primary anyway, only to be outmaneuvered by Murphy. The Tammany chief brought into the race not a political hack, as Roosevelt hoped, but James Gerard, Wilson's Ambassador to Germany. Gerard, without even bothering to come home from Berlin, swamped Roosevelt almost three to one. Once again Roosevelt learned the power of the regulars, at least in a primary, and saw the interrelationship of national and state politics. He learned his lesson so well, in fact, that he made his peace with Murphy a few years later and was even photographed with him in the Wigwam.

Roosevelt's reconciliation with Tammany paid off in 1928 when the regular Democrats, prompted by Al Smith, drafted Roosevelt for governor. It was one of the few genuine drafts in recent history; stricken by polio in 1921, Roosevelt had wanted two more years to exercise and strengthen the ravaged muscles of his legs. Once nominated, he campaigned with Rooseveltian vim and carried New York State for himself while Smith lost it and his chances of the presidency. As governor, Roosevelt had the ticklish experience of presiding over a minority party in the state legislature, and the harsher experience of dealing with the growing depression. Once again he came into conflict with Tammany; and once again the regulars showed their power when they elected a slate of delegates to the Democratic national convention of 1932 largely composed of anti-Roosevelt Tammanyites.

But it was not only Tammany that educated Roosevelt in the

exacting politics of state and nation. The two men who dominated American politics during his first 20 years of adult life, his Uncle Ted and his chief, Woodrow Wilson, were his true mentors. Through his cool blue eyes Roosevelt watched them appraisingly as they rose to the pinnacles and then came crashing down on the other side; he shared their triumphs and studied their defeats. And he never forgot the lessons they taught him.

Later, as President, Roosevelt liked to tell people about the specific things he learned from these two men. To feuding liberals he would mention Wilson's description of conservatives as having the striking power of a closed fist, while progressives were like a man trying to hit with an open hand. He told wordy subordinates about Wilson's (and his own) preference for one-page memos. He remembered Wilson's cyclical notion of politics—the idea that liberalism has its day and then ebbs away, that a President must work with this cycle —for example, he must get what he can during his first term, because the reform temper might slack off during the second. He liked to recall that Uncle Theodore had said to him, "If I can be right 75 per cent of the time, I shall come up to the fullest measure of my hopes." And he remarked, "I want to be a *preaching President*—like my cousin."

Still, it was the things that Roosevelt and Wilson did, not just their advice, that had the most influence on the education of Franklin D. Roosevelt. Above all, they had been *Presidents*. They had extracted every morsel of executive power from the Constitution and, especially in Uncle Ted's case, gone on to wield power beyond the letter of the Constitution. They had brought massive influence to bear on Congress; they had energized the executive branch; they had dominated their national parties. "T.R. and Wilson," Roosevelt said on the eve of becoming President, "were both moral leaders, each in his own way and for his own time, who used the Presidency as a pulpit." For the Presidency was more than an administrative office, more than an engineering job. "It is pre-eminently a place of moral leadership. All our great Presidents were leaders of thought at times when certain historic ideas in the life of the nation had to be clarified."

But there were certain lessons the two Presidents could not teach Roosevelt because they had not learned the answers themselves. How can a President maintain his influence in Congress during his second term? How can he induce party regulars and independents to work together for the common party cause? How can he straighten out relations between national, state, and local parties, each operating in a different context? Above all, how could a President of the Roosevelt-Wilson stamp fulfill their dream of party realignment out of which one party would emerge as clearly liberal in domestic policy and world-minded in foreign?

It was this kind of question—especially the last—that would test Roosevelt's political talent and intellectual power in the days after his inauguration at the depth of the depression.

Roosevelt and the Grand Coalition

His chin out-thrust, his face set and stern, Roosevelt looked at the great silent crowd standing before him in March 1933. "This is a day of national consecration. . . ." The phrase came through in a high, ringing voice. ". . . The only thing we have to fear is fear itself. . . . The nation asks for action, and action now. . . . We must move as a trained and loyal army willing to sacrifice for the good of a common discipline. . . . We are, I know, ready and willing to submit our lives and our property to such discipline, because it makes possible a leadership which aims at a larger good. . . ." Unless Congress acted, "I shall ask the Congress for the one remaining instrument to meet the crisis—broad executive power to wage a war against the emergency, as great as the power that would be given to me if we were in fact invaded by a foreign foe."

It was a call to arms against economic crisis, and there was no place for purely partisan action. Like Jefferson and Wilson before him, Roosevelt was starting his administration off on a high, non-partisan note. He would be President of all the people. Already he had moved to make his Administration bipartisan by giving big posts to progressive Republicans like Henry Wallace and Harold Ickes, the new Secretaries of Agriculture and Interior, and to independents like Frances Perkins, as well as to Democratic regulars such as Cordell Hull, Daniel Roper, and James A. Farley.

But unlike Jefferson and Wilson, who quickly reverted to partisan positions, Roosevelt carried on as nonpartisan head of the nation during much of his first term. A year after his Inauguration he was still playing down his role as Democratic leader. Early in 1934 he declined to take part in Jefferson Day celebrations. "Our strongest plea to the country in this particular year of grace," he told Democrats, "is that the recovery and reconstruction program is being accomplished by men and women of all parties—that I have repeatedly appealed to Republicans as to Democrats to do their part." He suggested that "nonpartisan Jefferson dinners" be held, with as many Republicans as Democrats on the banquet committee. Democratic leaders, who long had tried to pry Jefferson loose from the Republicans and make him an exclusively Democratic hero, were not pleased.

Roosevelt defended his nonpartisanship vigorously. The government was being run less for political purposes and more for the general good than it had been in some time, he told the National Emergency Council in June 1934. "In other words, we are thinking about Government, and not merely about party." When Charles Michelson, the hard-hitting ghostwriter for the Democratic National Committee, put out a partisan review of the New Deal's first year, Roosevelt had it withdrawn. The New Deal, he told a Wisconsin crowd in August 1934, "seeks to cement our society, rich and poor, manual worker and brain worker, into a voluntary brotherhood of freemen, standing together, striving together," for the common good of all. "Government," he told a convention of bankers two months later, was "essentially the outward expression of the unity and leadership of all groups." His role as President was as conciliator, harmonizer, unifier of all major interests. He was the master broker.

The policies of this master broker during 1933 and 1934 boldly attacked the depression; they also gave something to every major group. Businessmen got the National Industrial Recovery Act and permission to draw up codes of fair competition. Workers got, theoretically at least, the right to organize in unions of their own choosing. Farmers got the Agricultural Adjustment Act to limit production and raise farm prices. Reliefers got the Federal Emergency Relief Act. Small investors got federal supervision of traffic in investment securities. Debt-ridden home owners got readjustment of mortgage debts on small homes. Jobless young men got the Civilian Conservation Corps. Conservationists—and hard-hit Southern states—got the Tennessee Valley Authority. Taxpayers got a drastic economy program in the federal government and promises that the budget would be balanced. Fur traders got the Reciprocal Tariff Act of 1934. Internationalists got the Good Neighbor Policy and isolationists got Roosevelt's "torpedoing" of the World-Economic Conference in London. Radicals—and some businessmen—got recognition of Soviet Russia.

If the first New Deal had something for everyone, everyone had enthusiasm for the New Deal—and especially for the new President. Henry L. Stimson, Cardinal O'Connell of Boston, Walter Lippmann, Hamilton Fish, and William Randolph Hearst had applauded the Hundred Days. The adulation carried well into 1934. "To us," wrote a conservative farm leader, "you are the Andrew Jackson of the Twentieth Century." Father Charles Coughlin, the Populist radio priest cried, "I will never change my philosophy that the New Deal is Christ's deal." Pierre du Pont and other businessmen sent the President friendly letters of support. Hearst paid his respects at the White House, and the Scripps-Howard newspapers and such big-city newspapers as the *New York Daily News* warmly supported him. Left-wing labor leaders, conservative Southern congressmen, Texas businessmen, radical farm leaders—the President seemed to hold them all enthralled.

Still, the congressional contests of 1934 were coming along, under the inexorable calendar of American elections. Could the President remain a nonpartisan leader when his fellow-Democrats were struggling with Republicans for congressional seats? To a remarkable extent the President could and did. He stayed clear of many contests altogether. But where a non-Democratic Senator had gone down the line for the New Deal the President might support him against a Democrat. The classic case—and an instructive one for observant politicians—was Wisconsin's Progressive Senator Robert La Follette, scion of Fighting Bob. Wisconsin Democrats had put up one of their own against La Follette. But when Roosevelt campaigned in Wisconsin in August 1934 on a "non-political" tour, he let La Follette bask in his favor and he cold-shouldered the Democratic aspirant. In Minnesota the President played with the Farmer Laborites and left the state Democrats simmering with resentment. In California he withheld support from the Democratic candidate for governor, the crusading old muckraker Upton Sinclair, because of his "End Poverty in California" plan, and negotiated with Sinclair's Republican opponent. In some other states, though, the President supported Democratic candidates.

"I am trying to get across the idea," Roosevelt told reporters off the record, "that if we have the right kind of people the party label does not mean so very much." His tactics were handsomely vindicated at the polls. La Follette won in Wisconsin, the Farmer Laborites won in Minnesota, and Sinclair lost in California. But the remarkable thing was the increased Democratic strength in Congress. Ever since politicians could remember, Presidents had lost seats on the Hill during off-year elections. But Roosevelt had increased his House margin from 312 to 322 and his Senate majority from 59 to 69.

So, despite the President's honeyed words of nonpartisanship, the Democrats had won the election resoundingly. How long could Roosevelt continue in his ambivalent role as father of the people? During 1935 he shifted position. Strengthened by the enlarged liberal bloc in Congress, buffeted by conservatives in the Supreme Court, in Congress, and in the business community, and still groping to find dependable ways of coping with crises, he moved toward the "second New Deal" of reconstruction and reform. During the "second hundred days" of summer 1935 Congress passed the Wagner Act, the Social Security Act, a "share-the-wealth" tax law, holding-company legislation, and strengthened regulation of banking. It was not so much a strategic leftward turn by the President as the concatenation of a number of events that left him as a leader of a coalition.

It was not a radical coalition, for countless conservative Democrats were in it. It was not a Democratic party coalition, for many independents and some Republicans were part of it. It was not a bipartisan coalition, for the overwhelming majority of Republicans were out of it. It was a grand coalition of all the leaders and groups who were sticking with Roosevelt because of, or despite, the leftward direction of his Administration. It was, most simply put, a *Roosevelt* party. "There's one issue in this campaign," the President told Raymond Moley in 1936. "It's myself, and people must be either for me or against me." The President was moving beyond the classic

Democratic coalition of congressional factions in the South, city bosses in the North, and populist farmers in the West. He was, as Arthur Schlesinger, Jr. has said, building a new coalition of independent Democrats, progressive Republicans, trade unionists, intellectuals, and independents. He made special appeals to women, Negroes, and ethnic groups. He was picking up a generation later, the task of party reconstruction that Wilson had dropped with the coming of the first World War.

How many battalions could be crammed into the Grand Coalition? Roosevelt, hunting for every ounce of support he could get for the big test ahead, set no limit. La Follette, Senator George W. Norris of Nebraska, Mayor Fiorello La Guardia of New York City, and other progressives met with John L. Lewis, Sidney Hillman and other liberal laborites to form the Progressive National Committee to fight for Roosevelt's re-election—but not for the Democratic party. To tap the votes of independents, liberal Republicans, churchmen, and civic leaders the President set up a nonpartisan Good Neighbor League, which also backed Roosevelt in particular but not Democrats in general. The League aimed a special appeal to Negroes that culminated in a score of rallies in the big cities of the North. Special task forces were set up to capture the "women's vote," ethnic groups, and small businessmen. Meantime National Chairman Farley went about the job of mobilizing the regulars, and Southern Democrats awaited the automatic Democratic majorities in the Southland.

The Republicans, adjusting to the new day, shunted aside their conservatives and chose for their ticket two old Bull Moosers, Alfred M. Landon and Frank Knox. At first the Republicans took the initiative, while Roosevelt acted as though there were no campaign that year, and New Deal zealots like Ickes grumbled that the campaign was drifting. "Say, Steve," a reporter asked Press Secretary Stephen Early jocularly, "is this going to be a non-political campaign?" Farley, concerned almost exclusively with the Democratic party, was having his share of troubles. New Dealers wanted him to call off Democratic opposition to Roosevelt's liberal supporters in Congress who were not Democrats. Roosevelt endorsed Norris and ignored the progressive Senator's Democratic opponent. He indirectly induced Minnesota Democrats to withdraw their local tickets against Farmer Laborites. He refused to endorse James M. Curley, the Democratic candidate for Senator, over Henry Cabot Lodge in Massachusetts. Everywhere Farley turned, he seemed to find New Dealers flirting with independents and Republicans, and not for the sake of the Democratic party but to swell the votes of the man in the White House.

And when Roosevelt finally began his campaign swings in October he acted more like the New Deal candidate than the Democratic party candidate. He saw the party regulars as the heart of the grand alliance, but sometimes the heart seemed lost to sight. Roosevelt rarely mentioned his party by name; he usually acted, as Stanley High said, "not as a Democrat, but as a New Deal liberal fighting not for party success but for a cause." And rarely has a candidate made a cause so compelling and exciting as Roosevelt did in the fall of 1936. The passionate climax of the campaign in Madison Square Garden was a climax in Roosevelt's personalization of the cause. Never before in history, he told the tumultuous crowd, had the forces of organized money "been so united against one candidate as they stand today. They are unanimous in their hate for me—and I welcome their hatred!"

"I should like to have it said of my first Administration that in it the forces of selfishness and of lust for power met their *match*. I should like to have it said—" he paused to calm the clamorous audience, "I should like to have it said of my second Administration that in it *these forces met their master!*"

The Crumbling of the Coalition

It would have seemed inconceivable to any sensible observer, the day after the November 1936 election, that in two years the victor would be stumbling in retreat. For on that day in November Roosevelt was a political colossus. He had carried every state but New Hampshire and Vermont; he had swept the popular vote by the biggest popular plurality in history. Despite his personal campaigning—or perhaps because of it—he had created the most topheavily Democratic Congress in history, 334 Democrats to 89 Republicans in the House, 75 Democrats to 17 Republicans in the Senate. And his political coattails were long enough to help pull in a host of Democrats into state and local offices.

There was no letdown after the election in Roosevelt's militance. In his second Inaugural, delivered in dripping rain in January 1937, he declared that "the essential democracy of our Nation and the safety of our people depend not upon the absence of power, but upon lodging it with those whom the people can change or continue at stated intervals through an honest and free system of elections." Sitting a few feet from Roosevelt was Chief Justice Hughes; did the venerable politician-judge, reporters wondered, catch the implication for a court that had tried to limit the New Deal's power? Then Roosevelt turned to the challenge to American democracy.

"In this nation I see tens of millions of its citizens—a substantial part of its whole population—who at this very moment are denied the greater part of what the very lowest standards of today call the necessities of life."

"I see millions whose daily lives in city and on farm continue under conditions labeled indecent by a so-called polite society half a century ago.

"I see millions denied education, recreation, and the opportunity to better their lot and the lot of their children.

"I see millions lacking the means to buy the products of farm and factory and by their poverty denying work and productiveness to many other millions.

"I see one-third of a nation ill-housed, ill-clad, ill-nourished.

"It is not in despair that I paint you that picture. I paint it for you in hope—because the Nation, seeing and understanding the injustice in it, proposes to paint it out. . . .

"To maintain a democracy of effort requires a vast amount of patience in dealing with differing methods, a vast amount of humility. But out of the confusion of many voices rises an understanding of dominant public need. Then political leadership can voice common ideals, and aid in their realization. . . ."

Two weeks later Roosevelt exploded his "bombshell"—reorganization of the Supreme Court. For every Supreme Court justice who failed to quit the bench within six months after reaching seventy, the President would be empowered by Congress to appoint a new justice up to a total of six. This bold proposal was couched in evasive terms—the problem, it seemed, was simply judicial efficiency, congestion in the courts, not presidential power. But few were fooled. Roosevelt was trying to pack the court in favor of his New Deal bills. The proposal instantly divided Roosevelt's supporters on the Hill.

Like the defeat of the League of Nations 18 years before, the court-packing bill died more from slow suffocation than from outright opposition. The tiny band of Republicans in the Senate let Democratic opponents of the bill take the lead against it; hence Roosevelt could not convert the struggle into a straight party battle. Committee hearings prolonged the struggle. Hughes quietly provided the opposition with data disproving Roosevelt's charge of inefficiency. Newspapers hotly opposed the plan; New England town fathers called mass meetings; bar associations met and denounced. Most important, the Court made a sudden tactical shift; it upheld the Wagner Act and further obscured the real issue. Bad luck dogged Roosevelt: the resignation of an Old Guard member of the court gave him a vacancy that he promised to his loyal majority leader, Senator Joe Robinson, provided that Robinson got the whole bill through. But at the climax of the fight in July, the Senator fell dead in his hotel room. The stroke that broke Robinson's heart ruptured as well the bonds of personal and Senatorial loyalty on which he had been depending. In a week the plan was dead.

The defeat of the court plan was the forerunner of a series of congressional setbacks for the President. His proposal for a wages and hours law was ground to pieces between the Southern Democrats and the labor bloc in 1937; the next year it was resurrected in modified form, battered again by contending factions, and barely passed in an even weaker form. This bill was the last of the President's major reform measures to pass Congress. When the President asked the legislature for an administrative reorganization bill, he set off such an uproar on the Hill over the "dictatorship" bill that he was put on the defensive and had to tell the nation that he had no inclination to be a dictator. The bill was killed by the House.

By the spring of 1938 Roosevelt's program was deadlocked in Congress, his promises of 1936 and '37 unfulfilled, the one-third of the nation still ill-housed, ill-clad, ill-nourished. "For God's sake," telephoned a congressional spokesman to the White House, "don't send us any more controversial legislation!"

Worst of all, President and Congress were stalemated in a time of deepening recession. Late in the summer of 1937 stocks had slackened off, then dropped precipitously as wave after wave of selling hit the market. Suddenly it seemed like 1929 all over again. The Administration that had come into power during the Hoover depression now had on its hands the "Roosevelt recession." For months the President groped for an answer: then in March the stock market's slow decline turned suddenly into a panicky drop. The business downturn since September had been one of the sharpest in the nation's history. In mid-April 1938 the President proposed to Congress a three-billion-dollar spending program, and the Democratic legislators, frightened at the prospect of fall elections during a recession, voted him the money. Within a few months business was picking up, but a large lump of unemployment continued to weigh down the economy.

By the end of spring 1938, a year and a half after the landslide of '36, Roosevelt and the New Deal were on the defensive. His critics gloated. "The old Roosevelt magic has lost its kick," said one. "The diverse elements in his Falstaffian army can no longer be kept together and led by a melodious whinny and a winning smile." The magic spell seemed to be broken. What would Roosevelt do now? The answer came late in June in a fireside chat. The Seventy-Fifth Congress, elected on a platform "uncompromisingly liberal," said the President, had achieved some things, but had left many others undone. Now the congressional primaries and elections were coming up. The issue was squarely between liberals willing to try new remedies, including government action, and conservatives who wanted to rely on individual initiative and the kind of government America had had in the 1920's.

"As President of the United States, I am not asking the voters of the country to vote for Democrats next November as opposed to Republicans or members of any other party. Nor am I, as President, taking part in Democratic primaries."

"As the head of the Democratic Party, however, charged with the responsibility of the definitely liberal declaration of principles set forth in the 1936 Democratic platforms, I feel that I have every right to speak in those few instances where there may be a clear issue between candidates for a Democratic nomination involving these principles or involving a clear misuse of my own name. . . ."

Soon Roosevelt was off to the hustings. The presidential train zigzagged across the nation, stopping in key states, where the President gave mild approval to mild supporters, warm support to warm supporters like Alben Barkley of Kentucky, and elaborately snubbed his opponents. Then the President turned to his number one target, the venerable conservative from Georgia, Senator Walter George. At Barnesville, with George himself sitting a few feet away on the platform, Roosevelt said of the old senator:

"Let me make it clear that he is, and I hope always will be, my personal friend. He is beyond question, beyond any possible question, a gentleman and a scholar. . . ." But he and George simply did not speak the same political language. The test was in the answer to two questions: "First, has the record of the candidate shown, while differing in details, a constant active fighting attitude in favor of the broad objectives of the party and of the Government as they are constituted today; and secondly, does the candidate really, in his heart, deep down in his heart, believe in those objectives."

"I regret that in the case of my friend, Senator George, I cannot honestly answer either of those questions in the affirmative."

After stopping off in South Carolina and taking a sideswipe at the aged reactionary, "Cotton Ed" Smith, Roosevelt returned to Washington for a final effort against an old adversary, the urbane Millard Tydings of Maryland. At a press conference he accused Tydings—and he told reporters to put this in direct quotes—of wanting to run "with the Roosevelt prestige and the money of his conservative Republican friends both on his side." He lined up Administration people in Maryland against Tydings, and he stumped intensively in the state for two days before the primary.

By late September the returns were in—George, Smith, Tydings won sweeping victories, as did two or three other anti-New Dealers whom Roosevelt had opposed less outspokenly. So dramatic were the triumphs of George & Co., indeed, that they overshadowed earlier victories that Roosevelt had won in the border states—notably in Barkley's re-nomination. Also overshadowed was the most notable

Administration victory of all, the defeat of John O'Connor, chairman of the Rules Committee and a Tammany Congressman from Manhattan, who had used his key post to frustrate the President's measures. But O'Connor's defeat was not a personal victory for Roosevelt for he had not campaigned in New York. The job was done by two lieutenants who had spent weeks in Manhattan recruiting a good candidate against O'Connor, lining up Labor party backing through La Guardia, mobilizing Administration supporters in the Democratic party, and scrounging votes in the wards and precincts of the East side.

It was a bad defeat, but the nadir of Roosevelt's political fortunes was still to come. The Republicans staged a comeback in the November elections, almost doubling their strength in the House and picking up eight seats in the Senate. The Republicans lost not a single seat. Roosevelt had tried hard to pitch the whole congressional campaign on the old New Deal issues—prosperity, security, reform, peace—but now the old dependables did not work so well. The voters seemed concerned over vague and fearsome things like states' rights, "rubber-stamp" Congresses, dictatorship, the purge itself. Or they were diverted by local issues, or so it seemed to Roosevelt—a racetrack scandal in Rhode Island, corruption in Massachusetts, strikes in the Midwest. To be sure, the Democrats still had big majorities in both houses. But were they New Deal majorities?

They were not. During 1939 Republicans and conservative Democrats, mainly Southerners, combined to balk further New Deal reforms and to counter-attack the Administration itself. They used the classic instruments of the congressional party; investigations, control over Administration patronage through senatorial courtesy and other devices, and power through appropriations committees to cut funds for liberal programs. Not only were further reforms choked off, but the Administration's recovery policy was caught on dead center. Although business conditions had improved markedly since the year before, dead center still meant eight to ten million unemployed.

The New Deal, wrote historian Walter Millis toward the end of 1938, "has been reduced to a movement with no program, with no effective political organization, with no vast popular party strength behind it, and with no candidte." The Grand Coalition had shriveled;

a new anti-Roosevelt coalition was on the offensive. Such was the posture of affairs when war came in the late summer of 1939 and swung Roosevelt back to his earlier role of President of all the people, and to a new posture of Commander-in-Chief.

Roosevelt as a Political Strategist

"We'll have eight years in Washington," Roosevelt said to some liberal friends in 1932. "By that time there may not be a Democratic party, but there will be a progressive one." Afterwards these friends—Rexford Guy Tugwell, Harry Hopkins, Robert La Follette, Jr.—talked excitedly with one another about the boss's comment. Did he mean progressive with a big or little P? Did he want simply to liberalize the Democratic party, or did he hope to set up a new Progressive party, as his Uncle Ted had done? Would he repudiate the Democratic regulars—the conservative Democrats in the South, the machine Democrats in the northern cities? Would he bring progressive and independent Republicans into a liberalized Democracy? The questions went unanswered. Eight years and two presidential terms later, the liberal trio were still asking these questions and still wondering what Roosevelt really wanted to do.

The essential question still remains unanswered 30 years later. It seems clear that Roosevelt never thought seriously of deserting the Democratic party entirely and of creating a whole new Progressive party in its place. It is also clear that as a liberal he naturally wanted the Democratic party to be as progressive as possible, just as every Democratic President has wished in this century. But the core of the puzzle remains. How committed was Roosevelt to this goal? What effort and sacrifices would he make, what risks would he run, to achieve it? Was he interested in a strong and cohesive liberal party that would both sustain him and push him in a liberal direction? Or did he really want a party that would have a pleasing liberal countenance and a progressive tendency, but was so mixed in its make-up that he could easily master it, or at least prevent it from putting independent pressure on him?

Arthur M. Schlesinger, Jr., a distinguished historian of Roosevelt and his period, believes that Roosevelt's real objective was a liberal party rather than a "national party," that his early nonpartisan stance was put on to attract progressive Republicans and independents into the existing Democratic party as a first step toward rebuilding the party system along liberal-conservative lines. Schlesinger cites the facts that since the days of T.R. he had been sympathetic to the progressive strain in Republicanism, that he wanted to fulfill Wilson's effort of 1916, that he catered to the independent voters even at the expense of slighting regular Democrats, and that as President he kept close to Bull Moosers like Felix Frankfurter and Hiram Johnson.

Still the nagging question rises: was this an attempt simply to graft one more battalion onto Roosevelt's personal coalition, rather than to build liberal Republicans into a reorganized, realigned, and revitalized Democratic party? Was Roosevelt simply trying to maximize and make foolproof his personal popularity against the vicissitudes that afflict politicians, or was he trying to change the very essence of the Democratic party? The harsh test of his purposes was not simply what group of voters he wanted to pick up, but what he was willing to jettison. Was he willing to drop Southern conservatives? The old Cleveland or "Bourbon" wing in the North? The city bosses? It was precisely because such elements dominated state Democratic parties that independents and liberal Republicans declined to join the Democracy. Was Roosevelt a political strategist intent on building a coherent party out of a liberal majority, or was he more the master broker dealing neutrally with the conflicting groups in his coalition?

The answer is that Roosevelt acted as a broker during the early years of his presidency, that he later tried to reform and realign his party, that he lacked the political resources and the intellectual conviction to do the job, so that his final effort was too little and too late. In short, he wanted a liberalized Democratic party but was unable to take the necessary steps and unwilling to make the necessary sacrifices and commitments.

In assessing Roosevelt's role as party leader we must keep in mind the enormous effort and the huge political risks that party realignment would have required. If the President had been head of a simple, mass political party, organized on national terms, the job might not have been so hard. By moving closer to urban, labor, consumer, ethnic and Negro groups in the big cities, he would have alienated right wing elements in his party, but at the same time he would have strengthened the party's support on the left. His Uncle Ted, indeed, had tried an experiment along these lines in 1912. Believing that both parties had become too conservative, TR moved in on their left and had won a bigger popular majority for the Progressive party than did Taft for the Republicans. To be sure, such a party realignment would have demanded brilliant leadership to shake people loose from their old political moorings. It would have taken rare courage to alienate sizeable elements in his personal coalition that had also been bulwark of the Democracy since the days of Jefferson and Jackson. Still, FDR, like TR, had such brilliance and courage.

But the job of realignment called not for one brilliant and daring presidential coup on the national party scene. It called for a patient, steady, well-planned battle of attrition against a host of state parties and their leaders in congressional and state offices. It meant devoting endless presidential time and resources to a quiet, undramatic, and often cloudy struggle. Pennsylvania was an example of both the opportunity and the difficulties facing a presidential effort to reorganize and realign the Democratic party. This state in the mid-thirties had shown some signs of providing the materials for party realignment. Governor in 1934 was Gifford Pinchot, TR's old friend and fellow Bull Mooser. Pinchot had long led progressive Republicans in Pennsylvania against old time regulars like Boss Grundy. Early in 1934 Roosevelt suggested to Pinchot that he run for the Senate against the conservative Republican incumbent, David A. Reed, and that Democratic support might be forthcoming. It soon became clear, however, that the Pennsylvania Democrats would not nominate the Governor, for they expected to win with a man of their own. Roosevelt did not intervene with the Democrats to insist upon Pinchot. So the ex-chief forester had to run for Senator in the Republican primaries, denouncing Reed as a mouthpiece of the Mellons and lauding Roosevelt. But the President kept hands off the Republican primary; he would not even let Secretary Ickes, the old Bull Mooser, speak for Pinchot in the primary, and Reed won the Republican nomination. The Governor then tried to work out a new progressive Republican-Democratic ticket on which Pinchot would run for Senator with George Earle, the Democratic nominee

for Governor. But the regular Democrats had already nominated one
of their own, Joseph Guffey, for Senator, and they scented victory.
Why should they support a Republican who as governor had denied
them patronage and recognition? Pinchot turned to Roosevelt but
the President now was cool. He shrank from intervening at this
point against the Democratic regulars.

A bitter Pinchot wrote to Roosevelt that he wanted to support
the President but he could not stomach such unfit men as Guffey
and Earle. Roosevelt replied that he and Pinchot shared the same
goals but that Pinchot must learn to work in Pennsylvania, as
Roosevelt had learned to work in New York, "through many people
whom I did not like or even trust—but I have worked with them
and through them, in order to obtain the ultimate goal." Pinchot was
not propitiated. He supported his old adversary Reed against Guffey
(who won) and in 1936 he backed Landon against Roosevelt. By
1938 Pennsylvania was the scene of such noisy brawling among and
between liberals and conservatives in both parties that Roosevelt
compared it to Dante's Inferno.

New York City was another Inferno where Roosevelt dallied
with the notion of party reorganization. In 1933, he had intervened
adroitly to help elect as mayor the fiery Fiorello La Guardia, the
nominee of a fusion of parties but not a Democrat. In Democratic
New York La Guardia could not have won against a united Democratic party. What Roosevelt did was to inveigle Boss Ed Flynn to
nominate an independent Democratic candidate, Joseph V. McKee,
on an independent ticket, to run against the Tammany candidate,
thus splitting the Democratic ranks. McKee was persuaded to run
with vague promises of a presidential endorsement. But the nod
from the White House never came. In the end La Guardia beat the
two Democrats handily—just as Roosevelt evidently wanted him to.

In La Guardia the President had won a powerful new ally—and
one who would stand with him until the end. But where, wondered
the Democratic regulars, did this leave the Democratic party in New
York City? Their fears deepened as Roosevelt continued to play a
highly personal brand of politics. In 1936 the President encouraged
the formation in New York of a new organization, the American
Labor Party, to garner trade-union votes for his own re-election. The
ALP worked effectively for Roosevelt and other New Dealers, but

it also worked against many of the candidates of the Democratic regulars. Roosevelt pooh-poohed the arguments of the regulars that some day the Labor party would turn against the Democratic party as a whole—as indeed it later did. By 1938 the Democratic party in New York was in a muddle, the liberals were still divided, and the Labor party was still a splinter party that would later turn far to the left.

Wisconsin provided a third type of problem—and opportunity— to the President. There the progressive impetus within the GOP had burst through the party and brought the establishment in the spring of 1934 of a new Progressive party, under Robert and Philip La Follette. The Democracy in Wisconsin was now a poor third—"a fossilized, parochial group in the industrial cities along Lake Michigan," as Theodore White described it years later, "a receptacle for crumbs of Washington patronage, regarded in the words of its leaders as 'little more than a Polish-Irish marching society.'" When Roosevelt rebuffed the Democratic candidate for Senator in 1934, the hopes of the Democrats shriveled further. Thus the President had limited materials to work with in Wisconsin. He tried to mediate between Democrats and Progressives, but this inflamed the La Follette circle. By 1938 Philip La Follette was denouncing the New Deal and launching a new party, the National Progressives of America; the Democrats were still bumbling along (winning only eight per cent of the vote that year), and the Republicans were resurgent.

Clearly in the case of these three states—and in many others— Roosevelt was dealing with state organizations that could not be bent to his purposes by a wave of the wand. He was dealing with regular Democrats unwilling to combine with independents and liberal Republicans who had been fighting them in state politics for decades. Could the President somehow bring them together? Pennsylvania again provides a test. To obtain a Pinchot-Earle ticket, Roosevelt would have had to intervene months before the primaries. He would have had to offer some consolation prize to the Guffey forces; to arouse New Deal Democrats behind the joint ticket; to overcome those regular Democrats who would oppose Pinchot as a Republican; to invite independents and liberal Republicans into the Democratic party, to help them organize, and to lend them White House prestige. None of this was easy. The President might have been able to get Guffey to go along, but some other Democratic stalwart was sure to run for the Senate and to appeal to the regulars for their votes. Roosevelt men in Pennsylvania would have had to organize in the wards and precincts to overcome the entrenched organizations of the stalwarts.

Nor was this all. How would Roosevelt make a permanent place for Republicans in the revitalized Democracy? To be sure, he could clear the track for Pinchot and he could offer rewards to Pinchot's lieutenants. But what could he do for the local Republican politicians who were New Deal in sympathy but who had to calculate carefully as to their own place in the party scheme? These politicians were at the bottom of the political ladder, looking up; they had no use for the little Democratic bosses who were often conservative or corrupt; they knew that to turn Democratic at the grass roots might be to surrender themselves to such bosses and to block off future advancement. Willing though they might be to become national Democrats, to follow the progressive Roosevelt of the 1930's as their Bull Moose forebears had followed the progressive Roosevelt in his day, it was something quite different to become a local member of some reeking portion of the Pennsylvania Democracy.

It was stubborn facts such as these that prevented Roosevelt from converting into reality his wish for party realignment. Some New Dealers, worried about the decay and disorganization of the Democratic party as a base for progressivism, wanted to take a more long-range approach. They proposed to build up the Roosevelt or "presidential" wing pledged to the New Deal, to lift the party out of the ruck of local factionalism, apathy, and corruption, to weld liberals to the presidential party, and use that party to strengthen the liberals in Congress. They calculated that if Roosevelt could get control of Congress with solid liberal majorities, he could then reform the processes of Congress to put through the essence of his recovery program. Conceding the difficulties, they still contended that the President's popularity was so great, his political resources so huge, that he could do this job on a planned, long-term basis.

But such an effort would have called for a strategy—a comprehensive, long-term, persistent effort in a variety of states under a variety of conditions—and Roosevelt was not the man for this. It called for strong party organization and expert party organizers, but

Roosevelt had not developed such tools. Perhaps he saw the difficulties better than some of his advisers, or perhaps he missed a great opportunity. In any event, Roosevelt was the prisoner of the concessions he had made to the regulars—especially Southern Democrats—in gaining the nomination. He had recognized and hence strengthened conservative Democrats in Congress who had gone along with his program. He had overcome crisis after crisis by exploiting fully the magic of his personal leadership. As a pragmatic politician eager above all to win office, he was reluctant to divert the political effort necessary to improve the disheveled party organization. The personal traits that made Roosevelt a brilliant tactician—his dexterity, his command of many roles, his skill in thrust and parry, his nerve in facing some issues head on and evading others, above all his personal magnetism and charisma—were not the best traits for hard, long-range, purposeful building of a strong party behind a coherent political program.

The Two Roosevelts: An Epitaph

These reflections on "what could have been" might seem wholly academic except for one striking fact. Nobody—not the liberal advisers nor the progressive editors nor the academic intellectuals—nobody in the end was willing to make a more desperate commitment to party realignment than Roosevelt himself. For, after all his caution and dexterity, the master broker found himself in 1938 actually campaigning on his foes' territory in a mighty personal effort to oust them from office. And in 1944 he made a final try to solve the problem that had challenged him ever since he entered politics 34 years before.

The inheritor of the progressive, internationalist traditions in the Republican party in 1944 was Wendell Willkie. Four years before he had waged a slam-bang attack on Roosevelt, and both men had made dismal campaign concessions to the isolationists. As war neared and finally exploded on the nation. Willkie moved back to his liberal and internationalist moorings; he became one of the President's supporters and occasional advisers. In the Republican presidential primaries of 1944 he had been submerged by the followers of Thomas E. Dewey and Robert A. Taft, so now he was a man without a party. One day in June 1944 Roosevelt told his counsel, Samuel Rosenman, that Pinchot had been in to see him and had reported that Willkie had talked with him—Pinchot—about the possibility of party realignment.

"Well," Roosevelt went on to Rosenman, "I think the time has come for the Democratic party to get rid of its reactionary elements in the South, and to attract to it the liberals in the Republican party. Willkie is the leader of those liberals. He talked to Pinchot about a coalition of the liberals in both parties, leaving the conservatives in each party to join together as they see fit. I agree with him one hundred per cent and the time is now—right after election. We ought to have two real parties—one liberal and the other conservative. As it is now, each party is split by dissenters."

"Of course, I'm talking about long-range politics—something that we can't accomplish this year. But we can do it in 1948, and we can start building it up right after the election this fall. From the liberals of both parties Willkie and I together can form a new, really liberal party in America."

The President dispatched Rosenman secretly to sound out Willkie, who turned out to be highly responsive to the idea. But on one thing Willkie was insistent. He could not meet with Roosevelt until after the election. Under intense pressure to come out for Dewey and anxious to keep some leverage in the Republican party, Willkie feared that even an off-the-record meeting with the President would be misinterpreted by Republicans as an election sell-out to the Democrats. Roosevelt, on the other hand, wanted to pursue the matter before election, and here his reputation for cunning and indirectness tripped him up. The more the President pressed for an early meeting the more Willkie must have suspected his motives. Did the President really want basic party realignment, or was this just a Rooseveltian maneuver to induce him to come out for the Fourth Term, or at least not endorse Dewey? Leaks to the press about a possible meeting sharpened Willkie's suspicions. So the matter was put off until after the election. It was actually put off for good: Willkie died in October 1944, Roosevelt six months later. Such was the poignant ending to what may have been the best opportunity in a generation for party realignment.

It is symbolic of the differences between the two Roosevelts that

Theodore's last electoral effort was to break his party, while Franklin left his party largely intact but unreformed. The two men had contrasting styles: Roosevelt I was a compulsive idealist, utterly dogmatic, almost violent in his political reflexes and opinions, a man, as Henry Adams said, who thought in his hips. Roosevelt II was far more hard-headed, flexible in tactics, gentle and almost feminine in his political operations, a man who seemed to think in his finger tips. Yet at the core the two men were much alike: durably liberal and internationalist yet also conservative in the best sense; moralists who believed that the White House made a fine pulpit; basically hostile to the standpatters in their own parties, but willing to make many concessions for the sake of expediency; both imbued with a fine sense of *noblesse oblige,* both consummate actors, both equipped with extra-sensory political perception.

But the quality that most united the two men was their intellectual failure in the face of a common problem. Both men wanted to make their parties more durably liberal; both men failed in an operational sense (though the roles they played had a long-term effect). FDR's purge of 1938 was the counterpart of TR's party breaking-and-making of 1912: both efforts were last-minute, ill-prepared, desperate, and abortive. Both men were frustrated by the Madisonian system. Both men had to watch helplessly—TR in 1913-16, and FDR in 1938—as the party regulars rooted in state and local organizations reasserted control of the foundation blocks of the parties. In the end, both enterprises seemed to be such personal affairs that even the friends of the two men were left wondering whether they intended not so much to bring long-term party reform as to glorify the Roosevelts and strike back at their adversaries.

Both men, in short, were pragmatists who gloried in seeing politics as the art of the possible. They were superbly equipped to cope with their complex political environment; with the crisscrossing loyalties of friend and foe, with the jungle of party organizations and leaders, with the subtle machinery of a diffused political system. But in the end they were captive to the political forces around them rather than their shaper. They were, indeed, captives to themselves—to their habits of responding eclectically to the diverse people around them, of winning over opposing leaders rather than dealing with the power bases of those leaders, of improvising with style and gusto. They were both impatient with theory, remarkably effective in handling immediate problems, sensitively attuned to the play of forces around them. But they lacked the intellectual qualities necessary to a sustained effort for the long-term political goal they both shared. They were superb tacticians and courageous leaders, but they failed to achieve that combination of tactical skill and strategic planning that represents the essence of great political leadership.

8

EISENHOWER and TAFT: WHICH REPUBLICAN PARTY?

Dwight Eisenhower defeated Adlai Stevenson in 1952 by a margin of 353 electoral votes and better than 6½ million popular votes. The General cut deeply into the old centers of Democratic strength in the South and in the cities; he made big inroads among Catholics, union members, skilled and semi-skilled workers. He swept the suburbs as well as the Republican farm country. Four years later he boosted his popular margin to 9½ million votes. It was like 1920 all over again; in the twelve largest cities he drew 49 per cent of the vote and even won the old Democratic strongholds of Chicago and Jersey City.

But one constituency Dwight Eisenhower never carried. It was one of which he was doubtless unaware, for its actual voting power was infinitesimal; yet it might be, in the long run and in a special sense, the most important constituency of all. It comprised the his-

177

torians and political scientists who would compile the nation's annals, produce its history and government textbooks for schools and colleges, and ultimately render a verdict on America's leaders and parties. In 1962, 75 members of the historical establishment were polled as to how they evaluated the Presidents—as to which ones were great, which only near great, average, below average, or failures. The vote on Eisenhower was emphatic. He was rated, as a president, next to the bottom of the average group, somewhere between Chester Arthur and Andrew Johnson. In short—mediocre.

Although one of the voters on that occasion, I do not propose to discuss the rightness or wrongness of the verdict. But it is important to understand the criteria of the election. To the historian today, what does it take to make the grade in the White House? The five rated as great—Washington, Jefferson, Lincoln, Wilson, Franklin Roosevelt—"took the side of liberalism and the general welfare against the status quo," according to the poll-taker, Arthur M. Schlesinger, professor of history emeritus at Harvard. They "acted masterfully and farsightedly in foreign affairs." And they "left the Executive branch stronger and more influential" than they found it.

Most historians are Jeffersonians or Jacksonians or Lincolnians or Wilsonians. To them the great President is the strong President, and the strong President is the liberal and internationalist President. Walk through the stacks of any large library and the attention lavished on the strong Presidents and their administrations and their programs quickly becomes apparent. This is inevitable and perhaps desirable. But it means that we slight the weaker Presidents, and also the congressional leaders who have been conservative and "negative" and whose main role has been obstructing the strong Presidents.

If history is really written by the survivors, and if by some chance the Madisonian model should survive and flourish and the Jeffersonian model wither away, historians eventually might throw more light on some of the more obscure congressional leaders. They might consider a member of Congress who thwarted programs as worthy of study and understanding as a President who sponsored them. They might throw light on events that were as important as presidential inaugurations—for example, on the initiation some time in 1938 of the Democratic-Republican congressional coalition that has balked so many White House programs in the last quarter century. They might portray some of the obscure congressmen who attained power in their own quiet, unspectacular way.

On the day in March 1913 when William Howard Taft turned the presidency over to Woodrow Wilson before a huge and jubilant throng in the Capitol plaza, a freshman Representative from Massachusetts took his oath of office in a quiet ceremony that was ignored amid the pomp and ceremony of the mighty. His name was Allen T. Treadway; he was a Republican from the conservative mountain area of western Massachusetts; he was a Mason and a member of the local Grange; and he seemed—at the time—wholly unremarkable. It would take 30 years to discover that there was something remarkable about this man—his capacity to stay in office. During those years, while Presidents came and went, while the New Freedom gave way to Harding and Normalcy and then to Roosevelt and the New Deal, while the nation moved in and out of wars, depressions and booms, while dynasties rose and fell across the seas, Allen Treadway duly ran up his guaranteed majorities in the Berkshires and marked up term after term in the House. In 1942 he celebrated the end of his third decade in the House.

He was not the only survivor from the era of Taft. Sam Rayburn of Texas and Carl Vinson of Georgia had entered the House on the same day as Treadway. Other Democrats from the South and one other Republican from the rural North had managed to hold their seats. The most senior of them all was Adolph Sabath, who had represented his heavily Democratic district in Chicago since 1907. By the late 1930's all these men had risen to great influence under the rules of seniority. Rayburn was Democratic floor leader, Robert L. Doughton of North Carolina, was chairman of the Ways and Means Committee, Sabath head of Rules, Vinson chairman of Naval Affairs. And Treadway had become ranking Republican member of Ways and Means—and a 33rd degree Mason.

The Education of Robert Taft

It is not recorded whether Allen Treadway was on hand at the Capitol on January 3, 1939, when President Taft's son Robert took his oath as the new Republican Senator from Ohio, but he should have been. Not only was young Taft a living tie with the good Republican who had been President when Treadway was elected to Congress; he was the man who would lead the congressional Republicans out of their inertia and defeatism, re-shape their program, and make them an articulate and effective opposition to the liberals and internationalists of the New Deal and Fair Deal.

Taft was of the sort, moreover, to endear himself to durable regulars like Treadway. A stalwart party man like his father, Robert had begun at the bottom of the Cincinnati organization, helping out on the dull party chores, and then had started up the political ladder: state representative, floor leader, and Speaker of the Ohio House, 1921-26; state senator, 1931-1932, until he was carried down in the debacle of his hero, Herbert Hoover. He won his seat in the United States Senate in 1938 in the swing of the electoral pendulum back against the New Deal. When he arrived in Washington Republican leaders in the Senate, marking him as one of their own, gave him seats on three key policy committees: Appropriations, Banking and Currency, and Labor. From the start Taft was a good parliamentary hand: articulate, undramatic, conscientious, a strong committee man with his penchant for facts, figures, legal precedents, hard negotiation, and compromise. Fifty years old when he returned to Washington, he looked the part of the dependable legislator; he had the slight paunch, the thinning hair, the rimless glasses that made him as one with the solid Republican core of the Senate. He excelled in certain respects, though—most notably in sheer brain power and in adherence to the right Republican principles as he saw them. Soon he was the leader of the Treadways in both chambers.

For the next ten years almost everything went well for Taft in the Senate, and went badly outside. He became chairman of the Republican Policy Committee and in effect his party's leader in the Senate. He won re-election in 1944, despite the Democratic sweep of that year, and two years later he guided the congressional Republicans to victory in the House and Senate elections. He put the Taft-Hartley Act through Congress, even mustering a two-thirds vote to override Harry Truman's veto. By 1948 he was "Mr. Republican" on Capitol Hill. But he was not Mr. Republican off it. In 1940 he ran for the presidential nomination at the national convention in Philadelphia, only to lose to a rank outsider, Wendell Willkie.

In 1944 he stayed out of the race so that his fellow Ohioan, Senator John W. Bricker, could have a crack at it; Bricker lost to Thomas E. Dewey, who chose him for his running-mate. It was in this year that Allen Treadway finally retired from Congress—but Rayburn, Vinson, and Sabath were still going strong. Four years later Taft tried again. It looked like the ideal chance: Roosevelt was dead; Harry Truman was President and seemingly at the nadir of his popularity. But once again Taft ran into the smooth Dewey machine, which rolled up such a big vote on the second ballot that the Ohioan quickly capitulated.

For Taft the 1948 contest between Truman and Dewey provided both embarrassment and vindication. Embarrassment because Truman attacked the Republican Old Guard in Congress, while Taft, not being the candidate, was unable to counter on equal terms. Truman's tactic was nothing new; Roosevelt had ignored Willkie and concentrated on the three Republican congressmen, "Martin, Barton, and Fish," to the vast amusement of Democratic crowds. But Truman armed this weapon with a barb. Noting that the platform of the Republican convention promised solutions to problems of civil rights, housing, prices, agriculture, the President called a mid-summer session so that the Republican-controlled Congress could deliver on these promises. But this was Taft's Republican party that he was summoning back to Washington, and the Senator had no interest in redeeming the pledges made by the Dewey wing of the party. So Congress met, blustered, and recessed. Its failure to act sharpened Truman's denunciations of the "do-nothing 80th Congress" and helped him immeasurably to win his miraculous victory over Dewey in the fall.

Dewey's defeat was Taft's vindication. For years he had charged that the Republicans could not beat liberal, internationalist Democrats with liberal, internationalist Republicans. Now, for the third time, and against a Democrat who had lost big chunks of his party to Henry Wallace Progressives and Dixiecrat conservatives, this tired old strategy had failed. Was it not time to try a party regular? And who was more regular than Mr. Republican? But first he had to show that he could still win heavily in a big urban state. On this score the political calendar was just right, for Taft came up for re-election in 1950. Ohio Democrats played directly into his hands by nominating a drab candidate and by allowing union labor to move in and make Ohio a spectacular test of Taft and his labor policy. This test Taft met with a massive victory. Then he set his sights on 1952.

The Rout of the Regulars

The Chicago Stockyards, Wednesday evening, July 9, 1952: A burly man with rumpled, curly hair stood at the rostrum before 1200 Republican delegates and pointed a drooping finger at Governor Dewey sitting in the big New York delegation. "We followed you before"—here Senator Everett Dirksen undulated his finger limply—"and you took us down the road to defeat." The Taft delegates howled their resentment at their old foe; Dewey men answered with a chorus of boos and jeers, while the Governor sat stonily in his seat. A delegate fainted; heckling broke out between delegations; disturbances erupted in the aisles. "This is no place for Republicans to be booing any other Republican," Dirksen bayed, and slowly order was restored.

Old timers let their memories go back 40 years, when an earlier Republican convention was on the point of breaking up and another Taft was defending the Old Guard against invasion by irregulars. In 1912, too, the apparent issue had been the technical one of delegates' credentials but the real issue was who should speak for the Republican party: the regulars who worked in the party round-the-clock and round-the-year in lean times and good, or the independents who moved in on the party opportunistically when pospects looked bright? And once again the controversy centered in the South. Most of the contested delegates in the 1912 convention had been from the South; the Taft-controlled convention, by allowing these delegates to vote on their own contests, had re-nominated the President and had sent the Bull Moosers out of the conclave shouting "steam roller" and "naked theft." Would history repeat itself? Already the Dewey forces were ominously resurrecting some of the old war cries.

Since the nub of the 1952 dispute was the Texas delegation, a look at the pre-convention politics of that state tells much about the roots of the warring wings of the party. For decades the Taft wing of the party had been subsidizing a network of tiny Republican cells in Texas as in the rest of the South. Local Republicans lived off post-masterships and other Washington patronage, the recognition they got from the party greats, and their quadrennial treks to the party conclaves in Chicago or Philadelphia. Republican politics in the South was about as low-voltage as politics could get. The local big-wigs made no effort to broaden the party and bring in new people because the idea was not to win elections in the impossibly Demo-cratic South, but the reverse—to keep the party small so that the spoils from Washington need not be divvied up too widely. Every four years the Southern Republicans bestirred themselves to elect delegates who would go along with their friends in Washington—usually conservative men who supported the congressional wing of the party. Holding these meetings was no great trouble, though, for so few people took part that the whole business was often done in front parlors or in law offices. Nobody paid any attention, except the friends in Washington.

In Texas in early 1952, this peaceful order of things was sud-denly disrupted. For years a large body of Texan Democrats had been restive over the New Deal policies of their national party; they had deserted Roosevelt and Truman in national elections, but with little effect on the outcome. They might have joined with the local Republican party but that party was pledged to Taft, who had little appeal in Texas save to a faction of the regular Republicans. But in early 1952 the known availability of General Dwight D. Eisen-hower, then president of Columbia University, for the Republican presidential nomination acted as a catalyst; an anti-Taft Republican faction joined with anti-Truman Democrats and independents to wrest control of the state Republican enclaves from the Old Guard. Setting up a lively Eisenhower-for-President Club of Texas, the General's supporters laid plans to take control of the precinct meet-ings where delegates would be chosen to county conventions (which would choose delegates to the state convention, which would choose the Texas delegation to the Republican national convention). The Eisenhower men held practice caucuses throughout the state, care-fully instructed their people that they could vote in the Republican precinct conventions even though they were otherwise Democrats, and drummed up wide support for the General. The regulars were not idle. Denouncing these "one-day Republicans" they asserted that the precinct conventions were open only to those Democrats who would "burn their New Deal–Fair Deal bridges behind them and join with us in making Texas a two-party state by electing a Republican president and Republican state and county officers from constable to governor." Both sides poured huge sums of money into the battle.

The precinct conventions in May would have been highly comic if the adversaries had not been so grimly serious. The homes that had once served as convention halls for half a dozen people were now inundated. Taft men looked on in consternation as hundreds of Eisenhower supporters tried to crowd into their parlors. One hundred Eisenhower rooters showed up at the Fort Worth home of Taft's chief lieutenant in Texas (five people had attended the last convention); the poor man had to surrender his home to his adversaries and hold his own meeting out on the front lawn. This kind of thing happened in precinct after precinct: hundreds of Eisenhower supporters arrived, the Taft men challenged their right to take part in a Republican convention, the General's supporters proceeded to select their delegates, the Senator's supporters stormed out, held a rump convention down the street, and named their own delegates.

As the weeks passed the breach widened. More than a score of county conventions precipitated bolts by either Taft or Eisenhower men. Because of their historic control of party mechanics the regulars dominated the state convention and they let contested Taft delegates vote on their own contests. They quickly excluded the irregulars, who moved to a hall across the street, held their own convention, and selected their own slate of national delegates. Tempers had long since worn thin. Taft men charged that Eisenhower was backed by the *Daily Worker* and by the Political Action Committee of the CIO. Senator Henry Cabot Lodge, the General's campaign manager, denounced the actions of the regulars as "scandalous and shameful" and added that a man whose victory was based on Republican corruption could not raise his voice against Democratic corruption. Taft, expecting that the national convention would sustain the Texas regulars, rendered smilingly an un-Taftlike legal opinion: "Possession is nine points of the law." And after the national Republican committee, dominated by Taft forces, had awarded most of the contested delegates to the Senator, Eisenhower, by now on his way to the convention by special train, departed from his usual blandness to charge "chicanery" and "star chamber methods" and "smoke-filled rooms" at every whistle stop.

It was this steaming fight that was dropped into the middle of the proceedings in Chicago, along with a very similar contest from Georgia. And as luck would have it, the Taft and Eisenhower forces were evenly enough divided so that the disposition of these contests could tip the balance in the convention. Before the credentials committee, and then before the whole convention, spokesmen for each side cited state laws and Republican party principle to sustain their cases. Behind the scenes the Taft leaders, scenting trouble ahead, tried frantically to make deals with Eisenhower's men and split the disputed delegates.

But the Eisenhower leaders spurned any deal. For now they had what they saw as a supreme moral issue—the same issue that had racked the Republican convention of 1912—and moral issues could not be compromised. Much more useful to them than the few delegates that Taft would concede was the effect of the issue on uncommitted delegates holding the balance of power and on millions of Americans following the convention on television. With a fine sense of public relations, Dewey, Lodge & Co. set up the issue simply as: "Thou shalt not steal." Taft could cope with a legal issue over delegates' technical credentials. He could cope with a political dispute because such a dispute between reasonable men could always be settled by compromise. But when his opponents brandished the Sixth Commandment, William White has said, Taft was simply and wholly uncomprehending. "He had no genuine understanding of the *meaning* of what was afoot. He had come to Chicago to defend his general record and particularly his views of foreign policy; he recognized that it was these that really made him objectionable to so many powerful Eastern internationalist Republicans and independents. He felt therefore in the position of a commander who had prepared to withstand a siege against his capitol and main airfield only to find that his enemies were driving against the peony beds in the public parks."

Taft had a right to feel bewildered, for the issue of "Thou shalt not steal" was one of the most spurious moral questions that has ever influenced a convention decision. Certainly there had been "steals," and perhaps the Taft forces had "stolen" more than had the opposition. And certainly there was a real issue, but this was drowned out in the pious oratory. The real issue was the question of membership in the Republican party. Who was a Republican— simply the regular who stuck with the party and all its candidates, who worked in the party and made a political commitment to it? Or was it also the independent, the irregular who turned to the party when and if he liked its platform and candidates? A good case could be made out for both, for a party needs both regulars and ir- regulars; how much influence each should have is a complex prob- lem deserving hard thought.

What was presented to the convention was a grossly overstated moral issue and a hopelessly confused legal issue which together con- cealed the real political question. Neither party had settled the real question, for neither had clearly defined who should be party "mem- bers" and what their rights and duties might be. Indeed, party membership did not exist in the United States in any meaningful sense. The question of who was, and who was not, a party member had not been settled as a general proposition. But this was the real, though unseen, issue before the convention—the issue behind the limp finger pointed at Dewey, the boos and the jeers, the memories of 1912. And the convention was no more capable of coming to grips with the real issue than were American party leaders or the American people.

And because the issue could be resolved neither on legal terms nor on logical terms, it was settled mainly on the basis of power politics with the Sixth Commandment serving as one of the power plays. By winning the credentials fight the Eisenhower forces added to their own delegate strength; they also proved that Taft did not possess the majority for his nomination that he had claimed. The 607-531 pro-Eisenhower outcome of the first credentials contest (the Georgia dispute) was the crucial test; from then on the Eisen- hower forces held full command. The Senator, in the end, did not even force the Texas dispute to a vote because he feared another display of his weakness. His defeat came quickly. On the first nomination roll call Eisenhower rolled up 595 votes of the needed 604, against Taft's 500. At the end of the roll call Minnesota waved its standard wildly, gained the floor, and switched to Eisenhower; the rush began. The official vote after switching was 845-280; a hard core of Taft men stuck with their fallen hero.

The number of holdouts was significant; not for many years had a national convention adjourned among such sullen bitterness. In part the bitterness was simply anti-Dewey and doctrinal. Late in the proceedings, when the outcome was almost certain, Taft's campaign manager issued what an observer called one of the most extraordinary documents in party history. A broadside of newspaper size urged the delegates to: "SINK DEWEY!!" It read in part: "TOM DEWEY IS THE MOST COLD-BLOODED, RUTH-LESS, SELFISH POLITICAL BOSS IN THE UNITED STATES TODAY. . . . He is the greatest menace that the Republican has. . . . Behind Tom Dewey is the same old gang of Eastern Internationalists and Republican New Dealers who ganged up to sell the Republican Party down the river in 1940, in 1944, and in 1948. . . ." This ranting sheet was put out under the name of the Taft Committee.

But the feeling was personal as well as doctrinal. The hatred of the Taft delegates for the slick Easterners around Eisenhower stemmed from their enormous feeling for Taft. That feeling was deep and intimate. "They liked him," according to Richard Rovere, who was on the scene, "as a man and as a political combatant. They liked his record—particularly the fact that it was long. They liked his looks, they liked his voice, they liked his invalided wife. They liked him for the same reason that men everywhere like their old shoes and bedroom slippers: he fitted, he was comfortable, he was so well broken in that it was no chore at all to put him on. . . ." Beside him the General was a newcomer, an irregular, a boob—probably a liberal and internationalist, and perhaps even a Democrat.

Yet some of these delegates must have reserved a special kind of hate for themselves. These were the delegates who, vastly preferring Taft the regular, voted for Eisenhower the irregular. Why? Not because they thought Eisenhower would be a better President than Taft; they did not think this at all. Not because they thought that the General would probably win the Presidency, and that Taft probably could not; many regulars would prefer to risk defeat with a good safe man than risk victory with an outsider. The reason was simply crass self-interest. These delegates were the grass-roots party leaders who had the prime responsibility for electing Republicans to state and local offices in the fall. They calculated that Eisenhower, as a national hero, would have the same effect that other popular presidential candidates had had—he would attract to the polls millions of independent Republicans who would stay in the booth long enough to vote for the rest of the ticket. They wanted Eisenhower, in short, for the very reason they disliked him—his independence.

Right after his nomination Eisenhower walked over to Taft's headquarters. "I came over to pay a call of friendship on a great American," Eisenhower said before the television cameras. "His willingness to cooperate is absolutely necessary to the success of the Republican party in the campaign and of the Administration to follow." While some of his workers wept, Taft congratulated the General gamely and promised his help. But at the time these remarks were mainly ritualistic: Taft left Chicago deeply embittered and torn. He was now 62; his last chance at the presidency had almost surely gone. And he had lost to another "me too" candidate—and a man whose organizational Republicanism was deeply in question.

At his old family summer place at Murray Bay in Canada he pondered his course. He wrote a private memorandum in which he laid the blame for his defeat mainly on the power of New York financial interests, the anti-Taft propaganda of most of the newspapers, and the influence of most of the Republican governors. An old journalistic friend visited Taft and came back with the clearly inspired report that unless Eisenhower made assurances to Taft on specific policies, in writing, "General Eisenhower's chances of winning the support of Senator Taft of Ohio are about zero." It was a challenge that even a political amateur could recognize.

The General and the Senator

Several months before the convention Sherman Adams, Governor of New Hampshire and an ardent Eisenhower man, was struck by the chilling thought that the General on some vagrant occasion might have got himself registered as a Democrat and hence might not be eligible to enter the New Hampshire primary. So he had an inquiry sent to the county clerk of Dickinson County, in Kansas, where Eisenhower's boyhood home town of Abilene was located. The county clerk's answer was wholly revealing though not wholly literate. "Dwight" had never voted in the county so far as he knew. "Dwight's father," he went on, "was a Republican and always voted the Republican ticket up until his death, however that has nothing to do with the son, as many differ from their fathers of which I am sorry to see, the multitude believes in going into debt and see how much they can spend, it has become a habit & will sink this nation into bankruptcy."

"I don't think he has any politics."

The county clerk was dead right; Eisenhower had been about as non-political as was possible for a man who had been in the center of public and world affairs for over a decade. Born in 1890 in Texas, cut off from the domestic quarrels that broke out during the Taft and Wilson regimes, insulated from the main stream of American society by West Point and garrison life, he had disliked what little he had seen of politics. As the officer-in-charge of some Civilian Conservation Corps activities in Pennsylvania in the early 1930's he caused a small rumpus in Washington by choosing (probably by chance) exclusively Republican assistants; years later he said that he had been totally amazed that anybody had cared. But as commander in Europe during World War II and later as head of NATO forces he showed that he had a quality quite different from partisan politics—a consummate skill in mediating among warring generals and politicians.

And now in the summer of 1952, facing the ultimatum from Murray Bay, the General had to cope with one of the most partisan and proudly stubborn of American politicians. This would be Eisenhower's first major political decision, for the mechanics of his nomination had largely been controlled by Lodge, Dewey, and Adams. Here Eisenhower's elasticity on policy and dogma stood him in good stead. Inviting Taft to Columbia, he made what was quickly labeled by Adlai E. Stevenson, the Democratic presidential nominee, who was trying to drive a wedge between Eisenhower and independent voters, the "surrender of Morningside Heights." The Senator announced that he and the General were in full agreement on a set of policy statements that Taft had placed before him; it would now be possible, the Senator added, for him to campaign whole-heartedly for the ticket.

The appeasement of Taft heated up a struggle that was simmering within Eisenhower's campaign entourage between the somewhat liberal and internationalist independents, organized in Citizens for Eisenhower and other groups, and the regular, old-line Republicans operating through the Republican national committee and the state and local party organizations. The independents glumly accepted the Morningside Heights treaty as the price that must be paid Mr. Republican but they were appalled when the General went on to appease the radical right wing of the party. When Eisenhower, campaigning in Wisconsin, deleted from his speech a defense of his wartime chief, George C. Marshall, as a concession to Senator Joseph McCarthy, a telegram came from one of the General's leading independent backers, Publisher Arthur Hays Sulzberger of *The New York Times:* "Do I need to tell you that I am sick at heart?" And when the story broke about the "secret fund" of Senator Richard M. Nixon, Eisenhower's running-mate, the General kept him on the ticket despite the private advice of Governor Dewey and the public advice of the *New York Herald Tribune.* It was a measure of Eisenhower's flexibility and wide appeal that he was able to placate the regulars and still keep the support of millions of independents on election day.

Just as the regulars had calculated, Eisenhower carried with him Republican majorities into Congress, along with a host of Republicans in state and local offices. The majority in the Senate was precarious, but enough for Taft to realize his own Grand Design. This was simply to convert his informal and de facto leadership among Senate Republicans into formal and authoritative supremacy. He moved with the finesse of the complete Senate man that he was. He caused himself to be elected majority leader so that he would be the key liaison between the Senate and the Administration. He hopped from the Finance Committee to the Foreign Relations Committee both because he saw the key place of foreign policy in the new Administration and because he feared that the new chairman of Foreign Relations, Alexander Wiley, would be too internationalist. He saw to it that stalwart Taft men were in the key positions—a job made far easier because of the workings of seniority. Above all, his control of fiscal policy was buttressed by the elevation of Styles Bridges of New Hampshire and of Eugene Millikin of Colorado to the chairmanship of Appropriations and Finance. Millikin would also chair the Republican party caucus.

Quietly shouldered aside, again with the help of the seniority rule, were famous Senators who had been prominent in Eisenhower's pre-convention campaign. Only one or two anti-Taftites were placed on the Majority Policy Committee, which was headed by Senator William F. Knowland, conservative Senator from California. Nor did Taft confine himself to the upper chamber. Through his allies in the House, Joseph Martin and Charles Halleck, soon to be Speaker and majority leader respectively, and through powerful friends in the Rules and other key committees, Taft saw to it that the right men controlled the flow of legislation, timing of debates, and the procedure on the floor. Most of the new chairmen of the major House committees were to the right of Taft, and all were in the Allen Treadway tradition: John Taber of upstate New York, Appropriations; Dewey Short of the Missouri Ozarks, Armed Services; Jesse P. Wolcott of rural Michigan, Banking and Currency; Clare E. Hoffman, also of rural Michigan, Government Operations; Chauncey W. Reed of the rural area west of Chicago, Judiciary; Leo E. Allen of rural Illinois, Rules; Daniel A. Reed of upstate New York, Ways and Means.

By January 20, 1953, Taft was clearly and indisputably the boss of Congress. While Eisenhower had been busy constructing his Administration during the pre-Inauguration weeks, Taft had been busy constructing his. The Senator's group, indeed, seemed more unified over policy than the President's. Eisenhower, trying to placate independents and regulars, Dewey men and Taft men, liberals and conservatives, had come up with a Cabinet that cut across the party spectrum. The General had no influence over Taft's arrangements in Congress, but the Senator was an unseen presence in Eisenhower's Cabinet building. And a vocal one—he publicly termed "incredible" Eisenhower's choice of a union leader as Secretary of Labor. Still, it was an Eisenhower cabinet, with Taft types like Secretary of Agriculture Ezra Taft Benson neatly balanced against Dewey men like Attorney General Herbert Brownell, Jr.

How long could the President and the Senator work together? It was widely forecast that an early break was inevitable, but the prophets underestimated Eisenhower's plasticity and Taft's genuine desire to see the new regime—the first Republican Administration in 20 years—prove that it could govern. He set about "educating" the President in fiscal and labor policy. Eisenhower gave Taft complete access to the oval office, and met frequently with congressional leaders. Sometimes the frail alliance almost broke under the weight of the basic differences between White House and Congress; on one occasion, when he learned that the President would not be able to balance his first budget, Taft lost control of himself, pounded his fist on the Cabinet table, and shouted at the astonished President sitting across from him:

"With a program like this, we'll never elect a Republican Congress in 1954. You're taking us down the same road Truman traveled. It's a repudiation of everything we promised in the campaign!" But this was exceptional; most of the time Taft backed up the Administration and was even able to moderate obstruction from the radical Republican right in Congress.

Perhaps in the long run the General and the Senator would have broken off relations because of the political forces pushing them apart. But there was to be no long run, for in the spring of 1953 Taft was stricken by cancer. He went to his death as bravely and doggedly as he had fought his political battles. His departure from the Senate disrupted the precarious personal relationships on which the Eisenhower-Taft working alliance had rested. Eisenhower did not intervene as Knowland became the new majority leader. Younger, brasher, less skillful than Taft, ambitious for the Presidency, impatient, headstrong, Knowland could not control the anti-Administration forces boiling up on Capitol Hill even if he had wanted.

In the months following Taft's disablement Eisenhower's relations with Congress fell to their lowest point during his entire administration. Congress either postponed or turned down major White House proposals, including expansion of social security, the St. Lawrence Seaway, Hawaiian statehood, and raising of the debt limit. Taber's committee slashed a billion dollars off the appropriations for mutual security. McCarthy went on a rampage against the White House; meddled in State Department and Pentagon affairs; and in the end publicly apologized to the American people for having supported Eisenhower in 1952. The President had to combat the Bricker amendment, sponsored by Taft's junior colleague who wanted to cramp the President's power to conduct foreign relations. Worse than all this, perhaps, was the truculent ill will that marked the attitude of the congressional Republicans toward the White House.

The President could not understand all this. He felt that he had made every possible concession to the conservative, isolationist wing of the party. He had kept hands off the internal affairs of Congress. He had placated injured feelings. He had invited hundreds of congressmen to a long series of White House luncheons. He had wanted to display Republican unity, but they gave him no chance. How could they doubt his sincerity? Especially—and this is what galled the President the most—how could they doubt the military and foreign policy judgment of the man they had chosen President mainly on the basis of his experience in that area?

In his hurt and puzzlement Eisenhower began to wonder about the party he had led to victory. To Sherman Adams, now his chief assistant, he complained privately about the party's failure to face up to world conditions. Never a committed Republican, he now wondered whether the GOP had outlived its usefulness. His thoughts took a bold turn. What about a new party that would be "essentially his," that would be world-minded in foreign policy and middle-of-the-road in domestic matters? What about a realignment of parties so that moderate Democrats and Republicans could combine behind a centrist program? The President even cast about for a name for such a policy. What he wanted was a party of "conservative dynamism," or of "dynamic conservatism," as he said later, but he could not think of a good name.

Later the President had second thoughts. He feared that a new party might lead to a multi-party system, and his memories of the splinter parties of France made him wary of that. He recalled that the Bull Moosers in 1912 had not been able to survive. He decided that the only hope lay in the infusion of new young blood into the Republican party—a gospel he was still preaching long after he left the presidency. He learned first hand, moreover, how dangerous his speculations about a third party had been. In a rash moment Adams mentioned his chief's musings to Robert J. Donovan, a *Herald Trib-*

une reporter who was writing an account of Eisenhower's first term. At a White House meeting in 1956, shortly after the book appeared, Knowland seized on the episode and remarked acidly that the revelation would hardly be helpful to the Republicans in an election year. Donovan's report had, indeed, confirmed the congressional Republicans' suspicions about the President's Republicanism.

But long before this Eisenhower had gained a kind of party realignment, though not in the form he anticipated. In the off-year elections of 1954 the Republicans lost their slim margin in Congress. Eisenhower's coattails, so long in 1952, were not able to bring congressional victory when the President himself was not running. Eisenhower was not surprised that he got along so well with the new Democratic Congress, for time and again Democrats had supplied him votes he needed to get his measures through. But he was pleased by the easy relations he had with the Democratic leaders, especially with his fellow Texans, Speaker Sam Rayburn (in whose district Eisenhower had been born) and Senate majority leader Lyndon Johnson. Not only on foreign policy but in several critical areas of domestic policy the President gained vital support from sections of the congressional Democrats.

It is not certain, though, that Eisenhower ever realized that circumstances had brought him a viable middle way between the two parties. After the election of 1956, when he found that the Republicans had failed to regain Congress, he wondered whether he had been wise to run. After four more years he still had misgivings about his alignment of moderate Republicans and Democrats. He told Adams in July 1960 that he thought the Constitution should be changed to provide some guarantee that the "party of the President" would control the majority of Congress. It might help, he said, if the House were elected with the President every four years. How the President, after his experiences of 1953-54 with a Republican Congress, could have favored this kind of party government is not clear.

Still, the President had found a viable middle way in his working alliance with congressional Democrats, and in doing so he had upset the strategy of liberal Democrats as well as of right wing Republicans. The Roosevelt-Truman-Stevenson wing of the Democratic party found the party's congressional leadership guilty of "me-tooism" with Eisenhower, but the presidential Democrats, defeated in 1956, could do little about it. Their only recourse was of limited effect on legislation but of symbolic importance—the establishment under the Democratic national committee of an advisory council composed of liberal Democrats such as Adlai E. Stevenson, Harry S. Truman, Herbert Lehman, Estes Kefauver, Hubert Humphrey, and Mennen Williams, and with the support of Eleanor Roosevelt. The fact that Rayburn and Johnson declined membership in the council suggested that the cleavage between the congressional and presidential wings was at least as sharp in the Democratic party as in the Republican.

Eisenhower, meantime, happily dominated the middle way. He had declared himself a Republican in 1952, he told Adams toward the end, because some of his friends had convinced him that the Republicans were closer to his own beliefs. But, he said, he could as easily have been a conservative Democrat. "I feel pretty good when I'm attacked from both sides," he added a moment later. "It makes me feel more certain that I'm on the right track."

Summary: The Four-Party System in History

Early in these pages I advanced the thesis that under the Madisonian system personal factions would grow up around each officeholder and office seeker, from President to fence viewer, and would buttress the constitutional and legal checks and balances with political and human forces. The offices would give some structure and stability to the flux of political forces. The implication of this thesis is that if the structure of power-wielding offices remains substantially the same over time, the pattern of politics—of political factions, leader-follower relations, area groupings, for example—would also persist over time. The pattern would not always be very clear, of course. Fierce storms such as civil war, or long-gathering tides such as urbanization, or sudden squalls such as those personified by a Hearst or a Huey Long or a McCarthy, might wash over the familiar channels, but the old political patterns would reappear once the storm was gone.

The United States, with one of the oldest working Constitutions in the world, is a good place to test this theory. Despite wars and

depressions, despite vast economic changes and social transformations, we still have a President, a Congress with two equally powerful chambers, a Supreme Court with the power of veto, and a separate system of state and local government. The men in the White
House and on Capitol Hill still confront one another in much the
same posture of competition as they did a century and a half ago.
Rivalry between governors and legislatures, between national and
state politicians, between city mayors and state legislatures continues
unabated, as does the struggle of individuals and institutions within
each unit of government. Our economy and our national life has
become unified in many respects, while our politics has remained
largely factional and fragmented.

Still, as we noted in Chapter 2, politics too requires men to concert their activities, and politicians have long seen the need of operating within, or at least through, political parties. It may not be true,
as the paraphrase of Gilbert and Sullivan would have it, that every
man or woman that's born alive is a Democrat or Republican, though
most politicians have found it desirable to exploit the voting strengths
of one of the two major parties. But our excursion through American
history has suggested that to see the pattern of power at the national
level only in terms of two parties is grossly misleading. The balance
between one or two parties, on the one hand, and (at the national
level) over a thousand personal parties (one for the President, one
for each member of Congress, and at least one for each rival for the
office, in both parties), on the other hand, has been struck not in a
two-party power system, nor in a multi-party system, but in what is
essentially a four-party system. The four national parties are the
presidential Democrats, the presidential Republicans, the congressional Democrats, and the congressional Republicans. The groupings
that have been described as "wings" of the two major parties in these
pages are, in any meaningful sense, separate though overlapping
parties.

The oldest of these are the two Democratic parties—the congressional Democrats, who began as the Madison party in Congress,
and the presidential party, which was founded and built by Jefferson.
The symbolic founder of the Republican party was Abraham Lincoln; the congressional Republican party had its origin in the opposition to Pierce and Buchanan on the Hill during the 1850's, and

with the congressional Republicans who went on to fight Lincoln during the Civil War and to dominate Reconstruction. Today these four parties are as intact as ever: the Roosevelt-Truman-Stevenson-Kennedy presidential Democrats; the Willkie—Dewey—Eisenhower—Rockefeller presidential Republicans; the John Garner—Howard Smith—Harry Byrd—John McClellan congressional Democrats; and the Allen Treadway—Robert Taft—Charles Halleck congressional Republicans.

The sources and sustenance of the four-party system are several-fold.

1. *Institutional:* Obviously, the presidential parties are organized around, and oriented toward, the Presidency, and the congressional parties around Congress. But the institutional roots go much deeper. The national party convention is the bulwark of the presidential parties; not since Harding has a congressional Republican won a presidential nomination; not perhaps since Pierce and Buchanan have congressional Democrats captured a convention. Set up to move the presidential nomination out of "King Caucus," or the congressional party, the convention by and large has succeeded in doing just that, especially in recent times. The Robert Tafts and the Lyndon Johnsons usually do not win at Chicago or Philadelphia; when they win a nomination they usually fail of election, as Clay, Webster, Calhoun, and Blaine did in the last century. Often the congressional party controls the platform committee or the convention machinery, as in the case of the Taft men in 1952, but it cannot control the rank-and-file delegates because the latter represent a far broader stratum of the whole party coalition than do the congressional leaders.

But if the Presidency and the convention serve as the great bulwarks of presidential party power, Capitol Hill is the political home of the congressional parties. They control the machinery of Congress, the committees, the caucus and conference, the promotion system, the movement of legislation, procedure on the floor. They operate through a small coterie composed always of committee chairmen and sometimes of the elected leaders. The foundation of the congressional party is control of the legislative fiscal machinery, and this is also its oldest mechanism; it was the establishment and operation of the House Ways and Means Committee that marked the rise to influence of the first congressional party under Madison. Appointments and promotions to the fiscal and other key commitments have been a source of congressional party power; Robert Taft gained from this arrangement, just as Stephen Douglas ultimately lost by it.

2. *Electoral-behavioral:* Each set of parties has its roots in parts of the election system and in aspects of voting behavior. The electoral college, with its presumed bias in favor of the organized minority groups in the big states, compels presidential parties to cater to the urban masses and their liberal dogmas. The staggered election calendar, which causes half of Congress on the average to be elected in "non-presidential" years, usually slashes the number of congressmen elected on the presidential coattails; hence the regulars from the safer seats build up their seniority and their influence. The more competitive states and districts, which are more closely attuned to the national party balance, are automatically penalized.

Truman helped elect Fair Deal Democrats to Congress in 1948, but this group suffered a heavy toll in the next two elections. Eisenhower helped bring in a Republican Congress in 1952, but many of the more independent Republicans from the more competitive seats elected with him lost out in 1954. The same problem faced the Kennedy Democrats in 1962.

Because of these election forces we cannot assign all members of Congress to the congressional parties. There is a "presidential wing" in each party in Congress, but it lacks strength and stability because its numbers keep getting decimated. "Presidential" senators like Herbert Lehman and Paul Douglas, to be sure, could hang on to their seats on the Democratic side, and also men like Jacob Javits and John Sherman Cooper on the Republican side, but they lack a dependable number of supporters. Senators Stephen Douglas and John Kennedy won presidential nominations after they moved out of the congressional party.

The conflicting sources of presidential and congressional party strengths are due to voting behavior as well as election mechanics. Not only do the voters tend to elect congressmen on presidential candidates' coattails (especially the winning candidate), as in 1936 or 1952, but in a presidential election year they vote in terms of a different frame of reference than in off-years. Voting for both President and Congress in presidential years is heavily influenced by national issues and images, while the off-year contests are pulled into the narrower orbits of the state and local battles of governors, state senators, county commissioners and the like. Another difference between voting behaviors in the presidential and off-year elections is most important: Presidential contests draw regularly more voters to the polls than the off-year elections. Great presidential battles of the past have permanently enlarged the electorate: notably the Harrison-Van Buren "log cabin" contest of 1840, the Bryan-McKinley struggle in 1896, the triangular fray among Wilson, Taft, and Roosevelt in 1912, the Smith-Hoover battle in 1928 with its religious issue, Roosevelt vs. Landon in 1936, and Eisenhower vs. Stevenson twenty years later. Finally, the presidential contests draw a different kind of vote to the polls: lower income, less educated, more favorable toward government welfare programs, and less involved in ordinary politics.

3. *Ideological and doctrinal:* The four parties have been significantly divided in their ideas and policies. Today the presidential Democrats are liberal in domestic policy (i.e., favor the use of government to bring about a broader distribution of physical and psychic income) and internationalist in foreign (i.e., favor mutual accommodation with other nations in diplomacy, trade, aid, and military policy). The congressional Republicans stand at the opposite end of the four-party spectrum. In between are the presidential Republicans and the congressional Democrats, with the former more liberal and internationalist. This alignment has been true for several decades; but in earlier times the parties have occupied different positions in relation to one another. In general, though, both presidential parties have been more liberal (TR's party in 1906, Wilson's in 1916, Roosevelt's in 1936, Kennedy's in 1960) and both congressional parties have been more conservative.

The differences go deeper than policy; they go into doctrine and ideology. The presidential party has been the "popular" party, eager to broaden participation, espousing majoritarian and egalitarian doctrine. These parties have favored more activist government; they have responded more to the urban voters and their organizations. The congressional parties have sought to limit federal power, especially the authority of the President, as in the case of the congressional attempts to harass and hobble Johnson, Hayes, both Roosevelts, Wilson, Eisenhower, and Kennedy. The congressional parties idealize Madison and Calhoun; the presidential parties the strong Presidents, from Jefferson to Truman.

4. *Leadership and career lines:* The differences in the style and views of the more noted leaders—the men treated in earlier pages—are well known. Less obvious are the patterns of recruitment and promotion within the parties. For example, the presidential Republicans for decades have been drawing internationalist-minded men out of the universities, law schools, and metropolitan law and banking firms of the East: men like Elihu Root, Henry Stimson, John Foster Dulles, Douglas Dillon. Such men rise up the ladders of administrative, usually corporate or governmental, life. The steps toward eminence in the congressional Republican party are typically quite different: small-town lawyer in a heavily Republican area, district attorney (or its equivalent), state legislature, then national House or Senate. Their background is more parliamentary and less bureaucratic.

5. *Other Four-Party Tendencies:* Further variations can be noted, though of a more tentative sort. In foreign and military policy the two presidential parties seem to have a more European orientation, the congressional parties, especially the Republican, a more Asiatic or Oriental. Thus it was the Taft faction that flayed the Democrats for "starving" the Pacific campaigns during World War II, and for helping Europe at the expense of China afterwards. Different parties attract different journals and columnists: the *Washington Post,* the *New York Times,* Marquis Childs, the *New Republic* broadly support the presidential Democrats, while the *New York Herald Tribune* clearly favors the presidential Republicans and the *Chicago Tribune* the congressional Republicans. William S. White is a persuasive interpreter of the congressional Democrats. There is, finally, a geographical cast to the parties: the congressional Democrats are rooted in the South. The presidential Democrats draw their main support from the urban areas of the Northeast, Midwest, and West, the presidential Republicans from much the same area, but with heavier emphasis on suburbia, while the congressional Re-

publicans reap their best crops of votes in the rural areas of the North.

The four parties are not separated from one another by neat boundaries, though they are much more clearly defined than the Democratic and Republican. Nothing in the fuzzy politics of America can be neat. In particular, there is a major question of the place in the four-party scheme of the elected leaders of Congress. Are men like Lyndon Johnson or John McCormack or Everett Dirksen today, or Joe Martin or Henry Cabot Lodge or Champ Clark in earlier days, part of the presidential party or the congressional? The elected leaders' roles have varied so much over the years that we can generalize enough to say that they have served sometimes as bridges or umpires between the presidential and congressional parties, sometimes as spokesman for the congressional parties at the White House (i.e., Halleck), sometimes as the President's agent on the Hill (i.e., FDR's Robinson), sometimes as a kind of third force.

But even amid this irregularity there has been some pattern. When men of their own nominal party have occupied the White House, congressional party leaders have usually worked closer to the President; at other times they have become identified with, and exercised leadership over, the committee chairmen heading up the congressional party. The contrast in Taft's role before 1953 and after points up this dualism even in one man's career. Champ Clark, too, made the transition from independent leader to a presidential spokesman. Lodge's role in 1918-20 is typical of the congressional party leadership when the opposition has its man in the White House; Lodge tried to mediate between the congressional and presidential parties, but when the chips were down, he sided with the former.

Other irregular patterns can be discerned in the system. The presidential party usually allots the vice-presidential nomination to the congressional party, as a minor prize. FDR and Garner, Truman and Barkley, Eisenhower and Nixon, Kennedy and Johnson are recent examples that come to mind, though the practice goes back a long way. Sometimes the custom becomes ludicrous, as when Dewey chose Bricker to be his running mate, and when the conservative John W. Davis was teamed in 1924 with William Jennings Bryan's brother. On the other hand, the presidential party may withhold its favor from the congressional party, as Roosevelt did in 1940 in dropping Garner and choosing Wallace, and as Nixon did in 1960 in picking Cabot Lodge. But the pattern runs the other way.

Finally we may note some regular alternations in the control of the national party machinery. When the presidential party occupies the White House it almost always controls that machinery. Even Presidents suffering serious dips in popularity, like Taft in 1912 and Truman in 1948, can gain renomination. When the presidential party does not control the Presidency, on the other hand, its sibling congressional party can often get its grip on the party's national committee, elect one of its own as national chairman, and penetrate the machinery of the national convention. This was true of the Democrats in the 1920's and the Republicans in the 1940's.

Can the Supreme Court be viewed historically as a link in the four-party system? Only if we add another dimension: time. If, as Mr. Dooley said, the "supreme court follows the election returns," it has followed mainly presidential elections, and with a lag of ten years or so. Inevitably the power to declare national and state legislation unconstitutional has given the justices a role in policy-making that the presidents could not ignore. From Adams' choice of John Marshall on the eve of Jefferson's Inauguration in 1801, to Kennedy's nomination of Arthur Goldberg 161 years later, presidents have picked men who could be reasonably certain to sustain their programs. "I should like to know that Judge Holmes was in entire sympathy with our views. . . ." before nominating him, Theodore Roosevelt wrote to Lodge. Sometimes presidents err: surely Earl Warren turned out to be more liberal than Eisenhower could have expected, and Felix Frankfurter less activist than Franklin D. Roosevelt could have anticipated. Still, the Supreme Court has typically moved in the orbit of the existing or preceding presidential parties.

All this machinery—courts and congressmen, presidents and parties—would not be enough to sustain the four parties through history in the absence of a central organizing principle. This principle has been present from the start: the idea that the Constitution was properly designed to curb popular majorities, to fragmentize democratic government. But the idea has gained strength over time, as a result of events and ideas described earlier in these pages. The

Constitution, in a sequence well described by Edward S. Corwin a quarter of a century ago, changed from a source of national power to an object of popular worship, esteemed largely for the obstacles it interposed to national power, and finally became a protector of minority interests seeking escape from national power. The Madisonian model came to be enshrined in popular attitudes as well as in constitutional doctrine. Almost as old and as legitimate as Madisonianism, the Jeffersonian model of majority rule and executive leadership was forgotten as a proper alternative to the checks and balances, except during desperate periods of war and depression.

At the end, as at the start, we confront the Madisonian system. It has coalesced, at the national level, into four of what Madison would call factions and we call parties, but it is as durable and significant as ever. Questions arise. Are the underpinnings of the system changing significantly—the economic and social arrangements, the recruitment of leadership, the strength of ideas, the needs of policy? Are we confronted with a world situation that makes the Madisonian model obsolete? Is the Jeffersonian alternative possible and desirable? Before taking up these questions we must look concretely and critically at American politics as it operates today.

III

The Madisonian System Today

9

THE
BALANCE WHEELS
of POLITICS

J have advanced the thesis that under the Madisonian system personal factions would grow up around
each officeholder and office seeker, from President
to fence viewer, and would buttress the constitutional and legal
checks and balances with political or human forces. Governmental
offices would give some structure and stability to the flux of political
energy, for as Madison said, "The interest of the man must be connected with the constitutional rights of the place." Hence my thesis
implies that if the structure of power-wielding offices remains substantially the same over time, the pattern of politics—of political
factions, leader-follower relations, area groupings, for example—
would also persist over time. The pattern would not always be very
clear, of course. Fierce storms such as civil war, or long-gathering
tides such as urbanization, or sudden squalls such as those per-

sonified by a Hearst or a Huey Long or a McCarthy, might wash
over the familiar channels, but the old political patterns would reappear once the storm was gone.

This is precisely what has happened in America. We have recently
celebrated the 175th anniversary of the Constitutional Convention
with the proliferation of offices in that charter essentially as the
Framers gave it to us. In a more tranquil age Gladstone described
the American Constitution as the finest instrument struck off from
the brow of man. While few political scientists would say this today,
we can pay tribute to the marvelous resilience and durability of the
charter, its capacity to accommodate itself to the wrench of civil
war, to depressions, to westward expansion, massive increase and
spread of population, several world wars, urbanization, vast immigration and internal migration, cold war, and the demands of leadership
in the free world. It has co-existed with the expansion of the suffrage, the democratization of major sectors of government, and the
Jeffersonian impulse of strong Presidents. Above all it has survived
—no mean feat in a world littered with the scraps of paper once
destined to serve nations for the ages.

And with it has survived the Madisonian model of a variety of
different offices with mingled powers and separated constituencies.
We still have a President, a Congress with two equally powerful
chambers, a Supreme Court with its own source of authority, and a
separate system of state and local government. The men in the
White House and on Capitol Hill still confront one another in
much the same posture of competition as they did a century and a
half ago. Rivalry between governors and legislatures, between national and state politicians, between city mayors and state legislatures
continues unabated, as does the struggle of individuals and institutions within each unit of government. Our economy and our national
life have become integrated in many respects, while our politics
has remained fragmented.

In a flash of insight Woodrow Wilson said that Americans in
democratizing their government had stuck to Whig mechanics. No
ten words could better sum up the century of American constitutional development before Wilson, or indeed the half century that
followed. In our terms, the Constitution has embodied the Madisonian model in giving the checks and balances a formidable grip on

government, but it has also adjusted to the Jeffersonian strategy in permitting the democratization of the system, as in the direct election of Senators, and in co-existing so easily with political parties. The net effect of the embodiment of both models is that the Constitution and constitutional tradition legitimizes both models but clearly favors the Madisonian, for it encases the democratic impulse in "Whig mechanics."

How is the Madisonian system actually working today? How do the great balances operate and with what effect on government? Who takes part in the political process, who does not, and with what effect? How does the four-party system actually function—not just on the superficial level of filibusters and committees but at its base in the local political institutions and voting habits of the people? What basic changes are taking place that will affect the shape of politics and the strategies of the contestants? Since competing strategies affect the political process, what are the battle plans and alternatives of the major parties? What are the possibilities of presidential leadership—and what may prevent the President from playing his necessary role?

We will undertake, in short, a reassessment of the American system of government. And to do this we must make an inventory of our political and governmental resources. First we will look at people in—and out of—politics: voters, non-voters, partisans, non-partisans, politicians big and small, all comprising the structure of our politics.

Regulars and Irregulars

We begin with one of the most striking aspects of American politics—the fact that at least three-fourths of the voters consider themselves Democrats or Republicans and have done so for a hundred years. The durability of this party feeling is remarkable. No third party since the Civil War has polled more than one-fifth of the presidential vote, except for the 1912 Progressives, many of whom considered themselves temporarily displaced Republicans and voted for the Grand Old Party's state and local candidates. Party feeling is also able to survive sharp changes in voting. Asked by interviewers in 1952, the last year of the Truman Administration, "Generally speaking do you think of yourself as a Republican, a Democrat, an Independent, or what?" 27 per cent of the respondents called themselves strong or not-so-strong Republicans, 47 per cent strong or not-so-strong Democrats. Six years later the percentages were almost exactly the same. Most of the self-styled independents also leaned to one party or the other, and these leanings too showed considerable consistency over time.

This party feeling is a root factor in American politics. Most of the party regulars vote a straight party ticket; the stronger the party feeling, the straighter the party ticket. Hence a major party can be absolutely sure of gaining a good number of votes even when the times are not propitious for it, its candidates may be inadequate, or the opposition party may be running a Roosevelt or an Eisenhower. Party allegiance pervasively affects the partisan voter's way of sizing up public figures, his attitudes toward issues, his regularity in voting. It is a basic component in his capacity to lead and be led. The process is a two-way one, of course, or really a multi-way one; leaders and issues and elections can shape party regularity too. But the role of party identification as an original force in politics is marked.

Party feeling has this kind of original and durable force usually because that feeling is solidly based in the partisan's whole social and political matrix. Most partisans vote the way their parents did, or do. When parents are divided between the parties, the children are likely to be less partisan when they come to vote. Hereditary voting is not a result of parental indoctrination of the children in the proper way to vote, although sometimes this happens. It stems from the fact that the children are subject to the same sectional, economic, class, and status forces as the parents. "I was raised as a Democrat," or "I'm from a strong Republican family," are expressions one hears again and again in politicking or polling, and sometimes the remark is made in a tone of satisfaction tinged with resignation. People absorb their party feeling from curbstone talk in their neighborhood, from their church and school and social group, and these are likely to be interrelated and mutually reinforcing influences.

Party feeling also helps a person to organize his own thoughts about the complicated political world. There is a good deal of evidence that the average person with a grammar or high school education has little understanding of ideology. Terms bandied about by columnists and professors—"left," "right," "liberalism," "conservatism,"—may leave him cold. What he does glimpse is that parties seem to be made up of differing groups, or operate for the benefit of different groups. He has a practical grasp of who does what for whom, or against whom. An Ohio farm woman says that the Democrats "have always helped the farmers." A man in Iowa thinks of the Democrats as hurting taxpayers. The higher the political sophistication, the more the voter generalizes, the more he can organize specifics in terms of a broader frame of reference. Asked whether she liked anything about the Democratic party, a woman in a Chicago suburb said, "No, nothing at all." As for the Republicans, "Well, I think they're more middle-of-the-road—more conservative. . . . They are not so subject to radical change. . . . I like their foreign policy—and the segregation business, that's a middle-of-the-road policy. You can't push it too fast. . . . The labor unions telling workers how to vote—they know which side their bread is buttered on so they have to vote the way they are told to."

Even the most unworldly of people have a glimmering of what the parties stand for. The Republicans "stand up for a good clean Constitution," says a nightwatchman in Indiana. "They do more for the country and clean up Washington—never any drinking down there when the Republicans are in," says a Pennsylvania farmer. "They're better learned and scholared than the Democrat's men," says a retired butler. "Republican party is more of a party that promotes business and believes more in business principles," says a Michigan janitor. The Democrats, says a Bronx postal clerk, "are for the small working man, who is me." A Texas janitor: "I think Democrats are more for the workingman; give more help to the laboring class." A Georgia Negro maid of all work: "Yes, they don't be no depressions, when them Democrats is in. They just lets that money roll on and that's what I likes."

If party serves as a form of instant ideology for most voters, if the great majority of people seem to inherit their party preferences, is most voting a blind, irrational act? Not necessarily. To be sure, some people vote a straight party ticket, or vote for the same party in every election, simply out of habit, or because it requires the least thought. But hereditary voting in itself is not irrational: a wealthy son of a wealthy banker can have other reasons besides parental influence to condemn the high taxes and big spending of the Democrats, and several generations of Pennsylvania coal miners might find equally sensible reasons for backing several generations of Democrats. Voters also take their cues from group or party leaders who are more informed about political matters. Nor is the partisan voter oblivious to change in his economic or class situation. A millionaire rising from the ranks in Horatio Alger, Jr. style might seem a bit ridiculous voting for a liberal Democrat (on a narrowly economic basis alone), but this happens relatively seldom. People often take on new attitudes and change their voting behavior as they move into a new economic and social milieu.

Moreover, even the doughtiest partisan is not impervious to crucial historical events. The Civil War, jarring millions of Americans out of their customary party affiliations, still has its partisan effects today. The events of the 1890's also had a lasting impact. And millions of Americans today still vote largely in response to the Great Depression, in terms of what they feel to have been the Republicans' failure, and Roosevelt's success in overcoming it. "I dislike everything about the Republican party," a southern Californian told a pollster. "I was growing up at the time of the Hoover Administration. What a time I had, too. There was barely enough to eat. I don't think the Republicans wanted that, but they did nothing to stop it. Not until Roosevelt came along, and made things start to happen. . . ." American participation in world wars under Wilson, Roosevelt, and Truman also has left its stamp on voting behavior; the Democrats are often seen as the "war party."

The catalyzing event is especially notable for its lasting effect on the voting pattern. Things are never quite the same afterwards. The event smashes through the curtain of apathy around the voter, demolishes the old structure of attitudes, and pushes the voter out into the open, where he must shape anew his ideas and voting habits. And the catalyzing event leaves its mark for generations. Today millions of workers who never experienced the depression are still reacting to it, just as millions of Southerners are still casting their ballots in response to the trauma of Civil War and Reconstruction.

The regulars, then, are no less rational in their voting than the independents. The regulars, moreover, serve another function that should not be slighted. They supply the political cadres to operate the electoral machinery. These cadres man the party committees, choose party officers and convention delegates, help register voters, check lists at the polls, run party headquarters, put up placards, retail party propaganda on the sidewalk and the back stoop, and clean up the headquarters the day after election. Only a minority of the partisans, to be sure, do these jobs, and they often do not do them very well. But the burden of running the sprawling party apparatus would be impossible without the party activists, who serve as professional Democrats and Republicans just as other people serve as professional Elks or Sons of Saint Patrick or trade unionists or Legionnaires.

What about the nonpartisans, the irregulars, the independents? They are outnumbered by the regulars, but not overwhelmingly so, and they often hold the balance of power when the major parties are fairly evenly divided. Just as people have tended to underrate the partisans, they have glorified the independent. He is extolled as Rational Man, free of partisan bias, eager to consider candidates and platforms on their merits after careful and objective consideration. Election surveys have demolished this myth. "Far from being more attentive, interested, and informed," one study has concluded, "independents tend as a group to be somewhat less involved in politics. They have somewhat poorer knowledge of the issues, their image of the candidates is fainter, their interest in the campaign is less, their concern over the outcome is relatively slight. . . ."

Most independents, it seems, know as much about the candidates and issues as most adults know about teen-agers' television stars and the songs they sing. In both cases there are few known landmarks to be guided by. The typical independent drifts from election to election without a stable political mooring; he may shift his position casually during the campaign; he is affected by a television program he happens to see, an argument he overhears, a stray piece of gossip, the candidate's face, his wife's hat, or the ride to the polls that some party worker offers him. The picture should not be overdrawn. Many such independents cancel each other out; presumably those in 1960 who were mainly influenced by Mrs. Nixon's indefatigable charm were more or less offset by those who voted on the basis of Mrs. Kennedy's good looks. And most independents are not unaffected by the major historical and socio-economic forces that influence the partisans.

We must note, moreover, one type of independent who is quite the opposite of the rather vagrant type just described. This is the person, unaffiliated but highly motivated, who does take an interest, who does study the candidates and their position, who does vote in primaries as well as general elections. He switches parties between elections, or splits his ticket at the same election, not because of vagaries or inconstancy or ignorance, but because he imposes heavy demands on the parties and their candidates.

This man is the mugwump—a peculiarly American term for an especially American phenomenon. Originally an independent who turned against the Republican Stalwarts in the 1880's and backed Cleveland, the mugwump has existed all through our history and exists today. Statistically and sociologically he is hard to isolate. He is found in all classes, sections, and occupations. He may be either a liberal or a conservative in domestic politics. He may vote a fairly straight party ticket despite all his talk about voting for the man. But more often than not he is in the upper middle-class, he is a businessman or professional man or married to the same, and he splits his ticket. And he is almost always outspoken on some cause he believes in, especially lost causes, to the dismay of the party stalwart who wants immediate results.

The mugwump is not always a wholly attractive figure. His indignation is often righteous, his suspicions endemic, his criticism negative, his voice loud, and his manner peevish. It is always easy to poke fun at his solemn seriousness. He often tends toward Afghanistanism—concern over a problem in direct proportion to its distance away from him—and he often neglects immediate economic issues and denigrates the practical efforts that politicians, union leaders, and businessmen may be making. But he should not be underestimated. For decades he has been seizing on the great moral issues in America—free education, slavery, the secret ballot, clean politics, trusts, bossism, liquor, child labor, women's rights, civil liberties, prison reform, civic betterment, racial equality, international conciliation, "direct democracy"—and projecting them into politics. He charges these issues so full of moral content that anyone seeking out a neutral corner is automatically relegated to the side of the devils.

Mugwumps make up for their lack of numbers by the force of their moral positions and by the key places they hold in the political community. They are clergymen, teachers, lawyers, writers, intellectuals, newspapermen. They overrun PTA's, good government clubs, womens' groups, reform associations, forums, neighborhood leagues. They put issues and policies far above parties and candidates. Working through different organizations they can speak with a dozen voices. They worry and harass party leaders and candidates who would like to stick to the old, dependable, bread-and-butter issues. They are usually at odds with party organizations, although they often infiltrate and even organize, party clubs. If the party regulars supply ballast for American politics, the irregulars supply much of the motion and the zest.

We have been observing great aggregations of voters, Democrats, Republicans, and independents, who crowd the American political scene. But the picture is still flat and rather static. Leadership supplies the key dimension.

The Web of Leadership

Generations of Americans have been delighted by George Washington Plunkitt's analysis of how to become a statesman. "What I did was to get some marketable goods before goin' to the leaders," the Tammany leader said. "I had a cousin. . . . I went to him and said: 'Tommy, I'm goin' to be a politician, and I want to get a followin; can I count on you?' He said: 'Sure, George.' That's how I started in business. I got a marketable commodity—one vote. . . . I soon branched out. Two young men in the flat next to mine were school friends. I went to them, just as I went to Tommy, and they agreed to stand by me. Then I had a followin' of three voters and I began to get a bit chesty. Whenever I dropped into district headquarters, everybody shook hands with me, and the leader one day honored me by lightin' a match for my cigar. And so it went on like a snowball rollin' down a hill. I worked the flathouse that I lived in from the basement to the top floor, and I got about a dozen young men to follow me. Then I tackled the next house and so on down the block and around the corner. Before long I had sixty men back of me, and formed the George Washington Plunkitt Association. . . ."

What has been less noticed, perhaps, is that Plunkitt was describing a fundamental process that occurs at every level of political activity. Tocqueville described this process over a century and a quarter ago. ". . . A political aspirant in the United States," he said, "begins by discovering his own interest, and discovering those other interests which may be collected around and amalgamated with it. He then continues to find out some doctrine or principle which may suit the purposes of this new association, and which he adopts in order to bring forward his party and secure its popularity. . . ." Today social and political life has become more intensively organized than in Tocqueville's or Plunkitt's time, but within the institutional framework the basic process of leadership goes on. We hear so much about the top leaders *of* such groups as the Republican national committee or a Democratic city organization that we may overlook the network of leadership *in* such groups.

For the web of leadership stretches all through society. The husband who influences his wife, the parents who mold their children, the man next door who seems to know the score, the "opinion leader" constantly translating and purveying ideas to the man he drives to work or sits with at lunch—all these are leaders. They are all the more effective, perhaps without knowing it, because they talk to their followers face to face, have nothing ostensible to "sell," and may be trusted. The leader-follower network is elaborate and subtle. Observing a dozen youths lounging outside a drug store, we might dismiss them on first look as an idle gathering without meaning. Some years back a sociologist took a second look at such a group, studied it for three and a half years, and found a structure of leadership and followership, a pattern of internal relationships, and a significant role in the community (about all of which he wrote a notable study).

We talk about leaders and followers as though there were a sharp distinction between the two. There is a distinction, but it is not sharp. Not only do we have the chicken-and-egg problem of which comes first, leader or follower, we have the fact that most leaders are also followers, and that men are leaders in some matters and followers in others, and that the roles of leaders and followers shift over time. In this street corner group most of the youths held a specific and fairly stable place in a loose hierarchy, and most of them were both followers and leaders. The head of the gang, Doc, was a follower of other group leaders, including politicians. Moreover, even in the leader-follower relationship, the leaders must "clear" with the followers, must adapt their own attitudes or at least their arguments to the opinions of the followers, must adjust to followers' needs as the price of retaining leadership. The leader-follower relation, at least in our type of society, is mutually interdependent and hence is plastic.

The politician, building up his following, must deal with this web of leadership. He must draw support from people who are locked into countless semi-autonomous leader-follower relations of their own. He must find keys to these patterns of influence—to the grandfather who influences a whole clan, or the corner grocer who subtly affects a neighborhood. He must make their constituencies his own. But he discovers soon that their constituencies, too, are fluctuating and uncertain ones. Despite all the talk that Bill Smith can deliver his whole clan or a ward leader his whole block or a labor boss his whole union, leaders usually cannot deliver their constituencies. The politician only wishes they could. But he finds that too many other influences come into play, that there are too many sub-leaders and sub-groups and hostile and inactive followers. So he must work all up and down the line.

The rising politician, like Plunkitt, becomes the center of his own network of influence. He has marketable commodities—votes for himself and for his political allies. He is, indeed, a political entrepreneur, dealing in favors, smiles, handshakes, recognition, access, contracts, promises, appointments, legislation, out of which he hopes ultimately to gain a net profit at the polls. He pays out of his working capital at election time, and builds it up during campaigns. "I do a lot of things for people," says a New Haven party leader. "I keep working at it. . . . People come to see me, call me at my home at night. . . ." He described his clients—the woman whose husband was in jail for drunken driving, the fellow in trouble because he used some of his employer's money—much as Plunkitt described his clients 75 years before. "I just keep piling up good will," the New Haven man went on. "I'm always building up loyalty. People never forget. Anyone can do these things, but most won't do it. . . ."

As the politician expands beyond his precinct or ward, his following grows, becomes more elaborate and diversified. He can no longer hold his voters' loyalties through face-to-face contacts alone. He deals more now with party and group leaders. His aides work with leaders or sub-leaders in local clubs and associations. Since these groups are ostensibly nonpartisan (except when they have been taken over by the politician's organization), the lieutenants must win over sections of the group and capture the symbolic value of the group's name— hence such front groups as "Legionnaires for Jones" or the Republican Businessmen's League. But most associations have a semi-autonomous life of their own, which they do not wish to surrender to a politician or a party, for associations' memberships cut across party followings and candidates' constituencies. Hence a group's united support can rarely be "delivered on the barrelhead" despite all the promises a candidate gets. And as the leader broadens his constituency even further, his sub-leaders expand their own followings and hence gain a certain bargaining power with the top man if they wish to use it.

It is, indeed, mainly in the relationship between leader and his immediate sub-leaders that the dynamic quality of politics is found. The sub-leaders' bargaining power with the leader, and with the leader's rivals, depends on the leader's exclusive influence over his followers. But such exclusive influence is uncommon in American politics because followers are subject to the crisscross of many influences. And the top leader may have direct influence with the sub-leaders' followings; for example, in Franklin Roosevelt's fight with John L. Lewis for the voting allegiance of the miners the President could appeal directly to the miners through a separate political channel, the presidential election. The situation varies widely, of course. The old-time boss had his hands on so many levers of power and channels of influence that he could usually hold his lieutenants in line. Astute leaders like Roosevelt, by instinct or by design, took care to keep their lieutenants from building unduly autonomous followings. But even in the cases of strong Presidents and real bosses one finds that they still must play their broker role, yielding here and there, playing some sub-leaders off

against others, strengthening their own direct links with their constituencies, trying to detach sub-leaders and followings from rival
leaders, in the endless competitive jostle of American politics.

So we see the leader in the center of a giant network, somewhat
captive to his sub-leaders and his followings as well as commanding
them. The key link in this network is not the boss but the bargainer.
He trades both in the relatively hard currency of specific favors,
deals, and votes, and in the softer currency of unwritten expectations
and mutual obligations. This soft currency often provokes the press
and public into the suspicion that specific deals have been made
and contracts signed. But the political entrepreneur traffics much
more in long-term understandings which he must eventually honor
or lose his trading power. He prefers to do favors that build up a
balance of obligation, to be redeemed in whatever currency may be
useful at some future time.

Despite the genial atmosphere in which most political relationships
are enveloped, the brokerage operation is at heart rather imper-
sonal. Politicians, President Kennedy has said, do not have friends—
they have allies. It was his grandfather, "Honey" Fitzgerald, who
was reported to have perfected the "Irish Switch"—the art of pumping
one voter's hand while still talking to another, all the while beaming
at a third. As the politician operates in ever wider markets, his personal relationships become more fleeting and superficial, his friend-
ships more expendable. Despite the old theory that the politician's
chief motivation is to be deeply admired and loved, one student has
concluded that the distinguishing quality of the professional politician is "an inordinate capacity for multiplying human relationships without ever becoming deeply involved emotionally." Endur-
ing friendship is difficult, one candidate concluded, because "in the
frequent jumble of political atoms, the hostile and the amicable ones
often change places." There is much more fellowship than friendship. All this has its drawbacks for the politician as a human being,
but it greatly simplifies his task of ever broadening his constituency.

What type of men lead? Every type, because leadership cannot
be separated from followership, or taken out of the matrix within
which it operates. Hence leaders are as diverse as the ethnic, oc-
cupational, geographical, neighborhood, ideological, street-corner,
reformist, criminal, religious, family, military, or political groups they

lead. They are tall and short, handsome and plain, articulate and stumbling, intelligent and stupid, friendly and austere. Yet leaders share one characteristic that helps make them what they are. They take the initiative, go to their constituencies, keep things moving. The fact that their cues, in their cue-and-response relation with followers, are shaped at the start by what they think their followers will accept or reject, should not obscure the fact that the leader usually does move first and his constituency usually gives him a good deal of leeway. "I seen my opportunity and I took it," Plunkitt used to say, and Herndon once described Lincoln's ambition as a little engine that knew no rest.

Too, the ideological grasp and technical skill of the leader tends to be far greater in the higher than in the lower echelons of leadership. The city or county party leader, for example, is better informed about the issues, holds a firmer position on party policy, has more party spirit, than the rank-and-file leader or follower. He is less subject to social and ideological cross-pressures. Democratic and Republican leaders usually differ from each other on issues more sharply than the rank-and-file members of the two parties differ from one another. While the process is always circular, leaders keep the rank and file salient to and divided over issues much more than the reverse. This is an important fact, for it suggests the crucial role of leadership in provoking and sustaining competition and division in an electoral body that otherwise might grow inert with consensus. As Schumpeter put it some time ago, "the democratic method is that institutional arrangement for arriving at political decisions in which individuals acquire the power to decide by means of a competitive struggle for the people's vote."

The competitive, brokerage role of leadership is almost universal, though the exact mix of the competition varies with the situation. Sometimes the context is more stable and structured and brokerage is as patterned as the operations of a stock exchange. Sometimes the competition is so atomistic as to approach anarchy. In American politics an office seeker gathering sub-leaders and activists around him in a sortie for position may have a somewhat more unstable constituency than the head of a Masonic Lodge or of some other long established association. But the group leader, too, faces problems of competition, bargaining, and brokerage, as he seeks to maintain activity and unity in his order, deals with leaders of other groups, and tries to broaden his constituency. Both formal and informal leaders, both elected or appointed officials and self-chosen candidates for office, are part of the seamless web of leadership and followership.

The Anatomy of Balance

I have dwelt on the network of leadership because the existence of rich and abundant grass-roots leadership sustains a central thesis of this book and contradicts two competing theories. One of the latter might be called the plate-of-marbles theory. This is the idea that the American public is a great aggregation of atomistic individuals lacking ties with their fellow men, rolling hither and thither, colliding aimlessly. The other (and related) theory is the mass-mind concept that the great number of people are a kind of liquid agglomeration to be poured from receptacle to receptacle, homogeneous and indeed homogenized, easily exploited by factional leaders or charismatic rulers who cut through the frail web of formal group relationships and manipulate people almost at will.

It was some combination of these two related notions that lay behind Madison's fear of the "instability, injustice, and confusion" that, he said in the tenth Federalist, had been the mortal disease under which popular government had everywhere perished. Frightened by a mob that got out of hand, Madison underestimated the overlapping group memberships and the diffusion of group leadership that made his own society so stable; certainly he could not visualize a modern, industrialized, concentrated society as heavily latticed with overlapping, jostling, crisscrossing, mutually interdependent networks of leaders and followers as ours has become. He could not imagine a society such as ours today, with a swollen middle-class which not only acts as buffer and stabilizer between the very rich and the very poor but largely mans and runs the groups—church associations, sports, clubs, veterans' organizations, fraternal lodges—that cut across America's complex class system and provide ladders for men to climb up through that system.

This cellular structure is the basic source of stability in the American political system. "Each little society," Frank Tannenbaum has said, "such as a township, a parish, a rod and gun club, a musical society, or a chamber of commerce, is a code-forming and tradition-generating body. Each of these multiplies the ways of men with each other, and sets limits upon arbitrary power; for each in its own realm has authority and commands the support of its adherents. . . . The community is a compound of overlapping and contradictory policy-making bodies, each with its own variant of good and right." And the sub-leaders and sub-groups within these bodies help keep them in a balance that rivals the solar system's in complexity if not in regularity.

Not only are men's every day social relationships shaped in this cellular structure, but also their political attitudes and behavior. In some societies public opinion may fluctuate wildly in the face of events: rumors spread swiftly; people pour out of houses; mobs start toward the seat of government or the American embassy. But opinion in other countries is much more plastic or glutinous, like honey in a comb. "On the American scene mass opinion about most matters of political importance," Key finds, "possesses a high viscosity." Anchored by their crisscrossing group affiliations, people are generally sluggish in reacting to change. They receive different cues from different leaders and hence may be immobilized. Their party feelings insulate them against mercurial shifts. Political events, candidates, issues are viewed through partisan eyes and re-structured and stabilized and tamed in the process.

In the complex American society, of course, stability varies with the actual extent of overlapping group membership and other factors. Gabriel Almond found great mood instability in attitudes on foreign policy during the 1930's and 1940's. Americans shifted between moods of intervention and withdrawal, pessimism and optimism, tolerance and intolerance, idealism and cynicism. These shifting moods brought rapid changes in attitudes toward specific policies, such as dealing with the Russians. One reason for this instability, as Almond said, was that foreign policy attitudes among most Americans lacked intellectual structure and factual content. This lack in turn was due to lower participation in groups and parties that were relevant to foreign policy. Or consider the famous episode of Orson Welles' radio drama, *The Invasion from Mars*. People rushed into the streets; drove their families off to the hills; milled around wildly;

knelt down and prayed. They lacked the ordinary guidelines of information, experience, judgment, seasoned with native skepticism; the dramatic radio program had penetrated through the ordinary network of habit and restraint. For the time was 1938.

But these are exceptional situations. In domestic affairs, especially in the bread-and-butter matters that strike close to home, people easily fit most issues and events into their frames of reference. A political event or problem is harmonized with party feeling or political ideology. Asked in 1936 whether Roosevelt's actions might be leading toward dictatorship, respondents divided predictably: 91 per cent of the Democrats queried said no, 83 per cent of the Republicans said yes. Glittering personalities are subject to the same reevaluative process. Many (but by no means all) Democrats lost their enthusiasm for Eisenhower for President once he dropped his stance of nonpartisanship and gained the Republican nomination. The party balance works the other way too. Many Americans knew very little about Adlai Stevenson even in 1956; it was enough that he was the Democratic nominee. Said a Georgia poultryman: "He's a Democrat; that's all that's good about him."

If this kind of stability exists at any one time, there is also stability over time. Party feeling is highly persistent; the Michigan surveys among others proved that only events of tremendous intensity could shake most voters out of their traditional party moorings. But this does not have to be a static process. People stay with their parties because their parties stay with them, dealing with new problems in terms of old attitudes and symbols. Issues, too, have a kind of stability even though in motion. "Issues are typically introduced by a small vanguard normally toward the left, or experimental, end of the political spectrum, who are often aided by the circumstantial event," according to Berelson and his colleagues. "If successful, the issue wins its way slowly across the political field. At each point rejection turns to resistance, then to acquiescence, and finally to approval. After the initially 'radical' proposal becomes a *fait accompli* through acceptance in practice, it takes its place as a 'natural' characteristic of political life, and attention in the political arena turns to new matters. For example, social security had gone through all these phases within the lifetime of 1948 voters." This is the typical stability of issues and their "careers" in a balanced system such as the American; Russia or a Latin American republic might show a very different pattern.

On the face of it, the most stabilizing of all political forces over time should be the symbols and institutions and ideas that have support of a wide consensus: the Flag, Americanism, the Constitution, fair play, George Washington and Abraham Lincoln, and so on. The unifying function of these symbols should not be underestimated. But they lose their function unless they permit a changing set of subordinate symbols to invest them with meaning appropriate for new times and new problems. Americanism is not the same for 1965 as for 1900. The Constitution as symbol as well as instrument changes with the decades; at one time it was the symbol for protecting private property and states' rights; it may be in the process of becoming the symbol of civil rights and equal opportunity.

This shifting consensus is crucial, for neither change nor consensus by itself is necessarily a stabilizing force; stability rises from change-in-consensus. If Americans can draw together behind certain unifying symbols, can they also divide in such a way that long-run consensus is maintained? The evidence, not only from history (except for the Civil War) but from current analysis, seems to be that they can. For division is not a helter-skelter splintering of the population; division itself follows a pattern. On some issues, as Key says, a pattern of order in cleavage prevails.

These qualities of change-in-consensus and order-in-cleavage are especially notable on issues of domestic liberalism-conservatism, for these are the issues that voters can feel and see and touch. On well known issues such as fair treatment for Negroes, federal aid to education, federal guarantees of job opportunity, government subsidy of medical care, and government control of electric power, opinions tend to spread along a continuum. Some people want all these; some want none; many want some but not others. If some people wanted none and the rest wanted all, the dichotomy would imply an either-or confrontation between hard-core liberals and militant conservatives. But between the two are clusters of "soft" liberals and conservatives who act as both connecting rods and steadiers between the extremes. This is one more of the many sources of stability in a society that breeds countless tiny divisions rather than a few deep ones.

A final source of stability is competition among leaders. Without leadership at every level and in every cell, American society might be the pile of marbles or the fluid mass that some think it to be. Without vigorous competition leadership could degenerate into idle officeholding and spoils collecting. By constitution and custom we have established a multiplicity of elective offices which serve as the focus of competition. The party primary, the long ballot, and other developments have brought about a splintering of leadership within as well as between the major parties. Instead of becoming polarized in a contest for one or two crucial offices, the political struggle fragmentizes into countless skirmishes. This is one more source of balance and equipoise in the system—and one that has been carried to a dangerous degree.

When we view all the balancing and moderating forces pulsating through the web of leadership we get some notion of the profound and pervasive political stability of American society. We simply do not have the problem that so much troubled Madison. Occasionally mobs get out of hand; sometimes public opinion becomes so fitful that effective government and orderly change are impossible; occasionally extremist majorities take control of a community; and once or twice whole states have been captured by a semi-dictator playing on the fears and frustrations of the people, as in Louisiana in the early 1930's. But these are exceptions to the slow, orderly, and often sluggish movement of public opinion; and certainly the nation as a whole has not, at least for a century, been imperiled by dictators or civil wars or majority tyranny or the other disasters that Madison feared. The richness and diversity of our group life, the cross-cutting bonds that tie together members of diverse associations and classes, the vitality and competitiveness of leadership at all levels—these are all the true balance wheels in our society. The guardianship of our diversity, as David Truman has said, will emerge out of the affiliations of our guardians. The anatomy of the American body politic is the anatomy of balance.

The Outsiders

If there is a note of undue satisfaction in the foregoing appraisal of the balances in American politics, a change of mood is imminent.

Not only do these vast stabilizing forces raise again the question that Jeffersonians ask of Madisonians—why do we need extra balancing forces in the governmental system if we have so many in the social and political system?—but for a huge number of Americans the foregoing analysis is essentially irrelevant. These are the outsiders—the voteless, the nonvoting, the inert, the politically alienated, the uninformed, the "hard core of chronic know-nothings."

The extent of non-voting in the United States has been well publicized by moralists who like to charge people with dereliction of civic duty. The situation is easy to moralize about. The proportion of those eligible to vote who have cast ballots in presidential elections has shown a long-run decline since the 1870's and 1880's, though it has risen appreciably since a low point in 1948. A bit over 64 per cent of adults (over 21 years old) voted for President in 1960, a highwater mark since 1908. But this was still substantially lower than the percentage of eligibles who regularly vote in Britain and other Western democracies (apart from the massive "Ja" voting once required in Nazi Germany and the "Da" voting required today in Russia). Presidential voting, moreover, is only one test; participation falls off drastically in other types of contests. Fewer persons vote for congressional candidates than for presidential even on the same ballot. Many fewer vote for congressional candidates in non-presidential years than for presidential and congressional aspirants in presidential years. Gubernatorial contests during "off" (non-presidential) years also draw a lighter vote than during presidential; the total vote in the race for Governor of New York in 1954, for example, fell by around two million from the 1952 presidential participation. This drop in off-year voting has been one of the most persistent tendencies in American politics.

One might expect that voting would increase in local elections for city, town, and county officials, where the voters might know the candidates and the issues better. But no; while there are great variations, voting at such levels is substantially lower than for the seemingly remote presidential candidate. Voting is relatively low, on the average, in primary elections, in special elections, and on issues appearing on the ballot, such as constitutional amendments and state referendum proposals. If one were able to go through the enormous job of collecting and averaging the participation in all the elections for all public officials in the United States (even excluding elections of party officials and convention delegates) he would probably come out with a figure well under 50 per cent. In this gross sense, the United States is characterized more by non-voting than by voting.

Who votes—and who does not? Scholars have devoted much attention to this question, and happily their findings broadly agree. People between their mid-thirties and mid-fifties vote more than the younger or older. The turnout of men is roughly ten per cent greater than that of women. About twice the proportion of whites vote as of Negroes. White collar, professional, and business people vote to a much greater extent than semi-skilled and unskilled workers. The higher their education, or the higher their income, or the more urban their area of residence, the more people, proportionately, show up at the polls. People in the Far West have the best voting record; people in the South the worst. More Protestants vote than Catholics, proportionately, though religion itself is probably less a cause than social and economic factors. But all these are gross averages—it is also significant that millions of wives of young, rural, unskilled workers with grammar-school educations and low incomes *do* bother to show up at the polls.

Still, millions do not bother, or could not vote if they wished to. Some are the isolates—the bedridden, the non-English-speaking, the mentally incompetent, people in jail. Others are floaters—migratory farm workers, traveling salesmen, people moving to new addresses or newly arrived, hoboes. Others are not so much outwardly as internally isolated; they deprive themselves of the vote, though often as a result of forces beyond their control. They lack interest in politics; they see no relation between a political campaign and their lives; politics seems remote, complex, the business of other people; they see no duty to vote. Politics for such people is virtually meaningless. The Michigan study turned up a fair sample of such non-voters. "I'm not interested in stuff like that," they would say. Or ". . . don't believe in politics." Or "I don't care, I don't guess." Or ". . . they're all gentlemen when they go in as President but rascals when they come out. . . . I don't vote myself. I leave that for men folks." Or "I've never paid any attention to parties and have no interest in politics." Or ". . . prayers will do more than votes in keeping this country on the right path."

Then there are those who are legally barred from the polls: those who do not satisfy residence requirements, or were not able to register to vote, or who are aliens (years ago aliens were often allowed to vote). The largest numbers of these are, of course, Southern Negroes, barred from the polls by the poll tax, reading and understanding tests, and a host of other legislative and administrative devices. In certain counties of the South not a single Negro votes, or is registered to vote. Like whites, Negroes also do not vote because of lack of interest or of sense of involvement; Negroes, especially in rural areas, share these qualities to a marked degree, and the internal and external barriers to voting are mutually reinforcing. But even the Negro who breaks out of his milieu and wants to vote cannot do so in the rural South. He is the most outside of the outsiders.

Another and even more ominous type of nonparticipation is the result of voter alienation, a recent study has shown. That the locale for this study was Boston has the salutary effect of reminding us that the South is not the only place where the political pulse of the mass of people beats slowly. Boston in 1959 witnessed a particularly ugly and acrimonious contest for mayor between the incumbent and the president of the State Senate. So much money was spent, so many political bigwigs—including Senator John F. Kennedy—lent their names, so hard fought was the contest that a big turnout was expected. Actually the total vote fell off from the previous, milder contest; and interviews of Bostonians during and after the campaign revealed widespread feelings of political frustration, powerlessness, and cynicism, the product of years of experience with the corruption and irresponsibility of Boston politics. Again and again Bostonians told interviewers that both candidates were no good: "Neither candidate appealed to me. . . ." "Voting wouldn't do any good. . . ." "Felt they were all no good. . . ." "They tie up with racketeers—all of them do it. . . ." Some voters feel this way about candidates in all elections, but the startling finding in Boston was the sheer extent of the alienation; more than half of those who voted for one man felt that he would be no better in office than the other, and almost half of those who voted for the other man felt that *he* would be no better than the other. Comparable conditions, a later study showed, exist in the state as a whole.

So much for the passive end of the political spectrum. At the other end are the activists, the influentials, the "politicists." They talk politics, drive people to the polls, attend rallies, contribute money, put up posters, write letters to the editor, run for office. Politics is part of their life; they would no more fail to vote than fail to attend their son's high school graduation. Some are in politics as a business; a truck driver, hardly able to read or write, told an interviewer that he was not interested in the 1956 election. "I don't know nothing about that. I just vote the way the guy at the corner tells me. (Why?) Because he does me favor I just vote the way he says." And so he did. Clearly the guy at the corner had at least two votes, and the truck driver had none. The activists, however, are a small fraction of the population. The Michigan survey found that in 1956, a feverishly political year, only three per cent of the respondents belonged to a political club or organization. Ten per cent gave money or bought tickets or otherwise took part in a campaign, and seven per cent went to political meetings or dinners.

In between these extremes are the great number of Americans, voting in the exciting presidential elections and not bothering with many of the others, drawn sporadically into political activity but usually passive. For them politics is essentially a spectator sport. They are willing to watch the political arena, but their applause and participation depend on the nature of the campaign: whether the candidates run hard, whether they offer contrasting personalities or platforms, whether the outcome looks close. Abstract considerations like civic duty are not enough to propel them to the voting booths; they would no more take part in a dull election than attend a dull lecture. These on-and-off voters are found heavily among independents; the more intense the party preference, the more people vote.

How serious a problem is non-voting? Not serious at all, some students of politics believe, because the system is automatically self-correcting. The non-voters tend to be the less informed, less educated, less interested—the very people who deserve to have less political influence. Other observers go further. Studies have suggested, they point out, that non-voters generally tend to be less tolerant, less concerned about civil liberties, more nationalistic and even xenophobic, more authoritarian, and psychologically more inadequate and insecure. The people most inappropriate for the democratic process tend to keep out of it. Finally, some warn against a polity teeming with activists. Intensive political activity preceded the breakdown of political democracy in Germany, they point out. A democratic system needs political slack or looseness at the joints so that rising tensions will not immobilize and even destroy it.

One trouble with the theory of the self-corrective value of non-voting is that apathy is not neutral—it affects different groups differently. Those who vote least—the uneducated, the low income, the low-skilled—are often those who most need help from government and hence need most to influence it with their votes. Another trouble is that our system today is a long way from being taut with political zeal and tension. A lot more people could vote, a great many more could run coffee hours and check off voters at the polls, without taking up all the slack in the system.

To focus on the failings of the non-voters, moreover, is to miss the main problem. That problem lies in the political system itself. To a large extent we make non-voters. We make them through indefensible barriers set up by state legislatures and election officers. We make them through antiquated voting rules and procedures, such as residence requirements, which discourage participation more than they safeguard orderly elections. We make non-voters through our complex and confused electoral system which presents people with a bewildering array of electoral choices for offices that should be appointive. We make them through a registration system that, in contrast to the simpler methods in other Western democracies, forces a voter to go through an elaborate process of registering to vote wholly separate from the act of voting itself. We make non-voters by superimposing a whole extra set of obscure primary elections, usually devoid of meaningful issues, on top of the general election system, and adding elections at several local levels—town, city, county, etc.—to the state and national ones. We make them through state and local politics that mean nothing except the re-distribution of pork and favors among a few insiders. Above all, we make them by creating safe districts with the election outcome so certain that the excitement and vote-pulling power of real competition is lost.

Granted that some present non-voters would stay home no matter how much the political system was changed, we must still grasp the extent to which our polity breeds apathy and alienation. Low education and motivation, lack of information, privatization, poverty, passivity are not inevitable concomitants of a modern, affluent, urban society, at least to the extent that they exist in the United States. Society relentlessly writes political apathy into the lives of the poor, just as it writes social inequality and lack of opportunity. People are no more born politically apathetic than they are born bigots or chauvinists.

Nor need we be unduly deterred by fears of a flood of ignorance and knownothingism if the outsiders should enter the game of politics. Even drastic legal change, such as the 19th amendment allowing women to vote, produces slow alteration of voting habits. Abolish every barrier to voting and millions of Americans would still not vote. But other millions would, and more and more as they developed new motivation. Nor would their participation necessarily weight the political scales toward intolerance. The process of becoming voters would be part of a process of becoming more motivated to vote, and more committed to the rules of the democratic struggle, and hence of slowly breaking out of the mold of ignorance, apathy, and impotence that mutually reinforce one another and that are the real roots of intolerance. In short, the most effective techniques of enfranchising Americans—opening up and clarifying and vitalizing the political system—are the same ones that would make the new voter's participation more responsible. The elements of a democratic polity can be mutually reinforcing too.

Tocqueville was right: "I maintain that the most powerful and perhaps the only means that we still possess of interesting men in the welfare of their country is to make them partake in the Government. At the present time civic zeal seems to me to be inseparable from the exercise of political rights. . . ." And so today is Erik H. Erikson: "For the sake of its emotional health a democracy cannot afford to let matters develop to a point where intelligent youth, proud in its independence and burning with initiative, must leave matters of legislation, law and general policy to 'insiders' and 'bosses'."

All this raises the question of balance in the system. The real threat to a nation's political stability and gradual change is not a host of voters slowly but steadily being absorbed into the electoral process. It is a host of voters outside the system looking in, prey to a leader who might sweep them into politics along non-democratic channels. During Huey Long's rise in Louisiana political participation rose by about one half; it is doubtful that many of those new voters resisted his dictatorship. It was the radicalization of people who had not taken part actively in politics and who had been too young to vote that spurred the rise of German Naziism. No society can hold indefinitely a posture of stable equilibrium when it is weighted down by mass passivity, as Myrdal called it, surrounding a great lump of non-participants.

The Outsider Inside

Since this chapter and the next may reflect a churlish but loving attitude toward American politics and politicians, I must here declare an interest: I am a politician too. I am one of the ten thousand or so part-time politicians in both parties who attend committee meetings, junket to national and state conventions as delegates, organize rallies, telephone voters, and attend endless coffee hours. And once, for almost a year, I was a full-time politician, when I ran for Congress as the Democratic nominee in the 1st Congressional District of Massachusetts—the same rural and small-city district that Allen Treadway represented for 32 years. Since no Democrat had carried this district for 60 years, and only one since the Civil War, hoping to be a Congressman was not my only reason for running. I wanted the sheer experience, and I wanted to advance my education.

I was especially curious about three things. How much help would I get from the party in which I had been active so long? To what extent would the various candidates campaign together or separately? Above all, was it possible for a congressional candidate to run on national issues?

The answer to the first question began to come very quickly. Although I had been chairman of my local Democratic committee, the Democratic party made no special effort to recruit or draft me—I recruited myself. If I had waited for the joyful sight of a party deputation urging me to make my contribution to statesmanship, I would still be waiting today. I could have arranged a fake draft, of course, but no one would have been fooled. This confirmed an old rule in politics; drafts do not just happen.

After I decided to run in the primary I soon found that I was very much on my own. Many of my Democratic party friends gave me a great deal of aid, but the party committees officially were neutral between me and my Democratic opponent. Lacking organized party help, I built in each city and town a personal organization of party committeemen, Young Democrats, independents, union leaders, civic group activists, and even a few Republicans. Meantime my Democratic opponent, and the scores of Democrats running for a dozen other nominations, busily constructed their own campaign organizations, all of which overlapped one another in a baffling mosaic of concentric and cross-cutting circles. A small army of Republicans was busily campaigning for their party's nominations too; at every clambake, steakbake, and cornbake, I and the rest of this host of rapacious vote seekers descended on the bewildered picnickers like locusts; sometimes we outnumbered them.

The nomination won, I plunged into the general election contest against the Republican nominee. The Democratic party committees now endorsed me, of course, but it was soon apparent that these committees as such could give me limited help. In the small Republican towns, where I most needed aid and sustenance, Democratic committees hardly existed. Where they did exist, they had small memberships, practically no funds, few workers outside their own committees, and a narrow range of action. And they had the impossible burden of trying to elect Democrats to more than a dozen posts, from Governor to probate judge and register of deeds. They lacked even enough money to put out adequate advertising for the party ticket as a whole. When I approached the party chairmen for funds, occasionally they asked me to contribute to them, or at least to buy tickets to a dinner they were putting on; evidently the candidates were supposed to support the party rather than vice versa. As a result of all this I continued to lean heavily on my own organization, now bolstered by more party regulars and also independents. It was not the party organization but my personal following that distributed 30 or 40 thousand leaflets, mailed thousands of letters, rang countless doorbells, arranged coffee hours, put up posters, organized the climactic rallies, handed out cards at the polls.

There was an interesting mix of cooperation and conflict among the Democratic candidates for different offices. Each had his own organization, which he hesitated to share; each wanted help from the other; each had his exclusive sources of support that he could not or would not share. But there was a good deal of concerted activity too, especially between Democrats running in somewhat the same constituencies or holding a similar point of view. In my case I worked especially with Democrats running for state legislative offices in each district, because of our mutual interest in legislation, and with the candidate for United States Senator, who happened to be John F. Kennedy. We indulged, in short, in a continuous game of coattail grabbing (especially Mr. Kennedy's), but also in coattail avoidance.

Senator Kennedy could hardly have been more generous in extending his coattails to me. We made a film together, which I was allowed to put on television as much as I wished (and could afford), and we appeared together at party rallies and other ceremonials. Still, it was apparent that he was able to identify himself with issues in a way that I could not. It was not only that he was better known and had an ability to improvise in political situations—for example, taking the baton from a high school band leader and ending on the right beat. He had in eastern Massachusetts a big metropolitan area that gave him a solid and assured electoral foundation on which to base a politics of issues. And he could speak through a system of mass media that was organized on a statewide basis.

My situation was quite different. The 1st District is a giant inverted saucer, with isolated cities dotting the rim and the center composed of mountains, trees, small towns, and Republicans. The two television stations covering the district were both outside the district—one was across the state line in New York—so that whenever I used television I was guaranteed an audience of which at least 75 per cent could not vote for me. The chief morning newspaper was published outside the district. Most of the evening papers were Republican, and while all but one or two were fair in their coverage, they were not effective vehicles for publicizing a coherent set of policies. The district—and I think this is true of many others—

simply had no identity or coherence. Communicating with the voters was like trying to grab a handful of water. And my opponent would not debate with me.

I do not mean that we based all our efforts on an intellectual appeal. I preceded the main campaign with six months of door-to-door canvassing of carefully selected "local opinion leaders." We went in for the usual leaflets, matchbooks, bumper strips, blotters, sound trucks, and all the rest, and we even published our own newspaper in a city where the only newspaper, we felt, was not treating us fairly. But I hoped to supplement all this, and to give it some meaning, by relating campaign media to issues. Even our billboards urged that we "build jobs, schools, homes" rather than featuring just the name and picture.

My stand on issues did not interest the party regulars very much; it was enough for them that I was a Democrat. But I also needed strong independent support, and the independents or volunteers who became active in my campaign most decidedly were interested in issues. My talks to the regulars were reiterations of the party credo and were accepted as such. My talks to the mugwump type of independent provoked vigorous exchanges of ideas, and I was asked my opinions on unilateral disarmament, regulation of television, Israel-Arab relationships, population control, wire-tapping, and other subjects that might have seemed a bit esoteric to the regulars. The two groups never really met intellectually or physically. The mugwumps were wonderfully imaginative in thinking up publicity ideas and special campaign appeals and they arranged a magnificent climactic rally. But they did little of the pick-and-shovel work of the campaign, such as canvassing, registration work, driving voters to the polls, because they had never been geared into the operations of the local party organizations.

My chief memory of the campaign is a big room in some fraternal hall, with a bar in the rear—there always seemed to be a bar in the rear. After opening with the usual local references and pleasantries, I tried to deal emphatically with at least one national issue. I had to be emphatic to be heard over the buzz and laughter and tinkle of glasses at the bar. Although I was stressing bread-and-butter issues —this was a textile area caught in recession—I had to fight for my audience. And in the midst of my oratory someone was as likely as not to rise from a table in front of me, make his way noisily and un-steadily to the bar, and then, with all eyes following his uncertain progress, return triumphantly to his seat bearing four martinis.

This did not bother me. Who could doubt the relative importance of drink-in-hand compared to all the birds in the bush being dis-cussed by a speaker whose name you hadn't quite caught. But it symbolized the overpowering emphasis in the campaign on imme-diate and local specifics. There was simply no way—I believe that we tried every method except sky-writing—to lift the campaign out of the grip of local forces, geography (where the candidate came from), or ethnic, personality, and religious factors. My education was completed election night with defeat. I won 45 per cent of the vote; significantly, I did best in the areas where my opponent and I had both been unknown before the election, but I did worst in the textile cities that needed my brand of policies, or so I thought, but that remembered my opponent's faithful errand-running as a state senator. Despite the intensive stumping of both of us, almost half the eligibles failed to vote. In the elections since, the 1st District has been faithful to the memory of Allen Treadway. Today it is more incorrigibly one-party than ever.

10

THE STRUCTURE
of COALITION
POLITICS

"Ignorance is the first requisite of the historian, ignorance which simplifies and clarifies, which selects and omits," wrote Lytton Strachey in his preface to *Eminent Victorians*. However ironic Strachey meant this remark to be, it is a useful warning for anyone trying to find meaning in history. A long look at the growth of American politics shows a recurring pattern of four parties, especially in recent years. But this pattern may reflect the selecting and distorting process of the one who looks. A study of the raw materials of politics, as in the last chapter, shows some of the forces that might underlie a multiparty system, but Strachey's quip is as relevant to the political scientist looking for current patterns as to the historian looking for long continuing ones.

The crux of the matter is whether the phenomena make up a

234

superficial pattern or show structure and durability. We can ask with the sociologist, do the four parties make up a *system?* The word is used here in its technical sense—the system as a structure of inter-relations over time. The structure embraces a set of interdependent behaviors, roles, institutions and motivations; it has good internal communication and leadership; it is adjusted to basic political and social arrangements; it has existed for a long time and will continue indefinitely, barring fundamental alterations. To use a different formulation, institutions, ideas, interests, and individuals are in a condition of stable interaction and adjustment. The four parties are embedded in the political matrix; they are self-maintaining; their behavior and even their effectiveness, in policy terms, is broadly predictable.

To describe the four parties as a system is not to indulge in meaningless jargon. On the contrary, it is to pose the essence of the problem. If each of the four parties were simply a wing or a faction or a grouping in the two parties, each would possess qualities of impermanence, instability, fluidity, and fragility that would make them entirely different creatures from what they are. But as structures they must be viewed as stable, strong, and persistent. They will not collapse with the death of specific leaders, or a shift in party fortunes, or a tinkering with political machinery. This means, among other things, that the governing of the country is always in the hands of two or more parties, and hence we have coalition government, with the advantages and failings thereof.

This structure is not dead or static. We might picture it as a giant grid, with currents of political energy running back and forth from numberless centers to millions of sub-centers and back to the centers, and also running from sub-center to sub-center. Some areas throb with high tension; others receive no voltage at all and lie cold and dead; most throb feebly as they catch flickering bits of energy. Much of the grid remains stable; but in some places the linkages break off and form new connections, and sometimes a heavy jolt of energy leaves many connections broken and re-fused.

As we turn to the centers of national and state politics we see the high-voltage areas, where politics, as Mr. Dooley said, "ain't bean bag," but a "professional sport, like playin' baseball f'r a livin' or wheelin' a truck." Here the units glow with steady power, at times dully, at times striking off sparks. Here political activity is patterned and institutionalized in city halls and school boards, state capitols and executive mansions, White House and Capitol Hill.

Seeing this grid as a system not only enables us to see patterns and irregularities, and hence perhaps to predict political trends; it also saves us from oversimplification. The American political system today is under sharp scrutiny. The seniority system, the under-representation of urban voters dramatized by the Supreme Court decision in *Baker v. Carr,* the failure of Congress to enact the bulk of Kennedy's—or even Nixon's—program, has provoked calls for quick reform or simple surgery. But we must see these institutions as outgrowths of a system of power. They are rooted in sets of interrelationships that have great strength and durability. They cannot be cut off like a wart; they are built into the structure of American politics.

State Parties: The Shriveled Roots

The paramount fact about American political parties, is their organizational weakness at all levels, from local to national. It has taken Americans a long time to comprehend this fact. There is a conventional wisdom in politics as well as economics. Generations of Americans have been brought up on college textbooks that contrasted the weak national organization with the powerful party "machines" in the states and cities—even while these machines were disintegrating. Really strong party organizations run by party bosses (in contrast to the personal organizations of officeholders such as mayors or governors) hardly exist today. One of the few, the Democratic organization in Albany, New York, is so well preserved that it should be put into the Smithsonian before we forget what a political machine looks like.

At no level, except in a handful of industrial states, do state parties have the attributes of organization. They lack extensive dues-paying memberships; hence they number many captains and sergeants but few foot soldiers. They do a poor job of raising money for themselves as organizations, or even for their candidates. They lack strong and imaginative leadership of their own. They cannot control their most vital function—the nomination of their candidates. Except in a few states, such as Ohio, Connecticut, and Michigan, our parties are essentially collections of small cliques and they are often shunted aside by the politicians who understand political power. Most of the state parties are at best mere jousting grounds for embattled politicians; at worst they simply do not exist, as in the case of Republicans in the rural South or Democrats in the rural Midwest.

Is this too bleak a picture of party organization? If so it seems, we might try a few simple tests. How many of our neighbors are "card-carrying" Democrats or Republicans, paying regular dues to their party as they do to their church group or professional organization? How many of them take part in the affairs of their local parties, as they do in their lodge or union or the PTA? How many of them work for their party at election time, not merely for individual candidates?

This is not to say that party feeling or identification is unimportant; on the contrary, as the last chapter suggested, it is crucial. Our major parties do help keep alive great sets of fuzzy but powerful traditions, goals, and doctrines. Nor is this to assert that winning major party nomination is worthless; it is worth a great deal, but because of party sentiment, not party organization. It is to say that typically the American party is heavily faction-ridden, disorganized at the base, narrow in range of political action, limited in initiative and vision.

Why? Why is the American party, which was a prime agent in the broadening of American democracy, a rather decrepit institution in this Age of Organization? The answer lies in the enormous burden the party must bear and in some internal defects.

The enormous burden is, first of all, our system of federalism. State parties have a double role. They are independent and sovereign entities in their own right, charged with nominating and electing governors and other statewide officials. Each of them is also one of 50 foundations of the national party, charged with electing presidents and senators and congressional delegations. But this is not all. The state party is a holding company for a profusion of county, city, and town parties that must nominate and elect slates of candidates in those jurisdictions, and that must combine in a variety of ways to elect officials representing different parts of the electoral patchwork: state senators, district attorneys, and the like. The party is not only overburdened by the federal system, but also by the "long ballot" with its myriad offices and overlapping jurisdictions. The sheer operational job of the party is overwhelming.

The difficulty goes even deeper. To maintain organizational unity and fighting trim a party should be strong enough to have the intoxicating hope of victory, but not so strong that it grows fat and sluggish and prone to internal discord and disruption. The eternal dilemma of the state or local party is that if it is weak, politicians can ignore it as a route to office, while if it is too big, it disintegrates into factions. Parties need the stimulus of competition. But real two-party competition is precisely what is lacking in many states and localities. The parties, under our federal system, are overrun by national electoral forces that they cannot control. A Republican state party may have served the people well, but a Roosevelt sweep nationally can leave it impotent for years. A Democratic state party might have brought fresh approaches to state problems, only to collapse in the face of a national shift to Eisenhower. Two-party systems in the states are simply not free to find their natural balance of competition. And this may be even more true of parties in the localities. For reasons that may have little to do with the record of Democratic administrations in New York City, Republicans there have little chance of winning the mayoralty on their own. They are fighting something too big—the Al Smith-Roosevelt-Truman tradition of the national Democratic party. Democrats face the same problem in New Hampshire or Kansas.

Even where state or local parties are evenly balanced, the burden of federalism and the long ballot can disorganize the party. For competition carries its own danger: the likelihood that some of the party's statewide candidates will win, and others will fail. In about half of the elections in which a governor won office by a close margin of votes, V. O. Key, Jr. found that candidates of the opposition party gained one or all of the minor state offices. If one of the tasks of party is to concert the actions of its officeholders behind a party program, the state party is thwarted before it can start. It may find itself in the ludicrous position of trying to unite a lieutenant governor, a state commissioner of education, and an auditor against the other party's governor, treasurer, and attorney-general. The result is not party competition but guerrilla warfare.

Hence the eternal dilemma of many state (and local) parties:

swept into a majority or minority position by forces they cannot control, they are either unable to win at all, or they win too much, or they win some state offices but not others. The more-or-less rhythmic alternation of control of government by two competitive and united parties—the classic operation of the party pendulum—is hardly to be found in the states. And the party balance is even more frozen in most localities.

Both cause and result of this situation is the party primary. Adopted mainly as a response to the breakdown of competition resulting originally from the Civil War and more immediately from the realignment of '96, the primary has immensely complicated the effort of party leaders to recruit candidates, mobilize the party behind them, and organize a united party government when in office. The primaries are still pulverizing parties by opening the nominating process to leaders of ethnic and other groups, to "name" politicians, and to gifted self-promoters; by swamping the major party primary with too many candidates while starving the minority party with too few; by disrupting collective leadership in the party; and by catering to the vagrant, shifting, and individualistic forces in American political life. In this polity of free enterprise, hardheaded politicians gain nominations by playing up their party faith and gain elections by playing it down.

If state party leaders are generally impotent, who does run the political system? The answer is implicit in the foregoing: officeholders and candidates for office. These are the persons who recruit candidates for offices (including themselves), set up active organizational headquarters, raise most political money, put out the bulk of the more costly propaganda, mobilize most volunteers, conduct door-to-door canvassing, and even handle much of the job of getting people to register to vote and transporting them to the polls on election day. Sometimes state and local parties seem to be doing all this, but more often some candidate or officeholder is using the party for his own purposes, or perhaps using it in collaboration with other candidates or cliques. Significantly, most strong "party" leaders are holders of strong offices—for example, Mayor Daley of Chicago, Governor Nelson Rockefeller of New York, Senator Abe Ribicoff of Connecticut, former Governor Mennen Williams of Michigan, Governor Mark Hatfield of Oregon. The line between officeholder

leadership and collective party leadership is not always clear, and
the situation varies sharply from state to state, but the typical party
is a holding company for contending politicians rather than an independent source of control over political activity.

In most states, in short, the Madisonian model of politically fortified checks and balances is far more typical than the Jeffersonian
model of competitive parties and majority rule. The extent and effect
of this lack of competition between parties has been documented by
Joseph Schlesinger in an outstanding piece of research. By combining two basic tests of party competition in the states—the extent of
division of control of state offices between the parties and the rate of
alternation of control between the parties (that is, whether the
parties shifted control back and forth every few years, as against a
long period of control by one party followed by a long period of
control by the other party), Schlesinger was able to measure mean-
ingfully the real extent of competition for the major offices in each
state. (He did not include the Southern states because, of course,
Democrats win practically all state elections there.) In most of the
states, he found, most of the offices were non-competitive in this
sense. The governorship was the most competitive of the statewide
offices—far more so than attorney general or treasurer—but still not
highly competitive. United States Senator was not quite so competitive as governor. Least competitive was United States Representative—a fact of the utmost importance.

These findings underline a central fact about American state and
local politics: by and large, it is every man for himself, and the devil
take the hindmost. In our patchwork of electoral districts each candidate runs on his own, mobilizing his own majority, appealing to
his own electorate, bringing together his own unique combination of
group interests, independent voters, personal followings, party
cliques, and friends and neighbors. Sometimes politicians in one
party ally with one another, superficially at least, when they can appeal to a common electorate on the basis of common symbols and
promises. Even so, behind the scenes the candidates reach out into
special areas of support, even if they have to desert their fellow candidates in the process. They depend more on their own personal
followings than on the collective efforts of the party organization.
The inevitable result is that a party's successful candidates, still de-

pending on their autonomous personal organizations, often deal with one another in office as independent satraps—as indeed they often are.

The Congressional Party System

I have noted the heavy impact of national politics on state and local politics—how a presidential sweep of the nation, for example, can upset the competitive balance of parties in the states and leave a swath of one-party states and districts, with the resultant disintegrating and fragmentizing of state and local parties. Now we must look at the reverse process—how the structure of state and local politics, comprising personal organizations surrounding fairly autonomous politicians, reacts back on national party politics. The peculiar interplay in America of national political forces and state-to-local forces makes for a structure of politicians' motives, roles, expectations, and goals that comprise two political systems, the congressional and the presidential.

The base of the congressional system is the one-party district, as established and protected by the state legislatures. Though we hear much about congressmen's "safe seats," it is still hard to grasp the extent of non-competition in congressional elections. Almost half of the House seats never change party hands. Another quarter, roughly, switch only on rare occasions. Aside from great sweeps such as those of 1920 and 1936, about 150 Republican seats and about the same number of Democratic seats never switch to the other party. Reasonably competitive districts number about 125 out of a total of 435. Many Senate seats are also one-party, especially in the South, but not to the same extent as in the House.

These safe seats are only partly accidental in origin. They are also a planned result of the alignment of party forces in the states. The drawing of election districts (congressional as well as state) is in the hands of state legislatures. Most state legislatures are controlled year after year and decade after decade by the same party (at least in one house), and legislators naturally carve up the districts to benefit their own party. Actually, the hottest fights take place mainly within the dominant party as congressmen, to protect their districts, bring influence to bear on state legislators, state legislators

maneuver for their own electoral advantage (especially if they have
congressional ambitions), and intra-party factions engage in their
horse-trading. Sometimes state legislators act positively to protect
the congressional party. In 1962 the Mississippi legislature drove a
pro-Kennedy Congressman out of office by combining his district
with a highly rural and conservative one.

Note the difference between this kind of manipulation and the
shenanigans of gerrymandering. A state legislature can make every
congressional district approximately equal in population—and hence
absolve itself of the charge of gerrymandering—and at the same
time carve up the state with such expertness that some districts remain, or become, hopelessly non-competitive. Indeed, there is a
quiet but recurrent battle between state party leaders trying to
strengthen the state party as a whole, and the congressmen and their
legislative allies trying to fortify themselves in their part of the state.
The state leaders want to make as many districts as possible fairly
secure for their party, but not overwhelmingly safe, for they seek to
spread their party's strength widely in order to win as many congressional and legislative elections as possible. The congressman, on
the other hand, is a bit greedy; remembering the occasional horrible
examples of "entrenched" congressmen being unseated, he usually
wants to build up his majorities as high as possible. And given the
diffusion of power in the state party, the congressman can often get
his way.

Most one-party districts are made up of villages, small towns, and
small cities. They have a heavily rural bias. Compared to the larger
metropolitan areas, these districts tend to be more homogeneous in
social make-up and political attitude. They usually lack the political
competition and vitality that characterize more urban or mixed areas.
The major party, the local business interests, press and pulpit, the
community leaders combine loosely to represent the dominant interests in the area. Possible centers of dissent, most notably the opposition party, trade unions or ethnic groups, cannot carry the burden
of competition. The opposition, such as it is, fades away. The result
in these areas is not so much a loud and clear conservatism (which
might be logical in such a social and economic context) as confusion,
conformity, and negativism. But the congressman does not see it
this way. To him the grass roots are the source of common sense;

he would agree with Rousseau that there was more wisdom in small bands of Swiss peasants gathered under oak trees to conduct their affairs than in all the governments of Europe.

We must not exaggerate these urban-rural differences, given the blurring of social forces in America. Rather we must see how the political mechanisms are linked to dominant social forces in typical areas. The link is the politician—in this case the congressman. He does not relate himself to his district impersonally. He deals with its political life on his own terms, kindling some forces and tranquillizing or ignoring others. Thus he contributes to the political tone of the district as well as expressing it. The manner in which he does this turns on his perception of how his political behavior, given the political materials he must work with, can advance his political career.

Typically such a congressman has two major career choices. He can seek to stay in his congressional post and hence rise through the hierarchy in Congress. Or he can use his office as a stepping stone to bigger offices, such as governor or senator. Usually this is not a free choice, for it is influenced by the nature of his district as well as by his own motives and expectations. A man in a safe district often finds himself, as in upstate New York or downstate Illinois, representing a constituency quite different from the state as a whole. Rural districts in particular are likely to be more conservative than the state generally, or at least more opposed to prevailing political and governmental trends in the state. Republican congressmen from the upstate districts of New York, for example, are often at odds with their party's governor and senators. Hence it may be hard for such congressmen to "go statewide"; most of them hesitate to risk a safe seat for the arduous and risky job of appealing to the independents and moderates who might hold the balance of power in a statewide contest.

So the congressman from a safe seat usually follows the easy alternative: he stays put. He placates the dominant social forces in the district; "protects" his district against hostile outside forces; does a great many individual favors; lobbies for benefits for the district; maintains a friends-and-neighbors political organization that scares would-be opponents out of the primary or trounces them if they come in; and comfortably overwhelms the opposition party's candidate—if there is one—on election day. His main commitment politically is to the status quo. He wishes nothing to disrupt his easy relationships with the public officials and private interests that rule the area. He views with alarm the great issues that sweep the nation and threaten to disrupt the familiar and comfortable politics of his district. He does not want to broaden the franchise or encourage more voting, because this might disturb existing arrangements.

Naturally the one-party congressman fares best in the "off-year" (non-presidential) election. In presidential years the vote in congressional races is over one-third again as large as the comparable turnout in the off-years. Since presidential candidates arouse hosts of independent or apathetic voters who then stay at home in the congressional elections two years later, the one-party congressman faces his greatest risk when the opposition party offers a strong presidential candidate, like Roosevelt or Eisenhower. But such presidential candidates are exceptional, so that in presidential as well as off-year elections the typical one-party congressman is quite safe. And he remains invincibly local. By remaining in the orbit of his congressional area, he stays politically in the orbit of his party's local candidates and officeholders. Thus he operates in a world of political localism, for the electoral and other political forces in the area are largely activated by other local candidates. Hence the congressman, though a national officeholder, is almost as locally oriented as the district attorney or county commissioner, and almost as much beyond the reach of influence by the President or the national party. And this is one more reason he achieves his key aim: unbroken longevity in office.

Longevity in office—this is the crucial nexus between the man in the safe rural district and the congressional party in Washington. The mechanism is well known—the rule of seniority, which promotes congressmen up the committee ladder toward the chairmanship in accordance with his unbroken tenure on the committee. Our man in the safe seat has a wonderful incentive to stay put. He can, with any kind of luck, expect steady promotion to the top councils of the congressional party, regardless of merit. No other major Western democracy rewards its politicians with so much power for so little relevant accomplishment.

But it is dangerous to focus too much on the seniority rule in the committees alone, for this committee rule is merely one instrument, though a central one, in the allocation of power in Congress. Again we must think in terms of a system of power. And that system is today, and has been since 1938, essentially the same as it was in the 1850's, the 1890's, in 1910, and at other turning points in American history.

The leaders of the congressional party are, of course, men who have climbed the seniority ladders and hence the men who come from the safe, usually rural, districts. They are the chairmen, or ranking majority or minority members of the more important committees: the committees that tax and spend, that seek to control other central economic policies, such as prices and investment, that have major influence on the political status and personal privileges of other members of Congress (i.e., special appropriations for members' districts, or special bills affecting individual constituents), and that influence the traffic of legislative business—most notably the House Rules Committee. The statistics are conclusive. In a recent Congress the 217 most urban districts produced 26 per cent of the House chairmen in general, while the 218 least urban accounted for 74 per cent. But the imbalance of rural-urban power becomes even more significant if one notes the relative importance of the committees rather than simply their total number.

This imbalance of urban-rural control of committees is not accidental. The congressional party leaders are the same persons who make assignments to committees. In the House these choices are made by Democratic and Republican committees-on-committees, which are largely composed of rural representatives. Conservative influence in these selection committees is self-perpetuating; by taking on only those members who have already attained some seniority, the committees-on-committees automatically exclude freshman members from the more urban and mixed "swing" districts. Both committees, a careful study concludes, "are so constituted as to be virtually immune to immediate pressures brought about by electoral changes." Using this selection machinery, the congressional parties control access to positions on the key substantive committees and on the Rules Committee. Moreover, House members seeking committee assignments channel their requests through the "dean" or senior member of their state party delegation—one more concession to seniority.

The seniority system is pervasive. It shapes not only key committee memberships and leadership but the whole life and tone of the Congress. Freshman members find themselves treated like freshmen. As they learn the ropes—if they can survive their early re-election campaigns—they learn that the things they need for political survival, such as constituent favors and home-town projects, and the little considerations they want as employees on the Hill, such as office space or congressional patronage, depend on their cooperating with the congressional party leadership. "If you want to get along you've got to go along"—this hoary adage is one of the working principles of congressional life.

How the congressional party operates on a specific and vital front of public policy can be seen in the House Appropriations Committee. This committee, like the party as a whole, has its own set of roles and norms, rewards and penalties. Its ruling elements consider themselves guardians of the taxpayer's money; they are more prone to cut Administration requests than to shape positive policies of their own, though of course they allow themselves and their congressional allies local appropriations. They operate less as Democrats or Republicans than as elements of a coalition dealing with one another through bargaining, reciprocity, and a united front on the House floor. And appointments to the committee are mainly controlled, of course, by the chairman and senior members. Membership on the committee is not just a job, its members like to say, but a way of life.

The seniors are expert at compounding their influence. Consider Representative Francis E. Walter of Pennsylvania. Not only is he chairman of the Judiciary Committee Immigration Subcommittee, but also of the Un-American Activities Committee and of the House Patronage Committee. Hence he can withhold Capitol Hill patronage jobs from erring members, block private immigration bills (a special problem for urban congressmen trying to get around general immigration restrictions), all the while serving as an astute parliamentarian and as chief guardian of Americanism on Capitol Hill. Other, less noted congressional party leaders operate in the subcommittees of the Appropriations and other committees to compound their influence on the Hill.

I have been emphasizing the House seniority system here, but the Senate shows the same forces at work, though sometimes less visibly. Most Senators, like most Representatives, are lawyers, and about half the Senators in a recent session had begun their careers as state legislators or prosecuting attorneys. In the upper chamber like the lower, men from the safe rural states are more likely to get the choice committee assignments and more likely to acquire greater influence on the committees. Senators "table-hop" from committee to committee over the years to gain better berths, and a senior Senator requesting a vacant committee seat almost always gets it, unless, like Estes Kefauver, he has defied Senate norms. Senators from more competitive states are, of course, less likely to build influence in the upper body.

The Senate, like the House, has a set of standing committees that not only provide for division of legislative labor but, as Ralph Huitt says, are part of the allocation of political power. As in the lower chamber, committee chairmen control subcommittee appointments. Effectiveness on the Hill depends greatly on conforming with one's elders. The Senate's seniority system "results in the under-representation of liberals among the chairmen of both parties . . . ," Donald R. Matthews concludes. "The seniority system's bias against urban liberals of both parties tends to be self-perpetuating." And the right to filibuster—which is the power of a very few Senators to bargain effectively with all the rest—represents the Madisonian tradition in its most extreme form.

Helping to unite the congressional party is a common ideology. This ideology is, of course generally conservative (defining conservatism as opposition to the increased use of government to redistribute income in favor of lower-income groups) and isolationist (defined as opposition to greater political, diplomatic, and economic concessions and commitments to other nations). But this ideology is intrinsically negative; that is, it is hostile to major governmental trends in the 20th Century, although it offers grudging acceptance of welfare programs and other measures that have won wide support among voters. But on one matter the congressional party ideologists are most articulate and positive—defense of the congressional party system. States' rights, local elections, restricted franchise, minority rights, rural over-representation, checks and balances, congressional power, the danger of majority or "mass" rule, judicial review (at least in the old days), powerful committees, the seniority system, the fili-buster—in short, the Madisonian system in all its ramifications—arouse their stout support. And the ideologists in Congress are but-tressed outside it by able political thinkers, like James Burnham, by perceptive journalists like William S. White and David Lawrence, and by a host of newspapers, magazines, and commentators.

Congressional party leaders in both houses can exert a wide, though sometimes tenuous, discipline outside their chambers too. Congressmen report cases of Southern members being threatened with primary opposition backed with outside money unless they toed the line. In each house the Republican and Democratic congres-sional campaign committees, which for decades have operated largely apart from the national party committees, allot money to congres-sional candidates; and while the sum is not large, there are cases where the committees have given money to conservative candidates from safer districts at the expense of more needy aspirants from more competitive constituencies. The main party discipline of the con-gressional party, however, is internal. Significantly, the congres-sional party rarely takes prized committee assignments from members of Congress who bolt the presidential nominee.

Still, the main bulwark of the congressional party system is not this kind of conscious manipulation but, as I have indicated above, a whole system of local power patterns, electoral arrangements, voting behavior, career lines, and institutional arrangements and norms in Congress that together form an operating political system. For we must understand what the congressional party system is not, as well as what it is. It is not a tight, cohesive group of men, conspiring to-gether in a secret chamber and pushing the buttons on a nation-wide machine. It is a loose cluster of men, sharing a common con-cept of the public interest, convinced that they are protecting the nation against radicalism, benefiting from and in turn protecting a set of rules and institutions that bolster their power, and the product of local political patterns. These men deal with one another by bargaining and accommodation rather than by direction and com-mand. They are often divided over specific policies. They have the problem of cooperating across formal party lines between Democrats and Republicans, and across the physical and psychological gap separating Senate and House. And they must share some power with the formally elected leaders in each house, as we will see later. But what unites them is the common defense of a system that consolidates their influence on Capitol Hill. And that system, while not monolithic, is composed of social forces and political mechanisms that are mutually supporting and hence cumulative in their impact. Power in one part of the system can be parlayed into power in another. "The committees with their chairmen," a freshman congressman said recently, "are like a ring of forts."

The Presidential Party System

The head of the presidential party is the President. He sets its policies, confirms its ideology, appoints its leaders, and carries its hopes in the quadrennial crisis of the presidential election. Just as other parties are organized around other officeholders, so a party is organized around the Chief Executive. Beginning with Jefferson and Jackson the man in the White House has acted in varying degrees as "party leader." But he is not head of the whole Democratic or Republican party. There are great sections of the Democratic party beyond the control of President Kennedy today, just as many Republicans never really accepted Mr. Eisenhower as their party leader. But of that section of the whole party that we call the presidential party, the President is undisputed leader.

The President runs his party through a small political staff in the White House and through the chairman of the party's national committee. That chairman, like his own aides, is chosen by him and remains in office only as long as the President wishes. Other leaders of the President's party also remain at his sufferance: Cabinet members, top agency chiefs, and hundreds of administrative aides and operatives in the higher echelons of the Administration. These officials often appear to be non-political but in the final test they will support the presidential party. In the 1930's Harry Hopkins had a clear understanding of the close relation of relief activities to Roosevelt's re-election campaigns. In 1960, according to the testimony of the government official concerned, the Interior Department cancelled the sale of surplus tungsten in an effort to help Vice-President Nixon's election campaign. Some officials, such as the Secretary of Defense and heads of independent commissions, are less in the presidential party orbit, while others like the Attorney General or the Postmaster General hold offices that are much more partisan by tradition. And a few Administration officials may not be in the presidential party at all.

From Washington the presidential party fans out widely. Hundreds of Administration political appointees in the states and cities— federal attorneys, collectors of customs, federal marshals, and the like (except those who mainly owe appointment to Senators at odds with the President)—are expected to protect the Administration's local interests, at least where called on. Both in Washington and in the field the President's men also maintain close relations with many of the state party leaders, though some state committees are the possession of a potent Governor or Senator or big-city mayor, or are hopelessly divided between the President and the state leaders. The organizational reach of the presidential party typically does not extend below the state level, except perhaps in the choosing of national convention delegates.

The national convention shows the presidential party in its full splendor and power. The convention always endorses its leader in the White House, if he wishes it to—a fact of 20th Century history that Harry Truman remembered in the spring of 1948 and his adversaries in the party seemed to forget. The President's men write the platform, determine the content of the major speeches, decide which contested delegations will be seated, control the order of the business on the floor, and roll up the President's endorsement on the first ballot, followed by nomination by acclamation. Rebels are easily put down. The President also controls the nomination of his running-mate. If it is worth his while to make changes in the Vice-Presidency, as Roosevelt did in 1940, he can do so. Usually he does not make the effort, because the Vice-Presidency is not that important. All in all, the presidential party controls the convention as fully as the congressional party controls Congress.

The heart of national politics, Arthur Holcombe wrote, is the presidential campaign. So it is of the presidential party. Its candidate is the focus of the party's effort and the center of national attention. He dominates the national media and sharpens the national debate. He arouses and motivates millions of voters. The campaign is his supreme opportunity to arouse and shape mass opinion, to cut through the babel of voices, to show the voter the direct link between a national problem and doing something about it (i.e., voting for him).

This, indeed, has been the historic achievement of the presidential party—the immense widening of the electorate. "The rise of political parties and the extension of the suffrage produced the plebiscitary Presidency," Schattschneider says. ". . . The Presidency has in turn become the principal instrument for the nationalization of politics"— the destruction of old local power monopolies and sectional power patterns. From Harrison and Jackson in the last century to Eisenhower and Stevenson in 1952 and Kennedy and Nixon in 1960, it has been the presidential party contests that have spectacularly broadened the voting rolls. The reason is clear. The great incentive of the presidential candidates is to widen and "flatten out" their vote, to win states by dependable but not wasteful popular majorities, while the congressional party "bunches" its vote in safe districts.

The stunning impact of the presidential campaign is partly organizational. Roving through the nation, the President's men shake up sleepy committees, set up campaign organizations, raise money, recruit local party leadership. But the regular party organizations, no matter how efficient, are not able to mobilize the majorities that the presidential party seeks. So presidential party candidates establish auxiliary organizations to reach the millions of independents that the regulars disregard. This is an old practice; Horatio Seymour in 1868 set up the "Order of the Union Democrats" to bolster the listless Democrats with a vigorous new organization that could cut across party lines. More recently, the Willkie Clubs, Citizens for Eisenhower, Volunteers for Stevenson, Citizens for Kennedy and similar groups have conducted big campaigns separate from, and sometimes at conflict with, the regular organizations. Often they ignore or even "cut" the state and local candidates of the regular parties. Bad feelings always develop between volunteers and regulars. Sometimes the regulars slight the presidential candidate in return. Candidates for governor have been known to hold rallies without a single sign or poster for the presidential candidate of their own party—but the reverse also happens. Sometimes this uneasy marriage ends in disaster. In 1940 Willkie organized a huge force of volunteers through the Willkie clubs; during the war the regulars deserted him, in part because of his war-time support of Roosevelt, and they denied him renomination in 1944. Despite all the bickering, however, this bifurcation of presidential campaigns will continue as long as our parties retain their present character, for the presidential candidate must have machinery for winning independent and even opposition party votes.

Just as the congressional parties benefit from gerrymandered congressional districts, so the presidential party benefits from its own form of gerrymandering. This is the electoral college, which, by allotting all the electoral votes of a state to the candidate winning most popular votes in that state, puts a premium on the big urban states with their handsome electoral-vote plums. Since the big states tend to be highly competitive states, the winner-take-all arrangement plays up the importance of the organized groups, such as Negroes, Catholics, union labor, Jews, ethnic groups that supposedly control the balance of electoral power in the state. This control may be exaggerated, and usually is, but to the presidential parties, locked in fierce combat, this huge, supposedly deliverable vote, looks increasingly irresistible as election day nears. Kennedy's eleventh-hour emphasis on this vote in 1960, and Nixon's apparent unconcern for it when he flew to Alaska at the climactic moment, is bound to enhance the mythology of the electoral-college balance of power. The distortion resulting from the winner-take-all device further separates the bases of the presidential and congressional parties. But even without it, there would be some electoral bifurcation, for the presidential parties, as the more urban, liberally oriented party system, naturally direct their main appeals to the urban and suburban vote.

The career lines in the presidential party are significantly different from those in the congressional. The traditional path to the Presidency has been through a big-state governorship, the party organization around which is likely to be fairly parallel with the presidential party organization in that state (Stevenson in Illinois in 1952, for example). Few governors, on the other hand, rise to high places in the congressional party. Few Senators have become President in the past century, but we now know that the old rule that "Senators don't become President, with Harding as the exception that proves the rule," had a flaw in it (besides the notion that exceptions somehow prove rules). It was not Senators in general but Senators who were committed members of the congressional party that were ineligible for presidential party leadership (Harding *was* an exception to the rule). As if realizing this, John Kennedy moved steadily out of the orbit of the congressional party into that of the presidential during his years in the Senate. It was Lyndon Johnson's failure to do this, and Robert Taft's similar failure earlier, that fatally handicapped them in their quest for the nomination.

The career lines in the presidential and congressional systems seem to diverge at a deeper level too. While evidence on this is limited, it may well be that the presidential party draws on men who have risen through the bureaucracies of big business, universities, unions, large law firms, and state and federal executive departments. Many of these men are "political outsiders," as Mills has defined them; they have spent most of their working life outside strictly political organization. Congressional party leadership is mainly composed of one-time independent entrepreneurs, small-town lawyers, local law enforcement officials, and state legislators. We can guess that the differing vocational, ideological, and institutional worlds of the two groups—one more bureaucratic, hierarchical, and managerial, the other more individualistic and prone to negotiate and bargain— would have a significant impact on the nature of the parties.

All the foregoing discussion presupposes one crucial fact about the presidential party—that its leader is President. What about the presidential party that does not possess the White House? Things then, of course, are very different. There is no office around which the party can be organized, no office to lead it, discipline it, reward it. Defeated at the polls, the presidential party becomes apathetic and disorganized. No one speaks for it with a clear voice. The national chairman, as the executor of the defeated candidate's political estate, is powerless and must yield to the congressional party. The presidential party does not disappear, of course. Its head cut off, the body still lives, waiting for a new head and a new vitality. For the time being, however, it is impotent.

Such, at least, has been the traditional state of the out-of-office presidential party, but there has been an interesting change. After their defeat in 1956, notable presidential Democrats under the leadership of national chairman Paul Butler decided to establish a council to shape party policy and to focus attack on the Eisenhower

Administration. Its members came from the presidential party: Harry Truman, Adlai Stevenson, Herbert Lehman, Averell Harriman, among others, with Eleanor Roosevelt as consultant. The committee had little direct influence on policy and was ignored by the congressional Democratic party. But it helped keep alive presidential party doctrine among Democrats and posed well-publicized alternatives to the Eisenhower politics. Much more than the congressional Democrats, the council served as Eisenhower's Loyal Opposition.

That Senator Hubert Humphrey and other liberal Democratic legislators were members of the Advisory Council points up a puzzling but important fact: a large minority of congressmen belong to their presidential party rather than to the congressional. Many of these congressmen are freshmen who represent marginal districts, and perhaps were elected in a presidential sweep with the head of their presidential party. Kept in essentially a freshman status by the congressional parties, these members of Congress turn to the presidential parties for a political home. Otherwise, the congressional makeup of the two presidential parties varies considerably. Democratic members are mainly those who represent urban dwellers and who are not at home in the rural atmosphere of the congressional parties—for example, Democrats Emanuel Celler of New York, John E. Fogarty of Rhode Island, Chet Holifield of California, Edith Green of Oregon. Republican congressmen in their presidential party are much less numerous and represent more competitive constituencies; Jacob Javits of New York and Clifford P. Case of New Jersey are the outstanding examples. One reason some congressmen move into the orbit of the presidential party is that they see the need for the President's help in gaining re-election. The more marginal and competitive the congressman's district, the closer he will ordinarily be to the presidential party.

The borders between the congressional and presidential parties in Congress are not clear-cut. Many a congressman hedges his bets by shifting back and forth between the two camps, or by keeping a foot in each. And nothing is fuzzier than the role of the elected leadership of Congress—the Speaker of the House, the majority and minority leaders, and the various party conferences and policy committees. Indeed, an interesting question is whether the formal leadership belongs to the presidential or congressional parties. The answer is: it depends.

It depends mainly on whether or not the presidential party is in power. When it is, the leadership ordinarily lines up behind the President. It retains some bargaining power, as Taft did with Eisenhower in 1953. It can always revolt if put under excessive pressure, as Alben Barkley did against Roosevelt in 1944. But generally it goes along, and the meeting of the congressional "Big Four" or "Big Six" with the President has become one of the most durable institutions in Washington. A President's prestige is so great that his fellow partisans in Congress will rarely choose leadership hostile to him. Sometimes he is powerful enough to determine the choice himself. But usually the decision is made largely independent of the White House, as in the selection of Charles Halleck as Republican House leader in 1959 and the election of John W. McCormack as Speaker in 1962. This semi-independence can be of some importance, though; as Neustadt says, "the more an officeholder's power stems from sources outside the President, the stronger will be his potential power *on* the President."

When the presidential party does not occupy the White House, the elected congressional leaders usually move closer to the seniority leadership of the congressional party. This was evident in both Taft's and Johnson's majority leadership in the Senate, and is seen most notably today in Halleck's leadership in the House. The difficulty for the elected leaders, in contrast to the other sets of leaders, is that they lack firm institutional bases of support of their own. The policy committees, caucuses, and other party devices are insubstantial compared with the standing committees. If the majority leader and his whips lack a President to back them up, they are generally, and over the long run, drawn into the vortex of the senior leaders. Consider, for example, Rayburn's and Johnson's refusal to join the Democratic Advisory Council. They treated it as part of a somewhat different party—as indeed it was. Or consider Republican leader Halleck's attitude toward the Republican party platform of 1960. "We will take it out and read it from time to time," he said. "But the congressional people generally have very little to do with writing party platforms."

In this three-way tug of war much also depends on the skill of the elected leader. At times Taft through his experience and doggedness was able to act virtually as a third force in the Senate, as was Lyndon Johnson through his superb parliamentary skill and his grasp of the nuances of Senate life. But when the chips are down the elected leaders usually do not hold the levers of power. Sam Rayburn, despite all his prestige and support in the House, was never really able to vanquish Howard W. Smith, chairman of the Rules Committee. And, as we have seen, Henry Cabot Lodge finally had to yield to the Senate Irreconcilables in his fight against Wilson's League. One problem is that the Senate leader is not sure of his own constituency, as in the case of Senate Democratic majority leader Scott Lucas, who was defeated for re-election to the Senate in 1952. Another inhibiting factor is the fear of failure to be re-elected majority leader—the unhappy blow that Republican House leader Joseph W. Martin suffered in 1959. Unlike the seniority leaders, the elected leaders always face possible repudiation at the hands of one or both of their constituencies.

Another type of congressman who has a somewhat equivocal position is the member from a metropolitan, one-party district. He is ordinarily a Democrat responsive to urban interests and hence takes a liberal position on economic issues. At the same time he is the beneficiary of a seniority system that gives him special influence on Capitol Hill—though not so much influence as it gives rural representatives, who usually gain the most powerful chairmanships. Many such representatives of one-party urban districts end up in the awkward position of supporting the congressional power system at the same time that they support liberal policies, such as civil rights, that are blocked by that system. But the city men usually win by such big margins that their conflicting role positions on the Hill are not an electoral embarrassment, except possibly in a Democratic primary.

What of the freshmen congressmen and other congressional members of the presidential party? Sometimes they can turn to the elected leadership for help, but more often they are on their own. The freshman congressman quoted earlier as seeing the committee leadership like a ring of forts went on to evaluate his own side: "A coalition of Northerners, without interior lines of strength, is a tenuous thing. . . . We have no unifying philosophy. . . . We have no White House to cajole, threaten and promise. . . . The analogy with warfare that I have used is an accurate one. . . . The northern coalition, as the attackers, are spread out, with poor communications between one another and hence poor coordination. We have no base of power, with which to menace the chairmen on the one hand, or to discipline our own members on the other."

The President, as head of the presidential party, has no more vital task than to lead his presidential forces in Congress, to unify them, to give them interior lines of strength. For no section of the presidential party is more dependent on the President, nor more crucial to him.

Four-Party Politics

We can conclude that the pattern of national politics is essentially a four-party pattern. The Democratic and Republican parties are each divided into congressional and presidential structures, with all the elements that comprise the American type of party.

The division of Democrats and Republicans into two parties each is of course the immediate cause of the national four-party pattern. The four parties would not last long, however, if they lacked strong attitudinal bases in the electorate. They might not continue, for example, if people divided only over economic issues, for such a situation, combined with the tendency of politicians toward combinations, would normally produce two groupings, presumably of those who got smaller slices of the economic loaf against those who got bigger. At least two factors operate against such a simple two-way division in America.

One is the obvious fact that people divide over issues other than economic ones and—a crucial point—that the economic divisions are not congruent with the others. By "other issues" I mean those that have been variously called "moral" or "style" issues but that I will call "way-of-life" issues—that is, issues that pose choices about a nation's whole culture and way of life and that cannot be calculated in terms of immediate and tangible economic return for specific groups of people. Taxes, wages, social security, farm prices, tariffs, public housing are examples of economic issues; while civil liberties, women's rights, disarmament, immigration, corruption in government, defense strategy, racial tolerance and integration, government, and religion are examples of way-of-life issues. The presumed motivational appeal of the former, Berelson, Lazarsfeld, and McPhee suggest, is self-interest of a relatively direct and tangible kind, while that of the latter is self-expression and self-gratification of a more subjective, symbolic, and projective kind. Issues do not fall neatly into the two categories. An expansion of civil rights, such as job opportunity, or of immigration of certain types of workers, or of certain types of defense activities, could mean economic benefits or deprivations for various groups as well as psychic benefits or deprivations for a wider public. But the difference between the two seems sharp enough to affect the shape of our party structure.

Data on the non-congruence of economic and way-of-life issues are limited but highly suggestive. Polls indicate that there has been in recent years little if any relationship between persons' relative positions on domestic and foreign issues. "An interventionist position in foreign affairs was as likely to be taken by a domestic conservative as by a domestic liberal" in 1956, report Campbell and associates, "and the relative isolationist was as likely to favor social welfare activities in Washington as he was to oppose them." By cross-tabulating distributions of responses in 1952 to an "international involvement" question and a "social welfare activity" question, Key finds four combinations of opinion: isolationist-liberal, internationalist-liberal, isolationist-conservative, internationalist-conservative (with the last the smallest of the four in numbers).

Evidence on the non-congruence of economic and domestic way-of-life issues is even more limited but still suggestive. Much of it stems from historians' observations. The political parties have usually had their "conscience" and "cotton" wings. Under Theodore Roosevelt the Republican party numbered hosts of high-income business and professional men who looked on their party mainly as a weapon to attack the moral and social evils of the day. The Democratic party in Bryan's and Wilson's days and also more recently has numbered not only hosts of economic reformers but also workers and farmers who took a hostile or stunted view of civil liberties, women's rights, civil rights, civic betterment, and other way-of-life problems.

A second root cause of the four-party pattern is the disarticulation of the national and state party systems, stemming from the workings of federalism in a sectional society combined with some of our special political arrangements. The impact of national politics on state and local politics in our sectional nation has been noted in these pages—the creation of one-party states and districts. Balance and competition at the national level, especially in presidential contests, helped produce local noncompetition and imbalance, most notably in the South and rural North. These one-party areas tended to be ignored by presidential candidates, who concentrated on the swing areas, and hence the one-party areas became less important to the presidential parties, but they received extra representation in Congress because of the seniority system, and hence became the buttress of the congressional parties.

This double cleavage, institutional and attitudinal, between the presidential parties and the congressional parties is largely responsible for the conflicting positions that a President, whether Democratic or Republican, and a Congress, whether Democratic or Republican controlled, take on the crucial affairs of state.

Willmore Kendall has pointed to the curious fact that the Executive "is able, with good show of reason, to put itself forward on any particular issue as the spokesman for . . . lofty and enlightened principle. . . . The Executive tends, that is to say, to have the nation's ministers and publicists with it on 'peace,' the nation's professors and moralizers with it on desegregation, the nation's economists with it on fiscal policy and redistribution, the nation's political scientists with it on political reform and civil rights, etc. . . . The Executive is for world government, for the outlawry of war, for unselfishness in our relations with the outside world, for the brotherhood of man, for majority-rule, for progress, for generosity toward the weak and lowly, for freedom of thought and speech, for equality, for the spreading of the benefits of modern civilization to 'underdeveloped' lands, for science and the 'scientific outlook,' for civil rights. . . ." Congress, according to Professor Kendall, stresses other values: small group discussion in the community, deference to highly prestiged and presumably wiser citizens, and an anti-quixotic concern for the "realities, problems, the potential benefits and potential costs (and for whom?)" of presidential proposals.

Why this gap between President and Congress over way-of-life issues? Why, in Professor Kendall's own terms, do the two presidential parties win a much larger share of the "moralizers" and reformers and utopians than do the two congressional parties? Possibly—and here I can only speculate, for we do not have adequate data—because the most persisting major conflicts in American politics have been over economic issues; hence the national parties have offered the most meaningful alternatives in the realm of economic policy; so that if divisions of the voters over economic and way-of-life issues are not congruent, as we have reason to think they are not, millions of voters more concerned with way-of-life issues than economic ones have had to operate in a party limbo. They are simply not aroused by the state and local contests, including congressional contests, that turn on the old bread-and-butter issues; they have not been geared into the local two-party alignment over the years because they have had no meaningful alternatives presented to them on the issues that mean most to them: corruption, human rights, social reform, and the rest. Hence the voices of the mugwumps have often been ignored in the obscure politics of the local, often non-competitive struggle. But the presidential contest does reach and arouse such independents because their collective voice nationally is loud, and because in the sharply competitive presidential race the two candidates must move beyond the traditional economic issues and find way-of-life issues that may reach the uncommitted.

The consequence of the four-party system is that American political leaders, in order to govern, must manage multi-party coalitions just as heads of coalition parliamentary regimes in Europe have traditionally done—as the French did, for example, before De Gaulle. But the task of governing in a sense is harder in the United States, for the leaders' job is not simply to pick up enough parliamentary votes to form a cabinet, or even just to pass a bill. They must bring together the right combination of presidential party and congressional party strength to accomplish a great variety of tasks day after day and year after year. And the leaders' job is further complicated by the fact that continuous, effective government policy-making is impossible without a strong working alliance between at least some combination of presidential and congressional parties. For the presidential side and the congressional side each wields power not only in its own "constitutional" orbit but in the opposite side's orbit as well.

The extent to which the congressional and presidential parties share the same powers and hence can block each other is extraordinary. The President has a broad range of legislative power besides his veto: he can issue executive orders that have the force of law; he can draw up with other nations executive agreements that are as controlling under international law as treaties ratified by the Senate; he can make war "by the push of a button" and let Congress ratify it later, if at all. But Congress inserts itself into the executive process too. The Senate can refuse to confirm appointments—even one lone Senator can induce the whole upper body to withhold approval through the device of "senatorial courtesy." The standing committees closely affect administrative arrangements through their control of policy, and the appropriations committees and subcommittees have a profound impact through their control of funds. The more "independent" an agency or commission may be of the President, the more dependent it may be on a committee or faction of Congress. The relation, of course, changes over time. After the Civil War Congress tried to control the Administration through such means as the Tenure of Office Act; the act is long since gone but not some of the motivation behind it. Today the Army Chief of Engineers has legislative authority to plan public works and report to Congress without clearing with the President.

In less obvious fields too, the two-party coalitions, the congressional and the presidential, maintain countervailing institutional apparatus. The President can publicize an issue and influence public opinion by appointing a "blue-ribbon" presidential commission controlled by the President's men, and he and his lieutenants can set into action other varieties of Administration inquiries, probes, and explorations. Congress at the same time has its standing committees, including the Un-American Activities Committee, which can investigate at the drop of a hat, and it can set up special committees to conduct grand investigations.

The President can call Congress back into special session after it adjourns, but the houses can recess instead of adjourn and thus retain more control of their own operations. If the President can act on many matters through executive orders not subject to congressional veto, Congress can legislate, at least to a modest extent, through Concurrent Resolutions, which are not subject to presidential veto. Congress can limit White House legislative power by setting statutory expiration dates in the original act, as Ernest Griffith has noted, "as a device to circumvent a possible presidential veto of some future measure designed to change a particular policy to which it has given reluctant or experimental agreement." On the other hand, Congress has had to delegate to the President an immense amount of policy-making power. The bureaucracy of the executive department has grown enormously—but so has that of Congress. The General Accounting Office, which has a theoretically executive duty, supplies information on administrative lapses to congressional watchdogs.

An executive impetus and a legislative tendency confront each other at every junction. The executive impetus is to combine legislative and administrative power, to coordinate functions, to exert control from the top. Whether it is Elihu Root, Theodore Roosevelt's Secretary of War, trying (unsuccessfully) to nationalize the state guard, or Hoover and Truman trying to centralize administration, or Kennedy trying to reorganize the executive branch, the instinct of the executive is to integrate government for the sake of better control. The legislative instinct is pluralistic. Congress and the state legislatures, under the control of the legislative parties, seek to fragmentize the executive by means of individual or committee influence over administrative units, or control of specific budgetary items, or through hobbling the executive's power to reorganize. State legislatures have in some instances kept whole sections of the executive branch out from the governor's control, and have resisted efforts to shorten the long ballot, which gives state officials electoral strength independent of the governor.

This bewildering array of countervailing and overlapping powers compels American political leaders to piece together a new patchwork of party fragments, factional chieftains, congressional votes, constitutional usage, and bureaucratic officials in order to put through each major new program. Presidential party leaders do this through endless persuading, pressuring, manipulating, and bargaining. Congressional party leaders use the same methods to balk or modify Administration proposals, and their task is all the easier because of the many points at which action can be slowed or stopped in the narrow, twisting, and crowded legislative channels. Since each set of parties, congressional or presidential, is a coalition itself, action depends on the alignment of coalition with coalition.

Not that the presidential and congressional party coalitions are of the same type. The former, to use Dahl's apt expression, is an "executive-centered coalition." The President has means of direction and discipline unmatched by the congressional parties or by the presidential party out of power. He has a public position, a command of the media, a control over personnel, and a direct electoral link with the people that enable him to maintain and exploit a somewhat hierarchical system in the presidential party. The congressional party is led by a coalition of parties, allied through their common attitudes and mutual dependence, and with an internal party system marked more by bargaining than by hierarchy. The essential operational process differs: the congressional reliance on committees, with their tendency to protect an existing consensus over the status quo, contrasts with the executive emphasis on single-leader activism. The out-of-power presidential party, to use Dahl's terminology, is a network of "independent sovereignties with spheres of influence." But even this network, inchoate though it is, has the attributes of party —ideology, program, leadership, machinery, and existing or potential electoral support.

Any one of the four parties can—and does—coalesce with any one of the others. We take for granted the coalition of the Democratic presidential and congressional parties, and of the two Republican parties—though often we should not. The durable alliance of the congressional parties has long been publicized by liberals as the "unholy alliance of Old Guard Republicans and Dixie Democrats" in Congress. Less obvious is another alliance, holy or unholy, between presidential Democrats and presidential Republicans. These parties occasionally combine in Congress, as Republicans from urban and suburban districts support the proposals of Democratic Presidents. But the main focus of the presidential party alliance is in the foreign policy and fiscal agencies. Roosevelt's enlistment of Stimson and Knox in his Cabinet in 1940, Truman's appointment of a host of Republicans to foreign-policy and foreign-aid agencies, Eisenhower's choice of Texas Democrat Robert Anderson as Secretary of the Treasury, and Kennedy's retention of Douglas Dillon and other Republicans from the Eisenhower Administration and his selection of an internationalist Republican, McGeorge Bundy, as an assistant, reflect a wide community of interest between the two parties. The alliance is consecrated in the name of "bipartisanship in foreign policy," or the hoary slogan "Party politics stops at the water's edge." What mainly stops at the water's edge is not party politics in general but congressional party politics in particular. The real "unholy alliance" to a good congressional Republican is the historic coalition between the internationalists in both parties. And the internationalist newspapers that approve so highly of foreign-policy bipartisanship today were never so enthusiastic about it in the 1920's and the early 1930's, when it represented a coalition of isolationists.

No political system is neutral—certainly not the congressional and presidential. Power is inseparable from structure. It is not by chance that liberal and internationalist Presidents in this century have been "strong" Presidents, and that men like Taft and Harding are relegated to the ranks of the weak. The stronger the exertion of presidential power, the more liberal and internationalist it will be because of the make-up and dynamics of the presidential party. The stronger the exertion of congressional power, the more conservative and isolationist will be our national policy because of the structure of the congressional forces. The man who is all for liberalism and internationalism "as long as the President's power is not increased" (as for example in the trade agreements act) is a man who has not grasped the relation of ends and means, of power and structure. The man who favors cutting down the powers of Congress because it is "slow and inefficient" is cutting down conservative influence, whether he wants to or not. The structure of coalition politics is inevitably the structure of "who gets what, when and how" in American national politics. As the Madisonian system in being, it is also the structure of slowdown and stalemate in American government.

11

THE WHIRLPOOLS
of CHANGE

$\mathcal{T}$he thread of my argument has been that:

1. The Madisonian system, by establishing countervailing public offices around which would develop competing political organizations and power, forces leaders to govern by coalition, compromise, and consensus.

2. The Jeffersonian system, by organizing power more centrally and hierarchically through a national party led by the chief executive, permits leaders to govern more freely and vigorously and expeditiously, subject to majoritarian control in competitive elections.

3. The Madisonian has generally been the controlling system, despite the efforts of President and party to organize followings that could draw together the separate centers of power, and is the controlling system today.

4. Federalism immensely broadens the impact of the Madisonian system by establishing two levels of political competition, national and state; the greater the sectional feeling among the voters, the more the balance of two-party competition in many states is thrown out of articulation with the balance of competition in national party politics.

5. As part of this nation-state disarticulation, intensified by the Civil War and other "re-ordering" episodes, there have arisen numerous one-party districts in states and localities, the counter-effect of which on the national system has been to create centers of power in the congressional wing of each party at variance with the presidential leadership.

6. The four-party system is a result of these factors and of the non-congruence of the spectrums of popular attitudes on economic and way-of-life issues.

7. The Madisonian model, embodied today in the four-party system, has provided flexibility, accessibility, and representativeness in our governmental system, at the expense of leadership, vigor, speed, and effective and comprehensive national action.

So described, our Madisonian system seems to have a strikingly static quality. Quite so—for if politics is organized around the structure of offices, and if that structure has remained stable for 175 years, the patterns of political organization will be stable too. Still, the power of the offices has changed—most notably presidential power—and events like the Civil War and the Great Depression have transformed the party balance and some of the institutions too. No political system, as David Truman has reminded us, "is proof against decay and dissolution." Our task now must be to see the social and political changes that may transform both the governmental institutions and political organizations.

We must beware of simplistic notions of change in approaching this task. Orators like to talk about the winds of history and the currents of change, but these winds and currents often seem more blustery and choppy, swirling and eddying, than inexorably headed in a set direction. Not only do forces making for change interact unpredictably with solid or sluggish behaviors and structures but those forces often block rather than stimulate one another. The turbulent stream of change is forced out of a host of remote and immediate, direct and ancillary, personal and institutional forces.

The cause and impact of political change are especially hard to measure. The effect of an economic change, such as a drastic drop in farm prices, on social patterns, such as rural and urban population, is fairly predictable. But political change is the outcome of such a welter of economic, social, ideological, and institutional forces, combined with the erratic effect of personality and of sheer chance, that the political scientist must show a measure of humility in assessing political "trends." Still we must try, if only because the changes of the next ten years hold the possibility of major transformations in American politics.

The Cities and the Suburbs

America's own population explosion will have a major though not wholly predictable impact on politics. The sharp increase by 37 per cent in youngsters under 18 during the 1950's means that a huge group of young people will reach voting age during the 1960's. Although people in their twenties vote proportionately less than their elders, the sheer size of this added group will leave its mark on the voting tallies. The better educated—and the proportion of college graduates among young people is also rising rapidly—will be especially mobile socially, and volatile in their political affiliations and voting habits. Another consequence of a bigger voting population will be enlarged congressional and presidential constituencies, which may compel even more reliance on the mass media by presidential candidates, and less on individual favors, local personal organizations, and courthouse rings by congressional aspirants.

The distribution and nature of these present and future voters will be even more important than the size. We are nearing the end of an era during which the crucial political fact has been urbanization. The astronomical growth of the city is well known: a century ago only one out of four persons lived in communities of 2500 or over; now more than three out of every five are urbanites or suburbanites, and of those still dwelling in rural areas, over half were classified by the census as "rural non-farm." The cities are still growing, but the curve of growth has flattened out. Between 1950 and 1960 the population of cities above 50,000 grew about 13 per cent, of cities from 2500 to 50,000, a fraction more than that, while towns under 2500 and open country actually dropped a bit in population.

The era of heavy urbanization left a deep imprint on American politics. The cities were ports of disembarkation for immigrants from abroad and for Negroes moving up from the South. The cities gave the Democratic party a reservoir of votes that still serves as its base today. The cities, facing somewhat common problems and attitudes no matter where they were located, helped diminish the sectionalism that was such a pervasive factor in American national politics and helped realign our politics somewhat more along class lines. The cities, with their groups of "organized minorities," converted the winner-take-all mechanism of the electoral college into a key ingredient of presidential strategy and power. And the cities, with their heavy demands on expanded public services, introduced most Americans to the problems, burdens, and rewards of big government.

Now the explosion is in the suburbs. Again the growth is well known but still arresting. In the past dozen years suburban population has doubled—from about 23 million in 1950 to about 46 million today. Nearly a fourth of the population today lives in city suburbs. These suburbs are of many types, residential and industrial, low income, medium, and high, "old" and "new." But they represent, as compared with the rural and urban areas, a potential "third force" in American politics.

What will be the effect of this third force on the political life of the 1960's? Suburban voting is a good example of the situation where "inevitable trends" turn out to be not so inevitable after all. When the suburbs went heavily Republican during the Eisenhower years, it was theorized that exurbanites were being converted by the million into partisan Republicans. As the city people settled in with Republicans of the old suburbs, bought their homes and paid property taxes, fought for social status, joined suburban church groups and country clubs, they became assimilated into the Republican beliefs and systems of the community, it was supposed. In *The Ninth Wave* the novelist-political scientist Eugene Burdick invented the prototype of the converted suburbanite in Joe Wilson, formerly Jere Wilzwelski of Pittsburgh. As Joe changed from blast furnace stoker to junior executive, from downtown Pittsburgh to suburban California, from sedan to station wagon, he and his wife "put a Dewey sticker on their car and eagerly said harsh things about Truman, and finally even began to reconstruct their memory of Roosevelt and remembered him as a socialist, father of much-marrying children, fomenter of discontent, upsetter of the peace, and heard and believed that Eleanor had never loved him."

Other studies suggest, however, that the Joe Wilsons are not typical. Most suburbanites behave politically like other people: they respond mainly to parental influence. People bring their city beliefs with them, just as they do their city clothes, and the beliefs last longer. An analysis of Bucks County, Pennsylvania, showed that a heavy influx of workers in a new steel plant boosted the strength of the Democratic party fifteen fold, while Republican strength barely doubled. Not many Joe Wilsons here, evidently. A study of voting habits in heavily Republican Westport, Connecticut, revealed that most newcomers continued to vote for the same party, as did their parents. "If anything," the study said, "Democrats have retained more of their parental voting habits than have Republicans—and they have retained it both in the place of their prior residence and in Republican Westport itself." Often suburbanites *do* change parties or opinions, of course, but they may do so because of the changes that brought them to suburbia in the first place, such as a higher income or higher status aspiration rather than because of some magic impact of suburbia itself.

Neither the "conversion" theory nor the "transplantation" theory is wholly true, as Robert Wood has said. Everything depends on the nature of the suburb and of the people living and moving there, and these differ greatly. But one generalization about suburbia seems permissible. Suburbanites generally are less partisan than people elsewhere. They pride themselves on being independents, and they shy away from party activities and partisan associations. This may be due to the homogenizing impact of the suburb, or of the "middle position" of suburban white-collar people socially and economically, or of middle-class feelings about corrupt city bosses and machines.

This nonpartisanship bears a further look, for it may hold a clue to political change. What is it about parties that seems to attract suburbanites less than other groups? Could it be that they are less aroused by the issues which they feel have traditionally separated the two national parties? Since the divisive party issues have concerned economic matters—taxation, government spending, labor and farm policy, business policy, and the like—could it be that many suburbanites are relatively bored by the parties as they see them, not by partisanship in general?

Would a new kind of partisanship—that is, where parties took clear and competing positions on way-of-life issues such as foreign policy, education, government aid to the arts—evoke a highly partisan response, at least after a time? Evidence to answer this question is inadequate, but perhaps Eisenhower's election of 1952 is suggestive. After the Dewey-Truman battle of 1948 had been fought out on traditional party lines and the Democrats had won, the Republican party chose a man who was "above party," who accepted the welfare state but did not wish to extend it, who minimized economic issues and played up way-of-life issues such as "communism, corruption and Korea." Eisenhower's big pluralities in the suburbs were not just the automatic result of automatic Republican strength there; they were the results, in part, of decisions by the Republican party at the 1952 convention—especially its decision to choose the General over Taft, who could have been counted on to base his program mainly on the old partisan, or economic, issues.

If such was the case in 1952, it was nothing new. For generations political strategists have tried to shift from economic to way-of-life issues, or vice versa, according to their advantage. The Jeffersonian movement was an effort to change the bases of the national debate from those established by the Federalists to new ones of greater appeal to the potential Republican majority. Harrison in 1840 shifted the ground back to less economic issues. Bryan failed to establish the debate on his own terms in '96. Roosevelt in 1932 tried with some success to shift attention back from the way-of-life issues that had dominated the election of 1920 (League of Nations) and 1928 (Prohibition and Al Smith's urban style) to the economic issues so crucial in the third year of the depression. Kennedy's strength in the suburbs in 1960 may have reflected his success in immensely broadening the Democratic party's program as compared with 1948.

But our main conclusion from all this is not whether in a given instance the Democrats or Republicans have made a better mix of way-of-life and economic issues. It is that certain forces have produced in suburbia a large body of voters who may be somewhat more willing than others to respond to new party appeals and new political strategies. Political independents in the suburbs, more than any other group, may be responsive to bold leaders who stress issues of the mind and heart, and not just of the stomach.

Southern Politics: Rim and Heartland

For decades political analysts have been predicting a two-party South and Southerners have been perversely failing to vindicate the prophets. "In the South itself economic changes are tending to unsettle parties, the 'Solid South' is breaking," Ostrogorski said in 1910, and not an election comes along today that columnists do not see a party realignment just around the corner. But the heart of the South stays solid, at least in state politics. Today all the governors of the eleven Southern states are Democrats. All the United States Senators in these states except one are also Democrats, as are all but a handful of Representatives.

The trouble with the predictions has been their automatic conversion of economic and social forces into political trends. The basic forces have operated along the lines predicted: diversification of agriculture, growth and diversification of industry, urbanization and suburbanization, growth of industrial labor and of the white-collar class, migration of Negroes to the cities and outward to the North and West, the rise of a broader executive and white-collar class, some of it recruited from the North. The South, in short, has been caught up in the same basic forces as the North. "By and large," a sociologist says, "the class structure of the South has become more similar to that of the remainder of the United States. The relatively simple stratification of an agrarian society has been replaced by the more complex stratification of an urbanized industrial society. Also the differences in social mobility have been levelled off." But somehow these forces have had a delayed impact on politics. Labor has not been heavily unionized, Negroes have not been strongly organized, extension of the vote has been stubbornly resisted.

We can understand Southern politics better if we think of at least two Souths, and of at least four parties. Parts of the rim of the South have been competitive in presidential elections for many years. In 1928, and again in 1952, 1956, and 1960, Florida, Virginia, and Tennessee voted for Republican presidential candidates; Texas did the same, except in 1960. The mountain areas of Virginia, North Carolina, and Tennessee have been sending Republicans to Congress almost continuously since Reconstruction days. More recently Republican strength has spread from the mountains to other parts of the rim, especially urban areas. Republican candidates for Congress won in St. Petersburg, Dallas, and Alexandria or suburban Washington in 1960. The fact that Nixon almost rivaled Eisenhower's vote-drawing power in the South suggests that presidential Republicanism is in the South strongly, and to stay.

The Deep South, or heartland, is quite different. Georgia, Arkansas, South Carolina, Mississippi, and Alabama have never voted for a Republican candidate for President, and Louisiana has done so only once (Eisenhower in 1956). Republican congressional candidates from heartland rural districts still do not have a chance; Republicans may win a few hundred or even a few thousand votes at best. These are the valiant souls who run; often there is no Republican candidate at all. Eighty-three southern congressional districts were uncontested in 1958. State and local offices are also completely monopolized by Democrats. But the black belt knows how to revolt, even against Democrats. South Carolina, Mississippi, Alabama, and Louisiana deserted Truman in 1948 to vote for the States' Rights ticket. Mississippi in 1960 elected a slate of unpledged or "free" electors who voted for Senator Harry Byrd for President; about half of Alabama's electors did the same.

The chief difference between rim and heartland concerns the place of the Negro. The politics of the Black Belt (which of course is not coterminous with state boundaries) is still mainly the politics of race, while rim areas and the cities have become more entangled in the issues that grip most of the rest of the nation. The rim states will probably follow the trends of the border states of Missouri, Kentucky, West Virginia, and Maryland, which are still influenced by race issues without being dominated by them. As the border states become less and less like the South, politically and culturally, John H. Fenton has said, and more and more like the Middle West, the South becomes increasingly akin to the border states of yesteryear. "There is good reason to believe that the Border States represent a political and cultural model that the South is destined to copy." But not the Deep South—at least for some time. The Truman civil rights program and the Supreme Court's desegregation decisions sharpened the omnipresent feelings of Deep Southerners on the place of the Negro, and drew much of the state and local political struggle back into the orbit of race. Despite all the uproar over voting in the South, and the passage of federal legislation, Negro voting in the Black Belt remains minuscule; in some counties no Negro ever votes.

The future of Southern politics turns mainly on developments in three critical areas—the Democratic Black Belt, the cities and industrialized areas, and to a lesser extent, the mountain Republican districts. Barring a great upheaval, the mountain areas and the Black Belt will remain bastions of their respective parties. It is in the cities that the future will be fought out.

With their more mixed populations, the cities at present offer some hope to each party. Presidential Republicans can win big votes for candidates like Eisenhower and Nixon in Southern cities, especially in the suburbs, but congressional Republicans can win only a few congressmen and an occasional Senator. Congressional Democrats still gain virtually all the seats from the cities, and although their easy superiority is threatened, they can take comfort from the fact that the type of congressional Republican who occasionally wins is conservative politically and hence a likely recruit for the Democratic-Republican coalition in Congress. The presidential Democrats see their old predominance in Southern cities under siege by the presidential Republican party, and they are failing to mobilize the Negro and labor potential, but they are still able to combine enough rural votes to win heartland electors in presidential elections.

The problem is at root the familiar one of disarticulation between

national and Deep South politics. With their safe seats and their
influence with state legislatures, Southern congressional Democrats
can maintain the non-competitive, low-voting enclaves in which they
thrive, and from which they extract seniority for use in Washington.
They stoutly resist the intrusion of issues that might re-align voting
in their districts on a more national and less local (essentially race)
basis. They "keep the feds out" by maintaining personal organizations and by contending that the state parties are wholly separate
from the national Democratic party by rule and custom; by limiting
the main contest to the primary elections instead of the general; by
scheduling "off-year" elections; and through other devices. It is the
old dilemma: state politics cannot find a healthy, competitive two-
party balance because of the impact of history; the national two-party
balance is kitty-corner to the state so that there is no easy harmoniz-
ing of the two sets of party forces. Quite the contrary, the national
presidential party balance keeps the Southern state parties out of
balance, and the latter imbalance sharpens tension between the
Democratic presidential and congressional parties in Washington.

The future of southern politics turns on two Souths, and on the
relation between them. One South—the urban and rim part—is moving steadily into the two-party mainstream of American national
politics. Its people are voting more in terms of social class and economic divisions and less on the basis of older regional and racial
issues. This sector offers a promising source of votes to Republican
presidential candidates and to the Republican congressional party;
much will depend on how Republican party strategists deal with
these forces. The rural areas of the Southern heartland belong to
the congressional Democrats and will continue to do so for some
time; the real question is how soon they will split away from the
presidential Democrats for good. Standing somewhat to the side is
the Southern Negro who has broken out of his rural and racial
ghetto; he is politically in limbo, while he studies the presidential
parties for their civil rights promises and performance. He represents
the biggest moral and political opportunity to the strategists in both
presidential parties. What he does will turn largely on what they do.

Is Party Realignment Inevitable?

The future of the parties in the South raises the question of party realignment throughout the nation. Realignment is another one of those blessings or fates that we have long been promised but that never quite seem to materialize. Perhaps we would not recognize it if it did, for there is no agreed-on definition as to what we are talking about. Is party realignment a situation where the two parties in all the states are little replicas or miniatures, in policy and ideology, of the national parties? Or where all the liberals are Democrats and all the conservatives Republican in the states as well as nationally? Or where the two parties are competitive in each of the states and also nationally? Or where the leadership structure of the national parties is effectively integrated with the state parties? Or something else?

Behind these definitions lurks a major choice of alternatives. Students of politics differ over what shape they want the party system to take. Some value party unity or responsibility—that is, they want all the leaders and adherents of each major party, no matter what the area or office involved, to support roughly identical ideologies, programs, and policies, and to organize the party to govern on the basis of its ideology and program. A Republican legislator in Columbus, a Republican Senator from Kansas, a Republican Governor in New York State, a Republican President in Washington, would all stand for substantially the same things. They would work in harmony as fellow party members, and "Republican" would come to mean something—and essentially the same thing—in every part of the country and at every level of government. Advocates of this kind of party feel that it would lead to orderly, productive, unified, and responsible government.

Other students of politics prefer party competition. The trouble with party responsibility, they contend, is that many of the party's candidates could not follow the "party line" and still have a chance to win in certain parts of the country, or for certain offices. Republican candidates for governor of New York could not win on a conservative platform. Democratic aspirants for Congress in the Solid South could not win on a liberal platform set up in Washington. The great need, according to this view, is for the two parties to compete as vigorously as possible in every district and for every office. To permit candidates to compete, each party must be loose at the joints; it must let each candidate take the line that is most politically effective for each local situation, even if he must take a line at a tangent from the national party.

Since I can find values in both party responsibility and party competition, I propose a definition of party realignment that combines both concepts in modified form, though with more emphasis, perhaps, on the former. By party realignment here I mean a transformation of party leadership and rank-and-file support in such a way that the parties become broadly competitive for as many offices as possible, but not at the price of wrenching a local party out of the broad ideological or policy pattern of the national party. Under such a definition, a Republican congressional candidate in urban New York would place himself firmly in the presidential sector of his party, but would not be so liberal as to outflank the presidential Democrats on the left. By the same token, a Democratic candidate for the Senate in Alabama or New Hampshire would support a fairly mild brand of the New Deal or the New Frontier; but would not be so conservative as to outflank the Republicans on the right. Such a party system would permit flexibility to meet local conditions, but with a limit. It would not allow a local candidate or officeholder using the party label to follow so dissident a line that the image, the solidarity, and the integrity of the national party became tarnished.

If we define party re-alignment in this way, then—as a condition of affairs allowing each party both strength and flexibility to cope with a variegated society—what are the prospects for party re-alignment in the United States? One answer is that re-alignment has already begun. For the past 25 years, despite the Eisenhower victories, the presidential vote has been very close compared to the many lopsided majorities between 1900 and 1940. This presidential balance, moreover, seems to be based on a stable and rational division in the electorate. Since Al Smith's appeal to the cities in 1928 and Roosevelt's reforms of the 1930's, the Democratic party nationally has had special attraction for the lower-income, urban, industrial, liberal voters, the Republican for higher-income, rural-suburban, business, conservative voters. The contrast is not sharp, for both parties are middle-class in a middle-class society. But the differences have been significant. They have shown themselves in party platforms and in the presidential candidates themselves. Nothing has better symbolized those differences, as Paul David has noted, than the pairs of presidential candidates we have had since 1928, from Al Smith and Hoover in that year, to Landon and Roosevelt in '36, Dewey and Truman in '48, and Kennedy and Nixon in 1962.

Realignment has also been proceeding in the two-party politics of the larger states. States such as California, Pennsylvania, Illinois, and Michigan, which practically never elected Democratic governors in the first quarter of this century, have done so frequently since then; and Republicans have made some inroads on states once solidly Democratic. Almost all the larger states are highly competitive for governor today. Again this realignment meets our definition, for the gubernatorial candidates in the larger states appeal to roughly the same constellations of interests as do the presidential candidates of the respective parties. Such common support makes for at least potential harmony between the state and national parties, and hence for the national-state party articulation that was so disrupted by the Civil War, Bryanism, and the depression.

But this is not the whole story about party realignment, and the rest of the story is quite different. In most congressional elections and in many local contests, party competition is quite low, as we have seen, and the makeup of the local party is at variance with the national or even the state composition of the party. The safe seats represent a kind of party realignment in reverse. When state legislatures draw congressional districts that give one party a permanent majority, they are in effect diking off the national trends that otherwise would draw the congressional districts closer to the orbit of the presidential parties. The more competitive the congressional districts, on the other hand, the greater the party realignment as defined above.

Thus the erratic course of party realignment is more comprehensible if we view it in terms of four-party politics. The two presidential parties are the motors of national realignment, polarizing the electorate everywhere around their national doctrines and presidential candidates, moving into hitherto one-party areas and stimulating the minority party, as Roosevelt did in the Midwest in the 1930's and Eisenhower in the South in the 1950's. The congressional parties, on the other hand, fight to preserve the present alignment. Allied with local legislators and other officeholders who often have no party opponent at all, they preserve or expand the one-party districts that enable congressmen to resist the impact of the presidential party and the national competitive balance.

The decision of the Supreme Court in the Tennessee redistricting case, *Baker* v. *Carr,* and the remarkably quick follow-up in many lower courts, have raised hopes that rural over-representation in state legislatures, and later in Congress, can be corrected. Unhappily, rural power as such can be curbed without centrally affecting one-party districts. The target of the courts is the wide difference between the population of rural districts and of urban and suburban districts, while the basis of congressional party power is not so much rural over-representation (though this is a factor) as it is the one-party district. The courts could compel each state legislature to create congressional districts of mathematically equal size and still not meet the problem of the non-competitive district. The two problems are of course interrelated, and in the long run reducing rural over-representation should make for more competition. But how long this run will be will depend on a multitude of decisions by politicians as well as judges; certainly the congressional parties and their allies in the states will resist all the way.

Party realignment is not a trend; it is a struggle, with each side winning on its own favored ground.

There are other imponderables too. The present alignment and hopes for further realignment, turn on the supremacy of economic issues. But bread-and-butter matters are not the only basis of party alignment. Parties can also polarize around way-of-life issues—around foreign policy, church-state relations, civil liberties, federal aid to education, government and the arts, recreation and many others. Whether more congruence will develop between the economic and way-of-life policy alignments will depend on leaders and political decisions as well as on "basic trends."

So our answer to the question, "Is Party Re-alignment Inevitable?" must be no. In politics there are no inevitable trends; there are converging forces, some more powerful than others, and there are competing leaders, some more perceptive than others. Hence, political change comes unevenly, sporadically, with many a "backward" movement. Whether party realignment will proceed in the direction that its advocates want will depend in large part on decisions made by political leaders in the four parties, and on what the voters want or will accept.

This must also be our main conclusion about the other political changes discussed in this chapter. None is inevitable. The powerful forces of urbanization and suburbanization have been dulled in their political impact by the decisions of state legislators who maintained or extended district lines that augmented rural power. The Solid South is still a one-party area, despite the emigration of the Negro and the other economic and social trends that we noted, in part because there are intelligent men who want it to stay solid and so far have known how to help keep it that way. Politicians may spur the posing of new issues that operate at tangents to the economic questions around which realignment may be taking place.

There is, in short, the crucial element of choice, of decision. It is to the considered decisions of political leaders and parties that we must ultimately turn.

IV

Strategies
For
Tomorrow

12

WHICH REPUBLICAN PARTY?

*A*t breakfast in the Thunderbird Room of the Westward Ho Hotel in Phoenix, at the height of the 1960 campaign, Senator Barry Goldwater presented Vice-President Nixon to a thousand jubilant party workers. Meeting on their own special frontier, the Senator and the candidate were in good form. Nixon seemed overwhelmed by Goldwater's flowery introduction.

"Thank you very much, Barry," he said. "After that introduction, there really isn't anything I can add, because the sale, I hope, has already been made.

"But certainly I want you to know that Pat and I deeply appreciate the opportunity to attend this breakfast prior to the meeting that I understand will still be held outside in a little California dew this morning."

He had a special reason for talking with them before the public meeting. Nixon went on. "All of you are the people who make the party go. As Barry said. . . . I know this is the heart of the Republican party here. . . . It's going to be tremendously important not only to win this election at the national level, which we're hoping to do, but also to elect as many Congressmen and Senators as we can, and also to build the Republican party after this election and build it into a party which we know we can do if we work, and that's why I want all of you to know that I pledge to you that I shall talk to the Republican party all over the Nation, whenever the opportunity presents itself. . . . We have to strengthen our party. . . . We cannot do it unless we all stand together right up and down the line. . . .

"Frankly, if the time ever comes when I'm not proud of my party and proud of the candidates I'm running with, then, of course, the thing for me to do is to get out of the party. . . ."

Later in the day, at a Phoenix high school football stadium, Nixon addressed himself to a broader audience.

". . . . In this election it isn't enough to vote as your grandfather did or as your father did. It isn't enough simply to say, 'Well, this is my party label and I'm going to vote that way, because the other fellow has the same label. You've got to look beneath the labels. It isn't enough to vote on what somebody else tells you, someone who is the head of an organization to which you belong. . . ." And for the remaining weeks of the campaign Nixon pounded away at the theme of ignoring parties. The problem was bigger than party differences, he said again and again. "We've got to put America first and party second," he told a crowd in Wyoming. In his four-hour telethon on the eve of election he assured one questioner that if elected President he could work very well with a Democratic Congress, for "Congressmen, of course, are Democrats and Republicans, but they are Americans first. . . ." Yet everywhere he went he supported Republican candidates for Congress against Democrats, so that in this respect he was asking the voters to put party first.

The dilemma was not new. Nixon was facing the presidential candidate's eternal problem of holding the regulars firm while attracting independents and followers of the opposition party. But more than most candidates Nixon incorporated these contrasting

tendencies in his own political make-up and style. The story of
Nixon in 1960 was the story of a muffled struggle in the Republican
party expressed in the ambivalent political personality and mixed
tactics of one man.

At heart Nixon was a regular Republican who had entered national politics through the regular route of the congressional Republicans. His instinct was abrasively partisan; hence he could make statements about Democrats and the Democratic party that left his opponents livid. He was chosen Eisenhower's running mate in 1952
because he was a youthful and articulate spokesman for the congressional Republicans and the hero of the Hiss case; also he might help
appease the Taft forces. As Vice-President, however, he was increasingly drawn into the doctrine and operations of the White
House circle and hence into the orbit of the presidential party.
Within a few years he was saying freely that his role on the Hill
was to represent the President before the upper chamber, not to
mediate between White House and Senate. He was bored by his
formal duties in the Senate and welcomed every administrative and
diplomatic assignment that the President gave him. His conciliation
of Nelson Rockefeller in the struggle over the Republican party
platform, and his choice of an eastern internationalist, Henry Cabot
Lodge, as his running mate, put the final stamp on the image he
sought—that of a modern, traveled, internationalist, moderately liberal Republican.

But behind this image there was always the boy from Whittier.
Theodore White sensed this as he watched Nixon campaign in a
small Iowa village, passing through a file of flag-waving children,
stopping at the Harvest Festival. "For in such small towns he found
an echo," White said. "These people were his natural constituency,
his idiom their idiom. All the little anecdotes, the phrases ("Incidentally, now . . . Just listen to me now . . . You have to think
of the other fellow . . .") made him one of them. He was a small-
town boy and he understood them." Not surprisingly, it was in this
heartland of the Republican congressional party—Iowa, Nebraska,
Kansas, the Dakotas—that Nixon rolled up his biggest margins.

Caught between his small-town instincts for regular Republicanism and his politician's awareness of where the big voting blocs lay,
Nixon never made a clear strategic decision as to the conduct of his

campaign. He tried to appeal to independents as well as regulars, to Southern conservatives as well as Northern civil-rights supporters, to Goldwater stalwarts as well as Rockefeller Republicans. Hence at crucial points, when a decisive and dramatic act was called for, he was immobilized. This ambivalence lay behind his failure to act on Martin Luther King, his strange contortions on the Cuba issue. Above all, it made him look like a me-too candidate, aping much of the Democratic platform, without letting him present a really attractive program to urban and suburban independents.

Election Day, 1960, brought a temporary truce in campaign warfare between Democrats and Republicans, but it touched off a new stage in the old war between congressional and presidential Republicans. The issue of Kennedy and Nixon had hardly been decided when Goldwater attacked the Vice-President for his "me-too" campaign. "We who are conservatives will stoutly maintain that 1960 was a repeat performance of 1944 and 1948, when we offered the voters insufficient choices. . . ." Nixon, he said, had gambled the South for the industrial North.

While Nixon went home to California, Goldwater, Dirksen, and Halleck went back to their seats of minority power in Washington. They had four years to shape a winning strategy for the congressional Republicans.

The Congressional Party: Rearguard Strategy

Hostilities flared up between the presidential and congressional Republicans as soon as Congress convened in January 1961. Senator Javits urged his party to widen its appeal to urban voters, and Senator Kenneth B. Keating of New York, fearing that Goldwater might become the chief Republican spokesman, proposed a thirty-man "All-Republican committee" to shape party policy. Since its membership would include Eisenhower, Hoover, Nixon, and Lodge, and several Republican governors, along with senators and representatives, Keating hoped that the committee would be able to enunciate moderate, bipartisan policy for the two Republican parties.

The congressional Republicans would have none of this. They reacted to Keating's proposal as cooly as Johnson had responded to the Democratic Advisory Council years before. In contrast to the

Democratic leaders, Goldwater and his colleagues were able to block the presidential party's plan. Keating had to settle for a pyrrhic victory—a proposal by which Dirksen and Halleck would meet weekly with the national party chairman to discuss "the party's congressional policy." Full power over policy decisions would remain in congressional Republican hands. The presidential party protested in vain. A few weeks before leaving office, Eisenhower toasted Nixon in the White House, in the presence of Rockefeller and the congressional leaders, as "the head of the Republican party for the next four years," and the man who would "have my support and the support of all those who are here tonight." But after January 20, Eisenhower was back in Gettysburg, and Nixon back in California preparing for a strenuous battle for governor.

The congressional party now proceeded to take over the party machinery. Goldwater himself already headed the Senate campaign committee; chairman of the Congressional campaign committee was an equally conservative Republican, William E. Miller of upstate New York. A holdover from Nixon's campaign, Senator Thruston Morton of Kentucky, was still national chairman; soon Morton resigned and was replaced by Miller, who in turn was succeeded in the congressional committee by Representative Bob Wilson of California, another conservative. In assuming his new post Miller said that Republicans should be less concerned about their national "image" and should concentrate on winning congressional seats in 1962. "I think if we can minimize our concern about the big issues and concentrate on winning local elections we will be a lot better off." He discarded Morton's plan of using the national committee to serve as an oracle of policy guidance for Republicans. Technicians were brought over from the congressional committee to concentrate on congressional campaigns.

What chairman Miller was really saying was not that the party would put aside issues, but that these would be left to the leaders on the Hill. During early 1961 Goldwater was busy circulating manifestoes that defined the broad tenets of conservatism—a term that Goldwater, in contrast to Eisenhower and Nixon, was not afraid to use. In the House, Republican leader Halleck made clear that the congressional party would not be bound by the Republican party platform of 1960. He and his policy committee could speak for the party.

What were the tenets of this conservatism for the 1960's? Goldwater was explicit. Tax all incomes at the same rate, he urged, with liberal depreciation allowances. Reduce spending by withdrawing the federal government from welfare programs, and start no new programs if they called for increased taxes or deficit spending. Gradually end the farm-subsidy program so that farm prices could be determined on the free market. Block minimum wage increases because they would bring more unemployment, higher prices, and possible inflation. As for the aged, encourage profit-sharing and pension plans of employers by new and increased tax incentives.

In foreign policy Goldwater called for a mixture of intervention and withdrawal. Actively encourage captive peoples to revolt against communist rulers, he urged. In the event of a major revolt such as Hungary, confront Russia with an ultimatum forbidding intervention. If Russia rejects it, move American forces into the area. Make it clear that Russian use of long-range bombers or missiles would bring automatic retaliation in kind, leaving Moscow a choice between total destruction and local defeat. As for Cuba, eliminate the Castro government through an economic blockade and, if necessary, a naval blockade to keep out communist arms. On the other hand, Goldwater favored a drastic reduction in foreign economic assistance, limiting aid to military and technical help, and this only for nations openly aligned with the West against China and Russia. Disarmament was too risky, but the United States should stay in the United Nations, at least as long as it remained just a "debating society."

Like all good ideologists, Goldwater and his fellow congressional Republicans had a clear idea as to the relation of policy aims and governmental means. The main instrument of their whole program was states' rights. Goldwater stood for a cramped interpretation of the Tenth Amendment: powers not specifically delegated to the federal government in the Constitution, should be reserved to the states. Welfare activities, assistance to depressed areas, aid to education, housing subsidy programs, should be turned over to the states where they were not abolished outright. The states should pass "right to work" laws and restrict labor's use of political power. Along with states' rights, the congressional Republicans called for restriction of presidential power. In particular they saw the President's wide use of executive orders and executive agreements as inserting big government through a constitutional back door.

Equipped with this doctrine, entrenched in the machinery of Congress, the Republican congressional party spoke in 1961-62 for "respectable conservatism" in America. Goldwater was flanked by such Senators as Styles Bridges of New Hampshire (until his death), Karl E. Mundt of South Dakota, Homer E. Capehart of Indiana, Bourke Hickenlooper of Iowa, and by such Representatives as John Taber of New York, Clarence J. Brown of Ohio, Richard M. Simpson of Pennsylvania, Leo E. Allen of Illinois. These men in turn aroused and reflected the views of organized conservatism. They had editorial support from the *Indianapolis Star*, the *Chicago Tribune*, and the Hearst papers. They drew ideological nourishment from the *Reader's Digest*, the *American Legion Monthly*, the *National Review*, and from book publishers such as Devin-Adair and Henry Regnery. Their columnists numbered Raymond Moley, David Lawrence, Westbrook Pegler, and a host of locally known pundits, their commentators Fulton Lewis, Jr. and many an economic and religious fundamentalist preaching over the radio on Sunday.

"John T. Flynn is their Milton," Clinton Rossiter wrote of the conservative groups supporting the congressional Republicans, "Governor Bracken Lee their tax-resisting Pym (or Poujade), Vivien Kellems their Diana, Senator McCarthy their defunct and tarnished Galahad, William F. Buckley, Jr. their favorite Yaleman, Joseph M. Mitchell of Newburgh, New York, their ideal bureaucrat, the Intercollegiate Society of Individualists and Young Americans for Freedom their weapons with which to smash the tyranny of campus collectivism; General MacArthur the one man of the old generation they would have been happy with as President, Senator Goldwater the one man of the new generation to whom they seem willing to give the same kind of impassioned allegiance." Despite this passion, most of these conservatives tried to steer a wide berth from the Radical Right: the John Birch Society, General Walker, and like fanatics.

Despite this strength-in-depth, the congressional Republicans were the weakest of the four national parties during the first two years of the Kennedy Administration. To be sure, the Republicans as a whole were a strong minority numerically, but the congressional party could consistently marshal only three-quarters of the Republican membership in the House and less than this in the Senate. While the Republican congressional leaders held high ranking committee memberships, these men on the minority side of the congressional party suffered from the usual ambivalence of leadership: Halleck had to make occasional concessions to moderate Republicans to maintain party unity, and Dirksen, faced with a re-election campaign in his big swing state of Illinois, wandered far enough off the reservation to say kind things about the President. Goldwater crisscrossed the country to rally the forces of conservatism, but he could not begin to match the Kennedys' impact on public opinion.

In combination with the congressional Democrats, however, the Republicans maximized their power. Each party buttressed the other. In the Senate the congressional parties' coalition won all seven contests over civil rights issues in 1961, including the filibuster and federal aid to desegregating school districts. In the House the coalition killed the general school aid bill, defeated three public measures, and stopped two presidential proposals to reorganize regulatory agencies. On other matters, especially extension and broadening of New Deal "bread-and-butter" programs, the coalition failed. Its real score, however, lay not in measures passed or killed on the House or Senate floor but in those that never received full consideration in both chambers—medical care through social security, overhauling the tax structure, major civil rights measures—or that emerged in such debilitated form as to be unrecognizable.

Only one major issue potentially divided the Democratic and Republican congressional parties: civil rights. Northern Republicans, no matter how conservative, usually paid at least lip service to the notion of Negro rights. This was, after all, once a great cause in Northern rural and small-city areas, and Negro groups have some political influence there. But on this possibly divisive issue there was a magic elixir of harmony: states' rights. School integration was desirable, Goldwater said, but only if brought about by the states. So were Negro enfranchisement and other extensions of civil rights. On this formula the congressional Democrats were happy to settle.

Still, the congressional Republicans suffered from a heavy disadvantage. Its "image" was entirely negative. Aside from Goldwater's proposals for the liberation of the satellites, it was not clear what the party was for. "I would not say that the climate of the Republican congressional leadership is anti-intellectual," said Roscoe Drummond in the *New York Herald Tribune*. "It is just anti-idea, anti-initiative, anti-do anything." Was there any greater future for the party than to serve simply as a drag or anchor on presidential Democrats—or even the presidential Republicans? Was the politics of the congressional party never to be more than the politics of the rearguard?

Some of the activists in the party were contemplating these questions as 1964 drew nearer. But in four-party combat much depends on the strategies of the three other contestants.

The Presidential Party: Strategy of the Center

Typically, in a country with a two-party system, the "in" party bested at the polls retires from office with disappointment and perhaps bitterness, but with two great consolations. Now it can watch the "outs" try to deliver on all the outlandish promises they made on the hustings, and it can subject them to the same scorching criticism it has had to suffer during its own years in office. In the United States, however, there is something pathetic about the defeat of a presidential party. It does not shift smoothly to the opposition role; it disintegrates and disappears.

Such was the fate of the presidential Republicans at the end of 1960. The great party that had lost by a hair in 1960, that had rolled up a far bigger total of votes, cumulatively, than had the Democrats in the four presidential elections since Roosevelt, the party of great patriots from Lincoln to Eisenhower, as its orators said—suddenly this party was a shrunken thing without leadership, without a national rostrum, without structure, and soon the only piece of machinery left in its possession, the Republican national committee, was taken over by the congressional party, as we have seen.

But if the leadership had suddenly been decapitated, the great body of the party still lived, ready to sprout new leaders when the time came. And the party possessed by 1960 as coherent, specific, and positive a set of doctrines as it had owned perhaps since the post-Civil War days. These doctrines were embodied in President Eisenhower's proposals to Congress, the Republican national platform of 1960, and Nixon's campaign speeches the same year. Perhaps they had found their most cogent, forthright and prophetic form a year earlier, however, in "Decisions for a Better America," the report of an Administration-sponsored "Republican Committee on Program and Progress," under the chairmanship of a young business executive, Charles H. Percy. Composed of 40 leading citizens and experts, the committee was grouped into four task forces: on the impact of science and technology, on national security and peace, on human rights and needs, and on economic opportunity and progress. There were only two members of Congress on the committee, Dirksen and Halleck; this was intended to be emphatically a presidential party manifesto. And it was.

". . . Republicans believe in a central government vigilantly alert to the needs of the people and strong enough to defend the people, to help keep the economy in balance, and to make certain that a life of dignity is within the reach of every American . . . ," the report declared. "Government has a direct obligation, not only to provide the means for decent living and adequate care for those who are displaced by the changing needs of the economy to refit themselves for useful work. Every individual should have access to all the education he can put to use; the future welfare of the nation demands nothing less. This is a matter for concern and for action by the Federal Government. . . . The Republican Party stands for a strong, responsive Federal Government, opening and advancing economic opportunities for the American people . . . using its strength to ward off inflation and depression . . . restraining and disciplining any who use their power against the common welfare . . . regulating wisely when the national interest demands it. . . ."

There were, to be sure, the usual tributes to the American people as individuals, to self-reliance, preservation of state and local government, and the like. But these traditional concepts were balanced by a new emphasis on government, especially the national government. The preface said, for example, "The Republican Party believes strongly that self-reliance is the foundation of individual dignity— and no less strongly that you cannot talk of self-reliance or abstract dignity to people who are hungry, or out of work, or sick, or without the means to get the education or skills they need to support them- selves." And the more the report turned to concrete needs, the more it called for an active, wide-ranging federal role. If the report was balanced in its rhetoric, it was liberal on specifics.

This acceptance of government was enough alone to make the congressional party blanch. But in foreign policy the report went even further. It embraced bipartisanship fully and was intent only on improving the administration of it. On the economic front the committee favored "economic mutual assistance and development programs that meet the test of contributing to world-wide freedom; that are subject to meticulous country by country periodic reap- praisal; and that are progressively shifted to more economical bases of extended private investments and loans with political and finan- cial guarantees. . . ." The committee favored "a continuation of the policy of gradual, selective and reciprocal reductions of the barriers to a freer exchange of goods and services among free nations." And on the side of good will and tourism, the committee even urged the elimination of the fingerprint requirement for visa applicants.

This acceptance of the role of the federal government could prove decisive for the prospects of the Republican presidential party. The downfall of the Republican party in the 1930's was precipitated in large part by the refusal of Hoover and his colleagues and the busi- ness leaders of the day to use the right methods to attain the ends they wished. They meant well: they wanted to help the unemployed; they were willing for state and local governments to help the dis- tressed; some of them made personal sacrifices of their own. They simply stuck to the rigid principle that certain things, like unem- ployment insurance or old-age pensions, should not be undertaken by the national government. The Republican party is still wounded by the crippling effect of that doctrine. Political ends and govern- mental means are inseparable; Republican strategy and the govern- mental institutions through which Republicans operate cannot be divorced. The repudiation of the notion that federal action is auto- matically and intrinsically bad means that the Republicans are now in as free a position as the British Conservatives to contend with the opposition, not over whether federal power should be used, but how it should be used.

But a modernized doctrine, while necessary to win elections and govern the nation, is not adequate. What are the strategic choices facing the presidential party in trying to win the Presidency?

The problem is an acute one for the party today, for the omens of 1960 were not happy. A careful study of the returns by four University of Michigan analysts concluded that 1960 was a "reinstating election" in that, after losing two presidential contests largely because of Eisenhower's personal popularity and apparent non-partisanship, the Democrats once again drew to the polls and to their candidate the Democratic party-identified vote that had been greater than the Republican party-identified vote even during the Eisenhower years. The 1960 election was largely a straight party fight in which the Democrats mobilized one of their typical mid-century majorities. The photo-finish election results concealed this re-instatement because Kennedy's Catholicism lost him more votes than it gained him. "After two consecutive 'deviating' elections won at a presidential level by the minority party," the Michigan investigators sum it up, "the 1960 election reinstated the Democratic party. But short-term forces generated by the immediate 1960 situation once again favored the Republicans on balance. . . ." The candidates anticipated this possibility, of course—Kennedy in running as a Democrat and Nixon in appealing to independents.

Such an analysis would seem to darken the prospect of the presidential Republicans for 1964. For by that time, surely, President Kennedy would have largely erased the "Catholic" image by his actions in the White House, and the Republicans would lose the benefit even of this dubious advantage. And they would confront the further difficulty of trying to defeat an activist presidential incumbent—a feat that has not been accomplished in this century and, depending on one's definition of activism, was never accomplished even in the 19th century. Still, several opportunities may offer themselves.

One lies in the economic situation. Republicans are doubtless correct in holding that there is no point in trying to "out-promise" the Democrats on economic liberalism, or to try to outflank the Democrats on the left. The Democratic presidential party is too solidly rooted in the lower-income urban groups, labor unions, and ethnic minorities, the Republicans too historically tied to business, professional and white-collar groups to make Theodore Roosevelt's initial strategy of 1912 feasible in the 1960's. But the question of managing the economy is a very different one. The economic responsibilities of the federal government are now so massive and complex that any administration today is riding a skittish mount. The party that exploited the "Hoover depression" so mercilessly would be all the more vulnerable to riposte in the event of widening stagnation in the economy, or a real downturn. While much would depend on how the presidential Republicans played the issue, they would not face their 1932 inhibitions about promising effective action by the federal government.

A second opportunity is organizational. After every defeat, and especially after 1960, GOP statisticians computed how few votes the party needed in each ward to eke out a victory. Between elections business executives prowl the corridors of national and state party headquarters and make suggestions for organizational improvement. They have urged that fund-raising techniques be modernized, party staff and field forces increased, publicity improved, registration programs expanded, new membership clubs set up. For a party bursting with the kind of talented administrators who have, for example, put community charity on a businesslike basis, the Republicans are curiously backward in party organization, except in a few states like Ohio and Connecticut. Their main trouble, like that of the Democrats, lies in the personal organizations that often push the party organizations aside. The greatest operational test of the Republican presidential party will be its capacity to strengthen and centralize its internal organization in order to create a truly national party strongly and widely based in the communities.

Actually, this is more than an organizational test—it is a test of party-building, a test of whether the Republicans can make their party fit to win elections without military heroes, and fit to govern. Recognizing this need, leaders of the presidential party took the initiative in the summer of 1962, at a meeting with General Eisenhower at Gettysburg, in establishing an All-Republican Conference, designed to foster party unity through regular meetings and statements, and in setting up a Republican National Citizens Committee, aimed at providing a mechanism through which independent voters and dissident Democrats could support Republicans without embracing the party. Predictably, Halleck and other elected Republican leaders in Congress were lukewarm toward the idea, and Goldwater attacked the citizens group as a splinter group run "by the same people who caused most of our present party troubles" by straying from the party's "traditional principles." Still, a clearer voice in itself would not be enough. Everything would depend on the follow-up at the grass roots—on superior organization, better recruitment of candidates, more effective fund-raising.

A third opportunity is the biggest and most challenging of all: a deliberate effort to change the issue on which presidential elections are fought. No matter how much the presidential party builds its organization, it cannot come to grips with the presidential Democrats unless it can shift the axis of political combat. This is precisely what the Eisenhower forces did in 1952 when they played down the traditional bread-and-butter issues and played up emotional way-of-life issues such as "Korea, Corruption, and Communism." Eisenhower's great failure as a party leader was in not replacing these issues, which were rather ephemeral, with constructive appeals that could outlast his party headship. In hoarding his personal popularity he changed durably and decisively neither the image nor the substance of the presidential Republican party.

Can the presidential Republicans re-direct the thrust of national debate so that way-of-life issues might play a larger part and give the party a more secure footing in the decade ahead? The task seems formidable. The issue of domestic communism is less intense than a decade ago, and it is an issue that could kick back dangerously against the presidential party if it gained power, as in the assault of McCarthy against Eisenhower. Corruption is a perennial issue that stains each party's image impartially. To develop and pose dramatically new way-of-life issues would be difficult with a Democratic President dominating the news media from the White House. And the party is badly handicapped by the lack of a clear voice; here again the opposition presidential party pays the penalty of lacking the machinery of party discussion and national publicity.

The most hopeful issue for the Republicans is civil rights, especially if the Democrats cannot deliver on their campaign promises. The Republicans have at least three choices: they can return to their Civil War principles through a strong civil rights program

aimed at the voteless Negroes in the South; or they might choose
the congressional party tactic of leaving civil rights to the states,
while playing on Southern whites' racial fears; or they might adopt
an intermediate tactic of appealing to white Southern businessmen,
white-collar workers, and other urban and suburban voters with a
moderate civil-rights program that would keep to the right of the
presidential Democrats. The difficulty with the first tactic is that
civil rights have become inseparably linked with welfare issues, and
since the presidential Democrats have made a strong appeal to
Negroes north and south on both civil rights and economic welfare
and opportunity, Republicans would be hard put to outbid their opponents on this issue. The second choice would be retrogressive and
dangerous; as White has said, it could "only envision a new and
triple alliance between the Midwest farm belt, the racists of the Old
South and those political forces in the Northern suburbs that more
and more seek to exclude Negroes from their neighborhoods and
segregate them in the old core cities." Such a tactic would be out of
the question for a national party seeking at least some support in all
major groups. The intermediate choice of a moderate civil rights
policy that would attract the rising business elements of the South
would seem the most appropriate for the presidential Republicans
and for effective competition between the national presidential
parties.

For on this issue as on many others the presidential party has
a chance to serve the vital role of the great party of balance and consolidation. If there is a need for Democratic innovation, there is also
a need for Republican re-evaluation and synthesis. A period of rapid
change in governmental policy can well be followed by a period of
testing and taking stock. Nations, like people, must catch breath.
It was one of Eisenhower's failings that he could not dramatize the
impressive job that the Republicans did in the 1950's of retaining,
assimilating, and making acceptable the reforms of the previous 20
years. This is an honorable role, and one that would help the Republicans serve as a viable alternative to the Democrats, and as a
constant threat to them.

Can the presidential Republicans play this role? Can they find
their own vital center where they can shape a moderate and popular
alternative to the Democrats? Can they find in suburbia and in the

middle-class masses enough support for an enlightened conservative opposition? Can they press the Democrats so much on economic issues, and at the same time move ahead on way-of-life issues—as the British Conservatives did on the Common Market, for example— as to re-assert their old-time superiority? Their long-run prospects depend on whether after years of fluctuating between the Theodore Roosevelts and the Willkies on the one hand, and the Hardings and Goldwaters on the other, they can find their own mind, or soul. And this depends, in the short run, on how the presidential Republicans deal with the congressional party, in a system of four-party politics.

Coalition and Combat

One of the ablest strategists of the congressional Republican party is Senator Karl E. Mundt of South Dakota. For Mundt the frail and largely negative alliances of Democratic and Republican conservatives in Congress are not enough. For years he has urged "political engineering" that would enable the nation's conservatives in both parties to vote and govern together. Only in this way, Mundt says, can the liberals and radicals in both parties be stopped from socializing and bankrupting the nation. Mundt has offered a five-point strategy.

First, party re-alignment. "Let's get the people who think alike in this country and who think conservatively and in terms of a modification and limitation of the powers of the Central Government . . . into some kind of political party or political apparatus or political association or political instrumentalities so that they can vote alike for the same candidate on the same ticket regardless of what the party label is or where they live geographically." Mundt wants "Southern Democrats and rural Republicans" to vote together not only for equally conservative candidates for Congress, but for one conservative candidate for President.

Second, amend the Electoral College. For years Mundt and many Senate colleagues in both parties have denounced the winner-take-all machinery of the Electoral College and have urged Congress to "destroy the dictatorial power" of "a few huge American cities and

a handful of big so-called 'pivotal' States" that control conventions
and presidential elections. The South Dakotan has proposed a constitutional amendment, co-sponsored by Goldwater, Thurmond,
McClellan and other leaders of the two congressional parties, under
which presidential electors would be chosen in single-elector districts to be established by the state legislatures. A majority of electoral
votes would be necessary for election in the electoral college; if no
majority was achieved, the House and Senate would choose the
President in joint assembly with each member having one vote and
a majority of votes being required for election.

". . . One sodden drunk can fall off a park bench in Battery
Park of New York City," Mundt likes to say, "and hitting the
ground wake up and stagger and stumble into a voting booth on
election day, not knowing where he is, and, in the heat of the
election booth, to keep from falling on his face in his drunken
stupor, reach for an election lever as a support and accidentally pull
the election lever down, thereby determining the entire outcome of
a national presidential election. Do you all fully realize that this can
actually happen? That one vote cast by Mr. Stumble Bum in New
York City can put in action 45 electoral votes which mean more
than all of the votes cast by intelligent people voting unanimously
in 12 or 13 separate states of the United States. . . ."

Third, revise state election laws to "make it easier for people to
cross party lines." Since he seeks a bipartisan coalition of conservatives, the Senator wants state legislatures to relax primary election
requirements so that a Georgia Democrat, for example, could vote
in a Republican primary without losing his standing as a Democrat.
Here again Mundt's aim is unerring. Just as most liberals wish to
make parties more unified and competitive, Mundt prefers a loose
set of coalition arrangements that would maximize conservative
power. In the same vein, Mundt has praised James Byrnes of South
Carolina, Allen Shivers of Texas, and Harry Byrd of Virginia for
deserting the Democratic presidential candidate and supporting
Eisenhower.

Fourth, restore the two-thirds rule in national conventions. Mundt
feels that Roosevelt's elimination of the two-thirds rule in the 1936
Democratic convention was a milestone in the trend toward urban,

radical control of American politics. The South was stripped of one of its great defenses against the "banana-bunch" voters, as Mundt calls them, who "group themselves in ethnic, vocational, left-wing, or other pressure groups" to cast aside the "fine folks of the old South." If conservative Democrats could get the two-thirds rule restored, he thinks, Republicans might establish the rule for their own convention (for the first time). Both conventions might also destroy the unit rule, under which, Mundt feels, big-city delegates can control whole state delegations.

Finally, strengthen Republicanism in the Deep South. Mundt is less confident about this proposal because of the entrenched Democracy of the deep South. Still, he can hope: "If 500 of the most prominent Democratic families in South Carolina, for instance," he told a meeting of South Carolina bankers, "were to register Republican within any given month and publicize it widely, you could go far toward rewriting the future pattern for America. Thousands of your fellow citizens would be glad to follow such an example. There are ways that free men can escape from the trap you're in."

Is Mundt's dream realizable? Can conservatives in both parties be rallied and united in a coalition program to "escape from the trap" of widening urban control of politics, and the "banana-bunch domination" that comes with it? Certainly Mundt has a far better grasp of the relations of ends and means than many of his fellow conservatives and many liberals. But do the congressional Republicans have the political resources to do the job?

Mundt evidently sees two possible tactics for conservatives. The first would be to capture control of one of the national party conventions, and either establish the two-thirds rule, in order to block the nomination of liberals, or even gain the nomination of a conservative like Goldwater or Senator Richard Russell. This tactic looks almost hopeless. The convention is the arena of the party liberals and moderates; the cards are stacked against the congressional parties. Even if a Goldwater won the nomination, how could he rally the conservatives in both parties? Mundt can easily tell Southern Democrats that they should vote for a Goldwater or even an Eisenhower. Could he so easily urge South Dakota Republicans to vote for a Russell or a Byrd? And if he did, how many would cross

party lines? The power of ideology is great, but so is the power of
entrenched party conviction, as the polls of the Survey Research
Center have shown.

Mundt's second tactic is more subtle. He would change the
Electoral College not only to play down the "urban gerrymander"
in it, but to enable conservatives to align behind a conservative candidate in a presidential election in Congress. Under this formula,
the present winner-take-all systems would be dropped, and the district system set up. The latter would break down the present party
control of the designation of electors; instead local conservative
leaders could set up electors supporting a conservative candidate
for President (if both of the regular candidates were liberals). The
state legislature could be relied on to maintain or set up a districting
system that would over-represent rural voters. Out of this effort,
adapted to the situation in each state, would hopefully emerge an
electoral vote for a conservative candidate big enough to deprive
either of the presidential party candidates of an Electoral College
majority. The contest would be thrown into Congress, with each
member voting on his own. In this milieu—so significantly remin-
iscent of the selection of a premier in a parliamentary system—a
united bloc of conservative representatives and senators could play
the presidential parties off against each other and yield their votes
only for the election of a conservative in either party.

This, too, is an old dream, but Mundt's "political engineering"
might make it more feasible. Perhaps such a strategy could have
won in 1948 if more careful preparations had been made, including
the Electoral College change. Even so, such a strategy is always a
gamble depending as it does on the failure of any candidate to receive a majority in the Electoral College. It would intensify tension
between the congressional and presidential Republican parties, and
threaten future coalition arrangements between these two parties in
Congress. It would seem a reckless strategy, too, especially for conservatives, for it would plunge the country into a traumatic period
of confusion, uncertainty, and perhaps political chaos.

Some might contend that conservatives deserve one chance to
prove their argument that given the opportunity to elect a good
dependable conservative of the Goldwater type, a great majority of
the American people would do precisely this. Harding in 1920 and

Hoover in 1928, they remind us, were the two most successful Republican vote winners in this century. If nations were laboratories or courts of appeals, perhaps the bipartisan conservative coalition should have such an opportunity to make its clear ideological appeal. But Americans would hesitate to try the experiment; they would fear that the excessive polarization of the voters might disrupt the normal and healthy spectrum of American voting. Moderate conservatives in particular might fear that a conservative coalition regime would be followed by a powerful swing of the pendulum back to the left. And the time is neither 1920 nor 1928.

A coalition of the congressional parties to elect a conservative President seems doomed to fail. What alternative do they have? Their alternative is to stand pat, to continue their present rearguard tactics of delaying and devitalizing the programs they abhor. It is in this kind of political combat that the congressional parties maximize their power; it is for this that they are best equipped to battle. The time has long since passed when a congressional party could dominate the government, as the congressional Democrats did in the 1850's and the congressional Republicans in the late 1860's. This is sour advice for a party that would like, in its wilder moments, to restore McKinleyism at home and liberate satellite nations abroad. But there is no other choice, and the congressional parties might be all the more effective in concentrating their energies on rearguard operations instead of splurging them in a great presidential spree.

The more the congressional Republicans want to indulge in presidential politics, in short, the more they must coalesce with the party closest to them that was begotten and organized for such politics, the presidential Republicans. To serve as that party's collaborator on the right, to moderate its policies, to sustain and exploit the symbols and voting support of "regular Republicanism"—this is a limited but still honorable role for the congressional party. And it enables the Republican conservatives to maximize their opposition to what, after all, remains as their main political and policy adversary, the presidential Democrats.

The main question is not whether the party of Goldwater and Mundt and Halleck needs the party of Eisenhower and Rockefeller and Cooper, but the reverse. To what extent can the presidential Republicans coalesce with a party that faults their image as a

moderate, responsible opposition and handicaps their appeal to urban
and suburban groups? Until 1964 the presidential Republicans will
have no choice but coalition with the congressional party, against
the Kennedy Administration. They will have no agreed on leadership, and no unified strategy. Their presidential aspirants will be
busy traveling the country and reassuring gatherings of the party
faithful as to their safe, solid, and devout Republicanism. But once
the Republican convention of 1964 has chosen its man, the party
scene will change swiftly. The nominee will install his own national chairman, enunciate his own program, appeal to moderate
Republicans, independents, and independent Democrats. Remembering FDR's "Martin, Barton & Fish," and Truman's lambasting of
the congressional Republicans, he will try to hold his congressional
party in check. If victorious, the Republican candidate will deal with
the congressional party from a position of power; if the latter has
also won a majority of Congress and hence control of committee
chairmanships, the Republican President will find much of his
program stymied or watered down. He might find it easier to work
through a coalition with congressional Democratic leaders, as Eisenhower did from 1954 to 1960.

And so the cycle of four-party politics will go on. In the long
run, the congressional Republican dream of glory—control of the
presidential party and capture of the White House—might come
about through some stray combination of circumstances, through
some fancy political engineering, or through some national ordeal
that left Americans frustrated by centrist politics and hungering
for change and movement—even movement to the rear. But the short-
run hopes of the party lie in continued exploitation of the Madisonian politics of bargain and veto. Opportunism is the rule of the
day. Clarence Brown of Ohio, high-ranking member of the Rules
Committee, has said, "Sometimes I coalesce. Sometimes I don't."
This could be the temporary slogan of the congressional Republicans.

13

THE DILEMMA
of the DEMOCRATS

In March, 1956, there occurred on the Senate floor one of those complex struggles that confuse the tourists in the balcony and pare the newspapermen in the press gallery down to a hard core of the most conscientious. Only with the passage of time can we see that the episode was a milestone in four-party combat and was uncannily prophetic of the 1960 election outcome.

In the center of the struggle was a young Bostonian with a deceptively boyish air, Senator John F. Kennedy of Massachusetts. At this time Kennedy was known in Washington as a likable, freshman Senator, as the son of a millionaire who had served in high posts under Roosevelt, and as the victor over the "unbeatable" Henry Cabot Lodge, Jr. in 1952, the year of triumphant Eisenhower Republicanism. Before that contest Kennedy had served six years in the House but had not achieved a clear, political identity; he was a Fair Dealer on bread-and-butter matters, but he had criticized President Truman on foreign policy and he had deserted the presidential party line on a number of key issues. In the Senate he had won notice as a resourceful spokesman for New England interests, but he was still essentially a regional Senator.

The matter at issue in the Senate in March 1956 was the problem that had baffled the Founding Fathers 169 years before and had still not been successfully resolved: how to choose the President. After all these years the Electoral College was still a worrisome appendage of our political machinery; like the human appendix, it was useless, unpredictable, and always a possible source of inflammation. Both liberals and conservatives had long favored a constitutional amendment to abolish the "winner-take-all" system (giving a presidential candidate the whole electoral vote of a state, even though he won barely a majority of popular votes) in order to make it more attractive for Republicans to campaign in the Deep South and Democrats in the "Solid North."

The real issue, however, was not reform and "good government." It was power. Behind the long speeches and elaborate statistical complications was a careful campaign by two groups of hardheaded politicians to change, perhaps for good, the rules of the political game in order to benefit their own parties. These groups were the leaderships of the two congressional parties.

Spokesman for the congressional Democrats was Senator Price Daniel of Texas. Like his Southern colleagues Daniel had long been bitterly critical of the winner-take-all device that played into the hands, he felt, of the city bosses, ethnic minorities, and labor blocs of the big Northern cities. Democratic candidates for President had catered to these pressure groups and their radical welfare demands in frantic efforts to win the big pivotal states and their huge blocks of electoral votes. The remedy was simple. Change the system so that electoral votes would be divided proportionately to popular ones; if one candidate won 60 per cent of New York's popular votes, for example, let him have 27 of that state's 45 electoral votes and his opponent 18. Such a change would help the Southern Democrats because the Democratic presidential candidates would pay more attention to the one-party states and less to the big urban states. To be sure, the proportional plan, as it came to be called, would encourage the Republicans to strengthen their party in the South and cut into the topheavy Democratic pluralities, but this effort would take a long time, at least in the Solid South.

Spokesman for the congressional Republicans was Senator Mundt, who now seemed on the verge of realizing one of his five tactical plans. His proposal was different from Daniel's. Mundt favored the district plan whereby, as we noted in the last chapter, individual electoral votes would be cast for the leading presidential candidate in each district as drawn by the state legislature. His device would not only cut down on the big city blocs in the North, it would also allow state legislatures dominated by rural voters to maximize conservative influence in presidential elections—and in any presidential "run-off" that might take place in Congress. If the Daniel proposal would "de-gerrymander" the Electoral College to destroy its urban bias, Mundt's would "counter-gerrymander" it to insert a heavily rural bias.

By itself, neither of the two congressional parties had made much progress with its plan. The only hope lay in coalition. Since neither Daniel nor Mundt would accept the other's proposal, the leaders struck a bargain: they combined the two different bills into a curious "package deal" that would allow state legislatures to choose the device they preferred.

The package-deal proposal worked so well that a bipartisan group of 52 Senators joined Mundt and Daniel in formally co-sponsoring it—barely a dozen short of the two-thirds necessary for a constitutional amendment. It was not strange that Mundt won the support of Goldwater, Dirksen, Bricker, and a score of other congressional Republicans, or that Daniel won such co-sponsors as Byrd, Thurmond, and other Southern Democrats. It was curious that presidential Republicans like Irving Ives of New York and Ralph E. Flanders of Vermont, and a few presidential Democrats like Mike Mansfield of Montana, backed the package deal. The explanation is two-fold: a nonpartisan desire to remove the appendix for the good of the nation, and a Republican hope of improving the party's chances in the South.

The more that Kennedy studied this "hybrid monstrosity," as he later called it, the more he became convinced that urban liberals

in both parties should fight it. His negative reaction was fortified by
a letter from Arthur Holcombe, one of his government professors
at Harvard. Holcombe spoke for Madisonian balance. "Under present conditions," he wrote Kennedy, "the preponderant influence of
the big close states on the executive branch of the government
checks the disproportionate influence of the small and often more
one-sidedly partisan states in the Senate." Kennedy decided to lead
the counter-attack on Mundt-Daniel. His would not be a popular
cause; the proposed amendment, with its aroma of moderate, bipartisan reform, had won wide support in the press, though a few
liberal organizations and newspapers had set up an alarum when
they took a second look at the proposals, especially Mundt's.

On the face of it, Kennedy's tactic was simple: he thoroughly
mastered this highly complex subject, gained the Senate floor early
and held it, argued with his adversaries at every opportunity, poured
withering scorn on their "shot-gun marriage," and finally outdebated
and outvoted them. He never faltered. With statistics, with an impressive command of details of American political history, with
elaborate reasoning, sometimes with flashes of wit, he took on some
of the Senate's ablest members, all of whom considered themselves,
quite rightly, as experts on election machinery. He had powerful
support from Senator Paul Douglas of Illinois, but much of the
time he battled almost alone.

Kennedy knew, however, that fundamentally the issue was not
one of good will or reform: it was a power struggle. His hope lay not
in out-arguing the bipartisan coalition that knew precisely what it
could gain from the amendment. It was to convince the liberals—
and especially the presidential Republicans—that the proposals were
aimed against them and the strong, liberally oriented Presidency
through which they must realize their aims. To do this he dragged
out on the Senate floor the skeletons that most of the Senators were
hiding behind their torrents of oratory. The amendment was really
directed against Negroes, Jews, Catholics, and labor unions, he said.
It was a blatant attempt to strengthen conservative rural power in
the one-party states. It would not help the Republicans in the
South; the reason for Republican weakness there was not the
"winner-take-all" system but the "social, economic, and political

structure" which held down the vote and kept Negroes from voting. The amendment might foment splinter parties; did Southern Democrats want a labor party in Michigan and a civil rights party in New York? "The proposed system could change the whole political habits of the country, with results which are hard to predict now." One should not take down a fence until he knows why it was put up.

To conservatives, Kennedy said, pressure groups might mean Negroes or Jews or organized labor. But to others, the term might refer to farmers, doctors, veterans or the aged. All these groups had influence, some more than others, but candidates appealed to all groups. The groups tended to balance one another, and the system compensated itself; thus, if Negroes had less influence than their numbers warranted in the South, they had greater influence in the North. Kennedy's words reminded Senator Douglas, who was sitting nearby, of Madison and the Tenth Federalist. There, Douglas recalled to the Senate, Madison had held that in a federal nation "there would be so many divergent interests that they would in part cancel each other out and the general interest could be served more effectively." Kennedy agreed. "It is a system of checks and balances that has made the system work," he told the Senate.

Senate debate rarely changes votes, but in this case Kennedy achieved the near impossible. Not only did the Mundt-Daniel bill fail to muster the necessary two-thirds support, but no less than ten of the original sponsors, including Ives and Flanders, deserted the bill to which they had once subscribed their names. He had in effect swung the Republican presidential party in the Senate against the bill. He had defeated a congressional party coalition with a presidential party coalition—a job made easier by the fact that this time it was the conservatives who needed the two-thirds. Many other influences were brought to play, but Kennedy's role was central. "Your leadership in that battle was most skillful and decisive," Douglas wrote him.

However astute Kennedy may have been, one thing he could not know: that if the amendment had gone through, the new electoral mechanics would have elected Richard Nixon in 1960, or might have thrown the struggle into the Congress in January 1961. In the latter event, Congress might have exercised once again for the first time in over a century and a quarter, the power that many Framers had wanted it to have—the election of the President of the United States.

Kennedy and the Presidential Democratic Party

"One hundred and seventy years ago," Senator Kennedy told a Democratic rally in Virginia at the start of his presidential campaign, "Thomas Jefferson and James Madison left the State of Virginia and went to New York on a botanical expedition up the Hudson River. After they had caught fish and butterflies, they rode down the river and stopped in New York City, and there they met Aaron Burr, and the Knights of St. Tammany, and founded the modern Democratic Party, a party which has united the country and the city, the East and the West in the only and oldest national party in the history of the world." The flood-lighted crowd of 15,000 cheered.

"I come here tonight not on a botanical expedition, not to catch fish and butterflies, but I come to the home of this party with Lyndon Johnson and ask for your help. . . .

"I come today as a candidate for the Democratic party," Kennedy told a noon-day crowd in Bowling Green half way through the campaign. ". . . The history of this country moves in rhythms, back and forth, between progress and standing still, between liberalism and conservatism, and I believe in 1960 the choice for the United States is forward. I cannot believe that in the most revolutionary age that the world has ever known; in science, technology, in outer space, in the minds of men around the globe, I cannot believe that the American people are going to give their endorsement to a political party which says, 'You never had it so good,' which endorses the status quo, which endorses the past. . . .

"No Democratic candidate for the Presidency ever said that party labels are unimportant. Every Republican candidate every four years says, 'Don't pay any attention to the record of our parties.' . . . I say that party labels do mean something, if the party stands for something. No political party is of any use to the people, nor is any politician if he does not stand for definite principles and the principles that I stand for in this century are the same principles that Woodrow Wilson stood for in 1912, and which Franklin Roosevelt stood for in 1932, and which President Truman campaigned on in 1948, and my judgment is that their success abroad, the success of the foreign policies of those three Presidents, were directly tied to the success of their policies here in the United States. The Fourteen Points of Woodrow Wilson were tied to the New Freedom of Woodrow Wilson. The Good Neighbor policy was tied to the New Deal. And the Marshall Plan, NATO and the Truman Doctrine and Point Four all had their domestic counterparts in the efforts which President Truman made to lift our country forward. . . ."

As the campaign moved to its climax, Kennedy's attacks on the opposition became witty and biting.

"The Democratic party's candidates in this century never ran on slogans like 'Stand Pat with McKinley,' 'Return to Normalcy with Harding,' 'Keep Cool with Coolidge,' and 'Two Chickens in Every Pot with Hoover.' (Laughter.) I don't know what Dewey's slogan was because he never worked it out. (Laughter.) We know what Truman's slogan is. But there are children in the audience, as the Vice-President would say. (Laughter.) Our slogans have meaning. Woodrow Wilson's New Freedom, Franklin Roosevelt's New Deal, Harry Truman's Fair Deal, and today, we stand on the threshold of a New Frontier, for all Americans." (Applause.)

In winning the nomination Kennedy had won the leadership of the party of the Democratic presidential heroes. During the campaign he brought back to life the coalition that had ruled American politics since 1938. His political role had not always been this. As a congressman he had stayed out of the orbit of the Truman party. He backed the President strongly on domestic social and economic issues, but he criticized Truman's policies in the Far East just as he publicly regretted Roosevelt's concessions to Russia at Yalta. He deserted the presidential Democrats and supported the congressional Democrats and congressional Republicans on the coalition's biggest post-war victory—a constitutional amendment barring a presidential third term. With his safe seat and his mixed ideological background, Kennedy might have become one of those city congressmen who vote against the congressional parties on many economic matters but support the coalition on maintaining congressional institutions such as the seniority system.

But he chose differently. Widening his base to all of Massachu-

setts and then to New England, he campaigned intensively for the
Presidency for three and a half years before his triumph at Los
Angeles in August 1960. In the process he broadened the scope of
his own appeal. It was not enough to be a "bread-and-butter" liberal
who spoke for the economic liberalism of the New Deal and Fair
Deal. He had to attract also the support of Democrats and independents concerned about civil liberties, colonialism, the quality (as
well as the quantity) of public education, aid to developing nations,
McCarthyism, school desegregation, strengthening the United Nations and other international organizations, governmental support
for the arts, and a host of other such issues. This he did, in a series of
trenchant Senate speeches, magazine articles, and face-to-face exchanges with liberal leaders. Symbolically, his acceptance of the
presidential party tradition came on the eve of the election year when
he joined the Democratic Advisory Council, whose spadework on
liberal policy was to bear fruit in the Democratic platform of 1960.

It was a Jeffersonian image that the candidate projected in the
fall of 1960, as he made hardly a speech without boasting of his
party, invoking the party saints, and advancing liberal proposals. He
knew that he must attract to himself the tremendous breadth of
Democratic support. But if he recognized the strength of Democratic sentiment, he had few illusions about the strength of Democratic organization. He had always run on his own in Massachusetts,
working through his personal organization rather than the feeble,
faction-ridden party committees in that state. Most of the state
parties elsewhere he found to be little better than those back home,
and some even worse. Like Roosevelt and Stevenson, he had to set
up volunteer groups to spur and supplement the efforts of the party
"pros" (in New York, for example). None of this surprised Kennedy;
three years before the election he had written, "With a new breed
of respected, dynamic professional politicians coming into promi-
nence, we (Democrats) can no longer afford to continue in official
party positions tired or tarnished holdovers from another era—men
whose stature and activities inspire neither the enthusiasm of volunteer workers nor the respect of their communities—men who keep
busy by attending meetings, filing gloomy forecasts and complaints,
and fighting zealously to hold on to their position." Kennedy had

drawn a perfect bead on the state and local party politicos who run organized politics in most of the states.

But the Democratic party was something to win through, not to govern through. Whatever his Jeffersonian strategy on the hustings, however ardent his efforts to animate the Democratic coalition that could give him a popular majority, Kennedy remained a Madisonian at heart—he retained his view that progress could be made by operating within the traditional constitutional and political system, not by changing it. Heavy currents of political power out of the White House could energize the tangled filaments of government. "I believe that our system of checks and balances, our whole constitutional system, can only operate under a strong President," he said. Temperamentally the President found this the easier way, for he was an "institutional conservative" who spurned both comprehensive political reform and mechanical "gimmicks." Not only did he oppose Electoral College reform, as we have seen, but also a widely supported proposal to establish the post of administrative vice-president. "When it is not necessary to change," he liked to say, "it is necessary not to change."

Kennedy's election posed the question of whether a New Frontier could be created through the old machinery. The new President revived the traditional methods of presidential power. He went before Congress to propose major legislation. He made full use of radio, television, White House conferences, presidential advisory commissions, special assistants, in framing and publicizing his program. His legislative aides used all the time-honored methods of "blarney, bludgeon, and boodle," as Helen Fuller put it, in wielding influence on Capitol Hill. Kennedy met regularly with the legislative leaders, followed the course of bills carefully, intervened quickly with individual legislators, invited congressmen to receptions by groups, and had his aides pay close attention to their specific needs, whether a project back home or a special tour of the White House for a constituent.

With one exception, the President did not propose to change the system: Instead of altering presidential-congressional relations he depended heavily on a full exploitation of presidential authority—most notably executive orders. The exception was the Rules Com-

mittee in the House. Long before Kennedy took office this committee loomed as a formidable obstacle to his program. What to do?
Some advocated wholesale reform; as a minimum it was proposed
that Representative William M. Colmer of Mississippi, highest
ranking Democrat after Chairman Howard Smith, be dropped from
the Rules Committee as retaliation for bolting the national Democratic ticket in the campaign. But Rayburn, fearing that the seniority
system might be threatened, opposed this move. In the end the
Administration negotiated with Smith and other congressional
Democratic leaders a compromise whereby two Democrats and one
Republican were added to the committee, thus giving the Administration a narrow majority. So in the end the proposed change in the
system became a temporary shuffling of personnel.

The President was both leader and bargainer. He set the goals
in some of the most specific and compelling state papers in the
nation's history. He spoke to mass rallies on key issues like medical
care and foreign trade; and he dominated the headlines day after day.
When his back was against the wall, as in the fracas over steel price
increases, he struck back in controlled anger with the whole power of
the presidential party, including its connections ramifying into the
steel industry itself. But within the wheels of legislative policy-
making he was a conciliatory administrator of lubricants and pressure. He tried to fight on only one front at a time. Sometimes, as in
the case of an effort of Senate liberals to modify the filibuster rule,
he promised support for the change if the liberals came close enough
to marshal the necessary votes; since the President's help was needed
to marshal the original support, the filibuster remained intact.

Nor did the President take the lead in reforming or reorganizing
the national Democratic party. The national headquarters, under
one of the ablest state chairmen, John M. Bailey, served its traditional role as an adjunct to the White House rather than as a source
of over-all party leadership and executive-legislative teamwork. Ambitious programs were launched to mobilize local party support for
the President's program, with mixed results. The President aided and
abetted the efforts of Mayor Robert F. Wagner and Manhattan reformers to oust New York leaders Carmine De Sapio and Michael
Prendergast, but he publicly lauded old-line Democratic leader

Charles Buckley of the Bronx for his pro-Kennedy voting record in the House.

What mid-term verdict could be rendered as to the effectiveness of Kennedy's tactics? On economic issues that enjoyed consensus support—wages and hours extension, public housing, social security, for example—the Administration won some major victories, especially during its "honeymoon" in the spring of 1961. But where the President had asked for bold new steps to "get the country moving," and where the consensus was not so certain, White House bargaining and pressuring were not enough. The President lost out on major tax reform, establishment of a Department of Urban Affairs, federal aid for teachers' salaries and school construction, medicare, aid to higher education, long-term financing of foreign aid, new farm legislation, and even the rather moderate civil rights legislation that the Administration requested. The foreign trade bill was the President's only outstanding victory in 1962. Consolidation of the New Deal and the Fair Deal proceeded steadily; innovation on the New Frontier faltered.

Congressional Democratic Strategy

If a test of political expertness is the capacity to convert limited political resources into maximum governmental power, the most expert of the politicians in Washington today are the leaders of the congressional Democratic party. They represent a tiny fraction of the nation's electorate; the approximately 90 members of this party in the House are elected by about two million of the nation's sixty million voters. Those 90 members make up less than one-fourth of the House; they cannot by themselves muster enough votes even for a veto when a two-thirds vote is required. But they make up for their lack of numbers in the quality of their political craftsmanship, their grasp of the relation of policy goals and political means, and of course their control of congressional machinery.

Consider the party's unofficial leader in the House, Howard Worth Smith of Virginia. First elected to Congress in 1930, he represented for years the Arlington-Alexandria district across the Potomac from

Washington. During the 1930's, he survived intense opposition from the Roosevelt Administration. As his suburban area began to fill up with Republicans and liberal Democrats, many of them federal bureaucrats, Smith saw his one-party grip on the district weakening. Many a congressman might have given up under such circumstances, or gone down fighting, but not Judge Smith. He executed a tactical retreat to a more strongly fortified position, by moving out of the seat of his judgeship and law practice, Alexandria, into the interior of the state. The Virginia legislature obligingly carved out a new district for the congressman, so that he could stay in the House, keep his seniority intact and build his influence in the Rules Committee. Seated in the heart of Virginia's Black Belt, the new district seemed safe from urban penetration for some time.

Such political virtuosity could be displayed only in a congenial setting, of course, and this was supplied by the Byrd machine, one of the strongest personal organizations in America. Intellectuals who complain about the institutional repugnance of American society for political organization might do well to examine the Virginia system. Led by Senator Byrd and by his lieutenants in the state legislature, the machine operates through county officials and circuit judges to dominate the voting in primaries. Disputes within the organization are headed off in order to keep voting low. With a genteel but effective use of patronage the state leadership intervenes in the counties to enforce discipline, keep "obnoxious" candidates out of local races, and recruit new leaders. The remarkable feature of the organization is its durability and longevity. "A competent and shrewd state board of strategy, under the leadership of the Senator," V. O. Key wrote in 1949, "maintains a high degree of discipline over the local political leaders affiliated with the organization, which thus has a well-coordinated state-wide machine to bring out the vote in support of its candidates." The same could be said today; and the Senator is chairman of the Senate Finance Committee.

Not all the leaders of the congressional Democrats enjoy the political security of Smith or Byrd. Yet almost all are products of one-party states or districts in the South; lead small personal organizations composed of courthouse rings, local factions, friends and neighbors, that are strong enough to overcome primary opposition; tie in closely with "legislative" politics focused in the upper and lower chambers in their states; and, of course, accumulate seniority on congressional committees. Nor do all the leaders possess Smith's parliamentary astuteness. Yet John Rankin of Mississippi was able to "do the impossible" in the House a few years ago—convert the Un-American Activities Committee into a permanent committee, through a quick parliamentary stroke on the floor—and Southern filibusterers usually make up in wiliness and tenacity what they lack in numbers.

Like its Republican counterpart, the Democratic congressional party operates under collective leadership. If there is one focus of power, it is the House Rules Committee. The defense of the powers of this committee by the party leadership affords another striking case of the expert use of power.

The modern role of the Rules Committee dates back to Franklin Roosevelt's second term. Ironically, Roosevelt had no sooner "won the war" over the Supreme Court's role in striking down New Deal legislation (though he admitted he had "lost the battle" in the failure of the court bill itself) than Congress began to assert itself against the President after several years of "subservience." Perhaps this was the Madisonian formula at work, or at least the Madisonian spirit, for the President had no sooner got rid of the judicial check on his power than he faced a blunter check from the legislature. Strengthened by liberal Democratic losses in both houses in the mid-term election of 1938, Democratic and Republican conservatives combined to counter-attack the New Deal. The President failed in 1938-39 to enact major bills, including fiscal measures to break the "Roosevelt recession." The congressional Democrats launched a series of investigations of New Deal programs, including a "grand exposé" of the National Labor Relations Board by a committee headed by Smith himself.

The coming of World War II and of a new congressional consensus delayed a showdown between the presidential and congressional Democrats. During the Truman years the battle broke out again. Aroused by the bottling up or evisceration of major Fair Deal bills by the Rules Committee, and emboldened by the Truman "miracle" of '48, Administration Democrats, with the help of some presidential Republicans in the House, reformed the Rules Committee at the beginning of the new session in 1949. Under a new rule, if the committee failed to report a rule within three weeks of receiving a bill, the chairman of the legislative committee concerned was empowered to bring the measure before the House. Hailed as a body blow to Smith and the congressional coalition, the reform lasted just two years. In 1951, following an accretion of votes as a result of the mid-term election of 1950, the coalition quickly and quietly repealed the new rule. Smith lost his chairmanship when the Republicans controlled Congress during Eisenhower's first two years, but he had no difficulty in combining with the Republican members to thwart some of the major proposals of the presidential Republicans. And in 1955 he was chairman again.

The coming of the New Frontier in 1961 brought another assault on Judge Smith's domain, and as we have seen, with mixed success. The outcome of the battle, while helpful in easing the passage of some Kennedy measures, testified to the durability of the congressional party. Not only was Colmer left on the committee, but its authority was not touched. It seemed likely that Smith would be able to re-assert his old power as time went on. The rest of the congressional party's defense-in-depth—the seniority rule, the filibuster, the selection of new committee members, and, of course, its whole foundation of power in the one-party states and districts—was left intact. And the congressional party retained the backing of 40 or so congressmen, who came from one-party city districts and who would protect the existing pattern of power even though differing with the congressional Democrats on matters of policy.

Paradoxically, while the congressional Democrats have broadened their grip on political machinery over the last quarter century, the scope of their policy interests has narrowed. At one time the South was the source of much of the Democratic coalition's internationalism, as symbolized by the Southern-born Wilson and by Cordell Hull, a Tennessean. Economic and social conditions were so appalling in the South during the depression that some congressmen from that section, otherwise conservative in outlook, voted for major economic measures of the New Deal. And the South was an indispensable source of support to Roosevelt in his defense and war measures during 1938-41.

Much of this has changed now. With the growth in the South of industries sensitive to foreign competition, such as textiles, many of its representatives have swung to a more isolationist stand in foreign economic policy. The consensus on foreign policy is so broad that what remains of the political internationalism of the South no longer distinguishes it from many of the other groupings in Congress. Defense measures now receive unanimous roll-call votes. And most Southern heartland congressmen have reverted to solid opposition to presidential Democratic programs.

What distinguishing position is left for the congressional Democrats? Only one—and this casts its shadow over the future of the party: social segregation and political containment of the Negro. Forced on the defensive by the federal courts and the President, by Freedom Riders and lunch-counter sit-ins, the Deep Southerners have staked their political hopes to this cause. Through their strength in Congress they have blocked civil rights legislation. Through state legislatures they are keeping Negroes in the Democratic heartland voteless, and they are waging there a desperate—and so far successful—battle to resist school desegregation. And they wield party discipline; Southern congressmen contemplating a soft position on civil rights have been warned that they might face a segregationist in the next primary.

Like their Republican counterpart, the Southern Democrats have their dreams of presidential glory. In 1948 some of them switched tactics and nominated a presidential candidate on a States' Rights ticket and won over a million votes for him, but only by placing their electors under the emblem—the rooster—of the state Democratic parties. Their candidate, Governor J. Strom Thurmond of South Carolina, won 38 electoral votes in the heart of the Democratic heartland, Mississippi, South Carolina, Louisiana, and Alabama. The Southerners calculated correctly that in a close election their electoral votes might throw the contest into Congress. The Dewey-Truman outcome was close—but again the Southerners were frustrated by the mechanics of the Electoral College. Truman won without them. In 1960 Alabama and Mississippi withheld electors from Kennedy, but they still could not influence the outcome, even in one of the closest contests in presidential history.

What about Mundt's strategy of party realignment? The congressional Democrats are cool to the idea. Under which party label, they ask, would the conservatives of both parties unite? It will be a long time before conservative candidates can go to the regular Democrats of South Carolina and win votes as Republicans, especially with presidential Republicans like Rockefeller pressing for expanded civil rights programs up North. Far better, at least in the short run, to continue with a congressional coalition in Southern elections, with conservative Democrats winning in heartland rural areas and conservative Republicans gaining seats in urban areas along the rim.

The lesson for the congressional Democrats seems clear. Their best hope lies in continuing to do what they do so skillfully today: retain their entrenched power in the Southern heartland and in Congress. Today congressional Democratic leaders can vote against the Democratic presidential candidate and return to Washington to receive all the honors and emoluments of being Democrats. Not only did Colmer go back to his high place on the Rules Committee after his bolt against Kennedy; not one of the Senators and Representatives who backed Thurmond in 1948 was denied his committee chairmanship or regular assignment. Presidents grumble about these desertions but they need congressional support so badly that they give in, as even Truman did after retaliating for a time with his patronage power. The congressional Democratic leaders have an ideal strategy: they can oppose the presidential Democrats in elections and in Washington, all the while benefiting by the victories of liberal congressmen in the North, who will return to Washington to form a coalition in Congress with the congressional Democrats so that the latter may retain their chairmanships and their control of Congress.

Still, the congressional Democrats face one serious problem. Their absolute recalcitrance on segregation and civil rights may draw them into alliances with ultra-rightist nativist and even neo-fascist forces that might draw the party out of the orbit of the four-party system into an isolated and ultimately powerless posture. Such alliances would snap the present bonds that make possible coalition between the congressional Democrats and the other parties. In such an event, the question would not be whether the congressional Democrats needed the presidential Democrats. It would be whether the presidential party needed them—and could afford them.

What Strategy for the New Frontier?

"I am no Whig!" Kennedy said a year before he was elected President. "The job of the next President will be the hardest since Roosevelt. . . . The President must serve as a catalyst, an energizer, the defender of the public good and the public interest against all the narrow private interests which operate in our society. . . . The best the President can do is to track down the best talent he can get—people with ideas which are actionable—and then try, by his political management, by his mobilization of public opinion, by his hard work almost day by day in Congress and the nation, to bring along that more conservative and localized body."

How far would he go? he was asked. Was he not something of a traditionalist who had defended the American system of divided power seemingly down to the last check and balance?

"The Constitution is a very wise document," he answered. "It permits the President to assume just about as much power as he is capable of. If he fails, it is his fault, not the system's. I believe that the President should use whatever power is necessary to do the job unless it is expressly forbidden by the Constitution."

No one could doubt, after Kennedy's first two years in the White House, that he was an activist, pragmatic, wide-ranging, creative President who had exploited every traditional power of his office. But in 1962 the full use of traditional power seemed inadequate; Congress and the President remained deadlocked on major White House proposals. The President's techniques of pressure and bargaining, along with the failure of his major new programs to win enactment, encouraged the presidential Republicans. The stalemate in Congress also aroused complaints by some liberals that the Administration lacked a central purpose or vision or grand design, that it had bent before every gust of public opinion instead of coming to grips with its enemies, that the Augustan age of poetry and power forecast by Robert Frost had become a managerial age of empty rhetoric and manipulation.

Doubtless these critics underestimated the centrifugal forces operating on the President and the sheer intractability of the operational problems, especially those abroad, that pre-empted so much of the Administration's time. Still, it was clear by mid-term that the Administration was facing a widening gap between the slow progress of its program in Congress and its public hopes and commitments. For the President's shining rhetoric before and after his election, and his specific policy proposals following his Inauguration, were producing a revolution of rising expectations in his own country and overseas. Liberals who ran his agencies and embassies—indeed, the whole apparatus of the presidential party, which had a thrust of its own—were pressing on him, because they knew he wanted them to, their dreams of what could and must be done to make the country move forward.

This widening gap sharpened the dilemma of the presidential Democrats. Should the Administration continue with its vigorous Madisonian tactics, pressing ahead now here and now there, making a little progress at a time, but on many fronts, bargaining, negotiating, pleading, politicking, bending all its skills to make a coalition government work? Or was there another strategy that might make for long-term gains even at the risk of short-run stresses and hazards?

One possible strategy was the classic stroke of the presidential Democrats—the strategy of Jefferson and Jackson, Wilson and Roosevelt. This was a massive expansion of the electorate. By immensely broadening his appeal, as polls attested that he had done, by drawing new voters to the polls, and by converting independents and Republicans, Kennedy could win so "big" in 1964, according to this reasoning, that he could sweep a heavily Democratic majority into Congress. With assured support in both houses he could thus get his big program through Congress.

One trouble with this plan was that no matter how strongly the President ran in '64, no matter how large his congressional support, he would still face the congressional Democrats entrenched in power, as Roosevelt did during his second term. He would also face the handicap of being in his last term, with his power due to run out by the calendar. Moreover, the congressional party held one key to presidential party success in 1964 and for many years afterwards. This was the key to the Negro vote in the South. The greatest potential addition to Democratic presidential voting power, the Negroes would be denied the vote by the same party, working through

Southern state legislatures, that would be inevitably weakened if southern Negroes became enfranchised.

A second strategy assumed a big push in 1964 but went much farther. For this strategy was concerned not only for Kennedy's personal success in 1964, but for the success of the presidential Democrats for years to come. It recognized that the Democratic voting power of the last 30 years is not an immutable thing, especially since it is based more on historic circumstances than on organizational effectiveness. It notes that there are weaknesses in the present Democratic coalition; that the relative size and political effectiveness of organized labor is declining; that ethnic and religious groups may show less allegiance to the Democratic party, especially at the end of the Kennedy administration, as they become more assimilated into middle-class America; that Negro support for a party allied with racist Southerners will always be undependable; that the traditional Democratic rural vote in the Midwest is being dissipated by urbanization and migration; that the Democrats as a party may not be holding their own in the suburbs; and that the next presidential Republican leader may not duplicate Eisenhower's failure to convert at least part of his personal coalition into an organized national party following.

The second strategy proposes:

1. A root-and-branch reorganizing and strengthening of the presidential Democratic party. The party would continue to work through those state Democratic organizations that were nationally oriented and equipped to help national candidates, congressional as well as presidential. It would by-pass state parties that were weak or were the instruments of state politicians. In such cases the national party would establish its own congressional district organization, financed, staffed, and directed by the national headquarters.

2. A congressional as well as a presidential victory in 1964. The President would win so sweepingly that he would carry into Congress the kind of majorities that Roosevelt enjoyed after 1936. But unlike Roosevelt, the President would share not only his name and coattails in the election, but would share campaign funds, organiza-

tion, personnel; so that again unlike Roosevelt, the winning Democrats would have both the political support and the political obligation to back the Kennedy program. Hence 1964 would be a national party victory, not merely an Administration one.

3. Effective party control of Congress. Obviously the presidential party would have to clear away the institutions and procedures that today buttress the congressional party. It would energize the present, almost dormant party agencies—the caucus or conference, policy committees, and the like. Parliamentary procedure would be modified to allow a party majority to act. These changes would not subordinate the legislative branch to the executive. On the contrary they would allow Congress to legislate, to shape broad policy in concert with the President, in short to *act*. The presidential party leadership would be a leadership of both the President and majority leaders on Capitol Hill.

4. A permanent enlargement of the vote. In part this would come through unlocking the congressional barrier to Negro voting in the South—a move that would be possible only after the presidential Democrats overcame present congressional thwarting of effective voting bills. But the possibilities are much broader. The states restrict whites as well as Negroes. They maintain cumbersome voting procedures that discourage voting regardless of race—for example, registration requirements, absentee balloting, the requirement that a person must live in a state a year or two before he can vote even for national candidates. (Aside from the Negro, the most unfairly treated group of voters in America is the big mobile population.) So ultimately presidential Democratic strategy here would contemplate the feasibility of establishing through act of Congress a parallel system of local balloting for national offices that would be completely accessible, fair, and democratic—that would encourage voting.

5. The de-gerrymandering of Congress. Clearly the presidential party would have to destroy one of the bases of the congressional party, for reasons of both public equity and party power. Congress need only take seriously its lip service over the years, written into legislation, to compact and contiguous congressional districts, set up the technical machinery, and admit to its ranks only those members

elected on a fair basis. By the same token, the Electoral College should be de-gerrymandered too.

6. In the long run, a re-ordering of the presidential party's policy orientation, public image, and coalition make-up. The Democrats cannot live forever on the economic issues they acquired in the Roosevelt and Truman eras. As society has become more industrialized and suburbanized and affluent, the thrust of such issues has weakened. What will take their place, or at least supplement them? Clearly the way-of-life issues that go back in history and will go on as long as man concerns himself with more than matters of food, clothing, and shelter. Hence, as Arthur Schlesinger, Jr. has said, the Democrats must lead the way toward a qualitative liberalism. The relation of government to the arts, the quality of education as well as its quantity, civil rights as a means of recognizing the dignity of the individual rather than simply a bread-and-butter matter, a vast expansion of recreational facilities, government support of, and insistence on, superior use of mass media, urban renewal that would cultivate rather than obliterate the unique qualities of the city, and improvement in the tone, efficiency, imagination, and sensitivity of government itself—these are a few of the infinite possibilities of a *qualitative* presidential party program.

To describe such a strategy is to present the dilemma of the Democrats in its sharpest form. For clearly the presidential party could not undertake such an effort without a hard struggle with the congressional party leadership and its allies. Our politics is not made —our politicians are not made—for this kind of grand re-ordering of strategy. Yet the alternative is also unpromising—a continuation of the present tactics, and the consequent danger that the party could not live up to its commitments and to the ever growing needs of the country and that it would falter in the face of aggressive action by the presidential Republicans in 1968 if not 1964. And if the latter party should elect a man who was a strong party leader as well as a strong President, the Democrats might have to yield the initiative over both policy and party organization for some years.

The dilemma of the Democrats is also the dilemma of John F. Kennedy. He is a policy activist and liberal, and an institutional conservative, or at least moderate. He is suspicious of what seem to be grandiose and long-term schemes; he prefers to address himself to the concrete, the tangible, and the immediate. He is chary of total political commitments and dramatic controversies. He has experienced much of the "sheer damn cussedness of things" in politics and government. He has established a useful coalition with the presidential Republicans in foreign policy (and personnel), and heavy emphasis on his role as party leader might jeopardize the bipartisan support he needs in his operations abroad. Temperamentally he does not like to fight hard unless cornered, as he was in the steel price fight, and he may get enough bills through—or at least the tattered remnants of bills—to prevent the clear-cut situation that would make possible a dramatic confrontation with the congressional party. And he might fear a total lapse of government action while the battle within the government was fought out.

On the other hand, events can create problems of choice even though they do not provide the decisions. If there is anything about which the President is deadly serious, it is his program. If there is one charge he could not bear, it is that he would not govern. Not as a matter of abstract principle or party neatness, but to achieve his own policy goals, he will have to turn from Madisonian methods to Jeffersonian. And if there are great dangers in such a course, there are also great opportunities. The long overdue democratizing and strengthening and permanent vitalizing of our national government is not a bad cause to win on, or even to be defeated on. Certainly any man who grasped the nettle by the thorn, who staked his political hopes and reputation on a major advance in democratic government, as Lloyd George did in 1910 and Franklin Roosevelt in 1937, who inscribed his ideals of democratic government on the statute books of his country—such a man would have written for himself an imperishable new profile in courage.

14

STRATEGY
for AMERICANS

J have tried to describe the four parties today with
some objectivity—even more, to put myself in
the positions of their leaders, to share their aims
and outlook, to see the political world through their eyes. But I shall
not pretend neutrality or detachment. The chief results of the ideas
and institutions embraced by the Madisonian model are, I believe,
as follows:

1. We have been captured by that model, which requires us to
await a wide consensus before acting, while we have neglected, except furtively and sporadically, the Jeffersonian strategy of strong
leadership, majority rule, party responsibility, and competitive elections. Hence, government action has been unduly delayed, whether
measured by the progress of other comparable nations, such as
Britain; or by the ascertainable needs of people, such as the jobless of

the 1930's or the civil rights of minorities today; or by what the voters wanted or would accept, as reflected in the national platforms of both major parties and in the campaign promises of their presidential candidates.

2. Our four-party system requires coalition government, which is notoriously unable to generate strong and steady political power. To act, American leaders have had to gain the concurrence not simply of a majority of the voters, but of majorities of different sets of voters organized around leaders in mutually checking and foot-dragging sectors of government. The price of this radical version of checks and balances has been enfeebled policy, as major concessions have been made to gain the necessary support.

3. Hence as a nation we have lost control of our politics. We cannot collectively settle the elementary question of who may vote in national elections and hence we cannot extend the vote to millions of our fellow Americans, especially Negroes. We cannot exercise the primitive right of controlling congressional and presidential election arrangements, especially gerrymandering, rural over-representation, and one-party districts. We have lost control of political money and its misuse.

4. We lack popular control of the policy-making process. Our splintered parties set up barriers between the people and their national government rather than simplifying the alternatives, clarifying competing party doctrines, and allowing the victorious majority to govern.

5. Our government lacks unity and teamwork or, when it exists, it is often the integration of drift. Ideally, the winning party under a two-party system pulls together the executive and legislative branches in order to deliver on the party's (and candidates') promises to the people. But a fragmented party system cannot do this because the winning party is split into factions warring with each other.

6. We oscillate fecklessly between deadlock and a rush of action. Congress fails to act on crucial long-term problems; inevitably crisis comes, and the President uses his emergency powers. The Senate

kills a bill to control harmful drugs; then a drug causes babies to be born without limbs; the Senate passes the same bill unanimously. Congress slashes vital foreign aid appropriations, then passes mammoth arms bills with little debate and without a single dissent.

7. We can choose bold and creative national leaders without giving them the means to make their leadership effective. Hence we diminish a democracy's most essential and priceless commodity—the leadership of men who are willing to move ahead to meet emerging problems, but who are also sensitive to the rights of the opposition and subject to the results of a free and competitive election.

8. We cannot define our national purpose and mobilize our strength to move vigorously against the problems that beset us at home and abroad, or to exploit the enormous possibilities of urban man and world man in the last third of the 20th Century.

"If you ask me—as a historian, let us say—whether a country in the state this country is in today," George F. Kennan has said, "with no highly developed sense of national purpose, with overwhelming accent of life on personal comfort and amusement, with a dearth of public services and a surfeit of privately sold gadgetry, with a chaotic transportation system, with its great urban areas being gradually disintegrated by the headlong switch to motor transportation, with an educational system where quality has been extensively sacrificed to quantity, and with insufficient social discipline even to keep its major industries functioning without grievous interruptions—if you ask me whether such a country has, over the long run, a good chance of competing with a purposeful, serious, and disciplined society such as that of the Soviet Union, I must say that the answer is 'NO'!"

Toward Two-Party Competition

We need a new kind of bipartisanship. The two presidential parties should join forces in Congress and elsewhere just long enough to work out the rules of the game for a fair, orderly, and competitive battle between the two national parties for the decades to come. The presidential parties must singly and jointly overcome the arrangements that thwart political competition, that prevent them from broadening their electoral support, and keep them from dealing with the way-of-life issues that increasingly dominate the nation's future. This means that each presidential party must convert its congressional party into a party wing exerting a proper, but not controlling or crippling hold on party policy.

The overcoming of the congressional parties requires the curbing of the institutional buttresses of their power: the seniority system in Congress, the other minority devices such as Rules Committee veto and the filibuster, mal-apportionment and one-party districts in the states, and, if feasible, midterm elections for the House. It means the shaping of new party structures and procedures. Above all, it means that the parties must protect themselves as organizational entities. Today, as we have seen, they are holding companies for numberless state and local and "candidate" organizations over which they have little control. But some of these organizations—especially those built around officeholders—have a divisive and stultifying impact on the national parties. Other party organizations—especially those oriented around governors who share the national party's style and outlook—could serve as foundation blocks for the national party.

This uneasy relation between the national and local parties poses a severe intellectual and organizational problem. Most of those who favor stronger parties want the national parties to combine more closely with state and local parties for the sake of more party coherence, discipline, and responsibility. Certainly this is desirable when the presidential and state parties are enough akin in doctrine and policy to strengthen each other. But other state and local parties are so different in outlook and doctrine that the presidential party must disentangle itself from them and set up its own separate independent party, at least in the states and congressional districts, with its own officers, finances, and communications channels. This means, for example, that the presidential Republicans would work through the present state parties in New York or California or Michigan, but would work around the parties of Barry Goldwater and Karl Mundt in Arizona and South Dakota.

Members of the presidential parties can resolve this problem only if they keep in mind what end must be sought. The aim is to draw the congressional and presidential party leaderships to each other by drawing the two party electorates more closely together—more specifically, by combining the smaller congressional party electorates with the bigger, more inclusive presidential party electorates in the states. As far as possible the President and his party majorities in Congress should be elected by substantially the same electoral groupings, for the sake of clarity of policy, unity in government, and responsibility to the majority. To do this the parties must pay a price: they cannot be allowed to be all things to all men. In some states a nationally oriented Republican party might not be able to win; but it could still field candidates who would stage vigorous campaigns, put over the message of national Republicanism, and build toward the day when the Republicans would have a fighting opportunity in that area. Such candidates could "bend" the national platforms a bit toward local political needs but what they must not do—what the national party leaders should be in a position to prevent them from doing—is so to distort Republicanism that its national meaning and appeal is perverted and impaired.

Once the Democratic and Republican parties agreed on such assumptions, the specific elements of party consolidation would fall into place:

1. *The national government should control national elections.* There may have once been good reasons for states to control elections of national officials; there are none today. State control of national elections, indeed, is a violation of the Madisonian principle under which each level of government should regulate its own political affairs. It is ridiculous that a man who moves to Alabama or Mississippi must wait two years before he can vote for presidential candidates he has observed for years. It is tragic that state control of senatorial and congressional elections helps congressional leaders to keep their constituencies small, noncompetitive, and exclusive. Both presidential parties must open up the closed politics of these one-party enclaves and ultimately make them into fighting ground.

Republicans may object that enlarging the electorate would help the Democrats more than themselves. So it might, for a time. But in the long run the Republicans would have as much to gain, for the party balance would re-assert itself. The main problem for the Republicans is not a strong Democratic party; without a lively rival party it would not mean much to be a Republican; the main problem is a congressional party that frustrates the Republican party in becoming a formidable national organization.

2. *The national parties must build grass-roots memberships.* Colonels, lieutenants, and sergeants are not enough; the parties need the same foundation that every other big, politically active organization —the AFL-CIO, the Legion, the A.M.A.—already has: an extensive card-carrying, dues-paying membership. There must be a clear channel of direction and responsibility from party leaders to rank and file. This membership would be united chiefly by their common faith in their party's tradition, doctrine and policy. Hence they could operate effectively at any level, because they would be pursuing the same general objectives whether they were working at the local, state, or national levels.

Membership parties would call for more emphasis on party clubs and less on party committees, for clubs are the haven for party members and committees cater more to the parties' Kentucky Colonels. As the New York and California experiences have shown, the clubs encourage an open, vigorous, and policy-oriented politics. As that experience also shows, the clubs encourage a political independence and purism that will call for ingenious leadership if they are to sustain the old party organizations as well as rejuvenate them.

3. *The presidential and congressional parties must be merged organizationally.* There is no point in drawing a blueprint, especially since conditions will vary from state to state. One electoral change might have a helpful, though limited, effect. This is to alter the organization of the ballot so that candidates for President, Senator, and Representative would be placed in a separate box from candidates for state and local offices, and in such a way that the voters could choose a straight national party ticket simply by marking one party circle or by pulling one party lever. The form of the ballot, studies show, does have some influence on voting; moreover, every proper step should be taken to underline the key relationship of President to Senators and Representatives.

4. *New party leadership must be developed in Congress.* Clearly the institutional bases of minority and obstructionist politics, such as

the seniority system and the other devices described in Chapter 10, must go. A common defense of the seniority system is that it may be a poor way to run Congress but there is nothing better to take its place. This is nonsense, of course; hundreds of legislatures the world over choose their committees and leaders on other grounds than the accumulation of uninterrupted years of seniority. What the defenders of the seniority rule are really saying is that given our present congressional party system, a seniority rule is inevitable. And in this they are correct. By the same token, an end of the rule depends on the end of the system.

What would take its place? Representative, responsible, and vigorous party policy committees under the leadership of elected party officials and their whips. The arrangement would not look very different on the surface from the present majority and minority leadership and party and policy committees. But there would be a big difference; the elected party leaders of Congress, working with the President (or the "out" presidential party leadership) would be in charge of the content and handling of party measures.

The seniority rule and related arrangements have been in effect so long that they seem to have divine support. But they are wholly man made, and they can be removed by man just as they were instituted by men. What it takes is majority support for changes in Congress, determination, parliamentary resourcefulness, and persistence. This is where the bipartisanship of the two presidential parties is sorely, though only temporarily, needed. Supported by a Kennedy or a Nelson Rockefeller in the White House, the presidential party in Congress should pool its strength with the other presidential party to strengthen both Senate and House.

5. *The parties and their candidates should be financed on a mass, popular, systematic basis.* It is better that a lot of people give a little money than that a few give a lot. A large dues-paying membership should help on this score, and there should be legal restrictions on the total amount of money that one man (or one family) can contribute. Other specific steps could be taken. Political money in the national party should be put under the national chairman, who should be held accountable for its use. The national committee should allot money to congressional candidates much more gener-

ously than it does now. As a beginning, Congress should adopt the President's proposals based on the recommendations of his committee on campaign finance—especially those for government subsidy of certain campaign expenses.

6. *The national opposition party should be better organized and given a clearer voice.* Today the Republicans cannot oppose effectively and responsibly because they speak with two voices, through their two parties. The presidential party should strengthen its All-Republican Conference by giving it money, staff, and organizational effectiveness. It should stage an annual conference, much smaller than the national convention, where national policy could be debated and the party platform publicized and renovated. The national committee should become a vigorous, representative body for which the national chairman could speak authoritatively in advancing and defending his party's position on quickly changing events. He should be the acknowledged spokesman for the "out" party.

The "in" party might also do well to establish an annual conference and perhaps an advisory council. While the need is not so acute for the party in power, since it possesses the unrivaled rostrum of the White House, the President should take care to nurture embryonic party organizations toward the day when his party again becomes the loyal opposition.

These six proposals require only party and minor governmental reforms. With one possible exception, they do not call for constitutional change. (The exception is the nationalization of elections for national officials; but this aim could probably be realized by stringent congressional regulation of national elections administered by the states). Constitutional reform on the whole is not recommended, partly because it is so difficult. Still, as a capstone to these reforms, certain constitutional amendments would be extremely helpful and might achieve enough support to pass.

One of these is a four-year term for Representatives, to coincide with presidential terms. Today a two-year term for important office is an anachronism, as many states have recognized in shifting to four-year terms for governors and other state-wide offices. A two-year officeholder hardly has time to master his job; he is perpetually mending fences; he is unduly vulnerable to sudden gusts of public opinion. More important, the off-year elections usually raise havoc with the President's support in Congress, and of course form one of the bases of the congressional party system. Parliamentary democracies elsewhere find a four- or five-year term satisfactory for national legislators.

Extending the Representatives' terms to four years raises the thorny problem of the Senate. Politically, and perhaps constitutionally, it would be virtually impossible to shorten the Senate's tenure to four years, at least for the foreseeable future. We may have to accept the staggered six-year term, with a bow to the Framers.

A second needed constitutional change is repeal of the 22nd Amendment, but this would doubtless be more controversial than the proposal for a four-year term for Representative. Most political scientists (and most Presidents) believe that the anti-third term rule threatens a President's power during his second term, no matter how clear he makes his determination to choose his successor, for party and legislative leaders inevitably start moving into the orbits of other presidential candidates. But the impact of the amendment may not be crucial; Paul T. David believes that the amendment actually strengthens the "presidential wing" in both parties by partially balancing the weak position of the out-of-power presidential party, forcing the "in" party to deal seriously with problems of succession, and hence in making presidential party politics more competitive. I believe that the pulverizing impact of the amendment on presidential party unity more than offsets these advantages. In any event, the 22nd Amendment is less likely to be repealed as a result of general reform efforts than as part of a strategy to draft a highly popular President for a third term.

A final desirable constitutional amendment concerns the Electoral College. Today the system helps sustain the gap between the presidential and congressional parties, as we have noted; any change must be calculated in terms of its effect on the four-party system and on the coming of two-party politics. Perhaps the two presidential and the two congressional parties could hold a Four Power summit conference on this matter and adopt a compromise: if the congressional parties give up their gerrymandered and one-party districts (as far as possible) in congressional elections, the presidential parties would yield their own gerrymandering in the Electoral College. The presidential parties might offer, as a compromise, a proposal drafted by Professor Ralph Goldman and introduced into Congress by Senator Humphrey. This plan would eliminate the electors as such but retain the total number of electoral votes. The presidential candidate with a plurality in a state would receive two electoral votes (equivalent to its two Senators). The remaining 435 electoral votes would then be divided between the presidential candidates on a nation-wide basis, in proportion to the national vote for each. This proposal recognizes both state equality under the federal system and the Jeffersonian idea of the direct popular election of the President. Barring over-all change in the Electoral College, perhaps party leaders could at least agree on a simple reform to prevent individual electors from voting in defiance of the election mandate, and to correct some of the dangerous mechanical weaknesses of the present system.

All three of these amendments are desirable. But we must not stake our hopes on, or become too much diverted by, the possibility of constitutional reform. The more central need of party and governmental reform is challenging enough.

The Power in the People

I list these proposals in a mixed spirit of conviction and skepticism. Conviction, because I am sure we must adopt them for a more orderly, relevant, and effective politics. Skepticism, because I am well aware that I am only the latest in a long line of Americans, celebrated and obscure, who have urged changes to achieve that kind of politics. "The Constitution is not honored by blind worship," Woodrow Wilson wrote 80 years ago. "The more open eyed we become as a nation, to its defects, and the prompter we grow in applying with the unhesitating courage of conviction all thoroughly tested or well-considered expedients necessary to make self-government among us a straightforward thing of simple method, single, unstinted power, and clear responsibility, the nearer will we approach to the sound sense and practical genius of the great and honorable statesmen of 1787." Since then, A. Lawrence Lowell, Henry Jones Ford, Herbert Croly, Walter Lippmann, William Yandell Elliott, Thomas K. Finletter, and a host of others, including many working politicians, have dealt with the central problem in one fashion or another. Aside from a little fixing and patching, the results have been small. Why?

Americans have had the cushion of time. We have never been so close to the abyss, in domestic affairs (except when we went over it in 1861), that we felt much urgency about strengthening our political system. If that government could not cope with economic crises, if it could not deal with even as primitive a social problem as child labor, if it was a generation or two behind other modern nations in welfare programs, if it could not meet its international obligations, if Negroes were still segregated and discriminated against a century after Emancipation—we could wait until a large enough popular consensus could be achieved to allow our divided government to act. There is grave doubt now that history still allows us this cushion.

We have also suffered from a gimmick approach to political problems. Our genius at tinkering and improvising leads us to think that the most serious political problems can be solved by mechanical devices. In the old days it was the initiative, referendum, and recall; the party primary and proportional representation; nonpartisan ballots and honest election administration. Today there are proposals to solve executive-legislative deadlock and friction by question-hours, joint cabinets or councils, or mechanical changes in Congress. There may be nothing wrong with these proposals in themselves, but they have little bearing on the real problems of President and Congress, which are problems not of misunderstanding or of faulty communication but of who gets what—and who does not.

By the same token, Americans are skeptical about broad-scale planning or "social engineering," and often with good reason, for the American soil has not been hospitable to grandiose schemes of reconstruction. Communal utopias have withered in this soil, as have ideologies of the right and left, elaborate schemes of economic planning down to the last bolt and nut, and efforts to create whole new parties. But we may carry this disdain of planning too far. We have been highly successful in piecemeal public or private planning: witness the Tennessee Valley Authority or the Ford Motor Company. Many of the proposals made earlier in this chapter already exist in limited form. Puerto Rico has a party system and an arrangement

for partial government subsidy of election campaigns that could serve
as a model for the rest of the nation. An example of bold political
planning is Cincinnati where, back in the 1920's, a group of independents and liberal Republicans reconstructed the city's politics by
creating a new party system that drew the city out of the distorting
influence of national two-party politics and enabled it to establish
a new, competitive two-party balance of its own. Republicans in
several states have worked out modern methods of political finance.
During the Eisenhower Administration Democrats devised an advisory council that managed, against great opposition, to give the
national party a clear and eloquent voice. Republicans in Ohio and
Democrats in Michigan have shaped their state parties into impressive organizations for publicizing issues, getting out the vote, and
supporting their leaders who gain office. None of these efforts can
be called social engineering, but they raise some question about
American antipathy toward the possibility of effective political planning.

But the main reason, I think, that we have not come to grips with
our political problem is *intellectual:* we have been so enamored by
one model of government, the Madisonian, that we have failed to
comprehend the legitimacy and possibilities of what I have called
the Jeffersonian strategy of politics. We have not called the Madisonian model by that name; we have called it the Constitution (for-
getting that the Constitution can accommodate the Jeffersonian
model) and during most of our life as a nation we have, indeed, as
Wilson said, dishonored the Constitution by blind worship. We have
complained about government by barter, government by fits and
starts, government by minorities, and so on, but as a people we have
never squarely faced the philosophical assumptions on which that
government is built.

We have never faced them because we have never had to test
them against the assumptions of the competing model, the Jeffersonian. I will not repeat here the case for majority rule presented in
Chapter 2. But it may be useful to consider America's major in-
articulate premise against majority rule, for that premise has been
the main stumbling block to the use of the Jeffersonian strategy.

The basis of that premise has been a pervading distrust of the
people when organized in a national bloc or party. The people, yes

—but only in their separated, federalized, localized capacities. Popular government, yes—but not really popular rule by hungry majorities. Opposition to majority rule is not so blatant today as when Hamilton uttered his famous malediction on the people as a "great Beast." Nor do we have political theorists who condemn it with the brilliance of a John Calhoun. But anti-majoritarianism is still powerful as an intellectual and emotional proposition. And the genius of the Framers is operating every day through the Constitution to splinter and pulverize popular majorities.

The main trouble with anti-majoritarianism is that it sees not the people but a caricature of the people. If a popular majority really did constitute a great glob of mindless, herdlike persons, with the instincts of a mob, we would do well to build barricades against them at every strategic point. But there is no such thing as a nation-wide mass or mob; the people are divided by endless social, attitudinal, economic, and—as we saw in Chapter 9—political differences. There is no "herd instinct" nationally, no "mass mind," no "great Beast."

A more refined contention of the anti-majoritarians is that people are all right as individuals, but that somehow their good qualities are squeezed out in the mass. It seems likely that the opposite is nearer the truth. In their study of the voters of Elmira, New York, Berelson and his colleagues were struck by the frequent failure of Elmirans to live up to the long-accepted requirements of the democratic citizen: interest in public affairs, capacity to argue and think about politics, knowledge of issues and candidates, rational judgment, some sense of the general interest. But the requirements for the system of democracy, they conclude, are somewhat different from those for the individual. The system needs a proper balance between involvement and indifference, stability and innovation, progress and conservation, consensus and cleavage, individualism and collectivism. The basic argument for majority rule, I would contend, is that it guarantees enough of such qualities, in sufficient magnitude and mixture, to underpin the whole system of democracy. Mass majorities provide their internal sources of social health. This is the real power of the people.

A majority organized over the long run in a political party has a quality even beyond those noted by the analysts of Elmira. Continuing political parties are more than organizational conveniences or election devices. They are carriers of old attitudes; they embody popular hopes and aspirations; they make as well as follow opinion; they identify and pigeon-hole candidates; they try to anticipate future problems and needs; hence they link past, present, and future in the political behavior of the people. The Jeffersonian strategy, we must note again, is not majority rule alone, but majority rule embodied in a responsible party that has an independent role in educating, arousing, leading, and sometimes slowing up the people.

It is curious that majoritarian politics has won such a reputation for radicalism in this country. Actually it is moderate politics; it looks radical only in relation to the snail-like progress of Madisonian politics. The Jeffersonian strategy is essentially moderate because it is essentially competitive; in a homogeneous society it must appeal to the moderate, middle-class independent voters who hold the balance of power. A Jefferson, Lincoln, Roosevelt, or Wilson may seem to move ahead rapidly and hence frighten conservatives, but they are merely catching up for lost time in the journey of social progress, and their coming usually ushers in a period of consolidation and calm.

We must not repeat the mistake of the Madisonians by turning the Jeffersonian system into an infallible model, a rigid doctrine, an absolutist dogma. I wish only to suggest that the Jeffersonian strategy is as legitimate in theory and necessary in practice as the Madisonian, that it too can serve as a standard, and that the solution of our political problems depends, in the intellectual realm, on the extent to which we can exploit either or both models for the pressing needs of the nation. We have tended to think that the more we departed from Madisonian doctrine, the more we were violating basic democratic principles. This, I suggest, is unnecessary and perhaps dangerous. We can move, as conditions demand, between these two models.

Still, majority rule as a principle and the party as a practical system are not enough to make the Jeffersonian system an effective model. The third requirement is leadership.

Leadership: The Art of the Impossible?

Our fear of popular majorities has spurred our fear of popular leadership. The Madisonian dread of the man on horseback still lingers. No matter that we have never had a demagogue with an effective national majority, or that our most celebrated political free-booters, from Aaron Burr to Huey Long, had only state or regional followings, or that the Hearsts, the McCarthys, and the Birchites have been tiny minoritarians, not majoritarians. No matter that Presidents struggling to build and lead Jeffersonian majorities have met almost insuperable difficulties, as in the case of Wilson and the two Roosevelts, or that majoritarian politics puts a premium on moderate centrist doctrine and policy. The Madisonian model, with its anti-strong leadership bias, is still controlling.

Madisonians suspect that vigorous leadership is crucial to the Jeffersonian model of competitive parties and majority rule. They are quite right. Without strong leadership majorities are flaccid, parties inert. The relation of leader to people and party should be a pressing and compelling one. Without some tension between leader and led our political life would stagnate; rapid innovation and progress would be impossible. The Madisonian system finds its tension in the competition among struggling groups, multi-party factions, and mutually checking branches of government. The Jeffersonian system, a more hierarchical arrangement, finds its tension in the relation of leader and led, with the leader usually pressing his troops, like an army commander, and the troops usually restraining, but sometimes out-running, their leader.

Madisonian politics has a place for leadership, of course, but it is essentially brokerage. The leader responds to the amalgam of pressures working on him. He is a manipulator, a mediator, a master bargainer among the group pressures and fragmentized forces that the Madisonian model glorifies. At most the leader may point out a direction, enunciate principles and policies, and exert influence through persuasion, bargaining, and narrow forms of pressure.

The Jeffersonian leader must be much more than this. He must gain leadership of a big national party and guide it in seizing and holding majority status. He must publicize his and his party's program and goals with such clarity and conviction that he can help convert latent and amorphous popular attitudes into a powerful public opinion bolstering his cause. He must build structural support in his personal following by merging it with his national party organization or by creating new political units. He must keep his party eternally competitive and thus fulfill the first requirement of the Jeffersonian strategy. He must be willing to narrow his personal popularity if by so doing he can intensify and consolidate a working majority in Congress or the electorate. He must be willing in emergencies to take sweeping action, no matter how controversial, and then to appeal to the electorate for a majority, as Jefferson did in 1804 after the Louisiana Purchase, and Roosevelt in 1940 after the destroyer deal with the British.

The presidential leader must, in short, be more than a skilful manipulator or brilliant interpreter. He must be a constructive innovator, who can re-shape to some degree the constellation of political forces in which he operates. To reach the acme of leadership he must achieve a creative union of intellectual comprehension, strategic planning, and tactical skill, to a degree perhaps not paralleled since Jefferson.

Is such leadership possible in America? What would it require for a President of the United States?

Such leadership would require so strong a commitment to his program that the President would be willing to break with old traditions and take political risks, if these were necessary to realize the goals of his Administration. This would mean for a Republican President that he be willing, at least for the short run, to jeopardize support among highly conservative Republicans and in the more rural areas of the North; it would mean, for a Democratic President, that he risk losing the electoral backing of conservative Southerners —to such an extent that he might have to write them off and undertake the herculean task of building a new basis of Democratic support in the South, and one that would pay off politically only in the long run. Such presidential leadership would also mean extensive intervention in Congress. Not only would the minority devices of the congressional parties be swept away, but the President would have to throw himself into the legislative battle to fashion party machinery for the more effective debating and handling of legislation. Hence he would have to ignore the absurd "rule" (usually ignored in practice) that the President does not interfere in the legislative department. He must interfere, and openly so.

This intervention need not be the negative, abortive, and even vengeful action that it so often has been in the past. The President's job is to strengthen the presidential party machinery in Congress, not simply to circumvent or undermine the present machinery. Similarly, in the House and Senate elections he should intervene to help presidential party candidates for Congress, not simply to oppose the men who disagree with him. The trouble with Roosevelt's purge was not the objective, but the hasty, improvised, and negative way in which it was carried out. If he had strengthened the presidential party in selected states and districts, had recruited the ablest candidates, had seen that they had ample help on finance, registration, publicity, and other campaign needs—if, in short, he had worked through a local, indigenous unit of the presidential party instead of coming in from the outside, he might have come nearer to his goal of a more unified and liberal party. What congressmen in competitive districts need from the President is less to be coaxed, bribed, or threatened—they need *help*.

Nothing fails like failure, or is so educational. The purge was a failure; what is needed is a purge in reverse. The great task of the presidential party is to forge a new majority, just as the Jeffersonians and Jacksonians did, organized down to the wards and precincts, towns and villages, and effective in Congress as well as in the executive branch. Whether this task will be accomplished by the presidential Democrats under John F. Kennedy, or by the presidential Republicans under someone like Rockefeller, is one of the tantalizing questions of the future. Tantalizing—and epochal, for the presidential party that first gains control of its congressional party will dominate the politics of the center left or center right for decades to come.

It may be that Kennedy will be the first President to grasp the great possibilities open to a creative party leader. "Legislative leadership is not possible without party leadership," he said early in the year that he was elected to the Presidency. "No President, it seems to me, can escape politics. He has not only been chosen by the nation—he has been chosen by his party. And if he insists that he is 'President of all the people' and should therefore offend none of them—if he blurs the issues and differences between the two parties—if he neglects the party machinery and avoids his party's leadership—then he has not only weakened the political party as an instrument of the democratic process—he has dealt a death blow to the democratic process itself."

The cure for democracy, people used to say, is more democracy. A half century of hard experience has shown this cliché to be a dangerous half-truth. The cure for democracy is leadership—responsible, committed, effective, and exuberant leadership. The man and the party who take the lead in modernizing our political system, in establishing a majority party able to govern and a minority party able to oppose, will have helped put an end to the dangerous cycle of drift and deadlock in our national affairs. They will have enabled Americans to regain control of their national politics and to define and assert their national purpose.

Acknowledgments

Criticism of the American system of government is as old a tradition as the system itself. My indebtedness to the major critics, at least from Woodrow Wilson on, is clear, I trust, from the text and from my sources. Since World War II a number of younger political scientists have continued and invigorated that tradition with searching studies of the behavior of American politicians and the mechanics of American government. A number of these political scientists have criticized the manuscript of this book and my debt to them is enormous. They are Stephen K. Bailey, Dean of the Maxwell School at Syracuse University, author of a brilliant study of the Employment Act of 1946 and other studies of Congress, and a practitioner as well as a student of American government; Paul T. David, formerly of the Brookings Institution and now at the University of Virginia, who has an encyclopedic knowledge of the complexities of American government as well as a highly practical grasp of both the need and difficulty of reform; Duane Lockard of Prince-

341

ton, formerly a member of the Connecticut State Senate, an authority on the politics of the New England states, and a keen student of the obscure but vital struggles of state and local politicians; my long-time colleague, Jack W. Peltason, Dean of the College of Liberal Arts and Sciences of the University of Illinois, who has assisted and encouraged me with his usual generosity; and Austin Ranney, of the University of Illinois, author of a major study of the doctrine of party responsibility, among other works, whose criticism was all the more valuable because of his own somewhat more pluralistic emphasis. Samuel H. Beer of Harvard; Ralph M. Goldman, formerly of Michigan State University and now at San Francisco State College; George Goodwin, Jr., recently of the University of Massachusetts and now at the University of Rhode Island; and Lester G. Seligman of the University of Oregon, have also generously given me the benefit of acute comments and suggestions.

I am also grateful to my fellow political scientists at Williams, Mac-Alister Brown and Kurt P. Tauber, who reviewed parts of the manuscript; to Dean Robert R. R. Brooks of Williams, who made many useful editorial suggestions; to the helpful members of the staff of the Williams College Library, an ideal working place for a researcher; to Mrs. Margaret S. Thompson for discerning proofreading; to Stephen S. Cohen, for assistance on bibliographical research; and to Mrs. Louisa Blair, Mrs. Eugenie H. Fitzhugh, and Mrs. Mary Rita Healey for stenographic assistance. My wife, Janet Thompson Burns, assistant director of the Center for Development of Economics at Williams, made most useful suggestions from the vantage point of her broader view of a politically overdeveloped nation such as our own, as did students of the Center, notably A. S. Sholola of Nigeria, and members of my undergraduate course in American politics.

I am greatly indebted to the Rockefeller Foundation for financial assistance that enabled me to take time off from my teaching to work on historical and theoretical aspects of the "Madisonian and Jeffersonian models"; to the Social Science Research Council, for appointment to a Senior Research Award in American Governmental Affairs, which enabled me to travel to a number of states to interview officeholders, candidates, and party officials; and to the host of politicians who answered my questions and, I hope, greatly enlarged and deepened my understanding of American politics.

J.M.B.

Sources

Sources

CHAPTER 1

My main general sources on Madison are Gaillard Hunt, ed., *The Writings of James Madison,* 9 vols., New York, G. P. Putnam's Sons, 1901, and Irving Brant, *James Madison, The President, 1809–1812,* 5 vols., Indianapolis, The Bobbs-Merrill Company, Inc., 1941–56.

The Road to Philadelphia: My reconstruction of Madison's journey from New York to Philadelphia is based on scattered and fragmentary sources, but I believe this to be an essentially accurate picture. I have used Christopher Colles, *A Survey of the Roads of the United States of America, 1789,* ed., Walter W. Ristow, Cambridge, Belknap Press of Harvard University Press, 1961; Charles William Janson, *The Stranger in America, 1793–1801,* New York, The Press of Pioneers, Inc., 1935; Charles H. Sherrill, *French Memories of Eighteenth-Century America,* New York, Charles Scribner's Sons, 1915; "Patrick M'Robert's Tour through Part of the North Provinces of America," *The Pennsylvania Magazine of History and Biography,* Vol. LIX, Philadelphia, 1935; and Seymour Dunbar, *A History of Travel in America,* Vol. 1, Indianapolis, Bobbs-Merrill, 1915. Miss Selma Shapiro kindly assisted on research on

Madison's journey. On political affairs prior to the Constitutional Convention see Edmund Cody Burnett, *The Continental Congress,* New York, The Macmillan Company, 1941; Allan Nevins, *The American States During and After the Revolution, 1775–1789,* New York, The Macmillan Company, 1924; and Merrill Jensen, *The New Nation: A History of the United States During the Confederation, 1781–1789,* 1st ed., New York, Alfred A. Knopf, Inc., 1950. Jensen and other historians demonstrate that much of the criticism of the government under the Confederation was exaggerated, but I have tried to picture the situation as Madison saw it. The quotations from Madison are from his *Writings,* Vol. II, or from Brant, Vol. 2. In particular, for Madison's statement on the causes of faction, which anticipates his much-quoted paragraph in *The Federalist,* No. 10, see his *Writings,* Vol. II, pp. 366–67. I have used Madison's earlier version because *The Federalist* has often been treated as a rationalization of actions taken in the Constitutional Convention, whereas the Convention should be seen also as a realization of views held by Madison and his colleagues earlier.

The "Profound Politician" and "Scholar": On the Constitutional Convention, I have used the standard sources: Max Farrand, ed., *The Records of the Federal Convention of 1787,* 4 vols., New Haven, Yale University Press, 1911–37; Farrand, *The Framing of the Constitution of the United States,* New Haven, Yale University Press, 1913; Charles Warren, *The Making of the Constitution,* Boston, Little, Brown & Company, 1937. Carl Van Doren, *The Great Rehearsal;* the Story of the Making and Ratifying of the Constitution of the United States, 1st ed., New York, Viking Press, 1948, gives a good narrative of the discussion and picture of the setting. I have exploited John C. Miller's excellent *Alexander Hamilton Portrait in Paradox,* 1st ed., New York, Harper & Brothers, 1959, and other biographies of members of the convention. Brant, *op. cit.,* Vol. 3, traces Madison's role in detail and, I think, with balance. The description of Madison by the Georgia delegate (William Pierce) is from Farrand, *The Framing of the Constitution,* p. 17. I have used the Edward Mead Earle edition of *The Federalist,* New York, n.d. On the uses and misuses of *The Federalist,* see W. W. Crosskey, *Politics and the Constitution in the History of the United States,* 2 vols. Chicago, University of Chicago Press, 1953, pp. 8–11. E. S. Corwin, *The President; Office and Powers; History and Analysis of Practice and Opinion,* New York, New York University Press, 1941, analyzes early conceptions of the office. A. N. Holcombe, *Our More Perfect Union; From Eighteenth-Century Principles to Twentieth-Century Practice,* Cambridge, Harvard University Press, 1950, is indispensable for this period and, indeed, the whole growth of the Federal government.

The Theory of Minority Checks: See Miller, *op. cit.,* on Hamilton and *The Federalist.* E. M. Burns, *James Madison, Philosopher of the Constitution,* New Brunswick, N.J., Rutgers University Press, 1938, is a handy compilation of Madison's theories, but without sufficient regard for the changes over time. R. A. Dahl, *A Preface to Democratic Theory,* Chicago, University of Chicago Press, 1956, begins with a penetrating study of "Madisonian Democracy" that was indispensable to my own analysis; my quotation from him is from this book, page 28. The Hofstadter quotation is from Richard Hofstadter, *The American Political Tradition and the Men Who Made It,* New York, Vintage Books, Inc., 1948, p. 9; see also his summary of the ideas of the Framers. On the political setting in which the Constitutional fathers operated and the highly practical considerations that shaped their decisions, see the original and penetrating study, John P. Roche, "The Founding Fathers: A Reform Caucus in Action," *The American Political Science Review,* Vol. LV, No. 4 (December, 1961), 799–816.

CHAPTER 2

For Jefferson's reaction to the drafts of the new Constitution, see Nathan Schachner, *Thomas Jefferson,* 2 vols., New York, Appleton-Century-Crofts, Inc., 1951, pp. 343–46. The "botanizing expedition" has been both inflated and deflated by historians. Compare for example, W. E. Binkley, *American Political Parties: Their Natural History,* New York, Alfred A. Knopf, Inc., 1947, p. 78, and Schachner, *op. cit.,* Vol. I, 435–36. Probably it had little immediate party-building value but considerable long-term, symbolic importance for Jefferson's political leadership. Richard Hofstadter, *The American Political Tradition, and the Men Who Made It,* New York, Vintage Books, Inc., 1954, shrewdly describes the two Jeffersons.

The First Congressional Republicans: This attack of Jefferson on parties is quoted in Schachner, Vol. I, 367–68; the attack of the Philadelphian is quoted in N. E. Cunningham, Jr., *The Jeffersonian Republicans; the Formation of Party Organization, 1789–1801,* Chapel Hill, N.C., University of North Carolina Press, 1957, pp. 41–42. John C. Miller, *Alexander Hamilton,* describes Hamilton's methods as legislative leader for Washington. On the rise of the Republicans in Congress, see N. E. Cunningham, *op. cit.:* an impressive work of scholarship that corrects many earlier findings and which proves, in my view, that the first national party developed first in Congress around the Republican majority. It could be argued that the first really national party was a Federalist presidential party oriented around Hamilton, but his group, I believe, lacked the political roots in the country that Cunningham shows the Congressional Republicans to have developed. Cunningham, *op. cit.,* p. 72, is my source for the South Carolinian's complaint about disciplined parties, and P. L. Ford, ed., *The Writings of Thomas Jefferson,* Vol. VIII, New York, G. P. Putnam's Sons, 1896, pp. 316–19, on Jefferson's.

Jefferson Builds a Party: Jefferson's analysis of Federalist supporters is in Schachner, Vol. II, p. 571. Cunningham is indispensable on the organizing of the Republican party for the presidential campaign of 1800. Jefferson's analysis of the New York political situation is from P. L. Ford, *Works,* Vol. VII, p. 434. See Cunningham for correctives of the usual description of the New York City campaign. Nathan Schachner, *Aaron Burr; A Biography,* New York, Frederick A. Stokes Company, 1937, describes Burr's electioneering in greater detail, but exaggerates, according to Cunningham, the role of Tammany. Frank van der Linden, *The Turning Point,* Washington, D.C., 1962, treats in detail the infighting that accompanied the election of Jefferson by Congress. Jefferson's famous "What is practicable . . ." statement was in a letter to Dupont de Nemours, Jan. 18, 1802, quoted in Ford, *Works,* VIII, 125–27. The fullest treatment of Jefferson's political and legislative methods is still R. V. Harlow, *The History of Legislative Methods in the Period Before 1825,* New Haven, Yale University Press, 1917; see also L. D. White's comprehensive administrative history, *The Jeffersonians,* New York, The Macmillan Company, 1951. For views of Randolph from differing perspectives, see Henry Adams, *John Randolph,* Boston, Houghton, Mifflin and Company, 1882; and W. C. Bruce, *John Randolph of Roanoke, 1773–1833,* 2 vols., New York, G. P. Putnam's Son, 1922; W. E. Binkley, *President and Congress,* New York, Alfred A. Knopf, Inc., 1947, is my source for the Marshall statement.

The Theory of Majority Rule: Marshall's reaction to Jefferson's Inaugural is quoted in Nathan Schachner, *Thomas Jefferson,* 2 vols., New York, Appleton-Century-Crofts, 1951, Vol. VII, p. 665. A. T. Mason, *Free Government in the Making; Readings in American Political Thought,* 2nd ed., New York, Oxford University Press, 1956, contains the text of most of the Inaugural. I base my conclusions as to Jefferson's real political tactic in the Inaugural on letters he wrote at the time, Ford, *Works,* Vol. VIII, pp. 7–11, and on a remarkable article, *Conciliation with the Federalists* that Jefferson wrote and sent in 1803 to his Attorney-General to be printed in a newspaper as a letter from a Massachusetts citizen; this is reprinted in S. K. Padover, *The Complete Jefferson,* New

York, Duell, Sloan & Pearce, Inc., 1943, pp. 278–82. On the theory of majority rule see R. A. Dahl, *op. cit.*, especially chap. 2; Edwin Mims, Jr., *The Majority of the People*, New York, Modern Age Books, 1941; H. S. Commager, *Majority Rule and Minority Rights*, New York, Oxford University Press, 1943; and Austin Ranney and Wilmoore Kendall, *Democracy and the American Party System*, New York, Harcourt, Brace and Company, Inc., 1956. The Republican Party's moderate role under Jefferson is noted in M. J. Dauer, *The Adams Federalists*, Baltimore, Johns Hopkins Press, 1953.

The Checking and Balancing of James Madison: Agar, Harlow, Binkley, and White uniformly present the accepted historical picture of Madison as an "inert" President. Brant's *James Madison, the President, (1809–1812)*, shows that Madison was less inert in the war crisis than had been supposed, but it does not change the old picture of a *roi fainéant*. The Federalists' prediction about Madison is quoted in Brant, Vol. V, p. 12. Gallatin's letter of resignation to Madison is in Henry Adams, ed., *The Writings of Albert Gallatin*, Philadelphia, J. B. Lippincott & Co., 1879, Vol. I, 495. The term "administration party" was used by John Taylor and is quoted in Brant, Vol. V, p. 272. On Clay as Speaker see M. P. Follett, *The Speaker of the House of Representatives*, New York, Longmans, Green & Company, 1896. Agar's summing up of Madison is in *The Price of Union*, p. 198.

CHAPTER 3

On the decline of the Federalists see W. E. Binkley, *American Political Parties*. Excellent general sources on the election of 1824 are George Dangerfield, *The Era of Good Feelings*, New York, Harcourt, Brace and Company, 1952, and S. F. Bemis, *John Quincy Adams and the Union*, New York, Alfred A. Knopf, Inc., 1956. E. S. Brown, "The Presidential Elections of 1824–1825," *Political Science Quarterly*, Vol. 40, No. 3 (September, 1925), 384–403, leans heavily on the letters of a New Hampshire Representative. The Dangerfield quotation is from *The Era of Good Feelings*, p. 335.

The Flowering of the Parties: Robert V. Remini, *Martin Van Buren and the Making of the Democratic Party*, New York, Columbia University Press, 1959, emphasizes Van Buren's party objectives in enlisting in Jackson's cause; the quotations from Jackson are from pp. 130–31 of this book. See also Van Buren's autobiography in *Annual Report of the American Historical Association, 1918*, Vol. II, Washington, D.C., 1920. The Federalist conclave of 1808 is described as the first national nominating convention in S. E. Morison, "The First National Nominating Convention, 1808," *American Historical Review,* Vol. 17 (1912), 744–63. The reference to the convention as a means of concentrating the popular will is from *Niles' Weekly Register,* Vol. 48, May 23, 1835, quoted in P. T. David, R. M. Goldman, and R. C. Bain, *The Politics of National Party Conventions,* Washington, D.C., The Brookings Institution, 1960, p. 19, a definitive work on the subject. On the rise of national party machinery, especially the national committee, see R. M. Goldman, "Party Chairman and Party Faction, 1789–1900: A Theory of Executive Responsibility and Conflict Resolution," unpublished, Chicago, 1951, which is a source of many insights into the mechanisms of the national parties. On the scope and significance of patronage during this period see L. D. White, *The Jacksonians; A Study in Administrative History, 1829–1861,* New York, The Macmillan Company, 1956. On the suffrage, Chilton Williamson, *American Suffrage; From Property to Democracy, 1760–1860,* Princeton, N.J., Princeton University Press, 1960, reveals in passing the impact of enfranchisement on political ambitions as well as egalitarian attitudes. H. J. Ford, *The Rise and Growth of American Politics; A Sketch of Constitutional Development,* New York, The Macmillan Company, 1898, is a general description that takes up, if it does not always resolve, problems of intraparty relationships in the pre-Civil War period. Ivan Hinderaker, *Party Politics,* New York, Henry Holt & Company, 1956, supplies political diagrams and maps that are most helpful for a generalized view of the party battle. Some of the ironies of Clay's political career are treated in Clement Eaton, *Henry Clay and the Art of American Politics,* 1st ed., Boston, Little, Brown & Company, 1957. The Tocqueville quotation is from Phillips Bradley, ed., *Democracy in America,* New York, Alfred A. Knopf, 1945, Vol. II, 177–78. The quotation from David, Goldman, and Bain is from their volume cited above, p. 209.

Whigs: The Erosion of the Center: Holman Hamilton, "Democratic Senate Leadership and the Compromise of 1850," *Mississippi Valley Historical Review,* Vol. XLI, No. 3 (December, 1954), 403–18, gives Stephen A. Douglas his due credit in sponsoring the Compromise of 1850. The literature on the coming of the Civil War is stupendous; an admirable introduction to leading theories of causation is E. C. Rozwenc, *The Causes of the American Civil War,* Boston, D. C. Heath and Company, 1961, which includes excerpts from James Ford Rhodes, Charles A. Beard, James G. Randall, Allan Nevins, and other historians of the period. Herbert Agar's comment on the Whigs and their generals is from *The Price of Union,* Boston, Houghton Mifflin Company, 1950, p. 349.

On the decline of the Whigs, I have used A. C. Cole, *The Whig Party in the South*, Washington, American Historical Association, 1913; Paul Murray, *The Whig Party in Georgia, 1825–1853*, Chapel Hill, N.C., University of North Carolina Press, 1948; and H. R. Mueller, *The Whig Party in Pennsylvania*, New York, Columbia University Press, 1922. My conclusions on the decline of Whig congressional strength are based on figures from *The Tribune Almanac*, New York, Vol. I, 1868. Goldman and Bain, *The Politics of National Party Conventions*, p. 184, documents the failures of the Whigs to develop integrating machinery.

Democrats: The Strategy of Disruption: On the politics of the 1850's, I have used chiefly Avery O. Craven, *The Coming of the Civil War*, Chicago, University of Chicago Press, 1957; R. F. Nichols, *The Disruption of American Democracy*, New York, The Macmillan Company, 1948; and Allan Nevins' incomparable volumes, *Ordeal of the Union* (Vol. I, *Fruits of Manifest Destiny, 1847–1852*; Vol. II, *A House Dividing, 1852–1857*), New York, Charles Scribner's Sons, 1947; and *The Emergence of Lincoln* (Vol. I, *Douglas, Buchanan, and Party Chaos: 1857–1859*; Vol. II, *Prologue to Civil War: 1859–1861*), New York, Charles Scribner's Sons, 1950. The quotations from Nevins are from *A House Dividing*, p. 121. Two biographies that throw light on the personalities of two important Senators are G. M. Capers, *Stephen A. Douglas, Defender of the Union*, 1st ed., Boston, Little, Brown & Company, 1959, and David H. Donald, *Charles Sumner and the Coming of the Civil War*, 1st ed., New York, Alfred A. Knopf, Inc., 1960. On Democratic Party developments in the states see R. F. Nichols, *The Democratic Machine, 1850–1854*, New York, Columbia University Press, 1923. P. S. Klein, *President James Buchanan*, University Park, Pa., Pennsylvania State University Press, 1962, is a recent full biography.

Why Did the Parties Fail? On the Speaker and congressional committees during the 19th century see M. P. Follett, *The Speaker of the House of Representatives*, New York, Longmans, Green and Co., 1896; D. S. Alexander, *History and Procedure of the House of Representatives*, Boston, Houghton Mifflin Company, 1916; and L. G. M. McConachie, *Congressional Committees*, New York, T. Y. Crowell & Co., 1898. See David, Goldman, and Bain, *op. cit.*, for penetrating comments on party developments in the pre-Civil War period.

CHAPTER 4

The politics of Civil War and Reconstruction is such a rich field of learning and publication that a full statement of indebtedness would be impossible here. B. J. Hendrick, *Lincoln's War Cabinet*, Boston, Little, Brown and Company, 1946, gives a vivid and detailed account of the Seward-Chase affair and is the source (p. 324) of the quotation on the attempt of the legislature to seize the executive power. Harriet Beecher Stowe is quoted in W. E. Binkley, *American Political Parties*, New York, Alfred A. Knopf, Inc., 1947, p. 240. Lincoln's pleasure on his final day at the prospect of governing without Congress was noted by several intimates; see Herbert Agar, *The Price of Union*, Boston, Houghton Mifflin Company, 1950, p. 436.

The Seesaw of the Parties: E. D. Ross, *The Liberal Republican Movement*, New York, H. Holt and Company, 1919, treats that party's relations with, and contributions to, the post-Civil War Democratic party. Statistical material on party competition at the congressional and state level during the 1870's and 1880's is scattered; see the revealing figures in V. O. Key, Jr., *American State Politics: An Introduction*, New York, Alfred A. Knopf, Inc., 1956, p. 119; *The Congressional Directory*, Washington, D.C., which during this period presents congressional voting returns inconveniently in the members' biographies; *The Tribune Almanac*, New York; and E. E. Schattschneider, *The Semisovereign People: A Realist's View of Democracy in America*, 1st ed., New York, Holt, Rinehart and Winston, 1960. Woodrow Wilson recorded the disintegration of policy-making in *Congressional Government: A Study in American Politics*, Boston, Houghton Mifflin & Company, 1885. One of the fullest and liveliest general treatments of the period is Matthew Josephson, *The Politicos, 1865–1896*, New York, Harcourt, Brace and Company, Inc., 1938. On Cleveland's presidency see Allan Nevins, *Grover Cleveland; A Study in Courage*, New York, Dodd, Mead & Company, Inc., 1932, an admiring report; more critical of Cleveland and the Eastern Democrats is H. S. Merrill, *Bourbon Democracy of the Middle West, 1865–1896*, Baton Rouge, Louisiana State University Press, 1953, and H. S. Merrill, *Bourbon Leader: Grover Cleveland and the Democratic Party*, 1st ed., Boston, Little, Brown and Company, 1957. Paxton Hibben, *The Peerless Leader, William Jennings Bryan*, New York, Farrar and Rinehart, Inc., 1929, is a full-bodied life. Nevins refers to the "Senatorial clique" in his *Cleveland*. K. H. Porter, *National Party Platforms*, New York, The Macmillan Company, 1924, is a standard source for party pledges, including those of third parties. H. L. Mencken's social portrait of Bryan as a rustic is from his *Prejudices*, 5th series, New York, Alfred A. Knopf, Inc., 1926, reprinted in G. F. Whicher, ed., *William Jennings Bryan and the Campaign of 1896*, Boston, D. C. Heath & Co., 1953. E. E. Schattschneider, *The Semisovereign People* presents graphically some of the election results of the 1896 overturn. V. O. Key, Jr., "A Theory of Critical Elections," *The Journal of Politics*, Vol. 17, No. 1 (February, 1955), 3–18, shows the force of the straight sectional voting in New England; see William Diamond, "Urban and Rural Voting in 1896," *The American Historical Review*, Vol. 46, January, 1941, 281–305, and Key's comments on same in his footnote 12.

The Parties under Attack: On 1896 as a crucial election see E. E. Schattschneider, *op. cit.*, pp. 78–83 and V. O. Key, Jr., "A Theory of Critical Elections," *The Journal of Politics*, Vol. 17, No. 1 (February, 1955), 3–18. C. E. Merriam and Louise Overacker, *Primary Elections*, rev. ed., Chicago, University of Chicago Press, 1928, is a standard source. Richard Hofstadter, *The Age of Reform; From Bryan to F.D.R.*, New York, Alfred A. Knopf, Inc., 1959, Chap. 6 is an illuminating treatment of the attitudes of many progressives toward leadership and organization; on Herbert Croly see also Eric Goldman, *Rendezvous With Destiny*, New York, Alfred A. Knopf, Inc., 1952, and Croly's two major theoretical works, *Progressive Democracy*, New York, Macmillan Company, 1914, and *The Promise of American Life*, New York, Macmillan Company, 1914. California's dismantling of parties is described in D. R. Cresap, *Party Politics in the Golden State*, Los Angeles, Haynes Foundation, 1954, and discussed in J. Q. Wilson, *Intellectuals as Politicians*, unpublished, Chicago, 1961. A. N. Holcombe, *Our More Perfect Union*, Cambridge, Harvard University Press, 1950, offers a judicious treatment of present and past powers of the Speaker; see also G. R. Brown, *The Leadership of Congress*, Indianapolis, Bobbs-Merrill Company, 1922. On Cannon's rule and misrule see *Uncle Joe Cannon; The Story of a Pioneer American, as Told to L. White Busbey, for 20 Years His Private Secretary*, by L. White Busbey, New York, H. Holt and Company, 1927, and a more critical treatment, Blair Bolles, *Tyrant from Illinois; Uncle Joe Cannon's Experiment with Personal Power*, 1st ed., New York, W. W. Norton and Company, Inc.; Norris's activities are described in Alfred Lief, *Democracy's Norris; The Biography of a Lonely Crusade*, New York, Stackpole Sons, 1939, and in his autobiography, *Fighting Liberal*, New York, The Macmillan Company, 1945. B. C. La Follette and Fola La Follette, *Robert M. La Follette, June 14, 1885–June 18, 1925*, 2 vols., New York, The Macmillan Company, 1953, describes the progressive attack on "Aldrichism" in the Senate. The quotation is from Herbert Croly, *Progressive Democracy*, p. 343; see also his earlier more influential work, *The Promise of American Life*, M. I. Ostrogorski, *Democracy and the Organization of Political Parties, A Study in Extra-Constitutional Government*, New York, Macmillan Co., 1902, Vol. II, chap. 10, is a massive critique of the oligarchical tendencies of the party caucus.

American Hybrid: A Look Back and Ahead: The literature on political machines in America is long and luxuriant. D. W. Brogan, *Politics in America,* New York, Harper & Brothers, 1954, chap. 4, provides a knowing survey with numerous references to the literature. On party developments in the South see V. O. Key, Jr., *Southern Politics in State and Nation,* 1st ed., New York, Alfred A. Knopf, Inc., 1949, and C. Vann Woodward, *Origins of the New South, 1877–1913,* Baton Rouge, Louisiana State University Press, 1951. A. T. Hadley, *Undercurrents in American Politics,* New Haven, Yale University Press, 1915, perceptively noted the contemporary transfer of political power from party organization to groups of individuals. On the decline in voting see R. E. Lane, *Political Life: Why People Get Involved in Politics,* Glencoe, Ill., Free Press, 1959; the quotation is from p. 23. A. N. Holcombe's studies of the growth of parties and the shift from sectional politics to class politics are indispensable to a general understanding of recent party politics.

CHAPTER 5

The Tocqueville quotation is from *Democracy in America,* Francis Bowen, ed., Cambridge, Sever & Frances, 1862, p. 226. On antimajoritarian feeling, see the volumes by H. S. Commager and Edwin Mims, Jr. cited above.

The Colonel and the Boss: Theodore Roosevelt describes his early approaches to the organization, and his friends' reactions, in his *Theodore Roosevelt—An Autobiography,* New York, The Macmillan Company, 1913; see also H. F. Pringle, *Theodore Roosevelt, A Biography,* New York, Harcourt, Brace and Company, 1931, pp. 59ff. He described his reactions to his fellow legislators in his diary, a fragment of which has survived and appears in the appendix of E. E. Morison, J. M. Blum, and J. J. Buckley, *The Letters of Theodore Roosevelt,* 8 vols., Cambridge, Harvard University Press, 1951, Vol. II, 1469–73. This eight-volume edition of Roosevelt's correspondence, referred to below as *Letters,* is indispensable to understanding almost all phases of Roosevelt's political career. Roosevelt's remarks against serving as a guerrilla chief are quoted in Pringle, *op. cit.,* p. 88, and his remark about the reformers' myopia in a letter to Lodge, *Letters,* Vol. 1, p. 75. The adjectives used in portraying the reformers are all drawn from *Letters,* Vols. 1 and 2, *passim.* These volumes, pp. 871–77, and Roosevelt's autobiography, pp. 293–96, are major sources on Roosevelt's nomination for governor; see also the careful account in *Letters,* Vol. 2, App. II, p. 1474–8. Chauncey M.

Depew, *My Memories of Eighty Years,* New York, Charles Scribner's Sons, 1924, pp. 161–62, relates Depew's communication with T. C. Platt; see also the latter's more austere account in T. C. Platt, *The Autobiography of Thomas Collier Platt,* New York, B. W. Dodge & Company, 1910, pp. 367–69, a book worth reading for insights into the philosophy of a party regular, and dedicated appropriately to his "Old Guard." Roosevelt's *Autobiography* confirms the impressions of a "soft pact" between Platt and Roosevelt. The *Letters,* Vol. 2, pictures Roosevelt's touchy relations with Platt through the Governor's eyes. A long footnote by the editors (*Letters,* Vol. 2, pp. 1337–8) describes Roosevelt's nomination for Vice-President with emphasis on Platt's residual control; see also Platt, *op. cit.,* chap. 19. Hanna's famous reputed remark about Roosevelt as a madman is quoted in Pringle, *op. cit.,* p. 223. The estimate of Roosevelt's campaign travels is from a *New York Times* dispatch cited in Pringle, *op. cit.,* p. 225.

A *"Regular with a Conscience":* Steffens relates Riis's encounter with Roosevelt in his *Autobiography of Lincoln Steffens,* New York, Harcourt, Brace & Co., 1931, pp. 258–60. Roosevelt's presidential ambitions are indicated *inter alia* in *Letters,* Vol. 3, pp. 132, 136, 140. The description of Roosevelt as a "regular with a conscience" is from J. M. Blum, *The Republican Roosevelt,* Cambridge, Harvard University Press, 1954, a trenchant study that derives special authority from the author's associate editorship of the *Letters.* Roosevelt commented on his vice-presidential observations to William Howard Taft, *Letters,* Vol. 3, p. 12. For examples of Roosevelt's conciliatory approach to Senators during his first term, see *Letters,* Vol. 3, pp. 154, 155, 161, 201, 207, and especially his letter to W. H. Taft, pp. 450–51. His evaluation of the limits of his own power during the coal strike is from the same source, p. 332 (letter to Henry Cabot Lodge). Blum, *op. cit.,* chap. 6, and W. H. Harbaugh, *Power and Responsibility; The Life and Times of Theodore Roosevelt,* New York, Farrar, Straus & Cudahy, Inc., 1961, offer revealing accounts of Roosevelt's handling of tariff and railroad legislation. Roosevelt's comments on the matter are in *Letters,* Vol. 3, pp. 312, 317. Herbert Agar, *The Price of Union,* Boston, Houghton Mifflin Company, 1950, p. 650, quotes Roosevelt's famous statement about the canal. J. M. Blum, *op. cit.,* chap. 4, describes the President's forcing Hanna to back down, as a case study in Rooseveltian use of power. On the Missouri situation see *Letters,* Vol. 3, p. 688 and Vol. 4, p. 771. Roosevelt's effort to separate the debates over national and state questions is shown in *Letters,* Vol. 4, pp. 960, 983; and see the same volume, p. 987, for the Mr. Dooley comment.

Taft and the Congressional Republicans: Roosevelt's anti-third-term avowal is cited in *Letters,* Vol. 4, p. 1021, footnote 2. Mr. Dooley's famous remark is quoted in Eric Goldman, *Rendezvous with Destiny; A History of Modern American Reform,* New York, Alfred A. Knopf, Inc., 1952, p. 175. The quotations illustrating Roosevelt's shift leftward are from *Letters,* Vol. 6, pp. 1257–8, p. 1400 and p. 1369, respectively. See the *Letters, passim,* for Roosevelt's role in arousing, formally and informally, organized support for his program. His criticism of the "ruling clique" is from a letter to Albert Shaw, May 22, 1908, *Letters,* Vol. 6, p. 1033. Roosevelt's defense of Aldrich and Company is in a letter to Taft, March 19, 1903, *Letters,* Vol. 3, p. 450. My major sources on Taft's administration are H. F. Pringle's sympathetic *The Life and Times of William Howard Taft, a Biography,* 2 vols., New York, Farrar & Rinehart, Inc., 1939, and George E. Mowry, *The Era of Theodore Roosevelt: 1900–1912,* 1st ed., New York, Harper & Brothers, 1958. Pringle, *Taft,* p. 382, cites Taft's statement that his Cabinet appointees were selected with an eye to pleasing Congress. Mowry offers a perceptive account of Taft's relations with Congress. Pringle, p. 415, quotes Taft's "love letters" to Hale and Aldrich. The biographies of Aldrich, La Follette, and other congressional leaders, as cited above, offer illuminating sidelights on the Taft regime.

Conscience Without Regulars: Roosevelt attacked both the regulars and the "ultra-insurgents" in a letter to Elihu Root, Oct. 21, 1910, *Letters,* Vol. 7, pp. 146–49. B. C. La Follette and Fola La Follette, *Robert M. La Follette,* 2 vols., New York, The Macmillan Company, 1953, chaps. 31–35, offer a detailed account of Roosevelt's capturing of progressive leadership from the viewpoint of an "ultra-insurgent" rival. A short but highly revealing note by Alfred D. Chandler, Jr., "The Origins of Progressive Leadership," *Letters,* Vol. 8, App. III, based on a study of the backgrounds of two hundred and sixty Progressive Party leaders, stresses the urban, upper middle-class, independent background of Roosevelt's supporters. Richard Hofstadter, *The Age of Reform; From Bryan to F.D.R.,* New York, Alfred A. Knopf, Inc., 1949, offers a brilliant account of the intellectual background and problems of the Progressives. Eric Goldman, *Rendezvous with Destiny,* cited above, has an insightful chapter on Croly's influence on Roosevelt; recent Roosevelt scholars hold that Croly simply confirmed a trend in Roosevelt's thinking. The December 5, 1911, letter about Roosevelt's plans is in *Letters,* Vol. 7, pp. 450–52; the earlier letter, written as Vice-President, is from *Letters,* Vol. 3, p. 136; see also this volume, pp. 132–33. Root's reference to Roosevelt as a "thirsty sinner" is from Philip C. Jessup, *Elihu Root,* New York, Dodd, Mead

& Co., 1938, Vol. II, pp. 173–75; the rest of this letter (to Roosevelt) is worth reading. The Governor's appeal to Roosevelt and his reply are in *Letters,* Vol. 7, p. 511. The description of the Bull Moose Convention is from G. E. Mowry, *Theodore Roosevelt and the Progressive Movement,* Madison, Wisc., The University of Wisconsin Press, 1946, a basic work. E. E. Morison delineates a different morality from the Progressives in his fine biography of Stimson, *Turmoil and Tradition,* Boston, Houghton Mifflin Company, 1960. The reporter describing Roosevelt's seeming bewilderment at the convention is cited in Harbaugh, *op. cit.,* which provides a moving account of the stand at Armageddon.

CHAPTER 6

"Cabinet Government in the United States" appeared in the *International Review,* Vol. VII (August, 1879), pp. 144–63, under the name of Thomas W. Wilson. On Lodge's coeditorship of the *Review* see J. A. Garraty *Henry Cabot Lodge; A Biography,* 1st ed., New York, Alfred A. Knopf, Inc., 1953. Arthur S. Link, *Wilson: The Road To the White House,* Princeton, N.J., Princeton University Press, 1947, describes the critical reception; Link and Walter Lippmann, in an introduction to Woodrow Wilson's *Congressional Government; A Study in American Politics,* New York, Meridian Books, Inc., M27, 1956, (paperback version of original edition published by Houghton Mifflin, Boston, 1885), are among those who question the originality and profundity of Wilson's early analysis. Wilson's comment on the un-English quality of the separation of powers is from the *International Review* article cited above, p. 162. His continuing concern with leadership is reflected in the writings cited above and in those listed in Link, *op. cit.,* p. 535; and in a revealing essay written by Wilson in 1890 and published only recently in T. H. Vail Motter, ed., *Leaders of Men,* Princeton, N.J., Princeton University Press, 1952. Richard Hofstadter has a typically perceptive treatment of Wilson's formative influences, in *The American Political Tradition,* New York, Vintage Books, Inc., 1948, chap. 10. Link, *op. cit.,* chaps. 2–4, provide a full account of Wilson's battles at Princeton and his entrance into politics. Wilson's views of American government on the eve of his moving into broader academic politics and then into party politics were published in *Constitutional Government in the United States,* New York, The Columbia University Press, 1908. A. J. Warren, "The Development of Woodrow Wilson's Theory of the Presidency: Continuity and Change," in Earl Latham, ed., *The Philosophy and Policies of Woodrow Wilson,* Chicago, University of Chicago Press,

1958, pp. 46–66, is a useful summary and overview of the changes in Wilson's attitude toward the Presidency. A notable effort at psychological inquiry, gleaming with insights, is Alexander L. George and Juliette L. George, *Woodrow Wilson and Colonel House; A Personality Study*, New York, John Day & Co., Inc., 1956; the content of this volume is much broader than the title suggests.

The Scholar and the Boss: The remark about Wilson's jaw is taken from R. S. Baker, *Woodrow Wilson; Life and Letters*, New York, Doubleday, Doran, Inc., 1931, Vol. III, p. 80; there is a slightly different version in Link, *op. cit.*, p. 167. Wilson's acceptance speech excerpts are also from Baker, *op. cit.*, p. 79. Link, *op. cit.*, has a full discussion of Wilson's and Smith's understandings and misunderstandings. Baker, *op. cit.*, p. 127, is the source of the quotation "You poor scholar. . . ." See Link, *op. cit.*, p. 273, for newspaper comment on Wilson's first month in office, including the editor quoted. Link's own remarks on the decline of Wilson's fortunes are from *op. cit.*, pp. 297–98. James Kerney, *The Political Education of Woodrow Wilson*, New York, The Century Co., 1926, is an anecdotal account of Wilson's New Jersey years, by an editor who knew him. Wilson's 1912 campaign speeches have been published in J. W. Davidson, ed., *A Crossroads of Freedom, The 1912 Campaign Speeches*, New Haven, Yale University Press, 1956.

Master of His Party? The exchange between Wilson and Burleson on party appointments is from an interview of Burleson by R. S. Baker, March 17–19, 1927, Baker Collection; and cited by Arthur S. Link, *Wilson: The New Freedom*, Princeton, University of Princeton Press, 1956, Vol. I, pp. 158–59. This same volume and Link, *Woodrow Wilson and the Progressive Era*, New York, Harper & Brothers, 1954, report Wilson's concern over the condition of the Democratic Party in many states and his tentative plan to boycott some of the congressional standpatters. John M. Blum, *Joe Tumulty and the Wilson Era*, Boston, Houghton Mifflin Company, 1951, is invaluable for its details and comments on Wilson's role as party leader. Link, *Woodrow Wilson and the Progressive Era* portrays graphically Wilson's shift to urban progressives in 1916. Lippmann's tribute to Wilson as party leader appeared in the *New Republic*, Vol. 8, No. 102 (Oct. 14, 1916), 263–64. Marquis W. Childs and James B. Reston, eds., *Walter Lippmann and His Times*, New York, Harcourt, Brace and Company, 1959, especially chap. 11, "The Intellectual v. Politics," by A. M. Schlesinger, Jr., explains Lippmann's preconceptions about political organization. For the full text of Wilson's appeal to the people in 1918, see Baker and Dodd, eds., *The New Democracy*, Vol. 2. A. M. Arnett, *Claude Kitchin and the Wilson*

War Policies, Boston, Little, Brown & Company, 1937, pictures the re-actions to Wilson's later policies on the part of the anti-interventionist Democratic leader of the House.

Wilson v. Lodge: No Advice, No Consent: My main source on the later Wilson years are the companion volumes by Thomas A. Bailey: *Woodrow Wilson and the Great Betrayal,* New York, The Macmillan Company, 1945, and *Woodrow Wilson and the Lost Peace,* New York, The Macmillan Company, 1944, which are sensitive to the domestic and political as well as the foreign and diplomatic elements in Wilson's pre-dicament. The latter volume (page 47) presents a map showing states with "newspaper majorities for League, April, 1919," with specific results indicated by section; and (page 57) categorizes the Senate Republicans in terms of their attitude toward the League. F. L. Paxson, *Postwar Years, Normalcy, 1918–1923,* Berkeley, University of California Press, 1948, caps a three-volume work (*American Democracy and the World War*), that presents a comprehensive and detailed account of the Wilson years. For Lodge's role in the League episode see Garraty, *op. cit.,* and Karl Schriftgiesser, *The Gentleman from Massachusetts, Henry Cabot Lodge,* Boston, Little, Brown & Company, 1944. Lodge's packing of his committee is well documented; see the above biographies and M. C. McKenna, *Borah,* Ann Arbor, University of Michigan Press, 1961; and, for the Kellogg incident, David Bryn-Jones, *Frank B. Kellogg; A Biography,* New York, G. P. Putnam's Sons, 1937. Blum, in his study of Wilson, *op. cit.,* finds little effect on the Senate from Wilson's tour of the nation. The extremists' confrontation of Lodge is recorded in McKenna, *op. cit.,* chap. 10, and in the Lodge biographies. Bailey's *Woodrow Wilson and the Lost Peace* (p. 299) quotes *The New York Times* on the Republican convention. Merlo J. Pusey, *Charles Evans Hughes,* 2 vols., New York, The Macmillan Company, 1951, Vol. I, describes the role of a leading Republican moderate. Blum's books on Tumulty and Wilson add per-spective to a consideration of the defeat of the League. Kurt Wimer, "Woodrow Wilson's Plans to Enter the League of Nations through an Executive Agreement," *The Western Political Quarterly,* Vol. XI, No. 4 (December, 1958), 800–12, is a revealing explanation of that possible alternative.

Wilson as a Jeffersonian Leader: The quotation from Wilson on na-tional and party leadership is from *Constitutional Government in the United States,* pp. 67–68. J. M. Blum, *Joe Tumulty and the Wilson Era,* pp. 182–90, reports Tumulty's concern over neglect of the Democratic party during and after the war. Bailey, *Woodrow Wilson and the Great Betrayal,* pp. 214–15, describes Wilson's scheme to have Senators resign and run for reelection, and correctly terms it "fantastic." Austin Ranney treats Wilson's view of party in *The Doctrine of Responsible Party Government; Its Origins and Present State*, Urbana, Ill., University of Illinois Press, 1954, pp. 44–47; this volume is a most valuable study of prevailing ideas and problems in this area. The quotation from J. M. Blum is from his revealing *Woodrow Wilson and the Politics of Morality*, Boston, Little, Brown & Company, 1956, pp. 197–98; and that from Hofstadter from *The American Political Tradition*, p. 282, and also concludes his chapter on Wilson. R. S. Baker's, *Woodrow Wilson; Life and Letters,* Vol. VIII, *Armistice*, New York, Doubleday, Doran & Co., 1939, concludes his rich eight-volume study; for Baker on the postwar years see his earlier work, *Woodrow Wilson and the World Settlement*, 1st ed., New York, Doubleday, Page & Company, 1922.

CHAPTER 7

For the politics of the 1920's, I have relied heavily on William E. Leuchtenburg's vivid chronicle, *The Perils of Prosperity, 1914–1932*, Chicago, University of Chicago Press, 1958; for political ideas during the period see also James W. Prothro, *Dollar Decade: Business Ideas in the 1920's*, Baton Rouge, Louisiana State University Press, 1954. The English observer quoted was H. J. Laski, *The American Presidency; An Interpretation*, New York, Harper & Brothers, 1940.

The Education of Franklin Roosevelt: My main source on Roosevelt is my *Roosevelt: The Lion and the Fox*, New York, Harcourt, Brace and Company, Inc., 1956, from which I have taken occasional sentences; see also bibliography of this work, pp. 493–538. Works published subsequent to the above that I have used here are the first three volumes of Arthur M. Schlesinger's series *The Age of Roosevelt;* Vol. 1, *The Crisis of the Old Order, 1919–1933*, Boston, Houghton Mifflin Company, 1957; Vol. 2, *The Coming of the New Deal*, Boston, Houghton Mifflin Company, 1959, and Vol. 3, *The Politics of Upheaval*, Boston, Houghton Mifflin Company, 1960, all of which are masterly treatments of political men and movements. Rexford G. Tugwell, *The Democratic Roosevelt: A Biography of Franklin D. Roosevelt*, New York, Doubleday & Company, Inc., 1957, is especially informative on policy and ideological aspects of Roosevelt and the New Deal.

Roosevelt and the Grand Coalition: Schlesinger describes the Roosevelt coalition in detail in Vol. 3; see also Burns, *op. cit.*, chaps. 10, 11, and 14. Quotations of Roosevelt are from S. I. Rosenman, ed., *The Public Papers and Addresses of Franklin D. Roosevelt*, 13 vols., New York, Harper & Brothers, 1938–50.

The Crumbling of the Coalition: The material here is drawn almost wholly from Burns, *op. cit.*, chaps. 15–19; see especially the concluding sections of chap. 18 and chap. 19, which present an assessment of Roosevelt as a party and political leader in more detail. The Millis quotation is from "The President's Political Strategy," *Yale Review*, September 1938, pp. 1–18.

Roosevelt as a Political Strategist: Tugwell, *op. cit.*, p. 412, quotes Roosevelt's prediction on parties. Schlesinger's theory of Roosevelt's true purpose and role as a liberal party leader is in Volume 2, *The Coming of the New Deal*, pp. 504–505. Roosevelt's dealings with state Democratic parties and candidates in 1934 and 1936 are described in Burns, *op. cit.*, chap. 10 and chap. 14. T. H. White, *The Making of the President 1960*, New York, Atheneum Publishers, 1961, pp. 81–82, provides a searing picture of the state of the Wisconsin Democracy.

The Two Roosevelts: An Epitaph: The precise sequence of events in the Willkie-Roosevelt exchanges of 1944 remains somewhat obscure. M. N. McGeary, *Gifford Pinchot; Forester-Politician*, Princeton, N.J., Princeton University Press, 1960, p. 424, indicates that Pinchot was in touch with Roosevelt in 1944, but makes no reference to Willkie's proposal for party realignment at this point. S. I. Rosenman, *Working with Roosevelt*, New York, Harper & Brothers, 1952, chap. 24, has the fullest account, as Rosenman was the go-between.

CHAPTER 8

For the historians' voting on the President, see Arthur M. Schlesinger, "Our Presidents: A Rating by 75 Historians," *The New York Times Magazine*, July 29, 1962, p. 12.

The Education of Robert Taft: My main source on Robert A. Taft is William E. White's knowing and sensitive *The Taft Story*, New York, Harper & Brothers, 1954. Treadway's career is duly recorded in the annual volumes of the *Congressional Directory*, Washington, D.C. Harry S. Truman describes his congressional strategy in his *Memoirs*, Vol. 2, *Years of Trial and Hope*, New York, Doubleday & Company, Inc., 1956; the former President refers to the vivid summer session as a "special" session, but evidently Congress had recessed rather than adjourned.

The Rout of the Regulars: Paul T. David, Malcolm Moos, and Ralph M. Goldman, eds., *Presidential Nominating Politics in 1952*, 5 vols., Vol. 3, *The South*, Baltimore, Johns Hopkins Press, 1954, is a detailed treatment, in a pioneering study, of the state and regional preliminaries in the choosing of delegates to the 1952 national conventions. I have used especially chap. 14, which carries the Texas struggle into the national convention. On the 1952 Convention generally, see this same study, Vol. 1, *The National Story.* White, *The Taft Story, op. cit.,* pp. 177–79, describes Taft's bewildered reactions to the use of the "fair play" issue by the Eisenhower forces; I have quoted from this study, p. 177. For a more general treatment of the Republican party in the South see V. O. Key, Jr. and Alexander Heard, *Southern Politics in State and Nation,* New York, Alfred A. Knopf, Inc., 1949, chap. 13. The classic description of the confused state of membership in American political parties is Clarence A. Berdahl, "Party Membership in the United States," I and II, *The American Political Science Review,* Vol. 36 (February, 1942), 16–50; (April, 1942), 241–62. For a vivid report on the 1952 Republican convention see Richard H. Rovere, *Affairs of State: The Eisenhower Years,* New York, Farrar, Straus & Cudahy, Inc., 1956, from which I have quoted at pp. 27–29. Taft's memorandum on the 1952 nomination is included as Appendix A in Paul T. David, Ralph M. Goldman, and Richard C. Bain, *The Politics of National Party Conventions,* Washington, D.C., The Brookings Institute, 1960. White, *op. cit.,* pp. 186–87, describes Taft's uncertainties at Murray Bay.

The General and the Senator: My main sources on the early years of the Eisenhower Administration are Robert J. Donovan, *Eisenhower: The Inside Story,* New York, Harper & Brothers, 1956; Sherman Adams, *Firsthand Report,* New York, 1961; Marquis W. Childs, *Eisenhower: Captive Hero, A Critical Study of the General and the President,* New York, Harcourt, Brace and Company, 1958; and Rovere, *op. cit.* The report of the county clerk is quoted in Adams, *op. cit.,* p. 13, as is the telegram from Sulzberger, p. 32. White, *op. cit.,* pp. 211–12, describes Taft's views about Wiley as Chairman of the Foreign Relations Committee. *The Congressional Directory,* 83rd Cong., 1st Sess., March, 1953, Washington, D.C., lists committee chairmanships and other pertinent information. Taft's explosion at the cabinet table is described by both Adams, *op. cit.,* pp. 21–22 and Donovan, *op. cit.,* pp. 108–9. Both Adams, *op. cit.,* pp. 27–30 and Donovan, *op. cit.,* pp. 151–3, report on Eisenhower's misgivings about the Republican party and musings about a new party. There are discrepancies between the two reports, most notably in Donovan's indication that Eisenhower was considering a wholly new party, and in Adams' that the President was more concerned with realignment of existing parties so that President and Congress could work more closely together for a moderate program. Perhaps Eisenhower was not clear on this himself. Neither account makes clear just when Eisenhower indulged in these reflections. The President's later comment on the need of a guaranteed majority in Congress and on his pleasure at being attacked from both sides are from Adams, pp. 459 and 463, respectively.

Summary: The Four-Party System in History: This material is drawn from the foregoing chapters and from the references used therein.

CHAPTER 9

Woodrow Wilson's reference to "Whig mechanics" is in *Constitutional Government in the United States,* New York, The Columbia University Press, 1908 (Paperback, New York, Columbia University Press, 1961), p. 203.

Regulars and Irregulars: On the stability of party self-identification see the remarkable table in Angus Campbell, Philip E. Converse, Warren E. Miller, and Donald E. Stokes, *The American Voter,* John Wiley & Sons, Inc., 1960, a product of the brilliant and pioneering work of the Survey Research Center at the University of Michigan. Other general sources for this section are V. O. Key, Jr. *Public Opinion and American Democracy,* New York, Alfred A. Knopf, Inc., 1961, drawn from data at this center and a variety of other public opinion analyses and materials; and Bernard R. Berelson, Paul F. Lazarsfeld, and William N. McPhee, *Voting,* Chicago, University of Chicago Press, 1954, one of the most sophisticated community studies. Quotations from respondents questioned are all from Campbell *et al.* or from Key. The relation between party identification and the social matrix is stressed in the works just cited; see T. M. Newcomb, *Social Psychology,* New York, The Dryden Press, Inc., 1950; H. H. Gerth and C. Wright Mills, *From Max Weber: Essays in Sociology,* New York, Oxford University Press, 1958, and Muzafer Sherif and Hadley Cantril, *The Psychology of Ego-Involvements,* New York, John Wiley & Sons, Inc., 1947, for theoretical aspects of the relation between attitudes and cultural context. Herbert McClosky and Harold E. Dahlgren, "Primary Group Influence on Party Loyalty," *The American Political Science Review,* Vol. LIII, No. 3 (September, 1959), 757–76, is a recent treatment with many references. M. Brewster Smith, Jerome S. Bruner, and Robert W. White, *Opinions and Personality,* John Wiley & Sons, Inc., 1956, an intensive study of the developing attitudes of ten men, is a useful check on the gross results in the foregoing volumes. Campbell *et al.* and Key, both cited earlier, stress the difficulties of the less educated with ideological concepts. Berelson, *op. cit.,* treats the role of cross pressures extensively. The low assessment of the political involvement and knowledge, relatively, of independents, is from Campbell *et al., op. cit.,* p. 143. On the role of the Mugwump I have used, aside from the historical studies of the Liberal Republicans and Clevelandites of the 1880's, Richard Hofstadter, *The Age of Reform*, New York, Alfred A. Knopf, Inc., 1959, a critical appraisal, and Lorin Peterson, *The Day of the Mugwump*, New York, Random House, Inc., 1961, which focuses on his role in city politics and urban reform. That the reformist tendencies of sections of the middle class are not unique to this country is suggested by Seymour Lipset, *Political Man; The Social Bases of Politics*, New York, Doubleday & Company, Inc., 1960; Gunnar Myrdal, *An American Dilemma; the Negro Problem and Modern Democracy*, New York, Harper & Brothers, 1944; and Karl Mannheim, *Freedom, Power and Democratic Planning*, New York, Oxford University Press, 1950.

The Web of Leadership: For this and other of Plunkitt's sage observations see William L. Riordan, *Plunkitt of Tammany Hall*, New York, Alfred A. Knopf, 1948. Paul F. Lazarsfeld, Bernard B. Berelson, and Hazel Gaudet, *The People's Choice*, New York, Columbia University Press, 1949, first described effectively the role and influence of the local opinion leader; see also a discriminating analysis and extension of this theory, Elihu Katz, "The Two-Step Flow of Communication: An Up-To-Date Report on an Hypothesis," *Public Opinion Quarterly*, Vol. XXI, No. 1 (Spring, 1957), 61–78. The study of the local gang was William F. Whyte, *Street Corner Society; the Social Structure of an Italian Slum*, Chicago, University of Chicago Press, 1943. The remarks of the New Haven party leader are from Robert A. Dahl, *Who Governs? Democracy and Power in an American City*, New Haven, Yale University Press, 1961, p. 249. This book (p. 298) is also the source of the description of the politicians as multiplying their personal relations without involvement; this description is drawn from findings of Rufus Browning, "Businessmen in Politics" (Doctoral dissertation, Yale University, 1960), cited in Dahl. Stimson Bullitt, *To Be A Politician*, New York, Doubleday & Company, Inc., 1959, p. 63, describes atomistic relationships in politics and offers many other astute observations on the political world. Herbert McClosky, Paul J. Hoffman, and Rosemary O'Hara, "Issue Conflict and Consensus Among Party Leaders and Followers," *The American Political Science Review*, Vol. LIV, No. 2 (June 1960), 406–27, documents the differences between party leaders and followers; the fact that these findings are drawn from national convention delegates in both parties raises the question whether different responses might have been elicited from members of Congress and their subleaders. I have quoted Joseph A. Schumpeter from his classic *Capitalism, Socialism and Democracy*, 2nd ed., New York, Harper & Brothers, 1947, p. 269. My general notion of leadership stems from situational and cultural theories; see the works cited in Lester G. Seligman, "The Study of Political Leadership," *The American Political Science Review*, Vol. XLIV, No. 4 (December, 1950), 904–15, and in James M. Burns, *Roosevelt: The Lion and the Fox*, New York, Harcourt, Brace and Company, Inc., 1956, pp. 481–87, "A Note on the Study of Political Leadership."

The Anatomy of Balance: Robert M. MacIver, *The Web of Government*, New York, The Macmillan Company, 1947, and David B. Truman, *The Governmental Process; Political Interests and Public Opinion*, New York, Alfred A. Knopf, Inc., 1951, are general sources of the views of this section; Campbell *et al.*, and V. O. Key, *op. cit.*, underpin the general views with specific findings, mainly from the Michigan surveys. I have quoted from Tannenbaum's "On Political Stability," *The Political Science Quarterly*, Vol. LXXV, No. 2 (June, 1960), 161–80. The quotation from Key sums up a fruitful discussion of stability in *Public Opinion and American Democracy*, New York, Alfred A. Knopf, Inc., 1961, chap. 10. On instability of mood see Gabriel Almond, *The American People and Foreign Policy*, New York, Harcourt, Brace and Company, 1950. Hadley Cantril described the impact of Orson Welles's radio drama, and the significance of the impact, in *The Invasion from Mars; A Study in the Psychology of Panic*, Princeton, Princeton University Press, 1940. The Georgia poultryman is cited in Key, *op. cit.*, p. 244. The Berelson quotation is from Bernard R. Berelson *et al.*, *Voting*, Chicago, University of Chicago Press, 1954, cited above. An illuminating chart on liberal-conservative opinion distribution is to be found in Key, *op. cit.*, p. 165; see pp. 559–62 for the wording of the questions. Truman's comment on guardianship is from the last sentence of his volume, cited above, p. 536.

The Outsiders: The fullest treatment of political participation and non-participation in America is Robert E. Lane, *Political Life; Why People Get Involved in Politics*, Glencoe, Ill., The Free Press, 1959. Seymour Lipset, *Political Man, The Social Basis of Politics*, 1st ed., Garden City, N.Y., Doubleday & Co., Inc., 1960, provides a good deal of comparative material and questions some of the democratic assumptions about non-voting. The volumes by Key and Campbell *et al.*, cited above, generally substantiate previous research on voting turnout and differentials and also treat the subjective aspect of non-voting; the estimate of voting in 1960 is from Philip E. Converse *et al.*, "Stability and Change in 1960: A Reinstating Election," *The American Political Science Review*, Vol. LV, No. 2 (June, 1961), 269. Statements of non-voters are from the Michigan survey, cited by Key, *op. cit.*, p. 189. An imaginative and well-researched study, Murray B. Levin, *The Alienated Voter*, New York, Holt, Rinehart & Winston, 1960, documents voters' and non-voters' attitudes in Boston; quotations are from p. 59. The percentages on types of political participation in 1956 are from Campbell *et al., op. cit.,* p. 91. On the "low quality" of non-participants see Lipset, *op. cit.,* chap. 6; Philip K. Hastings, "The Voter and Non-Voter," *American Journal of Sociology,* Vol. 62 (November, 1956), pp. 302–307; and T. W. Adorno, *et al., The Authoritarian Personality,* New York, Harper & Brothers, 1950. Robert E. Lane, *op. cit.,* comments on some of the fears about non-voting; this volume, p. 344, is the source of my quotations of Tocqueville and Erikson. On Long and voting in Louisiana sce V. O. Key, Jr. *Southern Politics,* pp. 523–24 (see also his extended discussion of Southern non-voting in Part Five). Gunnar Myrdal's discussion of mass passivity and individual leadership in *An American Dilemma; The Negro Problem and Modern Democracy,* New York, Harper & Brothers, 1944, p. 715 is an important preface to a consideration of participation.

The Outsider Inside: For another view of a congressional campaign by the candidate, see the sparkling volume by Stimson Bullitt, *To Be A Politician,* cited above.

CHAPTER 10

Strachey is quoted in E. H. Carr, *What Is History?,* New York, Alfred A. Knopf, Inc., 1962, p. 13. The central analytical tool in this chapter is the concept of systems, or subsystems, as developed by Talcott Parsons and Robert K. Merton on the basis of earlier work by Weber, Pareto, and others and as carried on by a multitude of younger scholars. See Talcott Parsons, *The Structure of Social Action,* New York, McGraw-Hill Publishing Co., Inc., 1937; Talcott Parsons, *The Social System,* Glencoe, Ill., Free Press, 1951; Robert K. Merton, *Social Theory and Social Structure,* rev. ed., Glencoe, Ill., Free Press, 1957; Gabriel A. Almond, "Comparative Political Systems," *The Journal of Politics,* Vol. 18 (1956), pp. 391–409, and the work, among others, of Edward A. Shils and Marion Levy. S. Sidney Ulmer, ed., *Introductory Readings in Political Behavior,* Chicago, Rand McNally & Company, 1961, chap. 4, provides some judiciously chosen selections from such writers. I use the concept of "system" to mean a pattern of interrelations or a cluster of behaviors oriented toward certain goals, as a set of interactions tending toward equilibrium, as an integrated structure of patterned roles. Because of the elements of interaction, integration, and mutual reinforcement, a system has self-containment, stability, strength, durability, and perhaps predictability. There is some ambiguity in certain writings in this area as to the meaning of *role.* Here I have defined it somewhat more narrowly for my own purposes, as the patterned behavior of persons occupying any office, post, or other position, elective or appointive, formal or informal, in government, party, or organized group, that has political influence, a relationship with other political offices, and some permanence. For some of the broader variations and implications of role-taking, see T. M. Newcomb, *Social Psychology*, New York, The Dryden Press, Inc., 1950; Clyde Kluckhohn and Henry A. Murray, *Personality in Nature, Society and Culture*, New York, Alfred A. Knopf, Inc., 1948; and James M. Burns, *Roosevelt: The Lion and the Fox*, New York, Harcourt, Brace and Company, Inc., 1956, "A Note on the Study of Political Leadership." However difficult it may be to apply some of these concepts to the political process, given certain inadequacies in the available data, the concepts of system or structure and of role-taking are essential to both my method and my substance. For I am seeking to show that the congressional and presidential party systems are each, in their internal operations, mutually supporting and tending toward equilibrium and durability over time; and that these systems, because of their structural make-up, cannot be changed except by drastic action.

State Parties: The Shriveled Roots: No scholar can treat state parties without acknowledgement, even at the risk of repetition, to V. O. Key, Jr., especially in his *American State Politics*, New York, Alfred A. Knopf, Inc., 1956, which lays special stress on the role of the state party in a federal system. This work in turn has inspired numerous studies of specific states, using Key's formulations and statistical tools. I have taken some of my description of party disorganization from my article, "Two-Party Stalemate," *The Atlantic*, February, 1960, pp. 40–41. Key has developed the relation of party competition and party government in chapter seven of *American State Politics*; see also Duane Lockard, *New England State Politics*, Princeton, Princeton University Press, 1959, *passim*. The Schlesinger analysis is Joseph A. Schlesinger, "The Structure of Competition for Office in the American States," *Behavioral Science*, Vol. 5, No. 3 (July, 1960), 197–210. Much of this section is based on my own experience in Massachusetts politics; since Massachusetts has an enfeebled party organization (especially the Democratic) I may be open to some bias; but my observations of many other state parties, and interviews with party leaders conducted in 1959–1961, also support the general view in these pages. More work needs to be done on the recruitment function—or lack of it—of political parties (as compared with self-recruitment or with recruitment by party factions or leadership networks); two articles by Lester G. Seligman, "A Prefatory Study of Leadership Selection in Oregon," *The Western Political Quarterly*, Vol. XII, No. 1,

Part 1 (March, 1959), pp. 153–67, and "Political Recruitment and Party Structure: A Case Study," *The American Political Science Review,* Vol. LV, No. 1 (March, 1961), 77–86, are suggestive treatments. A few of the many studies that underline the weakness of state parties are Austin Ranney, *Illinois Politics,* New York, New York University Press, 1960; Daniel M. Ogden and Hugh A. Bone, *Washington Politics,* New York, New York University Press, 1960; O. Douglas Weeks, *Texas One-Party Politics in 1956,* Austin, University of Texas, Institute of Public Affairs, 1957; Joseph LaPalombara, *Guide to Michigan Politics,* East Lansing, Michigan State University, Bureau of Social and Political Research, 1960; Earl Latham and George Goodwin, Jr., *Massachusetts Politics,* rev. ed., Medford, Mass., Tufts Civic Education Center, Tufts University, 1960; and V. O. Key, Jr., *Southern Politics,* New York, Alfred A. Knopf, Inc., 1949, and Lockard, *New England State Politics,* cited above.

The Congressional Party Systems: On the urban-rural imbalance in state and national legislatures, see Belle Zeller, ed., *American State Legislatures,* New York, Thomas Y. Crowell Co., 1954, and Gordon E. Baker, *Rural Versus Urban Political Power,* Garden City, N. Y., Doubleday and Company, Inc., 1955. The differences between urban and rural political life have been widely, though perhaps not definitively, explored; see Robert E. Lane, *Political Life,* Glencoe, Ill., Free Press, 1959, pp. 77–78, 151; V. O. Key, Jr., *Public Opinion and American Democracy,* pp. 116–18, and the references cited therein; and Angus Campbell *et al., The American Voter,* New York, John Wiley & Sons, Inc., 1960, pp. 426–30. W. Lloyd Warner, *Democracy in Jonesville,* New York, Harper & Brothers, 1949, and Bernard R. Berelson, *et al., Voting,* Chicago, University of Chicago Press, 1954, cited above, provide case examples of rural and small city apathy. Key shows in his *Public Opinion,* chap. 5, that cities of 10,000 to 50,000 population (Berelson's city of Elmira, New York, had a population of 45,106) have many of the political characteristics of smaller communities. Richard Dewey, "The Rural-Urban Continuum: Real But Relatively Unimportant," *The American Journal of Sociology,* Vol. LXVI, No. 1 (July, 1960), 60–66, warns against seeing overly sharp dichotomies between urbanism and ruralism as such, urges attention to be paid to more crucial cultural factors, and supplies a most useful table showing forty elements in definition of urbanism as offered by various social scientists. On congressional career lines see Duncan MacRae, Jr., *Dimensions of Congressional Voting,* Berkeley, Calif., University of California Press, 1958, pp. 293–95; Donald R. Matthews, *U.S. Senators and Their World,* Chapel Hill, N.C., University of North Carolina Press, 1960, pp. 33ff; and Eric Goldman, *Rendezvous with*

Destiny. I believe that further research would indicate that the electoral roots of the congressional party are even firmer and deeper than I have suggested; see Robert H. Salisbury, "St. Louis Politics: Relationships among Interests, Parties and Governmental Structure," in Oliver P. Williams and Charles Press, eds., *Democracy in Urban America,* Chicago, Rand McNally & Company, 1961; John H. Bunzel, "The General Ideology of Small Business," *Political Science Quarterly,* Vol. LXX, No. 1 (March, 1955), 87–102; and Key, *Public Opinion and American Democracy,* pp. 485–86. On the fate of congressional candidates in presidential years, as compared with off years, I have used an admirable doctoral study, Milton Curtis Cummings, Jr., *Congressmen and the Electorate,* Cambridge, Harvard University Press, 1960. George Goodwin, Jr., "The Seniority System in Congress," *The American Political Science Review,* Vol. LII, No. 2 (June, 1959), 412–36, treats the subject soberly and systematically. The study I quote on the imperviousness of committees-on-committees to electoral changes is Nicholas A. Masters, "Committee Assignments in the House of Representatives," *The American Political Science Review,* Vol. LV, No. 2 (June, 1961), 350. On these matters generally, see one of the best analyses of the pattern of combat in Congress, Bertram M. Gross, *The Legislative Struggle,* New York, McGraw-Hill Book Company, Inc., 1953. Meg Greenfield, "The Melting Pot of Francis E. Walter," *The Reporter,* Vol. 25, Oct, 26, 1961, 24–28, and comment by Joseph L. Rauh, Jr., letter to the *Reporter,* Vol. 25, Dec. 7, 1961, p. 16, give some idea of Representative Walter's varied activities. The internal relations of the House Appropriations Committee are pictured with insight by Richard Fenno, "The House Appropriations Committee: The Problem of Integration," paper delivered at a panel of the American Political Science Association, September, 1961. William S. White, *The Citadel; The Story of the United States Senate,* New York, Harper & Brothers, 1957, and Matthews, *op. cit.,* describe the internal life of the Senate. The quoted comment on the Senate seniority system is from Matthews, p. 165. On the Senate committees see Ralph K. Huitt, "Democratic Party Leadership in the Senate," *The American Political Science Review,* Vol. LV, No. 2 (June, 1961), 333–44. James Burnham, *Congress and the American Tradition,* Chicago, Henry Regnery Co., 1959, analyzes Congress from a comprehensive conservative viewpoint. More work needs to be done on the operations of the congressional committees; Hugh A. Bone, "Some Notes on the Congressional Campaign Committees," *The Western Political Quarterly,* Vol. IX, No. 1 (March, 1956), 116–37, is a good preface; for a somewhat different view see David B. Truman, *The Congressional Party,* New York, John Wiley & Sons, Inc., 1959, p. 102; my own views are based also on interviews of committee members and staff, Washington, D.C. On the historical background of these committees see Goldman, *op. cit., passim.* Recent useful general works on Congress are Ernest S. Griffith, *Congress: Its Contemporary Role,* New York, New York University Press, 1956, and Roland Young, *The American Congress,* New York, Harper & Brothers, 1958. The Congressman quoted is the late Rep. Clem Miller (Dem., Calif.), in his newsletter to his constituents, Sept. 15, 1959. John C. Wahlke, Heinz Eulau, William Buchanan, and LeRoy C. Ferguson, *The Legislative System,* New York, 1962, is a pioneering study of legislative behavior at the state level.

The Presidential Party System: Important recent general treatments of the President are Richard E. Neustadt, *Presidential Power,* New York, John R. Wiley, Inc., 1960; Herman Finer, *The Presidency, Crisis and Regeneration,* Chicago, University of Chicago Press, 1960; Sidney Hyman, *The American President,* New York, Harper & Brothers, 1954; and Clinton Rossiter, *The American Presidency,* rev. ed., New York, Harcourt, Brace and Company, Inc., 1960. Earlier works still of great value are Edward C. Corwin, *The President: Office and Powers,* 4th ed., New York, New York University Press, 1957; Edward Pendleton Herring, *Presidential Leadership,* New York, Farrar & Rinehart, 1940; and Harold J. Laski, *The American Presidency, An Interpretation,* New York, Harper & Brothers, 1940. *The New York Times,* June 30, 1962, p. 19, carries a report on the Interior Department's action on tungsten during the 1960 campaign. On the President and the national convention see the authoritative study, Paul T. David, Ralph M. Goldman, and Richard C. Bain, *The Politics of National Party Conventions,* Washington, D.C., Brookings Institution, 1960, *passim,* and, on the President's hierarchical role, see Nelson W. Polsby, "Decision-Making at the National Convention," *The Western Political Quarterly,* Vol. XIII, No. 3 (September, 1960), 609–19. Angus Campbell *et al., The American Voter, passim,* Angus Campbell and Warren E. Miller, "The Motivational Basis of Straight and Split Ticket Voting," *The American Political Science Review,* Vol. LI, No. 2 (June, 1957), 293–312; and Warren E. Miller, "Presidential Coattails: A Study in Political Myth and Methodology," *The Public Opinion Quarterly,* Vol. 19, No. 4 (Winter, 1955–56), 353–68, throw considerable light on this difficult problem. The quotation of E. E. Schattschneider is from his iconoclastic *The Semisovereign People,* 1st ed., New York, Holt, Rinehart and Winston, 1960. On presidential "flattening" of the vote, see Charles Press, "Voting Statistics and Presidential Coattails," *The American Political Science Review,* Vol. LII, No. 4 (December, 1958), 1041–50. C. Wright Mills refers to the "political outsider" in his *The*

Power Elite, New York, Oxford University Press, 1956, p. 228. Donald B. Johnson, *The Republican Party and Wendell Willkie,* Urbana, Ill., University of Illinois Press, 1960, and Henry O. Evjen, "The Willkie Campaign: An Unfortunate Chapter in Republican Leadership," *The Journal of Politics,* Vol. 14, No. 2 (May, 1952), 241–56, depict graphically Willkie's difficulties with the party regulars. The Neustadt quotation is from *Presidential Power,* p. 42. Halleck's views on the party platform are quoted in *The New York Times,* Dec. 7, 1960, p. 50. My findings on the elected leadership of Congress differ somewhat, at least on the surface, with those of David B. Truman in his probing and scholarly study, *The Congressional Party,* New York, John Wiley & Sons, Inc., 1959. The difference is due mainly, I think, to his concern with the substantive policy positions of the seniority and elected leadership as a whole in a single Congress, the 81st, whereas I am more interested in the solidarity over time of a smaller, more powerful group of seniority leaders in maintaining the present system of influence. The quotation of the freshman congressman is from Representative Clem Miller, source cited above. My comments on the problems of organization and unity among the more junior congressmen are based in part on interviews with members of the Democratic Study Group, House of Representatives, 1959 and 1960.

Four-Party Politics: V. O. Key, Jr., *Public Opinion and American Democracy,* New York, Alfred A. Knopf, Inc., 1961, pp. 154–58, distributes opinions on foreign issues and domestic welfare policies in terms of a "four-party system"; I have modified his terminology slightly in my own formulation. Although polling results are too gross for attitudes to be categorically linked to the structural four-party system as I have formulated it, I believe that there is a relationship, and an interactional one, between the attitudes and the structure. I have taken the development of the concept of economic and way-of-life issues from Berelson *et al., op. cit.,* chap. 14, with a change of terminology. Stuart A. Rice, *Quantitative Methods in Politics,* New York, F. S. Crofts & Co., 1928, earlier made the distinction between economic and "moral" issues. Hofstadter, *The Age of Reform,* develops some significant aspects of the two types of policies. The quotation from Angus Campbell *et al.* is from *The American Voter,* New York, John Wiley & Sons, Inc., 1960, p. 197. Kendall's article is a masterful marshaling of ideological and institutional relationships from a conservative viewpoint: Willmoore Kendall, "The Two Majorities," *Midwest Journal of Political Science,* Vol. IV, No. 4 (November, 1960), 317–45; I have quoted him at p. 324 (emphasis subtracted). My emphasis on the partisan issue isolation of independents is somewhat at odds with survey findings that independents are somewhat less politically informed and motivated than party regulars. The question I am raising is whether this is, at least in part, a result of the fact that many independents are concerned with essentially non-economic issues over which the two major parties have not had clear differences. Bipartisanship in foreign policy is an example. The general works on President and Congress cited above provide data on the parallel systems of power; see especially Griffith on congressional power, from whom I quote (pp. 40–41). Robert A. Dahl develops his five patterns of leadership suggestively in *Who Governs?*, New Haven, Yale University Press, 1961, chap. 15. The phrase in the last sentence is, of course, from the title of Harold Lasswell's classic work.

CHAPTER 11

The quotation from David B. Truman is from *The Governmental Process*, New York, Alfred A. Knopf, Inc., 1951, p. 524. On theories of change see Morris Ginsberg, "Social Change," *The British Journal of Sociology*, Vol. IX, No. 3 (September, 1958), 205–29; Kimball Young, *Sociology, a Study of Society and Culture*, New York, American Book Company, 1942; especially chap. 6; Edward Hallett Carr, *What is History?*, New York, Alfred A. Knopf, Inc., 1962, especially chaps. 4 and 5; and Talcott Parsons, *The Social System*, Glencoe, Ill., Free Press, 1951, chap. 11.

The Cities and the Suburbs: On the relation between education and individual political change, see Eleanor E. Maccoby, Richard E. Matthews, and Alton S. Morton, "Youth and Political Change," *Public Opinion Quarterly*, Vol. 18, No. 1 (Spring, 1954), 23–39. V. O. Key, Jr., *Politics, Parties and Pressure Groups*, 4th ed., New York, Thomas Y. Crowell Co., 1958, pp. 272–79, presents a useful overview of urbanization and suburbanization. The Jere Wilzwelski portrait is from Eugene L. Burdick, *The Ninth Wave*, Boston, Houghton Mifflin Company, 1956, p. 286. Robert C. Wood, *Suburbia: Its People and Their Politics*, Boston, Houghton Mifflin Company, 1959, is a comprehensive treatment of the subject and a critique of some of the earlier literature on the subject. This work, p. 145, is also the source of the reference to the Bucks County Study: G. Edward Janosik, "The New Suburbia," *Current History*, Vol. 31, August, 1956, 91–95. The Westport study, by Dr. David Wallace of Columbia, was reported in *The New York Times*, Feb. 12, 1962, p. 25. Although Angus Campbell, *et al.*, *The American Voter*, New York, John Wiley & Sons, Inc., 1960, does not treat suburban areas as a special population category, for reasons stated on pp. 454–55, footnote 13, some of the data in chap. 16, "Population Movement," are suggestive for the study of suburbia. For references on economic and way-of-life issues, see notes for chap. 10.

Southern Politics: Rim and Heartland: The classic work on the politics of the South is V. O. Key, Jr., *Southern Politics In State and Nation,* New York, Alfred A. Knopf, Inc., 1949. Alexander Heard, who had a major role in this work, dealt perceptively with the long-run tendencies in *A Two-Party South?,* Chapel Hill, N.C., University of North Carolina Press, 1952. He quotes M. Ostrogorski from the latter's *Democracy and the Party System in the United States,* New York, The Macmillan Co., 1902, p. 420. On more recent political developments in the South, see M. D. Irish, "Political Thought and Political Behavior in the South," *The Western Political Quarterly,* Vol. XIII, No. 2 (June, 1960), 406–20. Rudolf Heberle, "The Changing Social Stratification of the South," *Social Forces,* Vol. 38, No. 1 (October, 1959), pp. 42–50, describes change from a sociological standpoint. *The Congressional Directory,* 86th Cong., 1st Sess., Washington, D.C., 1959, offers examples of Republican candidates for Congress in the Deep South winning a tiny number of votes. Campbell *et al., op. cit.,* pp. 276–82, probes the failure of Southern Negroes to vote more deeply than straight statistical studies have been able to do. Louis Harris, *Is There A Republican Majority?,* New York, Harper & Brothers, 1954, and Samuel Lubell's two books, *The Future of American Politics,* New York, Harper & Brothers, 1951, and *The Revolt of the Moderates,* New York, Harper & Brothers, 1956, offer stimulating discussions of Southern prospects. Penetrating recent treatments of the whole problem are Philip E. Converse, "On The Possibility of Major Political Realignment in the South," and Donald S. Strong, "Whatever Happened to the Solid South?" both being papers delivered at Duke University, July, 1962.

Is Party Realignment Inevitable? On this question in general, see the works cited for the previous section. The foremost statement of the case for party responsibility is still *Toward A More Responsible Two-Party System,* Report of the Committee on Political Parties of the American Political Science Association, *American Political Science Review,* Vol. XLIV (September, 1950), Supplement. Chairman of this committee was E. E. Schattschneider, whose other works on political parties are important in this field. On specific aspects of party realignment, see the admirable short studies: Paul T. David, "Comparative State Politics and the Problem of Party Realignment," in Stephen K. Bailey and others, *Research Frontiers in Politics and Government,* Washington, D.C., 1955; Paul T. David, "Intensity of Inter-Party Competition and the Problem of Party Realignment," paper presented at the annual meeting of the American Political Science Association, New York, 1957; and Malcolm E. Jewell, "A New Two-Party System?: Patterns of National Politics Emerging from State Party Trends," paper prepared for presentation at annual meeting of Midwest Conference of Political Scientists, Bloomington, Indiana, 1960. V. O. Key, Jr., "Secular Realignment and the Party System," *The Journal of Politics*, Vol. 21, No. 2 (May, 1959), 198–210, deals with long-range aspects of the question. On recent increases in gubernatorial competition, as compared with earlier years in this century, see Joseph A. Schlesinger, "Stability in the Vote for Governor, 1900–1958," *Public Opinion Quarterly*, Vol. XXIX, No. 1 (Spring, 1960), pp. 85–91 (which excludes twelve Southern states). For an essay loaded with implications for the problem see Schlesinger, "The Structure of Competition for Office in the American States," in *Behavioral Science*, Vol. 5, No. 3 (July, 1960), 197–210, especially pp. 209–10. Milton Curtis Cummings, Jr., *Congressmen and the Electorate*, a Harvard doctoral thesis, Cambridge, 1960, and Duncan Macrae, Jr., *Dimensions of Congressional Voting Behavior*, Berkeley, Calif., University of California Press, 1958, throw further light on congressional party competition. On evaluation and decision, see the impressive analysis, Henry A. Kissinger, *The Necessity for Choice; Prospects of American Foreign Policy*, New York, Harper & Brothers, 1960, especially chap. 7.

CHAPTER 12

Nixon's remarks are quoted from "The Speeches, Remarks, Press Conferences, and Study Papers of Vice-President Richard M. Nixon," *Final Report* of the Committee on Commerce, United States Senate, on Freedom of Communications, Washington, Nov. 28, 1961, pp. 596–97, 599, 1005, 1039, 1097. On Nixon generally see Earl Mazo, *Richard Nixon: A Political and Personal Portrait*, New York, Harper and Brothers, 1959, and R. M. Nixon, *Six Crises*, New York, Doubleday & Company, Inc., 1962. The observation of Nixon campaigning is from Theodore H. White, *The Making of the President 1960*, 1st ed. New York, Atheneum Publishers, 1961, pp. 277–78. Goldwater's postelection remarks were quoted in *The New York Times*, Nov. 10, 1960, p. 38.

The Congressional Party: Rearguard Strategy: The activities of the various Republican leaders in early 1961 are reported in *The New York Times*, Jan. 7, 1961, p. 8, and Jan. 16, 1961, p. 1. See also Paul T. David *et al.*, *The Presidential Election and Transition, 1960–1961*, Washington, D.C., Brookings Institution, 1961, especially the papers by

Thruston B. Morton and Paul T. David. Chairman Miller's statement on
party strategy was reported in *The New York Times,* July 24, 1961, p. 11.
The Goldwater program is taken here almost literally from a digest of it
in *U.S. News & World Report,* April 10, 1961, pp. 64–65; see also Goldwater, "The Future of Republicanism," *Human Events,* Vol. XVI, No. 4
(Jan. 28, 1959); and for the Senator's views on conservative party realignment, *The New York Times,* Nov. 10, 1960, p. 38. The excerpt
from C. L. Rossiter is from his *Conservatism in America; The Thankless
Persuasion,* 2nd ed., rev., New York, Random House, Inc., 1962, p. 171.
The estimates of coalition strength in the House and Senate in 1961
are from *Congressional Quarterly Weekly Report,* Vol. XIX, No. 44
(Nov. 3, 1961), 1796. Roscoe Drummond is quoted from Meg Greenfield, "Charles A. Halleck and the Restless Republicans." *The Reporter,*
March 29, 1962, pp. 27–30; see this article for a discerning general account of Republican congressional party policies and problems in 1961.

The Presidential Party: Strategy of the Center: "Decisions for a Better
America" was published in four parts (including a preface and the text
of an exchange of letters between National Committee Chairman Thrus-
ton B. Morton and Percy) by the Republican National Committee,
Washington, D.C., Fall, 1959. The University of Michigan study is
Philip E. Converse, Angus Campbell, Warren E. Miller, and Donald E.
Stokes, "Stability and Change in 1960: a Reinstating Election," *The
American Political Science Review,* Vol. LV, No. 2 (June, 1961),
269–80. The conclusions on Republican party organization are based on
interviews and observation by the author in Ohio, Michigan, New York,
Massachusetts, California, and other states. Angus Campbell *et al., The
American Voter,* New York, John Wiley & Sons, Inc., 1960, pp. 550–51,
deals with the prospects of an opposition party developing "new dimensions of opinion." The quotation from Theodore H. White is from his
The Making of the President 1960, New York, Atheneum Publishers,
1961, p. 360.

Coalition and Combat: This discussion of Mundt's strategy is taken
largely from an address of his to the State Convention of the South
Carolina State Bankers Association, Greenville, South Carolina, May 5,
1956, reprinted in the *Congressional Record,* June 4, 1956, and published in a pamphlet, "The Key to the Future of American Politics," with
a foreword by Senator John W. Bricker. I have also had the benefit of an
interview with Senator Mundt, Washington, D.C., June 5, 1962. There
have been extensive hearings on proposals to change the Electoral College system; a useful guide to the many recommendations is "The Electoral College—Operation and Effect of Proposed Amendments to the

Constitution of the United States," a memorandum prepared by the staff of the Subcommittee on Constitutional Amendments of the Committee on the Judiciary, 87th Cong., 1st Sess., Washington, D.C., Oct. 10, 1961. The quotation of Clarence Brown is from the Greenfield article in *The Reporter,* March 29, 1962, p. 29.

CHAPTER 13

For the Senate debate on Electoral College reform, see the *Congressional Record,* Vol. 102, Part 4, March 8–27, 1956; for highlights of Kennedy's remarks see pp. 5150, 5158, 5160–61, 5165, 5232, 5235–36, 5239–54, 5336, 5438. Douglas, p. 5250, referred to the "Fourteenth Federalist Paper," but clearly meant the Tenth. I have drawn my account of Kennedy's role in the battle in part from my *John Kennedy: A Political Profile,* New York, Harcourt, Brace and Company, Inc., 1960. Douglas' letter to Kennedy is cited in *ibid,* p. 174.

Kennedy and the Presidential Democratic Party: The selections from Kennedy's speeches are from "Freedom of Communication," Final Report of the Committee on Commerce, United States Senate, Part I, "The Speeches, Remarks, Press Conferences and Statements of Senator John F. Kennedy, August 1 through November 7, 1960, Washington, D.C., 1961, p. 42 (Alexandria, Virginia, Aug. 24, 1960), pp. 524–25 (Bowling Green, Kentucky, Oct. 8, 1960), p. 600 (Beaver Falls, Pennsylvania, Oct. 15, 1960). On Kennedy's political activities generally before his election, I have used my *John Kennedy: A Political Profile,* cited above. Senator Kennedy expressed these views on Democratic party professionals in *Life,* March 11, 1957, pp. 164–66. His view on the need for presidential leadership to make the checks and balances work was cited in the *New Republic,* Nov. 27, 1961. The expression "blarney, bludgeon and boodle," is from Helen Fuller, *Year of Trial,* New York, Harcourt, Brace & World, 1962, p. 104; she also provides a full treatment of the fight over the Rules Committee.

Congressional Democratic Strategy: A penetrating study of Representative Howard W. Smith is badly needed; I have depended chiefly on periodical sources. On the Byrd organization see V. O. Key, Jr., *Southern Politics,* New York, Alfred A. Knopf, Inc., 1949, chap. 2, from which I have quoted at p. 21. On the congressional counterattacks against the Roosevelt Administration, see James M. Burns, *Roosevelt: The Lion and the Fox,* 1st ed., New York, Harcourt, Brace and Company, Inc., 1956, chaps. 17–18. Roland Young, *The American Congress,* New York, 1958, pp. 122–23, describes the abortive Rules Committee reform of 1949. On the role of the Committee more generally, see James A. Robinson, "The Role of the Rules Committee in Arranging the Program of the U.S. House of Representatives," *Western Political Quarterly,* Vol. XII, September, 1959, 653–69, and Robinson, "The Role of the Rules Committee in Regulating Debate in the U.S. House of Representatives," *Midwest Journal of Political Science,* Vol. V, No. 1 (February, 1961), pp. 59–69. I have also used the text of a penetrating address on the Rules Committee by one of its members, Representative Richard Bolling of Missouri, delivered to the Midwest Political Science Association, Columbia, Missouri, May 11, 1961, on recent developments in the Committee. *Congressional Report,* a newsletter of the National Committee for an Effective Congress, Vol. 10, No. 1, March 4, 1961, provides an illuminating account of the Rules Committee struggle of 1961. An astute recent study that treats the strategy of the Southern Democrats is Allan P. Sindler, "The Unsolid South: A Challenge to the Democratic National Party," in Alan F. Westin, ed., *The Uses of Power; 7 Cases in American Politics,* New York, Harcourt, Brace & World, 1962, pp. 229–83.

What Strategy for the New Frontier? The quotations from Kennedy are taken from *John Kennedy: A Political Profile,* in turn based on an interview by the author, August, 1959. Some of the problems treated there are brought up to date in James M. Burns, "The Four Kennedys of the First Year," *The New York Times Magazine,* Jan. 14, 1962, p. 9, from which some sentences are taken here. Malcolm E. Jewell, "A New Two-Party System? Patterns of National Politics Emerging from State Party Trends," paper prepared for presentation at annual meeting of Midwest Conference of Political Scientists, Bloomington, Indiana, 1960, pp. 9, 14, 20, is a source of insights on basic problems of the Democratic party. Schlesinger's views on qualitative liberalism were expressed in "Where Does the Liberal Go From Here?" *The New York Times Magazine,* August 4, 1957, p. 7, and in "The Shape of National Politics to Come," pamphlet, n.d.

CHAPTER 14

The quotation from George F. Kennan is from a speech to the Woman's National Democratic Club, Oct. 22, 1959.

Toward Two-Party Competition: On the problems and possibilities of local clubs of political volunteers, see James Q. Wilson, *The Amateur Democrat,* Chicago, University of Chicago Press, 1962. Angus Campbell *et al., The American Voter,* p. 276, cite the effect of the form of the ballot on straight-ticket voting. My proposals for the reform of campaign finance are taken largely from Alexander Heard's indispensable *The Cost of*

Democracy, Chapel Hill, N.C., University of North Carolina Press, 1960, and from the recommendations of the President's Committee on Campaign Costs, 1962, of which he was chairman. My views on the role of the opposition party owe much to Paul T. David of the University of Virginia and to Stephen K. Bailey of Syracuse University. Bailey suggests the possibility of an eight-year term for Senators in *The Condition of Our National Political Parties,* Fund for the Republic, 1959, p. 15; although demurring on this matter, I have borrowed heavily from this set of trenchant proposals for party reform. For Professor Ralph Goldman's and Senator Hubert Humphrey's proposal for Electoral College reform, see "Nomination and Election of President and Vice President and Qualifications for Voting," Hearings before Subcommittee of Committee on Judiciary, U.S. Senate, 87th Cong., 1st Sess., June, 1961, Part 2, p. 351.

The Power in the People: Woodrow Wilson is quoted from his *Congressional Government* (Meridian ed.), New York, 1956, p. 215. For the view that mechanical devices or constitutional changes along the lines of a joint cabinet or a full-fledged "cabinet government" would be neither feasible nor effective in the United States, see my *Congress on Trial,* New York, Harper & Brothers, 1949, chaps. 8–9. The conclusions and reflections of Bernard R. Berelson *et al.* on democratic requirements are in chap. 14 of *Voting,* cited above. Campbell *et al., op. cit.* and V. O. Key, Jr., *Public Opinion and American Democracy,* 1st ed., New York, Alfred A. Knopf, Inc., 1961, both cited above, are the source, *passim,* of much evidence on the role of parties as embodiers and carriers of political attitudes over time. Wilmoore Kendall, *John Locke and the Doctrine of Majority-Rule,* Urbana, Ill., The University of Illinois Press, 1941, suggests that the concept of majority rule lies deeper and more securely in our intellectual heritage than some antimajoritarians have been willing to grant.

Leadership: The Art of the Impossible?: This section draws considerably from my study, *Roosevelt: The Lion and the Fox,* cited above, especially chaps. 10, 12, 18, and 19, and from my "Memo to the Next President," *The Atlantic,* April 1960, pp. 64–68.

Index

Index

Abolitionists, 71, 94, 117
Adams, Brooks, quoted, 51
Adams, Henry, quoted, 175
Adams, John, 29, 31-35, 37, 47, 50
Adams, John Quincy, 49-52
Adams, Sherman, 188-189, 193-195
Addams, Jane, 135
AFL-CIO, 328
Agar, Herbert, quoted, 44, 60, 104
Agricultural Adjustment Act, 157
Aldrich, Nelson W., 85, 91, 101-104, 108-112
alien and sedition laws, 31
Allen, Leo F., 191, 286
Allison, William, 102
All-Republican Conference, 292, 330
Almond, Gabriel, quoted, 219
American Labor Party, 170-171

American Legion, 328
American Legion Monthly, 286
American Medical Association, 328
Anderson, Robert, 263
anti-party reforms, 84, 90
Arthur, Chester, 76, 178
Articles of Confederation, 9, 14, 15, 31, 57

Bagehot, Walter, quoted, 121
Bailey, John M., 310
Bailey, Stephen K., quoted, 142
Bain, R. C., quoted, 57
Baker v. *Carr*, 236, 278
Ballinger, Richard, 111
Baltimore Sun, 128
Bank, National, 35, 43, 52
Barkley, Alben, 165, 201, 255
Barnes, William, Jr., 113

Barton, Bruce, 181, 300
Beckley, John, 30
Bell, John, 65
Belmont, August, 129
Benson, Ezra Taft, 191
Berelson, Bernard R., quoted, 220,
    258, 335
Biddle, Nicholas, 52
Black, Frank S., 97, 98
Blaine, James G., 76, 96, 112, 114,
    197
Bland, Richard, 78
Booth, John Wilkes, 73
Blum, John, quoted, 101, 146
Borah, William, 140, 145
Brandeis, Louis, 130
Breckinridge, John C., 65
Bricker, John W., 181, 201, 303
Bridges, Styles, 191, 286
Brooks, Preston, 64
Brown, Clarence, 286, 300
Brown, John, 64, 71
Brownell, Herbert, Jr., 191
Bryan, Charles, 150, 201
Bryan, William Jennings, 78-81,
    100, 122, 129, 133, 199, 258,
    270, 277
Buchanan, James, 63-64, 68, 196,
    197
Buckley, Charles A., 311
Buckley, William F., Jr., 286
Bundy, McGeorge, 264
Burdick, Eugene, 268
Burleson, Albert S., 131-132, 144
Burnham, James, 248
Burns, James MacGregor: cam-
    paigns for Congress, 229-233
Burr, Aaron, 26, 34-37, 45, 306,
    337
Butler, Nicholas Murray, 103
Butler, Paul, 253
Byrd, Harry F., 197, 272, 296-297,
    303, 322
Byrnes, James F., 296

Cabinet, 36, 119-120
Calhoun, John C., 49, 51, 53, 56,
    57, 69, 197, 200, 335
Campbell, Angus, quoted, 258
Cannon, Joseph C., 84, 85, 91,
    102, 103, 108, 110, 111
Capehart, Homer E., 286
Case, Clifford P., 254
Celler, Emanuel, 254
Chasc, Salmon P., 73
Chase, Samuel, 37
checks and balances, Constitu-
    tional, 6, 16, 20, 24, 36, 40, 87,
    120, 205, 247, 305, 309, 324,
    see also Madisonian system
Chicago Tribune, 200, 286
Childs, Marquis, 200
China, 4, 285
CIO Political Action Committee,
    184
Civilian Conservation Corps, 157,
    158, 189
Civil War, American, 65, 67, 69,
    71, 75, 82, 90, 209, 221, 238,
    266, 277, 293
Clark, Champ, 128, 129, 201
Clay, Henry, 44, 49-54, 56-62, 197
Clemenceau, Georges, 137
Cleveland, Grover, 75-80, 96, 97,
    122, 123, 211
Clinton, De Witt, 26
Clinton, George, 43
Colmer, William M., 310, 314,
    316
Columbia University, 183, 189
Compromise of 1850, 58, 61
Congress, 2-4, 8-10, 12, 17-19, 25,
    27-31, 35-43, 45, 46, 52-53, 55,
    59, 67, 68, 76, 78, 81, 91, 181,
    191, 196, 205, 241-249, 250-254,
    255, 256, 259-264, 278, 286,
    289, 293, 297, 299, 300, 303,
    305, 306, 309, 313, 317, 318,
    320, 324, 328-331, 333, 338-339;
    under Lincoln, 72-73; under

Congress (*Cont.*):
Theodore Roosevelt, 103-104, 108; indicted by Wilson, 120; under Wilson, 131-132, 144; under Franklin Roosevelt, 156, 159, 172
Congressional control of government: during 1850's, 58-61, 64-71; after Civil War, 74-75
congressional Democrats, 78, 144, 194-203, 254, 257, 263, 273-274, 287, 299-300, 302-303, 307, 311-316, 318, 320, 322
Congressional Government (Wilson), 120
congressional party system, 196-203, 241-249, 252-254, 259-264, 278, 287, 295, 299, 300, 305, 307, 326-327, 328-329, 331
congressional Republicans, 111, 120, 193, 196-203, 257, 263, 273-274, 283, 286-288, 290, 295, 297, 299, 300, 302-303, 307, 313
congressmen, one-party, 241-244, 256, 258
Constitution, 8, 10, 14, 15, 17-19, 22, 24, 28, 42, 75, 87, 90, 94, 104, 195, 205, 208, 221, 285, 317, 332, 334-335; 10th Amendment, 285; 14th Amendment, 3; 15th Amendment, 3; 17th Amendment, 86; 19th Amendment, 228; 22nd Amendment, 331
Constitutional Convention of 1787, 14-18, 205
Constitutional Union Party, 65, 70
conventions, political, 53-55, 57, 81, 83, 91, 293; two-thirds rule, 57, 68, 296, 297
Coolidge, Calvin, 139, 148, 151, 307
Cooper, John Sherman, 198, 299
Corwin, Edward S., 203
Costigan, Edward P., 135
Coughlin, Father Charles, 158

Cox, James M., 141, 149, 153
Crawford, William H., 49-51
Crittenden, John, 62
Croly, Herbert, quoted, 86, 114, 135, 332
Curley, James M., 161

Dahl, Robert A., quoted, 263
Daily Worker, 184
Daley, Richard, 239
Dangerfield, George, 49
Daniel, Price, 302, 303-305
David, Paul, quoted, 57, 277, 331
Davis, Jefferson, 62
Davis, John W., 150, 201
De Gaulle, Charles, 260
De Sapio, Carmine, 310
Declaration of Independence, 33
Democratic Advisory Council, 254-255, 283, 308, 334
Democratic party, 4, 51-53, 55-65, 67-68, 70-76, 80-82, 90-91, 96, 99, 104, 112, 116, 119, 123-125, 127, 130, 136-138, 141, 148, 151-154, 158, 163-171, 173-174, 177-179, 181, 183-184, 194, 200-203, 206-209, 213, 217, 220, 229-232, 236-238, 240, 248-249, 254-259, 263, 268-277, 281-283, 287-288, 291-297, 299-300, 302-303, 306-313, 315-316, 319, 321, 327, 334, 338; Gold Democrats, 79, 122. *See also* congressional Democrats, Democratic Advisory Council, Party Realignment, Presidential Democrats.
Depew, Chauncey, 97-98
Depression, Great, 3, 209, 266, 277
Devin-Adair (publisher), 286
Dewey, Thomas E., 173, 174, 181-182, 185-187, 189, 190, 197, 201, 269, 270, 277, 307, 315
Dillon, Douglas, 200, 264
Dirksen, Everett McK., 182, 201, 283, 284, 287, 289, 303

Doheny, Edwin, 149
Donovan, Robert J., 193-194
Dooley, Mr., quoted, 106, 107, 202, 235
Doughton, Robert L., 179
Douglas, Paul, 198, 304, 305
Douglas, Stephen A., 58, 61-65, 68, 70, 75, 94, 198
Dred Scott decision, 64
Drummond, Roscoe, quoted, 288
Dulles, John Foster, 200
du Pont, Pierre, 158

Earle, George, 169, 171
Early, Stephen, 160
Eisenhower, Dwight D., 4, 177, 178, 197, 199, 200-201, 220, 244, 249, 251, 253, 254, 255, 263, 268, 270, 272, 273, 276, 278, 282-284, 288, 289, 291-294, 299, 300, 301, 314, 319, 334; first presidential campaign, 183-190; as president, 191; on party realignment, 193
Electoral College, 75, 76, 252, 293, 295, 298, 302-306, 315, 321, 332
Elliott, William Yandell, 332
Emancipation Proclamation, 72
Eminent Victorians (Strachey), 234
Eppes, John W., 37
Erikson, Erik H., quoted, 228

factions, 18, 19, 22, 27, 47, 87, 153, 195, 204
Fair Deal, 180, 198, 302, 307, 308, 311
Fall, Albert, 149
Farley, James A., 156, 160
Farmer-Labor party, 158, 159, 161
Federal Emergency Relief Act, 157
Federalist Papers, 18; Federalist number 10, 18, 20, 218, 305; Federalist number 51, 20, 22

Federalist party, 26, 27, 29-39, 41, 43, 45, 48, 50, 53, 59, 77, 270
Federal Trade Commission, 133
Fenno, John, 29
Fenton, John H., quoted, 273
Fessenden, William Pitt, quoted, 71
Fillmore, Millard, 60, 61, 63
Finletter, Thomas K., 332
Fish, Hamilton, 158, 181, 300
Fitzgerald, John "Honey," 216
Flanders, Ralph E., 303, 305
Flynn, Edward, 170
Flynn, John T., 286
Fogarty, John E., 254
Folk, Joseph W., 105
Ford, Henry Jones, 332
four-party system, 7, 196-203, 206, 234-235, 257-258, 264, 266, 277, 288, 300, 301, 323-324, 331; See also congressional party system, presidential party system.
Frankfurter, Felix, 168, 202
Franklin, Benjamin, 14, 16, 33
Free Soilers, 61, 62, 63, 71
Fremont, John C., 63
French Revolution, 29
Freneau, Philip, 29, 31
Frost, Robert, 317
Fuller, Helen, quoted, 309

Gallatin, Albert, 42, 43
Garfield, James, 76
Garner, John N., 197, 201, 202
Garrison, William Lloyd, 71
Gazette of the United States, 29
George, David Lloyd, 137, 322
George, Walter, 165
Gerard, James W., 154
Gladstone, William E., 205
Goldberg, Arthur, 202
Goldman, Ralph, quoted, 52, 57, 332
Goldwater, Barry, 280-281, 283-288, 293, 295-299, 303, 326
Good Neighbor Policy, 158, 307

Grant, Ulysses S., 76, 94, 95, 100, 114
Greeley, Horace, 76
Green, Edith, 254
Griffith, Ernest, quoted, 262
Grundy, Joseph, 169
Guffey, Joseph, 170, 172

Halleck, Charles, 191, 197, 201, 255, 283, 284, 287, 289, 293, 299
Hamilton, Alexander, 10, 17, 18, 26-32, 34, 35, 37, 335
Hanna, Mark, 99, 101, 104, 105
Harding, Warren G., 139, 142, 147, 148, 149, 150, 151, 179, 197, 252, 253, 264, 295, 298, 307
Harriman, Averell, 254
Harrison, Benjamin, 75, 77, 96
Harrison, William Henry, 64, 199, 251, 270
Hartford Convention, 48
Hartz, Louis, quoted, 21
Harvard University, 119
Harvey, George, 128
Hatfield, Mark, 239
Hayes, Rutherford B., 75, 76, 200
Hays, Will, 149
Hearst, William Randolph, 128, 158, 195, 205, 337
Hearst newspapers, 286
Henry, Patrick, 13
Hepburn Act, 104
Herndon, William H., quoted, 217
Hickenlooper, Bourke, 286
High, Stanley, quoted, 161
Hillman, Sidney, 160
Hiss, Alger, 282
Hoffman, Clare E., 191
Hofstadter, Richard, quoted, 22, 83, 114, 122, 147
Holcombe, Arthur, quoted, 250, 304

Holifield, Chet, 254
Holmes, Judge Oliver Wendell, 202
Hoover, Herbert, 141, 142, 148, 149, 180, 262, 277, 283, 290, 292, 299, 307
Hopkins, Harry, 167, 249
House of Representatives, 28, 30, 36, 43, 50, 56, 74-76, 81, 84, 91, 103, 108, 137, 241, 244, 248, 255, 287, 296, 301, 326, 329-331, 339; Ways and Means Committee, 28, 36, 37, 71, 78, 110, 179, 191, 198; Speaker of, 36, 42, 85, 254; Rules Committee, 84, 85, 179, 191, 245, 256, 300, 309-310, 312-314, 316, 326; Naval Affairs Committee, 179; Armed Services Committee, 191; Banking and Currency Committee, 191; Government Operations Committee, 191; Judiciary Committee, 191; Appropriations Committee, 191, 246; Un-American Activities Committee, 246, 261, 313; Patronage Committee, 246; Judiciary Committee Immigration Subcommittee, 246
House, Edward M., 132
Hughes, Charles Evans, 135, 138, 141, 146, 149, 154, 162-163
Huitt, Ralph, quoted, 247
Hull, Cordell, 156, 314
Humphrey, Hubert, 195, 254, 332

Ickes, Harold, 156, 169
Income tax, 78, 107, 114
independents, 210-211
Indianapolis Star, 286
initiative, 83, 86, 333
Inland Waterways Commission, 108
International Review, 119
Interstate Commerce Commission, 103

issues, "way-of-life," 257-260, 270, 278, 321

Ives, Irving M., 303, 305

Jackson, Andrew, 47, 49-53, 57, 58, 60, 89, 143, 169, 249, 251, 318, 339

Javits, Jacob M., 198, 254, 283

Jay, John, 18

Jefferson, Thomas, 9-12, 15, 17, 24-30, 43, 44-47, 51, 69, 89, 156, 157, 169, 178, 196, 200, 249, 306, 318, 336, 338, 339; as Vice-President, 31; campaigns for President, 32-35; as President, 36-42

Jeffersonian system of government, 6, 32, 40-42, 46, 56, 59, 65, 66, 87-89, 92, 178, 203, 205, 206, 240, 265-266, 270, 308, 322, 323, 332, 334, 335, 336-338

John Birch Society, 286, 337

Johns Hopkins University, 76

Johnson, Andrew, 73, 74, 178, 200

Johnson, Hiram, 84, 139, 140, 168

Johnson, Lyndon B., 194, 195, 197, 201, 253, 255, 256, 283, 306

Joint Committee on the Conduct of the War, 72

Josephson, Matthew, quoted, 77

Kansas City Star, 128

Keating, Kenneth B., 283, 284

Kefauver, Estes, 195, 247

Kellems, Vivien, 286

Kellogg, Frank B., 139

Kendall, Willmore, quoted, 259, 260

Kennan, George F., quoted, 325

Kennedy, Jacqueline B., 210

Kennedy, John F., 2, 4, 6, 103, 197, 198, 200, 201, 216, 225, 231, 236, 249, 251-253, 262, 264, 270, 277, 283, 291, 300,

Kennedy, John F. (Cont.): 315, 316, 324; as a Senator, 301-305; campaigns for President, 306-309; as President, 309-311, 314, 317-319

Key, V. O., Jr., quoted, 90, 219, 221, 238, 258, 312

Keynes, John Maynard, 7

King Caucus, 49, 50, 54, 55, 197

King, Martin Luther, 283

King Rufus, 48

Know Nothings, 59, 61

Knowland, William F., 191-192, 194

Knox, Frank, 160, 263

Ku Klux Klan, 150

La Follette, Philip, 171

La Follette, Robert A., Sr., 85, 104, 106, 112, 113, 133, 150, 151

La Follette, Robert A., Jr., 158, 159, 167, 171

La Guardia, Fiorello, 150, 160, 166, 170

Landon, Alfred M., 160, 170, 199, 277

Lane, Robert E., quoted, 91

Lawrence, David, 248, 256

Lazarsfeld, Paul F., quoted, 258

leadership, congressional, 253-257, 262-263, 313-314, 328-329

leadership, presidential, 6, 175-176, 206, 212-218, 262-263, 336-340; as defined by Wilson, 121; Wilson on, 142-143; Wilson and, 143-147; T. Roosevelt and, 102-106; F. D. Roosevelt and, 168-173; Kennedy and, 310-311

League of Nations, 136, 137, 139-143, 145, 163, 256, 270

Lee, J. Bracken, 286

Lehman, Herbert H., 195, 198, 254

Leuchtenburg, William, quoted, 149

Lewis, Fulton, Jr., 286
Lewis, John L., 160, 215
Lincoln, Abraham, 64, 65, 70, 74, 178, 196, 197, 217, 288, 336; as President, 71, 72, 73
Link, Arthur S., quoted, 122, 123
Lippmann, Walter, 5, 121, 134, 158, 332
Livingston, Robert, 26
Locke, John, 21
Lodge, Henry Cabot, 102, 107, 119, 135, 145, 147, 149, 202; and League of Nations, 136, 138-141, 256
Lodge, Henry Cabot, Jr., 161, 184-185, 189, 201, 202, 282, 283, 301
Long, Huey, 195, 205, 229, 337
Longworth, Alice Roosevelt, quoted, 150
Louisiana Purchase, 36, 39, 338
Lowell, A. Lawrence, 332
Lucas, Scott, 256

machines, political party, 89, 95, 236
Madison, James, 24, 26-31, 33, 38, 46, 47, 51, 88, 120, 198, 200, 204, 218, 222, 305, 306; and Constitutional Convention, 8-18; and Federalist party, 18-23; as President, 42
Madisonian system of government, 6, 7, 16, 24, 32, 40-42, 45, 46, 57, 70, 87-89, 92, 102, 121, 146, 175, 178, 195, 203-206, 240, 247-248, 264-266, 300, 304, 313, 318, 322, 327, 334, 335-337; present-day, 206, 323-325
majority rule, 20-22, 39-41, 46, 86, 88
Mansfield, Mike, 303
Marbury v. Madison, 37
Marshall, George C., 190, 307
Marshall, John, 37, 38, 39, 202

Martin, Joseph, 181, 191, 201, 256, 300
Martine, James, 125-126
Matthews, Donald R., quoted, 247
McAdoo, William G., 132, 149, 150
MacArthur, Douglas, 286
McCarthy, Joseph R., 190, 192, 195, 205, 286, 293, 308, 337
McClellan, John, 197, 296
McCombs, William F., 129, 130
McCormack, John, 201, 255
McKee, Joseph V., 170
McKinley, William, 79, 80, 94, 100, 101, 104, 123, 199, 299, 307
McPhee, William N., quoted, 258
Mencken, Henry L., quoted, 79
Michelson, Charles, 157
Miller, William E., 284
Milliken, Eugene, 191
Millis, Walter, quoted, 166
Mills, C. Wright, quoted, 253
Milton, George Fort, quoted, 151
Missouri Compromise of 1820, 61, 63, 64
Mitchell, Joseph M., 286
Moley, Raymond, 159, 286
Monroe, James, 43, 47-49, 51
Monroe Doctrine, 104, 137
Montesquieu, Baron, 20
Morgan, J. P., 101, 129
Morris, Robert, 14
Morton, Thruston, 284
Mowry, George E., quoted, 110, 116
muckrakers, 82, 89, 107, 122
mugwumps, 86, 97, 114, 211-212, 232, 260
Mundt, Karl E., 286, 295-299, 303, 304, 305, 315, 326
Murphy, Charles F., 128-129, 153, 154
Myrdal, Gunnar, quoted, 229

Napoleon, 36
The Nation, 128, 135
National Conservation Congress, 108
National Country Life Commission, 108
National Emergency Council, 157
National Gazette, 29, 31
National Industrial Recovery Act, 157
National Labor Relations Board, 313
National Review, 286
Nebraska Bill, 61-63, 65, 67-68
Negroes, 3, 71, 74, 90-91, 133, 151, 160, 208, 221, 225, 252, 268, 271, 273, 274, 279, 287, 294, 304-305, 315, 318-319, 320, 324, 333
Neustadt, Richard, quoted, 255
Nevins, Allen, quoted, 62, 78
New Deal, The, 2, 157-162, 164-165, 171-172, 179-180, 183, 270, 287, 307-308, 311, 313-314. *See also* Franklin D. Roosevelt.
New Freedom, The, 130, 144, 149, 179, 307. *See also* Woodrow Wilson.
New Frontier, The, 276, 309, 311, 314, 317. *See also* John F. Kennedy.
New Nationalism, The, 115
New Republic, The, 135, 200
New York Daily News, 158
New York Herald Tribune, 190, 193-194, 200, 288
New York Post, 97, 128, 135
New York Times, 141, 190, 200
The Ninth Wave (Burdick), 268
Nixon, Patricia, 210
Nixon, Richard M., 190, 201, 202, 236, 249, 251, 252, 272, 273, 277, 280-284, 289, 291, 305
non-voting, 223-228

Norris, George W., 85, 160
Nugent, James R., 126-128

O'Connell, Cardinal William, 158
O'Connor, John, 166
O'Gorman, James A., 132
Ostrogorski, M. I., quoted, 74, 271
Outlook, 128

Padover, Saul K., quoted, 40
Panama Canal, 104
Parker, Alton B., 80
Parkhurst, Charles Henry, 97
parties, state political, 236-241
party realignment, 275-279; Wilson and, 131-132; F. D. Roosevelt and, 167-173; Eisenhower and, 193; Mundt and, 295; congressional Democrats and, 315-316
Payne-Aldrich Tariff Act, 111, 113
Pegler, Westbrook, 286
Percy, Charles H., 289
Perkins, Henry, 156
Pierce, Franklin, 59, 61, 62-64, 68, 196, 197
Pinchot, Gifford, 111, 112, 169-170, 171, 172, 174
Pinckney, Charles, 35
platforms, party, 55
Plato, 5
Platt, Thomas, 97-99, 101-102, 113
Plunkitt, George Washington, 212-214, 217
Polk, James K., 55, 56, 89
politics, public disenchantment with, 1-7
popular majority, *see* majority rule
Populists, 78, 82, 90, 91, 121, 131, 133, 150, 158
Prendergast, Michael, 310
Presidency, 2, 7, 17-18, 20-22, 24-25, 27-28, 38, 45, 56, 59, 87, 104, 120, 178, 205, 249-257, 259, 261-264, 286, 302, 304,

Presidency (*Cont.*):
308, 327, 329-333, 336-340; Wilson on, 142-143; F. D. Roosevelt on, 155
presidential Democrats, 195-203, 257, 263, 273-274, 288, 291, 293-294, 299, 307, 310, 313, 315-316, 318-321, 339
presidential party system, 196-203, 249-257, 260-263, 288-295, 298, 305, 308, 325, 326, 327, 328, 329, 331
presidential Republicans, 106, 196-203, 257, 263, 273, 288, 290, 292-295, 299-300, 304-305, 316-317, 319, 321-322, 326, 339
primary, direct, 82, 83, 84, 86, 90, 91, 222, 239, 333
Princeton University, 11, 119-120, 122
Pringle, Henry F., quoted, 109
progressives, 83, 84, 86, 112, 113, 116, 126, 131, 134, 155
Progressive Party (of 1912), 114, 116-117, 133-134, 145, 160, 164, 206
Progressive Party (of 1924), 150, 151
Progressive Party (of Wisconsin), 158, 171
Progressive Party (of 1948), 181
Prohibition, 270
The Promise of American Life (Croly), 114

Quay, Matthew, 101, 102
Quids, 43

Randolph, Edmond, 14, 15
Randolph, John, 37, 43, 45
Rankin, John, 313
Ranney, Austin, quoted, 146
Rayburn, Sam, 179, 181, 194, 195, 255, 310
Reader's Digest, 286

recall, 83, 333
Reciprocal Tariff Act, 158
Reconstruction, 74, 197, 209
Reed, Chauncey W., 191
Reed, Daniel A., 191
Reed, David A., 169-170
Reed, Thomas B., 77, 84
referendum, 83, 86, 333
Regnery, Henry (publisher), 286
regulars, party, 209-210
Republican party (Early 19th century), 26-27, 29, 30-31, 42, 44-45, 47-49, 51-52, 56
Republican party (since 1854), 2, 4, 95-98, 101-102, 104-108, 113, 116, 125, 127, 135-138, 141-142, 145, 148-151, 159, 163, 166-171, 174, 177-178, 181, 182, 183, 184-195, 206-209, 213, 217, 220, 230-231, 237-238, 248-249, 257-259, 263-264, 268, 277, 280-300, 302-304, 310, 312-315, 317-318, 327, 330, 334, 338; Radical Republicans, 71-76, 90; National Republicans, 53. *See also* All-Republican Conference, presidential Republicans, party realignment, congressional republicans.
Ribicoff, Abraham, 239
Riis, Jacob, 100
Robinson, Joseph T., 163, 201
Rockefeller, Nelson, 197, 239, 282-283, 299, 316, 329, 339
Roosevelt, Eleanor, 195, 254, 269
Roosevelt, Franklin D., 129, 136, 141, 149, 176, 178-179, 181, 183, 197, 199, 200, 201, 209, 215, 226, 238, 244, 249, 252, 255, 263, 264, 270, 276, 277, 288, 296, 300, 301, 306, 307, 308, 313, 314, 317-319, 321, 322, 336-339; early political career, 151-156; as President, 155-175; on Presidency, 155-156; and Su-

Roosevelt, Franklin D. (*Cont.*):
preme Court, 162-163; on party
realignment, 167-173
Roosevelt, Theodore, 79, 81, 84,
86, 95, 98, 100, 109-113, 123,
131, 133, 135, 151, 153, 155,
167, 169, 175-176, 199, 200, 258,
262, 292, 295, 337; as Governor
of New York, 99; as Vice-President, 101; as President, 102-108;
out of office, 112-115; runs for
President in 1912, 116-118, 130
Root, Elihu, 113, 116, 117, 138,
200, 262
Roper, Daniel, 156
Rosenman, Samuel, 174
Rossiter, Clinton, quoted, 256
Rousseau, Jean-Jacques, 243
Rovere, Richard, quoted, 187
Russell, Richard, 297
Ryan, Thomas Fortune, 129

Sabath, Adolph, 179, 181
Schattschneider, E. E., quoted, 251
Schlesinger, Arthur M., Sr.,
quoted, 178
Schlesinger, Arthur M., Jr.,
quoted, 160, 167, 321
Schlesinger, Joseph, 240
Scripps-Howard newspapers, 158
Schumpeter, Joseph A., 217
Scott, Winfield, 59-60
Secession, 31, 48
Senate, 16, 28, 30, 34, 42, 43, 52,
71, 75, 76, 81, 83, 86, 87, 91,
101-103, 108, 141, 180, 190, 241,
247, 248, 256, 261, 287, 296,
301, 302, 304, 305, 310, 324,
325, 331, 339; Territories Committee, 64; Finance Committee,
85, 101, 190, 191; Foreign Relations Committee, 136, 139,
190; Appropriations Committee,
102, 180, 191; Banking and Currency Committee, 180; Labor

Senate (*Cont.*):
Committee, 180; and the League
of Nations, 136-140
seniority system in Congress, 244-
248, 256, 259, 307, 310, 314,
329
separation of powers, 35
Seward, William H., 72
Seymour, Horatio, 76, 251
Sheehan, William F., 153
Shays, Daniel, 12
Sherman Anti-Trust Act, 133
Sherman, James, 112
Shivers, Allen, 296
Short, Dewey, 191
silver, free, 78, 79
Simpson, Richard M., 286
Sinclair, Harry, 149
Sinclair, Upton, 159
slavery, 2, 58, 61, 63, 67, 68, 72
Smith, Alfred E., 150, 151, 153,
154, 238, 270, 276, 277
Smith, "Cotton Ed," 165
Smith, Howard W., 250, 310, 311-
314
Smith, James, Jr., 123-124, 125-
127, 128, 129, 130
Socialist party, 66
Social Security, 2, 159, 220
Southern politics, 74, 82, 90-91,
182-185, 271-274, 313-314
Soviet Russia, 4, 5, 158, 285, 307
Square Deal, 81, 105, 110, 117,
122. *See also* Theodore Roose-
velt.
squatter sovereignty, 61, 62
states' rights, 3, 5, 25, 45, 57, 61,
69, 94, 166, 247
Steffens, Lincoln, 100
Stevens, Thaddeus, 71, 74
Stevenson, Adlai E., 177, 189, 195,
197, 199, 220, 251-252, 254, 308
Stimson, Henry L., 157, 200, 263
Stowe, Harriet Beecher, 73
Strachey, Lytton, quoted, 234

Sullivan, Roger, 128, 129
Sulzberger, Arthur Hays, 190
suburban politics, 268-270, 271
Sumner, Charles, 64, 72
Supreme Court, 37, 64, 159, 196, 205, 236, 273, 278, 313; F. D. Roosevelt's attempted reorganization of, 162-163

Taber, John, 191, 192, 286
Taft-Hartley Act, 180
Taft, Robert A., 173, 193, 197, 198, 200-202, 253, 255-256, 264, 270, 282; political career, 179-192
Taft, William Howard, 81, 84, 86, 106, 135-136, 138, 141, 146, 169, 179, 182, 189, 199; as President, 108-117; in 1912 campaign, 130
Tammany Hall, 34, 129, 132, 153, 154, 212, 306
Tannenbaum, Frank, quoted, 218
tariff, 63, 80, 103, 109, 110, 133, 143. See also Reciprocal Tariff Act.
Tennessee Valley Authority, 158, 333
Tenure of Office Act, 74, 261
Thurmond, J. Strom, 296, 303, 315, 316
Tilden, Samuel, 75, 76
Tillman, "Pitchfork Ben," 104
Tocqueville, Alexis, quoted, 57, 93, 213, 228
Treadway, Allen T., 179-181, 197, 229, 233
Truman, David B., quoted, 222, 266
Truman, Harry S., 180-181, 183, 192, 195, 197, 198, 200, 201, 202, 209, 238, 250, 254, 262, 263, 269-270, 272, 273, 277, 300, 302, 307, 313, 315, 316, 321

trusts, 83, 109, 115, 143. See also Sherman Anti-Trust Act.
Tugwell, Rexford Guy, 167
Tydings, Millard, 165
Tyler, John, 60

Underwood, Oscar W., 129
United Nations, 5, 308
urbanization, 267-268, 274

Van Buren, Martin, 89, 199; political strategy, 51-53; as President, 54, 56
Versailles Treaty, 143
Vice-Presidency, 250
Villard, Oswald Garrison, 97
Vinson, Carl, 179, 181
Virginia and Kentucky Resolutions, 31
Voting: city, 223-228, 267-268; suburban, 268-270. See also nonvoting.

Wade, Benjamin F., 71, 74
Wagner Act, 159, 163
Wagner, Robert F., 153, 310
Walker, Edwin, 286
Wallace, Henry A., 156, 181, 202
Wall Street Journal, 149
Walter, Francis, 246
Warren, Earl, 202
War of 1812, 48
Washington, George, 9, 10, 12, 13, 15, 16, 17, 27, 28, 29, 30, 35, 47, 178
Washington Post, 200
Webster, Daniel, 56, 58, 59, 60, 62, 197
Weeks, John, 149
Welles, Orson, 219
Whigs, 53, 54, 56, 57, 59, 60, 61, 62, 63, 65, 67, 70, 71, 90, 205; Cotton Whigs, 60, 149; Conscience Whigs, 60, 149
White, Theodore H., quoted, 171, 282, 294

White, William Allen, 77, 101; quoted, 148
White, William S., 185, 200, 248
Wiley, Alexander, 190
Williams, G. Mennen, 195, 239
Willkie, Wendell, 173, 174, 180, 181, 197, 251, 295
Wilson, Bob, 284
Wilson, James, 17
Wilson, Woodrow, 76, 119-121, 142, 144, 145, 149, 152, 156, 160, 178, 179, 189, 199, 200, 205, 209, 256, 258, 306, 307,

Wilson, Woodrow (*Cont.*): 314, 318, 332, 334, 336-337; as president of Princeton, 122-123; campaigns for Governor, 123-125; as Governor, 126-128; campaigns for President, 128-130; as President, 131-141, 154; considers realignment of parties, 131; and the League of Nations, 136-141; on Presidency, 142-143, 155
Wolcott, Jesse P., 191
Wood, Robert, quoted, 269